Lightworker's Log :-)

Transformation

SAM

Fourth Edition

Copyright © SAM/Lightworker's Log

ISBN 978-1-939890-13-9

Dedicated to the One within humanity that notes, "The shift to Heaven on earth increases as we forget the patterns of exclusion and move forward in time to its end."

Acknowledgements

Lightworker's Log :-) Transformation would not exist without the help of many people. Everyone noted within these pages taught me valuable lessons for which I am eternally grateful. Three ex-husbands helped me to take back my power and made it possible to cherish our beautiful children and grandchildren. Thank you for your treasured assistance! Family, friends, and spiritual teachers met through classes, workshops, seminars, and conferences helped to influence thoughts. They played a huge role in the development of this book. Sources listed in the bibliography also helped to shape *Lightworker's Log :-) Transformation* so more people can learn of the unseen world in which humanity resides.

Sincere thanks to my dear Canadian friend Eva Nolan for the drawing on the cover titled *The Sun Bird* copyright 2010. She knew immediately that it fit the book's message because it was inspired by the idea that an eagle can look at the sun and not have its retinas burned. Much thanks to Balboa Press as well for publishing this book in 2010 and therefore helping me to realize it's time to let go of all old energies.

I am especially thankful for ever-increasing recognition of that unseen guiding force many people identify as God.

Contents

Preface

Who am I? Why am I here? Is this all there is? Is there life after death? I began to examine these questions more thoroughly when messages from my departed son Daniel flowed quickly like a tsunami from the Otherside. Daniel's physical death marked the time to fulfill the contract made by our souls before birth. We agreed as souls to help humans realize we are really parts of God having a human experience. My contribution to the Shift of the Ages begins while purging lower, and more densely vibrating ego parts, honed through eons of earthly struggle and strife.

Part of a three book series, *Lightworker's Log :-) Transformation* details the continuing saga of my awakening in 2006. It documents a journey of ever-changing perception that blossoms into a pure state of grace, while studying *The Science of Mind* and *A Course in Miracles*. These books make it much easier to progress from a life filled with depression, desperation, illness, and limitation, to one of hope, tranquility, health, and joy.

A better world begins to manifest when I use the books as a guide to freedom. Increasing awareness of the power within us all helps to reshape life. I soon recognize that humans are co-creators in physical form. Trusting Spirit, I move beyond ego and fears to finally end decades of prescription drug use. My body begins to repair itself with the power of thought.

New experiences help to reshape thoughts lifting me from the bonds of limitation. Self-Mastery becomes a conscious goal, and as perception and beliefs change, experience creates a better reality. Increasing synchronicities help me to tap into an unseen world. My living conditions improve immensely by the end of the year.

This book illustrates the rising of Christ consciousness, demonstrates the strength of mind over matter, offers insight to the unseen world that guides humanity, and suggests how to tap into *All That Is*. Those of you who have not read the previous books in this series will still reap a great deal from this volume for it offers valuable insights to the largely unseen world. It also notes many messages that increasingly filled both sleeping and waking hours.

Certain words signifying aspects or attributes of the unchanging Vital Life Force within us, which many people refer to as God, are capitalized. *Italics* identify messages received in 2006 and while writing the book. They also note my beliefs while writing the book, lessons learned, and revelations after certain experiences.

Chapter One

Dawn of a New Year

"They themselves are makers of themselves."
James Allen – As a Man Thinketh

As the year 2006 begins, it's vital to set spiritual goals to answer the needs of my essence. A greater awareness of the divine nature within beckons after finally emerging from two years of grief and despair. This year I'll experience a heavenly state of grace, knowing without a doubt that humanity is part of the One.

It's time to put years of to do lists aside and concentrate on something much more important: how I feel about what I'm doing. The theme of Religious Science Fort Lauderdale's "One in Spirit" magazine perfectly reflects my thoughts for the New Year. I'm more optimistic about the future and ready to let change happen.

The concept of self-mastery invites me to learn and understand egos manipulative ways. This is the year eons of false beliefs in limitation, lack, and duality weaken and fade away. These old concepts, ideas, emotions, and attitudes are no longer useful. It will be easier to let them go as the year unfolds.

Studying *The Science of Mind* offers greater possibilities. I now welcome the thought of happier life conditions. Although many terms describe the unchanging Vital Life Force within us, due to my Baptist upbringing I still regress to the word *God*. This habit will continue to change as intuition heightens and the doorway to the Absolute opens, revealing more messages from the unseen.

I choose to be happy and full of love. This is the year negative experiences propel me to use the Law of God affirmatively, breaking the chains of bondage held with images from many lifetimes. These bonds of ignorance break with the realization that talk of discord results in discord, and time spent talking about sorrow only results in more sorrow.

Affirmations help to change the little mind that locked me in a sea of negativity for years. I'm reaching new levels of awareness, by religiously repeating an affirmation from *The Science of Mind*, while waiting for the next series of classes to begin.

"I partake of the nature and bounty of the All Good and I am now surrounded by everything which makes life worthwhile."

Life has never been easy so I don't quite believe the words. Yet, there are positive changes I can't deny. Life in general seems easier, and I'm more consciously aware of how thoughts and beliefs affect life on earth. Things are improving, for my right arm no longer goes numb while writing longhand. Now I'm happily summarizing parts of *The Science of Mind* onto small legal pads.

The three-fold nature of Universal Being enlightens me. Like everyone else, I am a unique form produced by soul, a blind force obeying the "Will of Spirit." My body is the effect of Spirit working through Law to produce form. It's clear that Spirit is the only self knowing and conscious actor of the three.

There really is a Universal Intelligent Presence that acts as Law. It's formless Stuff in the Universe that forever changes. Tiny points of light, the Stuff of Matter, are everywhere. They float in front of my open, amazed eyes, while sitting or lying in my beautifully sunlit room.

Sometimes I wonder if my soul still travels the astral highways Robert Monroe speaks of in books, for messages disrupt sleep. I wake often, remembering certain words, or bits and pieces, of what seem to be dreams. It's been many months since I experienced the delta waves of deep sleep.

Four known kinds of brain waves affect human thought. Delta brain waves are associated with the unconscious mind and occur in infants and adults during sleep. They are also present in the waking state of people who have strong intuition and psychic abilities. Frequencies in the delta stage are linked to the healing of mind and body.

Generally, beta waves appear during waking periods of sensory input and mental activity. Rhythmical alpha waves occur during meditation. Theta waves typically occur in children and adults right before sleep or when waking. Entering into the theta brain wave state allows us to access extrasensory perceptions and abilities. I'm more in tune with messages from the astral world during this state.

A smile forms upon remembering my companion on New Year's Eve, a magenta colored orb. Sleep comes quickly but words from an unidentifiable entity soon wake me.

Go to the path of God directly. Take care of all your brothers and sisters. And you shall be rewarded.

Eyes remain closed while my brain pictures a sofa. It has a white cloth holding a pattern of hearts and what looks like books on the top. Words flow forth. *Can a room hold but one God?* I fall back asleep after documenting the experience, only to awaken minutes later remembering the words *New Westchester*. James, my husband, knocks on the door to say he's going to visit Rachel and Abigail.

"Do you want me to take anything there for you?" he asks, already moving down the hall.

"No," I answer loudly while sitting up on the uncomfortable futon, confused, trying to remember how old my granddaughter is. "I'm waiting for an invitation to Abigail's birthday celebration."

I'm certain Abigail's mother Rachel already celebrated her daughter's birthday but can't comprehend not being included. Although our relationship is strained, I know things are as they should be. Thankfully, Rachel allows James to visit them. He's been a big help to her since her husband Daniel, my only son, transitioned to the Otherside.

After a quick bathroom trip, I fall happily asleep with my door still closed. The hole in the den ceiling consumes me so it seems safer to close myself off from the rest of the house. Repeated blessings continue to fill the house, and everything in it, with Love and Light.

Stifling heat in my chest seems eternal while kicking off the sheet hours later, remembering a vivid dream of Momma, Daniel, and my brother Terry's son, Joel. Details seem insignificant, but I document the dream anyway using a notebook from the top of a gray file cabinet that sits next to the futon where I sleep.

Momma stands at the kitchen sink, washing dishes, in the dream. Joel talks of poorly paid odd jobs as he agrees to fix a big window on the top part of our kitchen door for one hundred dollars. (Twenty-year-old Joel recently moved to another state, heartbroken over a failed relationship. He called his dad, upset about not making as much money as he had while in Florida. Several years ago,

Daniel replaced a piece of stained glass on our kitchen door.) A faceless man speaks to Joel.

"That's what Daniel did. Never short-sell yourself. Ask for more money and you will stay in business. If people have to pay more money, then they will think it (the work, the person doing the work) is worth it."

When I try to give Joel something, he gets onto a motorcycle and rides off with the faceless man who has a bike of his own. I follow them as Joel takes the lead. He speeds past everything in the right hand lane of a three-lane highway. The man follows closely behind Joel, as they drive on the dirt-filled, right shoulder of the road to squeeze past a big, red, flatbed truck. The path narrows, forcing Joel to stop his motorcycle. I see the faceless man catch up with him and hear what he says.

"This is what controls your body," he tells Joel, adamantly pointing to his head. "Not this," he says, pointing to his heart. "Don't be confused about what controls your body – the mind."

Joel and I always follow our hearts. At this point, I know Daniel is the faceless man, for he continues to search for ways to communicate with me during sleep, without jarring emotions.

The Science of Mind and other spiritual books fill time for the rest of the day.

Sleep is soon sporadic. I still sleep only on my back for my right side numbs in any other position. Bathroom trips occupy time. It's Momma's birthday when I open my eyes the next day at 5:15 AM remembering that Daniel spoke to me in a dream.

"You have to know the right time to pray," he said.

After documenting the communication, I try to fall back asleep. Minutes later, something like a picture show flashes behind closed eyes. On the left side of the movie are three golden objects; one of them is a telephone. The pictures change to three kinds of telephones on the right side of the movie screen. I see the words *she came to me*, in a gold color, and then a smile like a golden sun. Now I sense that either a woman asked for a child or someone passed.

Family celebrates Momma's birthday at Ruth and Naomi's house in the afternoon. We happily stuff ourselves with greasy pizza, cake, and ice cream. Family time always offers opportunities to practice a new way of being by silently repeating affirmations. Last years affirmation works wonders, silently repeated as the family makes fun of my new way of being.

4

"I do not react to outside forces because Spirit freely guides every aspect of my life."

Feeling the affirmation's power fills me with great faith that it's already done. Another affirmation honed for class helps whenever the negativity escalates.

"Love, Peace, and Harmony grow within me as I have positive interactions with all living things."

The power plays begin. Watching everyone use the negative ploys of interrogation, intimidation, aloofness, and pity me, to energize themselves is no longer enjoyable. It takes energy to build and maintain defense mechanisms and, even though we may not be aware of it, negativity drains our energy. I choose to get my energy by relying on the power within.

Remembering the peaceful serenity of the Light seen so long ago during my near-death experience at age sixteen calms me. I still secretly yearn to be on the Otherside, within *It*, where there's no awareness besides the Godhead, no separation. There's only a profound and abiding love.

Another affirmation silently repeated helps get me through the day.

"I am always in the right place at the right time. I increase my spiritual growth and lift my soul higher into the Infinite White Light."

As we sit at the dining room table, the white lace tablecloth stands out. It has a pattern of hearts, and what looks like books, the same pattern seen earlier on the cusp of sleep. Numerous orbs fill my digital pictures. After we eat, I show everyone the images along with some from our trip to see Sarah the previous October. Almost everyone ignores the spirit orbs saying my camera lens is dirty. Rebecca, my daughter, stays silent.

"Hooray!" I think later while viewing pictures taken with James' camera. "Other cameras pick up spirit orbs as well so my older digital camera is not a piece of junk after all."

The newsflash spurs me to continue snapping pictures while keeping results to myself.

Science of Mind (SOM) classes start, filling me with gratitude to imagine the possibility of a better world. Rev. Dr. Arleen Bump announces a travel tour to Greece, and the Greek Islands, resurfacing an old desire to widen horizons. Time volunteering and attending classes at Religious Science Fort

Lauderdale (later known as the Center for Spiritual Living – the Center), compliment self-growth, and uplifting materials, I'm drawn to hungrily consume.

My idea of evil changes forever, due to the teachings of Ernest Holmes who notes evil is an experience we choose to have that teaches us to choose differently. The Law of Cause and Effect is eternally operative. Realizing life experience is the result of thought makes change vital. I consciously begin to place thoughts into the Universal Creative Medium, to be acted upon by *It*, the Source of All.

The "World Healing Meditation" (repeated by fifty million people first in 1986) escapes my lips at sunrise. [1] The meditation is part of a daily ritual performed after something wakes me to begin the day. I now repeat three powerful words, "Peace, Love, Harmony," while sitting in a lotus position on my futon bed, facing east, with palms up on crossed knees. Sometimes, it's less than a minute before I feel, and see, the unseen. Palms vibrate as I watch the Stuff of the Universe, the matter of which makes all things.

The day's reading and treating begins by opening *The Science of Mind* to a random page. A yellow highlighter notes words, before structured prayers (treatments) set in motion the fundamental Law of the Universe, the Law of Love. Decades of formal prayer to a God outside me are gone. I know treatment expands consciousness, clarifies, and lets in the realization of Spirit. We connect to this Vital Life Force through treatment, and soon realize we're one with *It*. Using the Law of Love, I now consciously plant seeds in the subconscious Mind, knowing with God all things are possible.

Just repeating the word God makes a positive difference! In one of his groundbreaking books, *Life and Teaching of the Masters of the Far East, Volume 6*, Baird T. Spalding notes:

"Light and life is all one. You must give it one name always. You can never think of these things but that your body is vibrating at a higher attitude."

God's energy is everywhere. A sense of separation keeps us here, so we must look beyond the body to correct our disbelief in Oneness. Every time someone says "God" the body's vibration changes. And although other countries spell the word for God differently, the letters have the same vibratory influence. When we pray in full dominion, not begging or demanding, our body falls into

6

line and we become the God within. The most definite statement we can use is, "I Am God" or simply "I AM."

Only the mind is capable of illumination, the body is just a learning tool for the mind. What I see is an effect brought about by thought, ideas, and beliefs held by those living in the Soup of God. This mental medium, through which thought operates, allows me to know I can make a positive difference.

The daily ritual continues while repeating beliefs held by the Center. [2] I've always believed these things so it's wonderful to know others do too. Positive declarations free us from negative conditions, and change must start with children. They are the future of our earth, our conscious evolution back to the awareness that we are extensions of One. With that in mind, I say a treatment designed last year for children of earth, including Daniel, who I believe is reborn. [3] The treatment insures that humanity will be full of love, peace, and harmony, perfect and complete in the future. It will take many years but I trust the treatment works, especially for very young children, those with minds not poisoned by adults "stinking thinking."

The physical body allows Consciousness to function on earth. I'm quickly learning that the body we choose is a direct result of our awareness. Stress is a matter of perspective. It's important to remember that while thinking negatively takes energy and wears us down; positive thinking regenerates us. Discussing this with Rebecca seems vital after repeating her treatment for perfection, health, and limitless love, free of discord or disharmony. [4]

This dawn of a new day ends by switching off the closet light. The good Stuff of the Universe flows within, while my tired mind wanders for bedtime is still way after midnight. A sense that Spirit must create in order to express arrives on the brink of sleep.

The form that represents us, is just one of many forms our soul takes on, to help us realize we are not really a form at all. We are Light, one of the bodies within the One Body of the Universe. Forms always appear and disappear within that which is changeless and formless. We are as formless as our Creator is, One, living in a state of grace through the Power of God. Our reality is only Spirit, and we are in a state of grace forever.

:-)

Chapter Two

New Vocation

"What we are doing now, is learning to transcend conditioned consciousness in order to realize the Truth that there is only One–One Creator, One Creation—and that all things are formulated out of One Reality."
Helen Brungardt-Pope – For the Aspiring Mystic

The hiv nutrition business, so carefully nurtured in the past, now consists of weekly email updates about the company's website. Other business obligations no longer matter. I work wearing headphones, while singing softly to music, as sounds from the living room television (TV) rumble throughout the house.

Free time rearranges around visits to the Center. Wednesday evening's small group continues to satisfy, as I avoid Sunday services, which seem full of people seeking relationships. Classes help a great deal to take my mind off the family that appears more distant each day. I don't miss the more time-consuming business related work. It's replaced with class work from Rev. Bump's 102 SOM course. Understanding how the Mind of Spirit operates, for creative purpose, is much more important.

Sylvia happily travels with me back and forth to the Center. The jovial Jamaican seems to be my only friend. Our friendship grows as we share stories and revelations. The relationship will soon remind me that nothing happens by chance.

World wake-up calls continue, as news of the West Virginia Sago Mine explosion hits the newspapers, amid allegations of safety violations. Eleven men pass away, but the youngest one survives, because the others share their oxygen with him. Many of the men write comforting farewell notes for their families. Martin Toler Jr., wrote, "Tell all I'll see them on the other side. It wasn't bad. I just went to sleep. I love you Jr."

Feeling melancholy, I lift a DVD of Daniel from its case and leave the sanctity of my room to use the DVD player he gave us for Christmas years ago. I want to make sure the DVD works so everyone can see Daniel at his best. The player refuses to operate normally. It clicks repeatedly as I hear Daniel's quiet voice.

"They'll ask to see it when they're ready."

The DVD player continues to click and refuses to open.

"Alright, fine," I remark loudly to the air before walking back to my room. "Have it your way."

While using the bathroom later I notice the player is quiet and retrieve the DVD.

As I begin to piece this book together, the messages continue, making me wonder if they should go into the book along with the saga of my metamorphosis. Today is March 1, 2009 and I've heard that I'll be moving, and will "live alone with friends." I've always received these kinds of messages in plenty of time to prepare, but since my new lease is up in July, I'm a bit reactive.

"Get ready to move, for you will be moving on to a place of wonder and awe," echoes though my brain.

The answers come as usual when I ask questions. I'll have all the help I need, and will be, oh, so, ready to move on when it's finally time to go for things will change greatly by then.

I'm told there will be great storms here in Florida but I will be protected. The storms will feel like "ripples" to me, for I am consciously aware of the One. I am not to concern myself with these storms, for they're meant for those that are not consciously aware of our true BEing. It's not the first time I've been warned about dense storms in Florida. Yet, I wonder if these are weather related or just changes in consciousness.

I lie in bed not wanting to get up. It's been another long night of ascension symptoms where I wake repeatedly. I was unusually cold most of the night as atoms bounced off the walls of my body. It seemed like I had restless leg syndrome everywhere, for I could not stay still. And then the condition, last experienced in Egypt during 2008, where I brought up gobs of green gook and had 'ascension diarrhea,' arrived. This time it was worse.

I stayed in bed almost all day, from Sunday through Tuesday. On Wednesday, I got up to get my grandson Samuel from high school, went to the store, and returned to bed. Thursday brought the same tiredness with somewhat less distress.

Music remains a major part of life. The living room stereo fills the house with Christian music, while James works miles away.

Good energy rises within the house, prompting my soul to soar, as I continue blessing everything with Love and Light.

Musical thought is the language of souls. As Michael Newton explains in Destiny of Souls, unlimited musical sounds exist in the spirit world, where spiritual harmonics are building blocks of energy creation, and soul unification. I'm grateful that the souls of Daniel and I created a way to communicate, through music, in the physical world.

A message from Beliefnet inspires me after creating an account with the Huffington Post online. Thich Nhat Hanh notes mindfulness is the miracle by which we master and restore ourselves, by calling back our dispersed mind, and restoring it to wholeness so we can live each minute of life. Although not quite sure what he means, I am nonetheless ready to be restored to wholeness.

Weekly business search reports from the website continue to reveal people looking for information on nutrition and hiv/aids. Google Alerts on hiv nutrition greatly disappoint, for they rarely note subjects related to nutrition. They reinforce my old belief that information on the importance of hiv nutrition is sorely needed. I no longer feel compelled to devote myself to the cause, but spend countless hours praying and studying SOM.

The Universe again grabs my attention before the second week of the New Year. Uncaught bounce notifications, and failed email deliveries from the business website, fill personal email. I angrily delete them before reading the Beliefnet Buddhist Wisdom for the day, attributed to His Holiness the Dalai Lama.

"Anger or hatred is like a fisherman's hook. It is very important for us to ensure that we are not caught by it."

The synchronicity in life amazes as another email features the value of loving kindness. Annoyed over a Google Alert, with nothing to say about hiv nutrition, I think again and set my anger aside, still not recognizing it's time to fully cut the strings between my attention and the business so carefully nurtured in the past.

It's time to concentrate fully on a new life, and new way of being, but the habit of sending weekly business emails continues. The Universe acknowledges my effort by blocking access to the latest message. AOL and other subscribers report spam blockers hinder their email. Spammers' unwanted junk email, using my company's website domain addresses, arrives unhindered but legitimate email is discarded.

Messages from the Universe get more concise, as bogus requests to subscribe "out4138" to the business email list, from addresses using my business domain name, arrive. Fed up, I finally email a notice of my intention to sell the business formed in 1995. It seems reasonable to believe seven website domains, newsletters, handouts, and associated information will appear valuable, to someone other than me. Monthly website statistics show visitors in excess of seventy thousand people, from more than sixty countries.

Ego now prompts me to switch gears and follow email links to world news. Democracy Now reports of Ariel Sharon's major stroke, Jack Abramoff, and National Security Agency (NSA) eavesdropping on U.S. citizens, without court warrants. Beliefnet messages are much more appealing. The mysterious doors that will swing open, when a new perception comes that does not depend on structure, intrigues me.

Upon waking after an afternoon nap, I realize the CD player is playing a song faster than usual. *Let the children* fills my ears before I realize someone is in the front yard, very near my window. A quick peek, past light yellow blinds, reveal three men speaking Spanish. They stand around our beautiful, and very bountiful, four-foot Key Lime tree.

Sounds from a buzz saw assault my ears. I jump up from the futon, enraged with a realization. The dining room table holds several notices, from the State of Florida, noting diseased fruit trees in the area. As I approach the men, it's clear they've finished cutting down our healthy beloved tree. They talk to one another in Spanish, shaking their heads, as I yell, waving my arms about like a crazed woman. It's unthinkable that such a thing would be done without permission. Beside myself, ordering them off the property, I'm unaware that outer experience is a direct reflection of consciousness.

Local TV news the next day reports that the State of Florida's program to cut down personal fruit trees is now considered unconstitutional and has ended. Suffering may be useful for it leads us to the realization that it's unnecessary. Still angry over the loss of our beautiful tree, I begin to read. Robert Monroe reports in *Far Journeys* that it's very important to move toward a unified whole. The week's SOM study notes evolution depends on our ability to sense a unity with Nature. The tread of armies will cease when the knowledge of this unity comes and all feel brotherly love.

On the eighth day of 2006, I hear the words that change my life forever, as I lay in the twilight of waking from sleep.

My pre-birth vision into this life was designed to teach. To teach, I must learn. To learn, I had to suffer. I am now done with suffering. It is time now to teach here, in this life, on this plane.

My bladder burns as I ponder decades of illness. Ernest Holmes reports inner conflict; opposing desires that mentally conflict and produce lack of ease, cause most physical conditions. Is he right? Does disease really mean lack of ease (dis-ease), an unconscious experience operating through people? Is it true that only the mind needs healing? Is it truly possible to look past the illusion of sickness? Can I change my mind, about deciding to die, because the list of body conditions now covers more than half an 8.5 x 11 inch page?

It's time to more consciously create an enhanced life experience, by redirecting thoughts using Spiritual Mind Prayer Treatment. No longer begging during prayer time, I turn to the power within, that lifts thoughts to union with Creation.

I'm learning we exist in a temporally induced Mind experiment, and Truth is the absence of illusion. Thoughts will control us unless we control our thoughts. Since thought is constantly changing, forever taking on new ways of expression, it's possible to change one's circumstances just by changing thoughts. Holmes tells us, as long as we understand the mental cause of dis-ease and remove that mental attitude, we can heal it with the Truth. Consciously, and continually encouraging thoughts and desires, in harmony with ones true nature, always results in good.

Sometimes I get messages for others but am not sure when to communicate them. Two messages came today on March 5, 2009. One message is for me. The other is for my good friend, Michael the acupuncturist, who I see periodically, for Ba Gua Fa treatments.

Michael's wife of many years bears the burden of doctor reports noting breast cancer. She's had the surgery, and some radiation treatment, but she and Michael refuse chemotherapy, opting instead for less invasive methods that build, instead of destroy, the immune system. It's a trial for both of them, and other than offer a book by Louise Hay, I keep thoughts to myself. The messages came upon waking, before opening my eyes.

"There are always circumstances that seem beyond our control that pause us. We must define these circumstances in terms of living, in terms of how we wish to live. These circumstances are easily changed as we concentrate on the higher aspects of our being."

At this point, I realize this is a message I'm to give to Michael. I reach for my small tape recorder on the nightstand. The message continues.

"There are always circumstances that seem beyond our control in this illusion. These circumstances are not, necessarily, what they seem. There are ways to rid ourselves of these circumstances, and we must follow the tried, and true, method to do so. This method is the way we come back to the One, realizing that there is no limitation. That all are One, that we have never left, and shall always remain, in the bosom of the Lord. These friendly reminders help us to believe what is true.

"There are other ways to clear the emotions of dis-ease. These ways help us in becoming more alive with Source. These ways are the tried and true methods of the Masters. These emotional beliefs are not real. They don't fit into the mold. They are not a part of our natural self, for emotion is in itself human, and we are not human. To let bygones be bygones is a source of truth. Follow the path of wisdom to the Master within. That is the truth of the nature of our being. That is the truth of the nature of All.

"Relinquish the past, forget the future. Live in the Now, knowing the Now moment is the only true moment. This will carry you through. This will secure you in the life you wish to live."

After a short pause, I hear more words in my mind, and realize they are for me.

"The Being known as Truth is One. There can be no other. Stand clear of the chaos around you, turn to God. The God within will comfort and restore. There is none other. The truth has no value in this world, for it is unknown to the past, and the future. These words are spoken through you and not of you."

I am grateful beyond words for the One that speaks both to, and through, me.

I'm betting no dis-ease is incurable and console myself knowing there will be a time when pain ceases. No one will be unhappy. Holmes says the time will arrive in such a degree as we allow. It's vital to convince our consciousness that happiness was, and is, always there.

I'm eager to tap more completely into the Universal Mind, into which we think. It's imperative to avoid the negative stream of consciousness. Although it looks like a challenge, I'm ready and willing to look away from the conditions that plague me. It's time to concentrate fully on a different mode of thinking, and belief, knowing that mental treatment will change my life, for the better. Suffering lessens, as I begin to comply with the Laws of the Universe.

The following morning, I'm dreaming of doing something that my sister Ruth is not. *It's a progression* fills my brain at 5:54 AM. I rise reluctantly to repeat several treatments and study. Nearly three hours later, I fall back asleep and nap until one o'clock.

I strongly believe we write based on the knowledge we hold at the time, and that knowledge constantly changes. In my opinion, changing the future may be possible, by just changing the reality we live in. I'm fairly sure we live in more than one reality, with a wide variety of experiences, and outcomes.

In his groundbreaking book Conscious Dreaming, *Robert Moss notes, we become more conscious in life, when we become more conscious in dreams. Conscious dreaming allows us to change our personality, by first addressing dream situations. Once we realize we're dreaming, we can do anything, knowing we can change our thoughts and emotions.*

Unexplained tiredness overwhelms me. I nap again hours later, but rise with thoughts I prefer not to recall, before quickly falling back asleep. Minutes later, I promptly forget the same thoughts about Ruth. I then recall other words, for or about Terry, and quickly write them down. *You cannot embody those things, which you do not have.*

More words fill my brain at dawn.

It's time to awake to a brand-new day.

Daylight fills with prayer and spiritual studies. The "Sisters in Spirit" dinner hosted by Rev. Heidi Peck, later in the evening, opens new avenues to network and meet women of like mind. Rev.

Elle Bratland discusses changing life for good, through self-awareness, using positive self-talk, affirmations, visualization, forgiveness, and release. It's the first time I've heard we can "change the script" in which we live.

While checking email later, I learn an international photography organization selected my photo of the yard after Hurricane Wilma, as a semi-finalist in their contest. I'm soon outraged, after reading an online article in the *Sun-Sentinel*, which notes fraudulent methods of making money. It appears this company profits from the use of people's submissions, by preying on their vanity, selling them products related to their photos.

Compelled to share my "Florida Wilma" photo, because it displays so much more than the contrast of devastation and hope, I'm dismayed to learn the submission is not taken seriously. The memory of that day stands clearly in my mind. It's when I fully agreed to let Daniel go.

His essence stayed with Rebecca, Samuel, and I throughout the ravages of Hurricane Wilma, continually comforting me. Although few shutters were on the house, and we noted several vortex-like circles on the ground after the storm, only a few trees fell, all away from the house. I took the photo while feeling Daniel's presence, and was thrilled to see the loving magenta colored orbs in the sky. Overwhelming love, and gratefulness, surrounded me, as Daniel's words filled my brain.

"Are you sure you'll be okay without me Mom?"

Although I occasionally long for his presence, I've never regretted my reply.

"Yes," I told him with a full heart. "Yes, I'm sure honey. You go on and finish your business."

Remembering Rev. Bratland's talk, I forgive the company and once again move through the house, forgiving everyone in family photos. James pulls into the drive, home from his twice-weekly night job, as the last words of forgiveness leave my thin lips. I head back to my room, but leave the door open, in case he wants to talk. When he settles down on the living room couch, and the TV comes to life, the door is quickly closed.

There's one more person I need to forgive, and with a start, I realize it's me. Ruth's pending trip to Michigan prompts memories of an impropriety made in my late teens, when living with her and a friend. I sit down, and write a letter of apology, to the man who so kindly opened the doors of his house, and heart, knowing that all is forgiven before drifting off to sleep.

After several years of sprouting forgiveness, I have completely stopped forgiving, for this is an illusion, and it's not necessary. I now recognize everyone as a perfect part of One. Gary Renard notes, "If there is no world, then there's nothing to forgive, and recognizing that fact in the events, situations, and people you see is advanced forgiveness, because now you're not forgiving other people for something they've done, you're recognizing that they haven't really done anything. So you're actually forgiving yourself for dreaming them. That distinction is vital. Without it, you're doing the old-fashioned kind of forgiveness, which can't undo the ego."

:-)

Chapter Three

Changing Beliefs

"Dreams must be heeded and accepted, for a great many of them come true."
Paracelsus

Change the time of fishing to get the most fish.

The words wake me on Joy's birthday. I rise to use the bathroom wondering if Rachel will have a party for her mom. After silently wishing Joy a happy birthday, I drift back to sleep. More words fill my head minutes later.

I will show the way to those good of heart.

My eyes open upon remembering Ruth needs a ride to the airport. Still unemployed, and now depressed, she's going to visit our friend Sara in Michigan. The thought gets me off the futon, to search through old journals, for the perfect words to help her realize she's not alone.

Quotes and a poem, written during my depression days in 1978, seem adequate. Other writings, and three stories written for college English classes, noting turning points in my life, are set aside as well. While reading them, it's easy to see how far I've come from the crazy days, of repeated ups and downs, when Ruth and her partner Naomi routinely helped with the children. After a night at the drive-in with the kids, and opening my carburetor when the car flooded, I'd written what was then a flash of wisdom.

"Many obstacles block our way, but if we are wise enough to maintain patience, the light is everlasting inside."

The only obstacles are the ones we choose. It's vital that Ruth knows I'm ready to help whenever she's ready to ask. After a quick meal, I pull a new spiral bound notebook from the file cabinet to write her a note about documenting thoughts. I imagine Ruth using the empty pages to doodle on as she waits for her flight and head to my car.

Thirty minutes later, I'm at her door with a cheerful hello.

"Are you ready to go?"

"Just about," she says lifting a suitcase before setting the house alarm. "I hope there aren't any calls for work while I'm gone."

We discuss her job search on our way to the airport. When we arrive, I offer her the empty spiral notebook with my writings and the ghost poem written in her late teens.

"Are you sure you don't want this?" she asks holding up the faded white paper with her poem. "I gave it to you."

I assure her it's okay to keep the poem of ghosts seen while sleeping on my living room couch in the late 1960's.

"I don't need this," she says handing me back the empty notebook and other papers, before quickly heading toward a smiling luggage handler.

As the man happily takes her bag, I shrug my shoulders, get into the car, and head back home for a nap before class.

My view of life has changed drastically but confusion now muddles thoughts. Did God make us or are we a part of God that lost its way? Is it possible that as parts of the conscious whole we decided to be more, and after various adventures, and experiences, became unconscious of our divinity?

Currently in 2009, I'm sure of one thing. Humans are parts of God living in a Matrix of unlimited possibilities. This world, this earth, and everything I see, is part of a game, an illusion that is not a part of God. This earth game is only one of many, many, other games played on an infinite number of planes. Playing the game here has become more difficult since I'm more aware of the Infinite Intelligence that surrounds us and reacts to thought. The game endpoint is when we all realize we're part of One and unify in Love.

Emotional energy is prized highly in this game of life. Part of the game is developing emotional energy to its most effective condition, love. Since Infinite Mind responds to mental states, it's vital to control emotions, which control our environment. Although they offer opportunities for learning, emotions such as worry, anger, hatred, jealousy, and greed are negative and destructive. Love renews the soul and reigns supreme for Love is God.

The energy of Love, how much and how well we love, is the subject of much discussion. Holmes tells us:

"Love is greater than all else and covers a multitude of mistakes. Love overcomes everything and neutralizes all that is unlike itself."

There's nothing but love Emmanuel notes. It's all love, from the fires of our sun and the stars in the sky, to the cells of our body and the consciousness in our hearts. The expansion of love comes through our heart upon self-acceptance. When we truly love and accept ourselves, we are free to expand that love to others.

To love fully and richly is the calling of the God within. Every loving act adds more Light and power to the Godhead. Becoming a generator of "Original Prime Energy," as described in the book *Far Journeys*, is the major reason we're here on earth. "Original Prime Energy," also known as "Super Love," is an indestructible synthesis of emotional thought and action. Super Love is the power source that helps us to escape this dream world.

We know energy expresses itself as waves, and particles, and the consciousness of the observer determines how energy will behave. Research at the Human Energy Systems Lab documents investigations showing that love is an invisible attractive force, which transcends most boundaries and barriers, including physical death.

The heart's electromagnetic signal is a form of invisible "light" or photons that radiates out into the vacuum of space, allowing us to interact with loved ones, regardless of distance. "Super Love" is never affected and is not dependant upon manifestation in physical matter, or activity. This catalyst helps to end eons of lives on earth. There's no doubt that I must love everyone as I loved Daniel consciously, and unconsciously, radiating love into the Soup of God.

Today's waking message is short and sweet. "Let me forget the patterns of exclusion as I move forward in time to its end."

Sometimes I go days without remembering what I've done. Messages received day and night frequently remain lost in the body's circuits. Evenings are something I'm beginning to look forward to increasingly as volunteer efforts expand. Now I'm in charge of the music system and passing the tithing basket for the Center's Wednesday night service. Feeling empowered by Karen Drucker's music, I discretely slip in a few dollars from my hidden stash before circulating the basket.

Like-minded energy attracts the same. There are no exceptions. Spiritual and Universal Law insures that when we tithe all our needs are met once the time is right. What we send out into the universe comes back to us. It materializes in physical results. Author Mark Victor Hansen eloquently notes in *The Miracle of Tithing*, "A tithe is not a debt we owe, but a seed we sow!"

Everything, including money, is energy. I've always thought tithing was connected only to church. I'm happy to know it is not. Tithing is about making a difference in the world. It's wonderful to know that volunteering at the Center, helping family members, and offering bottles of specialty water to the homeless is a form of tithing. The Universe always returns this energy in motion.

It's clear there's work to do as I review *The Science of Mind* while preparing for class after the service. Knowing thoughts and emotions determine reactions, and mold the body, in my case with sickness, makes it easier to forge ahead. Changing my dominant mental and spiritual state is vital if I'm to reflect the Wholeness of God. There's no doubt I must work on emotions, which often overwhelm me, causing increased physical suffering.

It's time to let go of the past and create in the here and Now. Spiritual Substance is always around us waiting to form. I know faith molds undifferentiated Stuff of Matter and brings into manifestation the focus of creative imagination. The Presence of God is always around and the Law will work as I transcend past experience releasing old mental reactions.

Singh notes in his book <u>Commentaries On A Course In Miracles</u>, *since the past exists only in the memory of the brain, it's an indulgence of the ego to relive it. Bringing the past into the Present serves only to bewilder and depress.*

Sitting in the bathroom, I know I'm not alone even if Daniel is reborn. His presence embraces me. After taking my camera from its perch on the dresser, I return to take a picture. Numerous orbs meet my expectation. One of them is much brighter and denser than the rest. It's heartening to think Daniel lives on in another form.

Words of encouragement embrace my ears when waking during the night. I rise in the wee hours to write, *Yea, though I die, yet shall I live.*

I'm still lying on the futon when Rebecca telephones at 10:00 AM.

20

"I'm stuck up here at my first stop Mom," she says exasperated. "Can I borrow your car? Mine's broken down again."

I leave the house minutes later thankful she's only ten minutes away. Rebecca stands next to her car in the almost empty lot when I arrive. She gratefully slips into the passenger seat.

"You know, Ruth's plane was delayed after you dropped her off at the airport," she says in a soft voice.

"I had no idea," I reply shaking my head in wonder. "When I drove her to the airport I tried to give her some things to read and a journal to write in but she refused them. I was just acting on instinct."

"Well you can't make people do things you want them to," she resolutely notes turning her head toward me with a broad smile. "You know that Mom. Anyway, did I tell you about Lydia? She's still trying to have lots of kids."

"We haven't really spoken since your grandma's birthday."

"Lydia just got out of the hospital after going in for a D&C," she informs me while nervously pulling the scarf around her neck. "She lost four liters of blood, nearly died, and almost had a hysterectomy."

"I didn't realize they were trying to have another child so soon. The baby isn't even a year old yet."

I try to tell her it's how people live, how they consciously and unconsciously think and act that causes these things. She doesn't want to hear it.

"I've got enough to think about with this car trouble Mom. I don't need to burden her with your beliefs too."

"Jeremiah would be happy to help you any time. He told me so the last time I saw him."

Rebecca starts to cry quietly.

"This is when I miss Daniel the most. He always bailed me out whenever the car broke down."

Her voice wavers and then gets stronger as she continues.

"I'm not going to ask Jeremiah for a thing. He and Daniel were tight but he hasn't called me once since Daniel died. I'm not even sure I can get through the day without going to the emergency room again. This pain never seems to end."

"We're all in this together," I reply forcefully. "Even though we have our own things to deal with, we don't need to face them alone. Just remember he's willing to help if you're willing to ask. And thoughts are things."

Rebecca quickly jerks her head toward the side window where it stays for the rest of our short drive.

After she drives away with my car, I quietly repeat two treatments for her upon settling back in the sanctuary of my room. The phone rings when I'm done shortly after eleven o'clock. It's Rebecca saying she meant to call her own phone for messages. I smile happy to know she's already in Boca Raton at work, evidence in my mind that the treatments worked.

Feeling smug, I leave my room to watch Democracy Now hearings of a Supreme Court judge. It seems wise to record the next show, a documentary on nuclear war. Exhaustion soon overwhelms me. I decide to nap but ask for a dream of the future, for the good of all humanity, before falling asleep.

A vivid dream wakes me two hours later. I was watching four-year-old Abigail in what appeared to be something like an apartment building. It was a wide, open, area with the ocean to our right. I heard that some ice (glaciers) fell and many homes were swallowed into the earth. Abigail stood waiting for me in a fenced play area outside. My feet were bare so I turned to find shoes.

Rachel came in and asked if I knew what happened. I told her yes, and Abigail was outside waiting for me. We planned to try and see the phenomenon. "We might be able to see something if we look toward the northeast," I said. It seemed like we were in a location close to where we could see such an event and still be safe. I left to put my sandals on to join Abigail and Rachel. That's when I woke up.

For the next two mornings, I hear things I cannot document.

A change in perspective is wonderful to nurture. The world of form is just vibrating energy organized into a particular configuration by the frequency of our consciousness or intention. In Spiritual Alchemy, *Christine Page M.D. notes if it can be thought then it must exist somewhere in universal awareness. When we see what could be future events in dreams we can change them by choosing differently. By making that change we wake to a different reality.*

For instance, Rebecca often had a vivid nightmare where James and I drowned after crashing through a bridge in the Florida Keys during a rainstorm. She finally repeated her dream in great detail. I slipped it into the back of my mind but brought it forth when circumstances matched her vision. As James and I drove through a sudden rainstorm in the Florida Keys, I had him slow down before we crossed a bridge. No one can say that we avoided an accident but Rebecca never had the dream again.

Currently, I do a few things to change the past and future, thereby ensuring a better Now. I revisit past events, change the memory of them, and periodically ask to wake up in a dimension with a better outcome for humanity, and myself.

:-)

Chapter Four

Undercurrents

"As the emotions become balanced and our minds clear and open, we start to remember who we are, beyond our name, nationality and the drama we're playing out in the moment."
Christine Page – Spiritual Alchemy

Samuel is hungry when I pick him up from school. I promise to buy him a piece of pizza when we're shopping. James has taken charge of our finances but I'm still able to withdraw small sums of money. I'm thankful nothing is said when it's used for food. We stop at the credit union on our way to the Costco's in Davie. This time I withdraw $200 from the checking account, instead of the usual $100, because I need to refill four medications. I now use eight, of thirteen prescribed drugs.

Rebecca meets us after work. We shop together, making it easier for me to meet my urge to share. It feels good to know we can still help her by splitting the large packages of food. Colorful boxes of tissue decorated with penguins go into my cart while waiting in the long drug refill line. Rebecca sits waiting patiently with Samuel in the food court, while he happily woofs down greasy pizza.

It occurs to me the focus of my awareness must be different. I must imagine new, healthy possibilities, envisioning a life of travel, where I snorkel, hike, and participate in physical activities, joyfully pain free. A shift will soon change conditions as I embody the Truth, directing conscious thought more clearly, to visualize wholeness and health.

I follow Rebecca and Samuel home happily listening to "Faceless Man" playing on the portable CD player. "Next time I see this face I'll say, I choose to live for always. So won't you come inside and never go away." I sing forcefully with raw emotion, clenching my left hand, and jerking it down, before pulling into Rebecca's long, gravel driveway.

Minutes later, we divide large packages of food. I quickly recall how it feels to feed an ever-hungry adolescent boy.

The rest of the food is stored away after arriving back at the house on 47th Drive. I pull brown medication bottles out of white bags, remembering a time when they weren't needed. I want to revisit that time but ego informs me it can't be done.

"Remember all the drugs you tried before you found the right combination to keep the pain at bay?" ego asks loudly.

I hesitate to change remembering my low quality of life before taking Elmiron for interstitial cystitis. I'm still juggling meds, to get the best results, with the least side effects. The Pamelor, taken first, gave me almost unbearable headaches, particularly when I was out in the sun, along with a propensity for sweets, and weight gain. I soon switched to Sinequan but after a week had to stop because of disturbing and horrific nightmares.

The more medications I take the worse I feel. After years of researching P450 interactions, I know drugs can decrease, or increase, the effectiveness of others. It's a never-ending task to make sure drugs are effective. Many drugs decrease liver function and some cause conditions that require more prescriptions. Even after consciously cutting dosages, while repeating treatments for wholeness, I still swallow medications around the clock.

Many drugs create intestinal disorders and I'm tired of dealing with them. Mealtimes and food choices also interfere with medications. There are so many "rules" to follow it's a full-time job to remember them all. Some require an empty stomach, while others must be taken with food. I'd love to eat or drink anything, without suffering, and am tired of omitting certain foods. It's been a long time since I've been able to drink a tall glass of grapefruit or orange juice. Sometimes, it's easier to ignore what I've learned.

Filled with anxiety, I calm down with thoughts of rebirth. This year I'll change my life for the better. As spiritual studies progress, I'll finally stop judging and talking about others. I'll learn the fine art of establishing joy, after ridding my mind of the sorrow that's consumed it like a fire-eating dragon. My body will begin to heal, without the use of prescribed drugs, as I release the past.

Healing is the changing of vibrations from within. A Course In Miracles *notes to be born again is to let the past go, foregoing condemnation and looking only on the present. Creative Energies lovingly mold the body, back to wholeness, as we attune to the Divine within living tissue. Many spiritualists note prayer, particularly group prayer, raises body vibrations to wholeness.*

Colors and sound are also fundamental forces of vibration that promote healing from the Divine. Both can raise the healing properties of Christ Consciousness when used appropriately.

It feels good to be grateful. I'm happy the Universe is listening while I repeat a preference to see only birds, caterpillars, cocoons, and butterflies. I'm so very tired of picking up palmetto bugs and fleas, to release them outside, and strongly prefer the butterflies, for they represent transformation.

Later in the day, my nutritionist friend Mary sends jokes through email. She's tired and discouraged to think she'll always be the breadwinner as her husband slips further into a state of debilitating illness. After reminding her it's vital to recognize and deal with traumatic events to avoid nightmares and ill health, I share quotes savored when my own state of mind wallowed in the self-pity of ego's reign. One from Dr. Albert Ellis reminds me of my recent decision to be more responsible for myself.

"The best years of your life, are the ones in which you decide your problems are your own. You don't blame them on your mother, your environment, the ecology, or the President. You realize that you control your own destiny."

I'm ready minutes later to immerse myself in a different world when Rebecca drives us to see the Off-Broadway show "Movin' Out" featuring songs by Billy Joel. The extravagance of my belated birthday present overwhelms me while watching the actors on stage at the Broward Center for the Performing Arts. I notice the similarity, between the main character and myself, as he reviews the past and finally sets his life back on track.

The next morning, I hear something very profound, but cannot write it down. I can state with joy that throughout the less than four hours I slept, something cradled me, once again, in the arms of Love. A strong sense of love, of comfort, of safety, of arms holding me, as in a cradle while I slept, still surrounds me. There was no sense or thought of sex, only the pure love of being held by one who truly cares for another, without abandon. I gratefully fall back asleep hoping the feeling will return. It's a feeling unmatched by anything of this world and I welcome it with joy.

Sometimes the wooden and metal wind chime, hanging in the middle of my ceiling, warrants attention when Daniel's essence makes itself known. Waking minutes later, with a smile upon hearing chimes, I repeat the morning ritual before sleeping again.

James is gone, fishing once again, when I rise for the last time at ten o'clock. It's a day for me to be human, relax, and watch TV. I schedule programs to watch up to ten o'clock at night but throughout the day receive messages, which I cannot write down.

I'm up at dawn on Monday. James is home due to Martin Luther King Day. The wooden and metal chimes softly clang, as I repeat treatments, before reading and falling back asleep. The word *pair, pair* repeats inside my brain upon waking. I listen intently, receive a message, but can't write it down. It seems like a lot is now happening that I can't write down, maybe just for now...

James again asks when I will get a paying job later in the afternoon. I retreat to my sunlit room after telling him my working days are over. He announces it's time for me to empty the den file cabinets. We shared the room for years in the late 1990's, while he tied fishing flies and I tended to business, but now the room is his.

The Universe is telling me it's time to move on. I march into the den to remove another part of my old identity. More than twenty years of aids research, most of it on nutrition, fills cabinets and the computer stand. Several hours later, I'm exhausted from shredding years of work. I stop to take a nap when my head begins to hurt.

The day passes quickly. Although Terry McBride is speaking on joy and abundance as our birthright at the Center, I don't feel compelled to go. The body I'm in seems to require much more rest now. I fall happily asleep earlier than usual.

The noise as James gets into his shower the next morning wakes me at 6:00 AM. A comparison between Daniel and Terry runs through my brain. The evaluation offered a reason why Daniel was chosen instead of Terry. I'm not sure what he was chosen for, but perhaps it was his faith in God, that was the deciding factor. As usual, I fall back asleep but wake when James pulls out of the driveway thirty minutes later.

Sunrise is still forty-one minutes away but it seems as if parts of the sky are light already. I remember spending much of yesterday shredding past work. An almost unbearable amount of heat is coming from the middle of my chest. My head still hurts on the top, all around. A lovely bird, my God-given alarm system, announces it's time to repeat treatments and meditate.

Hours later while checking email, and feeling wholly alone, I offer Mary love as she deals with new trauma stemming from her husband's illness. A Beliefnet message attributed to Swami Chetananda consoles me.

"When you are with someone you love very much, you can talk and it is pleasant, but the reality is not in the conversation. It is in simply being together. Meditation is the highest form of prayer. In it you are so close to God that you don't need to say a thing-it is just great to be together."

Rhythmical alpha waves, occurring during meditation, help to neutralize disharmony, allowing regeneration and rejuvenation of body cells. Knowing these waves disappear during sleep, I try to stay awake to meditate. Again, I cannot write down what I remember, but I can say I'm happier than ever before. It's so cool to get these messages and know there is a time to look forward to! I am meeting my destiny and even though James and I will part, we will both be happy in time. Now back to drinking lots of water and getting more restorative sleep.

At 6:15 AM, it's time to begin reading. Winds seem strong, like a tropical storm, when I recall hearing, *awake and be free.* Our weather is odd. It reminds me of waking one day last month to see fog on roads. The mayor from New Orleans was on TV saying God is punishing us with hurricanes and blood clots. Ariel Sharon was in an induced coma for days; perhaps he is gone, passed now. Pat Richardson, the famous preacher, says the same. God is punishing us. I know the earth will suffer greatly in the years to come. James is still here but getting ready to leave. I softly repeat treatments and the usual meditation before sleep beckons once again.

The telephone soon rings loudly. I wake with Momma's words in my brain only recalling my first name. Maybe Momma is beginning the process of passing, her body no longer a complete and perfect host for her soul to grow. I've learned from SOM classes that in order to be permanently well we must be poised, peaceful, and happy. The soul deserts it, and functions on another plane, when the body is no longer a fit instrument. It seems like a long time since Momma's been poised, peaceful, and happy.

Although I thought I had no fear, I do fear Terry may interfere and try to prolong Momma's life. There still seems to be a karmic connection between them and our brother Amos. Momma is the only one who ignores Amos' addiction to crack, while Terry always points it out.

Thought is the movement of ego, independent of God. Words promote separation for they came into being with thought, which came after the separation from God. Ego also rose from the separation. It feeds on our continuing belief in disunity. There is no separation and our inner calling is to end this illusion.

Fear is one of the greatest denials of the reality of God and a barrier to growth. A Course In Miracles notes fear came into existence when the illusion of separation from God began. It's our identification with the body, values of the brain, and personality, but it's not natural to us. There are no opinions, judgments, or unforgiving thoughts when we enter the Mind of God.

Fear is always the cause of illness and places an incredible burden on the physical body. Emmanuel notes, "Fear is the necromancer who takes a functioning, beautiful physical being and transforms it into precisely what you fear."

When the body is no longer disrupted, it's able to function harmoniously. We begin to experience great moments of illumination when finally ridding ourselves of fear. The lifting of the veil begins and we remember who we really are, spirits having a human experience.

Everything is energy and everything is Spirit. Our bodies are shadows of our divine essence, each on certain vibrations out of tune with the higher frequencies, unless we take the time to reconnect with Source. The essence is within, always prompting us to see beyond the illusion, to recognize that we are gods of matter.

Walter Starcke notes in It's All God, "Until we can look right at human conditions and simultaneously be aware of what we see and the fallacy of appearances, we divide rather than reconcile."

I say a treatment for Momma and return to sleep. She is a good soul, and I know is, and has always been, in the hands of God.

Upon checking email later, I'm saddened by Cosmo Baker's announcement of Wilson Pickett's passing. I offer a prayer for his soul before reading the daily message from Beliefnet. It offers words of wisdom I relate to, noting ignorance is the failure to discriminate between the permanent and the impermanent. I've spent most of my life in ignorance, and now realize it's time to awaken, even though my family does not understand.

It now seems vital to rid myself of the past. Yet, sorting through twenty years of paperwork, on hiv nutrition, tires me out. It's hard to decide what to keep. I soon give up and fall fast asleep.

Minutes later, I wake hearing, *she's not ready, she can't go now. I cannot take her now. She still has something to contribute to the world.* I rise confused to continue the day.

Rebecca still has my car. She stops by in the early evening to report on Momma's huge stomach bruise. It's getting better. Maybe Momma decided to go on with less pain. I can only hope as I answer the day's email.

A Christian researcher answers my request for information about a past life regression by asking for details. I relate the life regression in 960 A.D. as an old woman called "Samantha" who is slain by the King's soldiers, for harboring the Christian James.

"Interesting," he writes. "I guess the most useful place to begin, if you want to verify the historical accuracy of your vision, would be to determine who ruled Samaria then, and whether or not they were actively persecuting Christians. I'd say you need an historian, not an amateur genealogist. Sorry I can't be more help."

His email offers a link to the American Bible Society. I follow it hoping they'll help me verify the past life. Not knowing where to start, I relate the beginning of my current life.

"I planned to get pregnant at 15-years-old, to have someone who would always love me, and whom I could always love. Many things happened along the way since my son's birth. We always held a deep love for one another. He passed at age thirty-seven on 4/4/04. Since his passing, I've had many extraordinary experiences.

"I sense my son has shown me there is more to life than what meets the human 'untrained eye'. I've always known this but the sense of it increases daily. I started doing my own life regressions using the instructions from Dr. Weiss' second book, taped in my own voice.

"After I did a few on my own, I then paid a licensed Ph.D. who led me through and verified the first life regression. I needed a prescription from my doctor to see her, and diagnosed with many conditions, got one for high blood pressure. I didn't tell this professional anything about myself. My faith in God is strong."

I relate the regression and add a bit more about myself.

"I have always been a humanitarian. For the last twenty years, I've owned a small business but it's been difficult to continue the work. I now have a new mission. The world is getting more erratic and more people will try to make some sense of it all. I'll help as many as I can, and now, am just trying to put some pieces together to get a better understanding of whom, why, and when.

"Nope, I do not do dope, am not high, or greatly religious. I have always believed in a higher power and myself. I started classes at Religious Science and much of what I read in *The Science of Mind*, and hear in the classes, is just verification of what I already know. Thanks for your kind consideration."

The man answers my query quickly but notes he can't find a thing that gives a Rebekah as the mother of James and John.

Rebecca phones to ask if James and I will come for pizza and a movie. Since she still has my car, we drive over together but barely speak. Surrounded by an undercurrent of tension, it flows between us while watching *Star Wars*. Rebecca discusses finances and health as the film unfolds. She sounds fearful of many things, but when I point out there's no reason for limitation, she gets upset.

"I'll always be here for you Rebecca," I tell her loudly, "even though I may not be able to help. Just remember thoughts manifest into things."

"There you go again talking about how you're going to haunt me after you're dead," she says heatedly. "I know how to get rid of spirits so you won't bother me."

"I'll always be there for you and Samuel," I reply.

Discussion abruptly ends.

Rebecca wakes James at the end of the movie while I'm in the bathroom so he can drive us home. The silence is deafening. I feel wholly alone in my beliefs and wonder if anyone else will realize this earth is not our real home.

At one point in time, there is something within us that notes there has to be more to life than what we see. Emmanuel tells us it's because there's a cellular memory of being beyond physical manifestation in the perfection of Oneness. Crossing the threshold of physicality, we entered into separation, forgetting the essence of Self.

:-)

Chapter Five

Ego Pushes On

"We are all of One Mind, though it has not yet dawned on you, and all questions and all answers are known to the One Mind, thus known to you. Yet your sight is veiled, and you perceive only the shadows and not their source."
Dennis William Hauck – The Emerald Tablet: Alchemy for Personal Transformation

Sometimes I dream of jobs worked long ago. This morning I remember helping Jezebel at the bakery. The dream seems real making me wonder if we live parallel lives as noted in many of the books I read. Am I, as described in *Destiny of Souls*, one of those extraordinarily ambitious souls leading a parallel life?

Time is not linear, as science leads us to believe. We live many lives, human and non-human, simultaneously in other realities parallel to this one. Our souls work through many layers of reality at the same time affecting others lives as well as our own. Other planes of consciousness love and protect humanity. Acknowledging the awareness of these realities brings us closer to the truth.

The basic teachings of Michael note billions of parallel universes, co-existing in the same space, but in different space/time fields than ours. A new parallel universe spins off, assuring that all possibilities of each personality play out, every time we make a major decision.

In his bestseller, The Divine Matrix, Gregg Braden reports our world may be a projection of events happening in an underlying reality, a reality we change with our thoughts. Our thoughts transform the possibilities of deeper realms into physical reality. Even without fully understanding the scientific logic, it seems reasonable for everything is energy.

Emmanuel tells us souls exist in many realities and it's impossible to place them geographically. When we're ready to receive guidance in the way of unity and not in a dependant

32

childlike way, intergalactic communication will become a part of everyday existence. Ultimately, all is one, all is here, and all is now.

Author of It's All God, *Walter Starcke, reminds us to be grateful for this state of being. He notes:*

"Thank God that this world is a parallel universe to which we can return not only for a refresher course when we need it, but also where we can rejoin our human/spiritual friends for a class reunion and share our experience with those who are still bewildered."

An email announces my nomination as Amateur Photographer of the Year later in the afternoon. The message invites me to speak about the story behind my "Florida Wilma" photo at "the most prestigious gathering of professional and amateur photographers ever assembled." I'm thrilled to see the Annual Convention and Symposium is held in Las Vegas, Nevada. The sender writes of cash prizes and "very special awards" for my photographic achievement, including applause from fellow photographers, and a Commemorative Award Medallion honoring my dedication and achievements at a weekend full of sessions.

Before reading the fine print, returning to Las Vegas sounds exciting. Disappointment sets in upon reading I must pay my own expenses and complete the "Artist's Proof" for a book I can buy when it's published. I don't expect a reply to my response that this appears to be a ruse to make money.

The house on 47th Drive no longer feels like home. There's something much grander on the Otherside. It now seems wise to detach from this illusionary world, while still sharing love. I joyously email friends about *The INDIGO Evolution* movie showing at the Center. They're alarmed when I note the Center is a mere two blocks away from James' house.

The usual body numbness wakes me near dawn. I'm saying something about all good, how something will be used only for all good. James is in the shower. It's 5:33 AM. I fall back asleep asking to wake an hour before sunrise.

A short time later, snoring wakes me to recall a dream. I was crying out for Joseph after calling Mattie to no avail. A figure dressed in black was choking me. My throat now has the same constricted feeling it does when I lay down sometimes too tired to stay awake. It makes gurgling sounds as it fills with a thick green fluid. Maybe this is just a response to the *Star Wars* movie we saw days ago.

James eats, scraping the bowl, in front of the TV, as he watches the news. The sound wafts down the hall to my room. The morning ritual flows quietly from head to lips as he leaves for work. After completing spiritual work, I switch gears to clear physical remnants of my past.

It's time to start another life by acknowledging lessons and putting what went before aside. For nearly five hours, I plow through what seems like mountains of aids/hiv material. Some of it is easy to discard but many items hold memories difficult to abandon. I place them in a shipping box remembering Rev. Bump says we must rid ourselves of old mental reactions to transcend experiences. Changing the past through different perception changes the imprint for everyone because thought waves circulate throughout space. Tiredness soon overwhelms me and I fall quickly asleep.

Ruth's voice rings through my brain moments later.

"Momma, she's gone Samantha."

I rise to read about dis-ease in *The Science of Mind*. It is clear sickness is an experience, an effect caused by lifestyle, including thoughts. The illnesses that seem to consume me must be released. I've had enough limitation and know the Law of Cause and Effect will operate in my favor. The next step is to stop taking the blood pressure medication prescribed by the Internist. It will be easy to do since I've already decreased the dose and sequester myself in a peaceful sunlit room. I smile at the thought and drift back to sleep.

There's barely time to eat before class when my eyes open again. Rebecca still has my car but I don't mind the walk to the Center. It's a pleasure to be able to move through fresh air without feeling the heat of summer. Feeling rejuvenated, I walk briskly going a few blocks out of my way to prolong the adventure.

Class offers a string of 'holy instants' where I suspend judgment and look upon others as God's holy children. I've stopped looking at people as a body and see everyone as the same when at the Center. New volunteers making coffee for the 12-step program become friends just like the previous week's recruits. They all seem to love my hugs and it makes me feel good to give them. For some mysterious reason the feeling of oneness doesn't seem to last for long elsewhere.

I sit with the office administrator, Rev. Kandi Haggerty, at the back of the classroom while Dr. Bump describes the difference between prayer and treatment.

"We need a volunteer to head up the hospitality department," Kandi announces with a sly grin during our fifteen-minute break. "Can you commit to setting up the coffee station on Sundays?"

I've recently resigned from several volunteer commitments related to hiv/aids and do not want to become overloaded again.

"I come on Wednesday nights because I like the smaller crowd," I answer softly with a smile while reaching for a fresh pot of coffee. "And mornings are not my thing."

"Well," she says turning her head to look at the hospitality schedule on the refrigerator, "as long as you can get volunteers for the two Sunday morning services just coming on Wednesday won't be an issue. I can help you schedule volunteers for classes and special events."

"I'll schedule Sunday volunteers for now," I tell her not really knowing how, "but I'll feel more comfortable if you get someone else. I'm backing off from volunteer duties."

I don't realize the agreement will help me become more involved with the Center and the people who come there.

Checking email after arriving home, I search for a message from Rebecca to no avail. Several emails to her remain unanswered. We live in different worlds, but I make one more attempt to reach her, sending something funny about teenagers, which sounds a lot like Samuel. Ego comes out of hiding as I continue our last conversation typing quickly.

"I will **not** be with you or Samuel always if you do not want me to be. Live in fear or not. It is your choice. You have, and daily use, your ability to shape your life. Your life is what you say it is and nothing else." Continuing to allow my old overbearing ego to vent, I add a quote from Anguttara Nikaya from the days email hoping she'll read it.

"Luminous is this mind, brightly shining, but it is colored by the attachments that visit it. This unlearned people do not really understand, and so do not cultivate the mind. Luminous is this mind, brightly shining, and it is free of the attachments that visit it. This the noble follower of the way really understands; so for them there is cultivation of the mind."

It doesn't occur to me that the message is really for me as I end my email sweetly letting Rebecca know my love will never change. Many hours later, I realize much of the discord between us stems from my own judgment and forgetfulness, which she is too polite to acknowledge.

Words from an unknown source wake me the next morning.

Love is all there is in this perfect world of love, peace, and harmony.

James shifts through his closet for work clothes as the train roars by on the railroad tracks four blocks away. The day begins and soon I'm weeding through email. Although research briefs, digests, messages from various professional journals, Democracy Now, and Kaiser Reports will never be put to use, as in the past, I still find myself downloading them out of habit.

Email petitions concerning health care and insurance hold attention, sapping positive energy. It's appalling to think insurance companies may limit access to usual doctors and subject me to repeated tests. Personal experience reveals the health care system is failing miserably. Nowadays, due to greed, there's too much administration and too few dedicated health care professionals.

I've learned all we can count on here is change. The more tests and operations we have the weaker our body gets. That's why I decided two years ago not to have any more tests or operations. Currently, I take much fewer medications and have less pain. I think it's due to my spiritual studies. It's great to know the body I inhabit is not the real me. I can change it with my thoughts.

An email of thanks for the business website makes ego happy. Despite increasing disinterest in hiv/aids, detaching seems difficult as I check website statistics to find they increased. Perhaps I can funds my new humanitarian mission by selling the business to someone who will carry on the work. The clock now reminds me it's time to dress before leaving the house to volunteer at the Center.

Minutes later, I'm looking forward to seeing *The INDIGO Evolution* as I move through the large classroom putting green tablecloths on brown tables. The work prompts memories of my catering days, serving others, and supporting a family, while attending community college. Those days are past. Now it's time to create different memories, of abundance and joy.

Returning home, I type quickly documenting another day, of light, of love, of self-fulfillment, of belonging, and of sadness.

Today was another day of separation from blood relatives but union with my new chosen family.

"We all as humans have a lot more abilities than we use. After seeing *The INDIGO Evolution*, I'm elated to know I am not alone. My telepathy with Daniel and Rebecca, and their children, confirms our unity as Indigos, people who realize, at one point or another, that they have an increased awareness of their abilities.

"Spalding notes the great power contained in mental telepathy, *God speaking to God*. Every child born is a perfect Christ child. Only human thoughts lower it. Rebecca, Samuel, and Abigail all know they are different from what most people believe as the norm but, as life, uncertainties often delay us from following through on our life mission.

"It was encouraging to see there are more children and adults diagnosed with attention-deficit hyperactivity disorder (ADHD), attention-deficit disorder (ADD), or labeled weird because they think without limitations. We are here to make the world a better place.

"The thing to remember is that our abilities are no stronger or different from other humans. We just are more conscious of them. I sense it's vital to nurture these abilities, rather than allow the 'veil' to cover consciousness with the acquisition of useless material possessions, and negative words of discouragement concerning Indigo judgment and visions.

"Many Indigo children are born with memories of past lives, and waiting to be born to their chosen mother. I know Daniel chose me just as I manifested him. I think Rebecca chose me too but only she knows that, for now at least. I'm pleased and hopeful that recent visions will come true. My head hurts more and my heart is too heavy to continue trying to mend this body while fighting off negativity and ungratefulness. Yet, I must forge ahead to pave the way.

"Reading ahead in class work, I see Holmes notes emotional attitudes and ideas of tension, fear, conflict and struggle result in physical pain. Grief, shock, loss of love and fear result in problems with the heart. Perhaps my blood family will recognize and use their powers of manifestation in their next incarnation. We can choose differently and get different results.

"I await deliverance from this unstable world to join my spirit family and try to open closed minds from the Otherside, if not my birth families, then others. I will always continue to make this world a better place no matter what form I take on. I will never go back to the unconscious state again. My next life will begin near the end of humanity. But at least then, I'll have all the tools needed to wake the others. And, yes, I know Daniel and Rebecca's spirits will be with mine in the end as we strive for peace, love, harmony, and unity with all things, as One."

Suddenly exhausted, I stop typing and take a quick shower before saying bedtime blessings. Ego is happy to have pulled me further into the illusion of separation. Sleep fills with quickly forgotten messages when waking throughout the night.

Another night of sleeping only on my back, still feeling the bars of the futon below, makes it difficult to rest. I decide to shop for another foam mattress after finishing the usual morning prayers and study.

There's a CD you'll love at the thrift store fills my brain.

A caterpillar sits directly in my path as I walk out the door. Looking down at its motionless form, I note if it wants to come into the house, it must climb up by the doorbell before I return. I slowly pass it and drive the short distance to search for bargain CDs at my favorite thrift store. Even though I have less than three dollars in my pocket, I know it's enough.

Karen Drucker's "Hold On To Love" sits in a cluttered CD bin. I've wanted it ever since hearing its signature song at a Wednesday night service. The CD looks brand new and cost a dollar so I rifle through the used cassette tapes as well. A cassette by Poison sits securely in its original case. I search through the songs and see it holds "Something To Believe In." Daniel asked me to get the song more than a year ago.

As I move on to another discount store to charge a foam mattress, it occurs to me that one day; soon, I'll have my very own place. And I will feel comfortable in every room. It seems impossible, yet when I see a shower curtain with penguins on it in the markdown bin; I add it to my cart for a new space. I'm beaming from ear to ear while charging purchases to my Visa credit card.

The drive home is easy despite an increase in cars due to tourists. My eyes rest on a caterpillar by the doorbell at the den door. I sense it's time for the caterpillar to transform into a butterfly. The thought pleases me for I'm still hoping to pass during the night. I've designed a colorful yellow, orange, black, and brown butterfly, in my mind, and plan to use the form as a signal to let my family know all is well from the Otherside.

With a smile, I enter the house to unload packages before returning for the caterpillar. I get a plastic cup and take it out into the back yard. Leafs and flower buds from the night blooming jasmine go into the cup before telling the caterpillar it can enter as well. The caterpillar clings to my fingers and tickles me with its countless furry legs. After a few minutes, it worms its way into the cup. I place it on my bookshelf, pour a bit of water into a bottle cap, and place it beside the cup before walking away.

After placing the foam under the futon mattress, I log onto the Internet. "The Futurist" Robert Downey, Jr.'s new CD, plays in the background as I switch between checking email and studying. Shortly before class, I open *The Science of Mind* to a random page and suddenly feel as if Homes speaks directly to me, for I'm still hoping to leave the physical plane as soon as possible. It's not just the physical body, which still seems very cumbersome, but the remembrance of what lies on the other side of the veil of forgetfulness as well.

Holmes notes we live on three planes of life at the same time, physical, intellectual, and spiritual. "To attempt to desert any one of these, to the cost of the others, is abnormal."

I'm no longer concerned with these planes but wish to pass beyond them to that place of pure Oneness where only love, peace, and joy exist. After closing, and reopening, the book to another random page, I'm faced with page 489. It's a short discussion of mental expansion. I know I'm an inlet for God and now consider consciously becoming an outlet of the Source within. Can I move thoughts out of perceived limitation and reflect the greater glory of God? Daniel told me it's a gradual process. I now welcome the change more fully knowing that changing beliefs form new patterns of thought.

Dr. Bump tells us later in class that the Law is always working in everything we do, say, or write. It's clear I still use limiting language after filling out the class worksheet. My written answers reflect a contrast of changing consciousness. While I'll always be peaceful and spiritual, ego counts on my family to be disruptive and negative. I believe my work is God's work, for the greater good, and decide to use more "freeing language" in the future. It's clearly time to consider the results of my thoughts and make them positive, life giving, and for the greater good.

We are beings of Power, masters of thought and builders of environment and destiny. Because our thoughts create the material world, we transform by renewing our mind. Charles Fillmore notes in *The Twelve Powers of Man*, "The mind generates an energy that contacts the universal energy, and causes circumstances and events to fall into line for the attainment of the latent ideal." Careful thoughts and actions create ideal outer conditions.

:-)

Chapter Six

Connections

*"Out of the One comes the many expressing the diverse faces of the
One and when they are fully expressed they naturally reunite,
recreating the One."*
Christine Page – Spiritual Alchemy

Juggling old earthly issues while deciding what's now pertinent to ever-changing consciousness puts me between Heaven and hell. Taking classes at the Center is what I'm to do but the number of people requesting information on newsletter subjects, covered many years ago, haunts me. There's still a need for information on hiv nutrition. The question remains. "Can I end the old mission without feeling guilt?"

Although hurricane season ended months ago, the business equipment, including a desktop computer, remains stored in the closet. It no longer seems necessary to have the computer act as an answering machine. I've even placed the telephone in the hall. Most house calls are for James and I don't want him in my room anymore.

A laptop computer, portable CD player, numerous pictures of family, Abigail's wrapped birthday presents, and the crystal figurine Daniel gave me years ago fill my work area. The crystal reminds me that I deserve nice things. Since Daniel's been physically gone, no one outside of the Center reminds me of my value. I realize it's time to, as Daniel would say, put on my big girl panties and remind myself.

A lit candle remains on my desk twenty-four hours a day but I don't know why. I'm also compelled to put a filter into the air conditioning vent in my room even though the unit is off.

The recumbent bicycle Daniel lugged home from the store for me sits unused as I check email. Democracy Now reports Cindy Sheehan, whose son Casey died in Iraq on the same day Daniel transitioned, was arrested at the State of the Union address after unveiling a T-shirt with an anti-war message. Authorities dropped charges and media coverage the next day.

It's storming outside. I'm glad to be safe in my room feeling positive energy. Life is a contrast of worlds as I shift through thousands of unread listserv messages for personal correspondence. Email from medical, health, and political groups no longer matters. Messages from Beliefnet verify new beliefs. Yes, life is a matter of balance. Work consumed every waking moment for many years but those days are over. Now I'm easier on myself, resting as desired, and limiting outside ventures to a bare minimum.

The furry, red, electronic Christmas Furby stares at me but rarely speaks. I miss its sporadic chatter. Inspirational music plays in the background as I use gift cards received at Christmas to buy movies online. They're more than enough to order what I want. What a grand feeling to buy things without a second thought!

The day is almost over when I telephone Rachel. Her answering machine records my monthly loving message. It's impossible to determine if Abigail gets the monthly greeting cards. I continue to send them hoping she does. Abigail's next card sits safely in the mailbox as I drift off to sleep.

Numerous experiences and revelations occur during slumber but I can't disclose them now; perhaps they are not to be shared at all.

Sunshine climbs above the horizon when I wake thinking something is different. I'm lying on my stomach and there's no right-sided numbness! It's been years since I've felt this good. I've slept on my back to avoid right sided numbness for so long that I was beginning to think doctors were right. Now I'm positive there's no need for spinal surgery.

The Science of Mind sits on the floor. I pick it up, close my eyes, and open it to a random page. My finger points to "Arise, My Spirit" on page 536. "Arise, my Spirit, arise and shine," it begins. It's reassuring to know that love, peace, and harmony will continue to fill days even though family avoids me because I no longer fit in the old unhealthy mold. The family closeness nurtured for years is gone. I tell myself it's okay, as it must be, and it's all good.

The twice a day ritual still includes a treatment for Rebecca. I'm happy to check email when it's complete. A collection of jokes with animated pictures, from our Michigan friend Sara, delights me. It sure would be nice to have a friend nearby. I thank Sara before sending slide show links to a classmate named Leah.

42

Replying to business email distracts me from my new mission. I still can't ignore requests on subjects researched in the past. After answering a message received several weeks before, I decide to contact the people on Daniel's list, offering Suggestions for the 21st Century penned the previous year. (5)

"I think the 'times' are rapidly changing," I write hurriedly as if someone might stop me. "These words came to me several months ago. They are things I try to do to keep what's left of my sanity ;-o. Rough days are ahead. Take care of yourselves and remember I will always be with you in spirit."

A storm drifts by outside but it doesn't bother me. Nighttime blessings are complete by 3:30 AM. Before drifting off to sleep, I ask to wake in three hours to complete the morning routine.

Good journey to you fills my head three hours later.

The heavy rainstorm has passed. My stout, red candle, on the computer desk a few feet away, is half-full but the flame is gone. I rise quickly, use the bathroom, and re-light the candle before repeating the day's ritual. It's Saturday and James is sleeping across the hall so I will not be as loud.

Sleep beckons as usual after meditations and treatments are complete. The telephone wakes me a short time later. It sounds like James has a cold as he talks to someone on the phone and sure enough, he tells the caller he does. A treatment noting his perfection escapes my lips before falling back asleep.

A short movie passes by closed eyes less than an hour later. It looks like a picture in a journal or magazine, pure white, but two thirds of it is a profile of Daniel, the right side of his face. I'm pleased, and see a few more things but fall back asleep forgetting what they are.

The sound of my door slamming shut jolts me to wakefulness. I lie still wondering how the door could have opened, and then slammed shut, because it was closed before I drifted off to sleep. Now, I recall Daniel smiling, and looking great, like he did when we went to my brother Aaron's Michigan wedding with Amos. I think I shall always get to hear Daniel's voice in my head. Even though we are all spirits taking on different forms, his voice is the one that makes me want to do what I hear. I smile remembering the many times Daniel's essence said, "Go to bed, you're working too hard." Things like that help me to restore balance and prepare for what's to come.

It's beginning to rain again. I think the storms will continue... Catastrophe drives us toward positive change and that's the only kind of change I want to focus on.

James peeks his head into my room later in the afternoon. "You spend a lot of time on that laptop," he says. "Show me the money. Where's the money? Where do you keep the money you make?"

My bladder begins to burn upon detecting a note of sarcasm. I turn around slowly after sending an email. "I'm still trying to sell the business so I can fund my new mission helping everyone to wakeup," I reply as calmly as possible. "There is no money. You have all the power and money now."

"Do you think your new mission will bring any money into this household?" he asks, before turning away and muttering something under his breath.

It's time to work on abundance. This is the first time in many years that I have not had a few thousand dollars put away for emergencies or family vacations. I sign with relief knowing there's a few hundred dollars hidden away after cashing in my individual retirement account (IRA) last year. Bon Jovi's latest CD plays on the portable CD player as I reach for *The Science of Mind*. The book opens to page 532 and I'm calmly guided to read "Complete Confidence." Yes, my confidence in the All Good is complete.

My mind strays moments later. Some people are not taught how to love or it is battered out of them at an early age. We take care of what we love. First, we love ourselves, then others. Look around this house. It's literally falling apart with peeling paint from the den ceiling, food dropped on the floor and left there, and a hole in the porch ceiling for three years now. There's love in my one room. Look around. You will see it.

Music fills the room as I type a presentable list of published newsletters to show potential buyers of the corporation. Yet, I sense big changes, big dreams, and big troubles ahead...

Everything is part of the Greater Plan. In her groundbreaking book, Conscious Evolution, Barbara Marx Hubbard explains a strategy that is now changing the doomsday approach to one of a positive nurturing shift of consciousness. Millions of people are realizing they have a role to play as nurturing co-creators for a better world. Conscious evolution, being

44

aware of our role as co-creators with the process of evolution, is spreading quickly throughout the globe.

New proactive groups form periodically but the ones I am most familiar with are Hubbard's Foundation for Conscious Evolution (BarbaraMarxHubbard.com), Redfield's Global Prayer Project (CelestineVision.com), and Joseph Giove's Common Passion (CommonPassion.org). Each group offers opportunities to globally connect with others through teleconferencing, Internet Webcasts and face-to-face. Their get-togethers create positive, loving, energy filled opportunities that nurture humanity, our atmosphere and beyond.

The old world is quickly collapsing as more and more people no longer believe in the old "story." World-changing harmonious events are a joy to participate in as people from all over the globe bring forth all that is within to evolve the world to a state of unconditional love. Although each group has their own way of reaching out, their collective power assures our goal of evolving humanity, consciously and ethically.

I'm so very tired of waking, going to the bathroom, and falling back asleep. Words from a song fill my brain in the wee hours of the morning. *Who says you can't go home?* I try to fall back asleep after recognizing Bon Jovi's new hit but more words enter my brain on the cusp of sleep. *He went quickly, freely, with no pain, for he knew his true being.* These waking words are welcome for I relate them to Daniel's passing.

Blessings and treatments flow from head to lips minutes after sunrise as God's Power flows through me. Only time will tell if false beliefs remain to hinder the process of manifestation. Yet, I can reject them after recognizing that they make me feel depressed, sick, or jealous.

Now I'm prompted to check the NOAA/National Weather Service online for information on weather in space. Venus is up before sunrise in the southeast sky. It explains why I'm compelled to search the heavens throughout the night.

Messages during meditation, concerning my Michigan friend Ester, prompt me to telephone but there's no answer. I push thoughts aside and leave the house to refill a prescription. The drug store blood pressure monitor reveals a pressure of 127/72. It documents a vast improvement from the days of higher blood pressure hovering constantly at, or near, 172/90.

A conscious decision to look only at what I want, ignoring things that compete for attention, comes later in the morning while reading *The Science of Mind*. The prayer on page 185 becomes part of my daily routine.

"Perfect God *within me*, Perfect Life *within me*, which is God, come forth into expression through me as that which I am; lead me ever into the paths of perfection and cause me to see only the Good."

It's becoming increasingly clear that everything has origin in thought. Life is finally a constructive program that robs no one and creates no delusions. My thoughts are positive, life giving, and for the greater good, for I know we reap what we sow.

Sometimes it's hard to conceive of things as already accomplished, especially when the body's pain calls for attention. Today I ignore the pain knowing it's possible to produce harmony out of what appears as chaos by controlling emotions. It's easier to do as long as I go between my room and class.

Words ring through my brain minutes after lying down to nap. "These are some heavy-duty remarks," I think before falling back to sleep.

Hours later the telephone rings just one time. Now the toilet is running, as if recently flushed, so I began to walk through the living room to see if someone is in the house. The den motion detector light is on.

I concentrate but hear no message trying to make sense of it all. Why did the phone ring once? Why is the toilet running? And why is the den light on? Thoughts of Aunt Lois in Michigan and calling Ruth cross my mind but the telephone gives me an off the hook signal when I pick it up in the hall. The den phone is just plain dead.

So again, I wait on *Thee*.

Ruth telephones a bit later complaining that my computer is messing up the phone. She's the one who called. I calmly let her know we no longer have an answering machine and the business computer has not been hooked up to the telephone line for a long time. It's been in the closet since last summer.

She surprises me by asking if I'll walk with her in the park. It's clear either Ruth has something on her mind or James has spread the word that he'll be out of town for two days. I agree to meet her tomorrow morning at eleven o'clock. She reports Amos is out of jail and back on the streets before we end the call. I quickly design a treatment for him. [6] Amos is fifty-years-old today.

It's now easy to see how many of us choose to avoid the voice of our soul through the avenue of addiction. We use addictions to mask our fears and block emotions. Any addiction deprives others, and us, of true intimacy with God and limits the potential for full realization of the Soul. I'm surprised to note my favorite addictions listed within the pages of Spiritual Alchemy. *Some addictions, including my all time favorites, are perfectionism and faultfinding, being a martyr, workaholic, overly serious or the opposite, constantly talking, excessive exercise, and being a professional patient dependant on others.*

Sylvia doesn't answer when I arrive at her door before the Wednesday service. The Section Eight housing unit hall stinks like three-day old fish so I quickly depart to take my station next to the sound system. The service is short and, as usual, refreshing.

It feels wonderful the next day to get out of the house and into fresh air with someone to talk with. Ruth and I walk a few minutes before she asks me a loaded question.

"How are you and James doing? Are you getting along any better or still at each others throats?"

I figure James must be up to something and reassure her as much as I can while explaining my beliefs and new mission in life.

"None of us understand this mission of yours," she tells me honestly. "Why can't you just act the way you used to? Why do you always have to be different?"

"Because since Daniel passed over to the Otherside I've been able to see things differently," I reply touching her arm as we walk between two calm lakes. "It will turn out okay. Don't worry."

As I discuss how we are all the Christ in God, as it says in *The Science of Mind*, a plane begins to write in the clear blue sky. I smile as words form directly in front of us. "U + God = :-)."

"Look at this grand demonstration!" I exclaim loudly pointing up into the air. "You know I don't believe in coincidences."

Ruth looks up quickly and replies with a cynical sneer. "It's just the Jesus man I read about in the paper. He's rich now and has nothing to do since he's retired. He's around here all the time."

"It's not a coincidence Ruth. You know we were meant to see the message right now as I talk about how we are parts of God. Look, there's even a smiley face."

Ruth looks up at the sky again and shakes her head from side to side. "There's no way you can convince me it's a special message for us."

I give up trying, thankful that we've had a good walk. It's been a time of joy for me to be able to share what's going on in our lives. We agree to take turns picking up Momma before meeting to walk at the park twice a week until Ruth gets a job. A "Pr" appears in the sky as I drive out of the park. By the time I get home, the sky reads: "U + God = :-) Praise Jesus."

Two caterpillars sit near the doorbell. I allow them to climb into my outstretched hand after unlocking the door. They crawl slowly into the plastic container and hide under the fresh leaves placed in it earlier. The other caterpillar is motionless. I wonder why it has no cocoon but after placing a few drops of fresh water in the container begin to study for class.

A few hours later, Rebecca calls to invite me to see another *Star Wars* movie tomorrow night. It's been a number of weeks since someone in the family contacted me so I know James called the family. Rebecca admits he called to tell her he'd be out of town but tries to convince me she planned on calling anyway.

Later, Space Weather News reports NASA's Cassini spacecraft is tracking an intense lightning storm on Saturn. The powerful bolts are causing the spacecraft's radio instruments to "crackle" like the crackles from a car's AM radio when driving by thunderstorms. I don't know how, but feel it affects humans too. The moon looks full with a ring around it and summons me to take a picture. Two white orbs are prominent in the photo I take before slipping off to sleep.

Rejoice in the beautiful day rouses me to wakefulness the next morning. I joyfully rise to repeat the morning ritual before going online. It's easy to ignore an email broadcasting Dick Cheney's hunting accident by focusing on the day's message from Beliefnet.

"Don't go by gossip and rumor, nor by what's told you by others, nor by what you hear said, nor even by the authority of your traditional teachings…"

Rev. Peck's "Sisters in Spirit" monthly dinner offers a way to connect with a wonderful group of empowering women. I sit quietly after dark listening to Dr. Nathalie Campeau discuss her ideas of boosting energy on demand. My heart soars as she talks about the power of our hearts so I decide to make "Heart-Smiling" a habit. It's easy to help with the clean up as we all share laughter and love.

After arriving back in my room, I log onto the Internet to check email. It's been two years since the transition of a friend, and now, I'm saddened to see I failed to follow a motivation link he sent before taking his own life. I forward the link to friends and relatives wishing he'd truly believed in what it says.

"All is as it should be," I tell them. "It's less hostile as I do daily treatments to keep it that way. I am happy in my own white light room."

It's time to try a different attitude because most of my life is spent in judgment acting upon something before it acts on me. From now on, I'll consciously try to maintain an unbiased position, uncover the Truth, neutralize, and erase false beliefs. Trauma becomes obsolete as I remove myself from drama and omit the words wrong and problem, replacing them with inappropriate and issue. The daily prayer ritual continues to include a treatment concerning love. [7]

:-)

Chapter Seven

Letting Go

"The second we have individually experienced the slightest
transformation of consciousness, we are a new person and the past
becomes obsolete."
Walter Starcke – It's All God

The electronic list at Daniel's memorial website provides an avenue to reconnect with his friends. "We are all good," I report to the list, days before what would have been his thirty-ninth birthday. As Daniel said, "Life is good. The World is good. Enjoy yourself."

A quick peek at the clock reminds me it's time for class.

It's delightful to walk under clear skies amid a cool breeze. I happily set up the beverage station upon arriving and find another way to tithe. It feels very good to share my favorite decaf herbal tea and Splenda at the table.

Beau approaches me with a wide grin during the break. "You're a Course student, aren't you?" he says with a knowing look. He repeats the words more like a statement than a question.

"What course do you mean?" I reply, filled with curiosity.

"*A Course In Miracles*," he answers clasping one of my hands in his. "It's a popular work channeled by Jesus through a woman named Helen. When you talk it's clear your beliefs reflect what's in the Course."

"You're the second person in the last couple of months that's asked me if I'm a Course student."

"Apparently, it's time to begin your Course studies," he announces as Dr. Bump calls for our attention once again.

I sit down and make a note to get *A Course In Miracles*.

The next morning I wake remembering a dream in which I talked to my Internist. He asked how I was. I told him my blood pressure was down to 127/72 without medication. "I took your advice and started exercising," I'd happily noted.

"Remember to eat better," he said with a grin and warm hug. "I'm taking some time off to be with family and slow down. Take care of yourself."

Dream details sit on a yellow legal pad before sleep overwhelms me.

We supply the word by sharing our skills wakes me moments later. I rise quickly to make pasta salad for our family's Sunday get together.

After another day of study and prayer, I'm ready to sleep but slumber does not come easily. My brain insists on remembering years of birthdays. They'll be no more birthdays for Daniel. Sleep finally claims me as soothing music blares though headphones resting on my chest. It's impossible to keep headphones on my ears because the volume level knob on the portable CD player broke.

James leaves the house Sunday morning before I wake. I'm glad he's spending a few hours with Rachel and Abigail before meeting the family to share what would have been Daniel's birthday. After meditation and treatments, there's still time to update Daniel's friends. It seems appropriate to note that after life is when it matters. Pictures, videos, and voice messages document daily life, hopes, dreams and sometimes our struggles, failures, and losses. They give us a way to measure progress as functional human beings, but after life is when it really matters.

Sharing a bit of myself with listserv members, I note the wonderful feeling of being home as soon as I walked through the Centers' doors in May 2005. It's amazing so many people at the place Daniel's soul prompted me to enter have been members for forty years, or more. I always feel 'in the flow' whether there for classes or services.

Fingers slowly type as ego dictates, relating the self-imposed solitude of my fifty-fifth birthday. It's meaningful for that's the day I designed the Spiritual Mind Treatment for Children, without fully realizing that words turn into things, thoughts that can come true.

"Originally, the treatment was for Daniel's soul," I gladly reveal, "for I sensed his essence returned in a new form and I wanted to nurture his soul's spiritual growth. Yet, while writing the words, it occurred to me that all children are the future of humanity. Holmes notes since role models influence children, sometimes it's necessary to teach parents how to think about their child. Hoping to spur greater thoughts, I designed the treatment for all children, and not just for Daniel, who would have been thirty-nine today. The treatment is my way of helping children to grow up healthy, free of any dis-ease, fear, or addiction."

The clock reminds me it's time to go. I head quickly for the door deciding to leave my camera behind. James arrives at Ruth and Naomi's minutes later with his digital camera. We greedily pore over photos of Abigail. She wears a bright red top with pink shorts while jumping on her new trampoline. I'm happy to hear she still goes into her clubhouse to "talk with Daddy."

After dinner and a quick game of pinochle, I head home before James to work on Daniel's memorial website. It seems important to share thoughts, again noting as the spirit that was known as Daniel continues to evolve, so must I. Holding on to the human is fruitless. I know his human form is gone, never was, and it's truly time to let go. I must encourage spiritual growth in all humans as I do in myself. To hang on to a human's life is to hold them back spiritually. I no longer wish to do that. I'm eternally grateful his soul continues to evolve into an even greater awareness of his True Self, pure Spirit.

When Daniel was about three-years old, I read a saying about children that I didn't understand. I recently read an old book and found the same words within it. I understand what the words mean now. As noted in *The Prophet* by Kahlil Gibran:

"Your children are not your children. They are the sons and daughters of Life's longing for itself. They come through you but not from you. And although they are with you yet they belong *not* to you.

"You may give them your love but not your thoughts. For they have their own thoughts. You may house their bodies but *not their souls*. For their souls dwell in the house of tomorrow, which you cannot visit, not even in your dreams.

"You may strive to be like them, but seek not to make them like you. For life goes not backward nor tarries with yesterday.

"You are the bows from which your children as living arrows are sent forth. The archer sees the mark upon the path of the *infinite*, and He bends you with His might that His arrows may go swift and far.

"Let your bending in the archer's hand be for *gladness*; For even as He loves the arrow that flies, so He loves also the bow that is stable."

Sleep comes quickly after uploading the new Web page.

"Time to wake up Mom," Daniel's voice says the next day.

It's the only thing heard that can be documented.

The Science of Mind sits nearby so I open it to a random page. Holmes notes on page 496, think on things that are of good report, of the Truth, and in doing this God will supply our needs. A desire to share the wonderful feeling of Oneness blossoms into a Spiritual Mind Treatment for Samuel because he's on my mind. [8]

The day's reading is enlightening as I switch from *Conscious Evolution* by Barbara Marx Hubbard to *Soul Work* by Anne and Charles Simpkinson.

Later during class six of the 102 SOM series, Dr. Bump discusses healing through spiritual treatment. I decide to write a treatment for each condition noted in *The Science of Mind* textbook. Even though we won't cover these pages, nor are they covered in the next series of classes, I sense it will be homework for a more advanced curriculum.

Sylvia calls days later from a rehabilitation hospital where she's recuperating after surgery on her left knee. She's not happy about skipping Dr. Bump's last class for it's about what the mystics taught. It's comforting to know I'll always receive inspiration when turning to the One as I design a treatment of wholeness and health for my like-minded friend. [9]

After parking my car the next day in front of the small rehabilitation hospital's entrance, I'm surprised to see Mary leaving the building.

"Hey, I didn't know you worked here," I announce while giving her a warm hug.

"It pays the bills," she replies wearily looking down at the pavement, "but I do work longer hours."

Before we part, I tell her about Sylvia. I'm happy to hear she'll see her the following day.

"Oh, my angel," Sylvia says turning her small head slowly away from the nurse as I enter the smelly room. "My angel Sam is here."

"How are you my friend?" I ask bending down to kiss her plump cheek.

Small brown eyes accented by luxurious black eyelashes sparkle with her reply. "I've told the doctors I will heal much faster than they think," she says pulling her hand out from under mine to clasp it firmly.

"Then I shall design another treatment for you when I get home," I respond brightly placing the first treatment on her stomach.

The Science of Mind helps to design Sylvia's treatment as soon as I get back home. It's a bit of a challenge but I'm pleased with the results. [10] I know the treatment will work if she wants it to.

Sensing a transformation within, I try to verify it. Photos fail to show a change in physical appearance. The energy between my room and James' feels different too so, I try to document it as well, but again, no visible changes appear.

Sleep is still irregular. I'm up many times throughout the night hearing messages but usually not remembering them, drinking sips of water, using the bathroom, and returning to bed. This time I remember hearing that I need to buy water for something will happen with the water supply. My throat often feels extremely dry as if I have not drunk fluid for days. Yet, I eliminate much more fluid than I take in. Copious amounts of urine, regularly flowing from my body, amaze and startle me.

The next day starts before sunrise upon hearing, *prepare the way further*. After a sip of water, I use the bathroom, and return to my room to complete the morning routine.

Later while reading *The Science of Mind*, I see that ideas and attitudes of fear, tension, conflict, and struggle greatly contribute to the manifestation of pain. It makes sense considering the past so I design a treatment for pain. [11] It's added to the notebook that holds several others including one for health, peace of mind and unity, and one for my grandchildren. [12, 13] Hours later, I design a treatment for headaches to add to my growing library of cosmic assistance. [14]

Walking to class at the Center is a joyful experience. I take notes for Sylvia as Dr. Bump speaks. Learning that mystics have a deep inner sense of Life and their unity with the Whole thrills me, for I've held that sense for many years. Holmes notes, all we can know about God is what we directly experience, and what we believe others have experienced.

:-)

Chapter Eight

Breakthrough

"We need to shift our outlook unreservedly into that of a world which is evolving. I believe that the universe is an evolution. I believe that evolution proceeds towards Spirit. I believe that Spirit if fully realized is a form of personality. I believe that the supremely personal is the universal Christ."
Teilhard de Chardin – Christianity and Evolution

The Universe continues to tell me it's not necessary as I work on the business website in March. Most of the seven domain names are not redirecting to the proper Internet address. Spam with attached viruses, supposedly coming from the business, continues to affect me and I suspect clients as well.

Odd dreams wake me in the middle of the night. I'm standing in front of a mirror looking at my teeth. The gum around one looks odd. When I try to touch it, two of my teeth fall out into my outstretched hand. I'm walking through a crowd of adults now. One pulls me back, and says with a smile, "The girlie wants to present you with something."

Instantly wide-awake, I take it as a sign to talk telepathically with four-year-old Abigail, offering love and hope for the future. This new way to unite is much different from writing of weather and cats. The communication is on a higher level and much more joyful than sending monthly cards.

Emilytine stands in front of her mother's apartment when I arrive to escort her to the hospital in the evening. She's a large, vibrant Jamaican wearing a very colorful dress that clings to her plump body.

"I've brought some good food for mother," she tells me placing a bag of delicious smelling food on the back seat.

Emilytine thinks it odd that her mother is friends with a younger "white girl" and asks if I too live in a Section Eight housing project. When I reply no, she looks out the window on the passenger side trying to hide a look of surprise. I tell her we hold the love of

Spirit and the Center in common. She's clearly not pleased with her mother's new choice of religion either. We finish the thirty-minute drive in silence.

Sylvia is ecstatic to receive Emilytine's gift of food. She's not happy about the diabetic, low fat, low-salt regimen her doctor ordered. "There's not much I like on this menu," she tells us pointing to the selections while holding it out for us to see. I make a mental note to contact Mary knowing she'll offer Sylvia appropriate foods that aren't offered on the menu.

Back at the house on 47th Drive, fear enters my brain upon reading Democracy Now reports of an issue that first came to my attention two years ago. Government and major corporation plans, to track Americans with radio frequency identification (RFID), reminds me of the movie *1984*. RFID is a technology that uses tiny computer chips to track items at a distance. Major corporations are working to install RFID chips on consumer products and other tests are set to begin.

After wasting precious hours online, I learn that the latest edition of *1984* costs nearly $100. Today's Beliefnet message, attributed to Buddha, centers me after ordering a much cheaper copy of the original movie. Yes, I must forget the things ego knows and recognizes in order to evolve. A stronger need to concentrate on the Self within overwhelms me.

Years later, the movie DVD will sit in the trash, still in its original packaging, unopened, for I clearly recognize the vast power of thoughts, words and deeds. Everything is energy that continues to exist because we feed it with our attention!

While lying in my sunlit room upon the black futon, now open to allow more sleeping space, I think of family who seems lost in the dream. Holmes notes when filled with anger, hatred, and resentment we're filling our body with poisons. But anger can be turned into love. I'm adamant about discarding the judgment, verdicts, and opinions that poison my human form. Once again, I vow to act in ways that support a new life-affirming consciousness.

Life continues to be a mix between designing treatments for fatigue, insanity, lung trouble, and vision [15-18] to answering business emails that last year would have been addressed weeks ago. I've now designed at least twenty treatments.

Most of what I read resonates strongly while studying the condition of constipation. A bowel issue diagnosed in the early 1990's still seems to plague me. Holmes notes constipation is often a belief in limitation or bondage. The many times I've fearfully entertained restricting thoughts looms before me like a scary nightmare. It's time to change false beliefs and replace them with life-affirming ones as I design a new treatment for constipation. [19]

Knowing thoughtless words allow conditions to continue makes a difference. We always experience the belief we project. Spalding notes every mine-set responds to a certain vibratory influence or frequency. Everything we think about affects our health, wealth, and happiness. Conditions change only as our thoughts progress.

Getting rid of fear is as easy as realizing our essential nature. I treat faithfully with zeal, recognizing the ability to do anything I wish. There will be no more limiting thoughts of fear. I am full of love and an open channel for good. Spirit guides while doubt, distrust, worry, condemnation, and fear fades away.

Rev. Mary Jo Van Damme Rance and her husband Rev. Gerald Rance conduct a new Sunday night service at the Center. Their loving message fills with passion for the work of Spirit. A handful of people sit in the audience but I know the service will grow for they share their message from the heart. My own heart soars as Jody Ebling encourages us to sing with her. I'm delighted to support them by setting up refreshments and passing the tithe basket.

The next morning, before fully waking, I see Momma happily sitting at a table full of food as if she's the one responsible. A banner on the wall notes, "Daniel's Party – Making a New Destiny." Eyes open as I smile at the thought, fueled to repeat the daily ritual.

During self-study, I design treatments for skin and issues with arms and hands. [20, 21] A stressful conversation with James later in the day leads to the design of several more treatments. [22-24] It's easy to write treatments while identifying with Source. After acknowledging the Oneness, *It* envelops me. The Mind of God is my mind as I accept my good. My body will soon be healthy again using the power of Mind. Gratitude overwhelms me repeating each treatment while releasing it to the action of Law.

Ego draws me back into the world hours later. Trying to amend an application for a registered business trademark makes me feel out of my league in the physical realm. I quickly vow to complete the process another day and fall soundly asleep.

My brain fills with the words *black plague will return* the following morning. *They will strike out the attitudes that are not their own...* I cannot comprehend the rest. A lot more is said but I can't remember it. Daniel soon pops in and plants a thought into my head, as I design a treatment for feet and legs, and another for false growths. (25, 26)

"The world is good," he reminds me. "Life is good. Enjoy yourself."

I smile remembering a Keys vacation that now seems longer than five years ago.

The day passes quickly while studying for class. It's time to experience increased consciousness in a new way as we review Spiritual Mind Treatment for self. The walk to Dr. Bump's last 102 SOM class seems too short. It's a pleasure to envision an enjoyable life while walking and repeating the newest treatment for perfect physical health.

Later in the predawn hours, I ask to know something for my highest good and fall back asleep. Aunt Hagar is soon delighted to see me in a dream. The memory of our separation in both miles and thought tugs at my heart when I wake for the day. Thirty years of resentment and anger for no apparent reason rise to the surface as ego fights to keep me grounded in life's delusion. It's an easy decision to telephone Ruth for Aunt Hagar's telephone number.

In my experience, the best way to address ego is to focus on positive activities. I use music, writing, spiritual books, constructive endeavors like gardening, and friends of like mind to keep centered in Christ Consciousness. Anything positive that doesn't dwell on the ego is good because the more we dwell on ego, the more we try to kill it, the more we recognize it and make it real.

Yet, it's best not to actively ignore it. We must acknowledge that ego helped us to survive. Acknowledging thoughts and replacing them with positive ones works well. Sometimes when ego seems difficult, I'll thank it for the suggestion before moving forward to a constructive endeavor. I do allow it little victories like locking the door at night but draw the line at most waking thoughts.

I've also addressed the ego by telling it how grateful I am for its help in getting me though many rough situations in the past. Since these phases are now complete, it's time for ego to rest and enjoy the passenger seat while Inner Self takes on the task of driving.

The trick is to get into the habit of overlooking ego thereby ignoring it without realizing what you are doing. It's a sort of mind training, the same way our minds were trained to believe all the things we believe now. The same way our mind was trained to forget the things that are real when we first came here.

The telephone on the other end of the line rings twice before Aunt Hagar answers. Her voice sounds the same. "Hello Aunt Hagar," I say with gladness in my heart recognizing it's time to correct the past. My heart soars when she sounds genuinely happy to hear from me. We replace what went before with apologies and words of love that flow smoothly from God-driven lips.

The rest of the day is well spent, praising God for the unerring direction that always serves to lift my spirits. In the early evening, I extend the four-block stroll to Wednesday's service to increase exercise efforts. It's the only exercise I get but an improvement over recent years. Upon entering the building, I hear the cool-down music of the aerobics class. Memories of dancing to Richard Simmons's first oldies video fill my brain. I make a mental note to try aerobics again.

The next morning I ask to know something for the greater good before falling back asleep. It's not too difficult to do for it's been another restless night and I'm exhausted. I soon dream of airline threats before visioning a sequence where I'm very insistently telling Ruth we have to buy land. We're in a place named Urban, or Urbin, in Illinois living in a big trailer, had just moved there, and Rebecca is about three-years-old. I tell Ruth we have to start building the basement, with the secret door leading below, like the drawing I wrote in the back of one of my books a few weeks ago. There is more but I dare not write it...

Thinking the dream occurred due to a popular Christian book series, of doom, I push it out of my mind. It's a short day of study. After prayer, meditation, and class work, I use *The Science of Mind* to design more treatments. [27-29] *Walking in the Garden of Souls* and *The Afterlife Experiments*, which seems much too left-brained to keep my interest, occupy time before retiring.

The night sky interests me. Something unexplainable rises due east from Fort Lauderdale, and returns back to where it came from before 6:00 AM. It's bright and spooky, because it's big, and doesn't move with the stars but seems to scan the ocean between 12:30 to 5:50 AM.

The mysterious object remains unexplained even after hours spent online to find an answer. News of sky views include information on zodiacal lights, stretching upward from the western horizon, forming a pale luminous triangle visible from places with dark skies. I wonder if that's related to what I'm seeing.

NASA Science News reports solar minimum has arrived. Sunspots have all but vanished but the most intense solar maximum storm in fifty years is coming. I wonder if this is a precursor of what's to come. Researchers expect old magnetic fields to re-appear, as big sunspots between 2010-2012, with the first sunspots of the next cycle appearing in late 2006 or 2007. Solar Max, the next sunspot cycle, will be thirty to fifty percent stronger than the previous one and is expected to be underway by 2010 or 2011.

Scientists at the National Center for Atmospheric Research (NCAR) note, "Predicting the Sun's cycles accurately, years in advance, will help societies plan for active bouts of solar storms, which can slow satellite orbits, disrupt radio and other communications, and bring down power systems." I'm interested in hearing about these predictions for I know the sun affects humanity as well.

Solar activity has increased considerably over the years. Scientists link geomagnetic activity to a mixture of strange phenomenon impacting earth, and humanity. Common space weather disturbances include solar coronal mass ejection (CME's – clouds of magnetized gas propelling solar material out into interplanetary space), coronal holes, and solar flares.

The geomagnetic field is increasingly unsettled with active conditions each time CME activity occurs. CME's and intense solar flares can cause radiation poisoning in mammals. Shock waves from these events typically strike earth's magnetic field within twenty-four to thirty-six hours.

We now use satellites to lessen the effects of earths constantly changing magnetic fields. Yet, smart power grids, GPS navigation, air travel, financial services, and emergency radio communications can all be knocked out by intense solar activity.

Now that class has ended, we have almost an entire month to wait for the next series of lessons. I don't let it stop me from learning. Today, I study the condition of paralysis with great interest. Several doctors informed me last year that I'd be paralyzed in two years without spinal surgery. I've decided they are wrong.

Holmes notes paralysis can be caused by a thought of restriction, a very emotional nature, and often stubbornness and resistance to heal. It sure sounds like the cause to me for I've always felt restricted and very emotional. The stubbornness that got me to where I am today has often been a liability. With a flash of distaste, I recall looking forward to surgery. It offered a break from my hectic life as a single mom.

It's time to erase thoughts of yesterday, put the past behind, and place my full trust in Universal Consciousness. I focus only on positive statements to design a treatment for paralysis with myself in mind. (30) Healing represents a change in consciousness, awareness of the presence of Love (God) manifesting itself. God knows no past and a consciousness of the One Indwelling Presence now fills my spine. I'm free to feel God's energy flowing through me.

Conscious Dreaming by Robert Moss is one of several books I peruse before bedtime. After several years of erratic rest, I'm finally sleeping fairly regular periods, from ninety minutes to four hours, on my stomach, back and either side. At daybreak, I had one more dream that related to two dreams the night before. The dreams lead me to believe it's time to trust Source even more and go further than ever before.

The two dreams last night had the same theme. I woke up after the first one remembering my sister Sarah telling me to lock the door. We'd been in a room with Momma as Sarah walked around and noticed the door wasn't locked. Momma was a foot away from the door as Sarah loudly asked in fright if she locked the door, even knowing she had not.

I watched her fearful attention turn to the half-open window in front of her. It had a white wooden frame. Knowing she was upset by it, I walked over and closed the window. That's when she told me to lock the door. (Since I've settled into my new home, I rarely concern myself with locks for I've been led to a safe neighborhood.)

In the next dream, I was with a handful of people as we settled into airplane seats. The plane was strange, with two black cords on the floor where we secured our feet before the flight. When

I attempted to place my feet securely within the cords they slipped through and seemed to go outside the airplane.

I sat in the front row, which appeared to be facing where most airplane wings would be. It was odd because there didn't appear to be anything that separated the plane from the atmosphere. I was frightened and anxiously thought the plane had better footing when you sat in any of the back rows.

A glass door was ajar to my near left so I pushed it shut. The stewardess noticed and told me she thought she shut it. Another glass door to my far left was open a bit as well. And then I realized the entire plane was open to the atmosphere and calmly woke up.

I look at these two dreams, and not even recognizing others, know I need to go beyond the door, the window, without fear knowing and trusting in God. And although I do that consciously, subconsciously there still seems to be a block. I must subconsciously unblock that block and go beyond where I've never gone before. I must trust that the Will of God will be done and all is well.

I had a lot of dreams the next night but not much remembering. However, in one dream there were a lot of people with me. We decided to put black cloth over the windows so no one could see in. At one point in the dream, I saw an open window and pointed it out to the group. Everyone was concerned. Someone was going to go outside to shut it. I saw the crank handle on the inside of the window and closed it without going outside.

Again, the message seems to be pushing me to go out beyond the windows. Although I'm not sure what that means, I think it concerns this illusionary world. For some time I've thought it's just an illusion and the less I get involved the better. Sometimes when I'm in lower vibration situations, I get very uncomfortable, feel limited, and have to get out quickly.

Yet, I have to find more ways to participate here on earth. As long as I seem to be here, I have to find a way to go beyond these windows that I keep closing, to go beyond these doors, parts of the plane, out into the unknown, for God can't work through me, God's Will can't be done through me, unless I'm out there in the world. Spirit will continue to lead and guide me towards what I'm supposed to do as long as I'm here. Of this, I am certain.

:-)

62

Chapter Nine

Ego versus Self

"Everything from the past, every teaching and every concept is as of this moment obsolete."
Walter Starcke – It's All God

Excitement fills the air as I dress to volunteer at Deepak Chopra's event. It's truly delightful to drive with several other women to the convention center. We quickly set up the Center's table. After what seems like only minutes, I'm free to sit at the back of the auditorium. Dr. Chopra is captivating as he talks about the human body's ability to renew itself each month. I feel in the midst of like minds as he discusses the hidden dimensions of life. It's a joyful feeling that I want to increase.

Viewing the Center's website hours later further boosts my faith. I nod agreeing with Ernest Holmes for there's no power that can free us but ourselves. A quote from Rev. Jim Lockard in "Creative Thought" magazine inspires as well. I resolve to heal of all dis-ease while repeating a treatment for perfect health before following links to Space News.

A "penumbral" lunar eclipse is visible from eastern parts of the USA and Canada, all of Europe and Africa, most of Asia and South America, and Western Australia. Reports note the sun over Egypt is turning blue, a side effect of very fine particles in the air kicked up by seasonal dust storms. The moon is shaking with "shallow moonquakes" that researchers don't fully understand. Other planets may be shaking too.

Ruth and I meet at the park on Monday afternoon. This time, we leave Momma at home. She doesn't want to sit on the bench waiting for us to make our roundtrip through the small park. We force ourselves to walk further than before but still don't see eye-to-eye. Ruth invites me to see Sylvia Browne with her and Rebecca on Wednesday before we part.

The evenings' "Sisters in Spirit" dinner offers a way to meet Lauren Lane Powell, a singer and dynamic speaker. Her timely discussion about boosting self-esteem and releasing old patterns of poverty thinking is full of passion.

Women flock around her when the talk ends but I look through her rack of Goddess dresses. Although I long to own one, the $125 cost makes purchase seem impossible. Envisioning me in the dress is even more difficult. My mind is still unconsciously stuck in limitation while my body quickly passes through the door to walk the four blocks back home.

A message from the Association of Biblical Counselors garners attention before bedtime. It's a link to downloadable resources for ministry. I ignore the links to information on subjects such as marriage, anxiety, anger, depression, and tolerance wondering why someone sent them.

Two days later, Ruth, Rebecca, and I are driving to downtown Miami through rush hour traffic. The James L. Knight Center appears much older than our local theatre as we make our way to three seats near the middle of the room. Ruth is sorely disappointed when Sylvia Browne discusses many things I relate during daily walks. Our long drive back home fills with banter about the seen and unseen.

Ego pulls me back in with world news just when I start making headway in the spiritual realm. The urge to share news reports with email buddies is strong. I pass on bulletins of increased global hurricane intensity, attempts to censure President Bush, government secrecy, flaws in Florida's voting machines, the Middle East war, and my favorite, the "national food uniformity" labeling law. It's unthinkable that Congress would pass a law removing our right to know what's in the food we eat.

It's only the beginning, I think to myself while designing a treatment for nerve troubles and another for asthma and hay fever. (31, 32) "I Represent the Principle of Perfection" beckons me for the fifth time in less than two months. It's within the pages of *The Science of Mind* as I close my eyes and stab a finger at the place where it begins.

Although I know God is in each of us and study daily, it's still difficult to embody the Divine Perfection within fully. Ego fights for control, trying to keep me from being centered in Christ Consciousness. The video camera hasn't worked for several months but now I sense it will. Pushing thoughts of body aches aside, I begin to videotape family photos.

There are ten albums to video as I note, "Pictures are important because they show our history and help us to remember the good times. They help us remember where we were so we can determine where we want to go."

It's a time-consuming task to painstakingly video each photo but I'm compelled to tell everyone about their ancestors. Ego tells me storms may destroy the albums and I may go Home soon. Daniel's presence fills the room as I discuss photos in the first album. The wind chimes begin to tinkle as a pink color sporadically covers certain pictures. Blue, white, and magenta colored orbs begin to appear as I video trying to ignore them.

My monologue wavers between past and present. I talk about feeling tired, taking a nap, and being refreshed by angels during sleep. Noticing a quote by Theodore Roosevelt taped to my computer desk, I pause to repeat it.

"Do what you can, with what you have, where you are."

It takes several hours to record the first ninety-minute tape. The finished video reveals subtle changes in the room's atmosphere, as pink-colored substance, slowly flows past black and white photos. My voice fades in and out and at times is difficult to hear. I call it a night, say my blessings, shower, and go to bed.

Completing video projects, usually with music, served to lift my mood and focus on tasks rather than concentrate on living conditions. One reason I did this was to rid myself of ego by leaving the past behind. Each video documents, my state of mind while making it, and the experiences I'm having. It's interesting to note that the photo albums were not destroyed by storms but left behind the next year when I finally moved on to experience different atmospheres. The DVD's used for this book were already stored at Rebecca's house.

Feeling pressured to put the past behind after dawn, I again weed though files in James' den but soon change rooms. I'm on a roll, shifting quickly to the china cabinet in the dining room removing awards, plaques, and certificates of recognition received for years of work in the field of hiv nutrition. Everything fits in a shipping box along with other memorabilia. "1982-2004 - This was SAM," I quickly write on the box with a big black marker. A feeling of overwhelming loss consumes me while lying down to sleep.

James retires for the night as I rise to meditate using the guided meditation CD Isaiah gave me last year. The field of wild flowers near Ruth and Naomi's Michigan house looks serenely peaceful in my mind's eye. I walk though it picking flowers while slowly moving uphill. My right hand reaches down for a bright yellow dandelion. I place it in my hair before making a wish. Then I disperse a parachute ball into the wind with one swift blow.

Scents of fresh evergreen fill the air as I make my way over to a row of tall, dark green, pine trees to the left. I lie down under the first two relishing in the luxury of free time while taking in the immense, clear blue sky.

After a few moments, I rise to walk nearer to the lake on the right. Water shimmers in bright sunlight but doesn't hurt my eyes, as I become one with *It*. I'm in 'the gap' but don't recall what is said or heard. Ever-permeating Love envelopes me while sending white light, out from the core of my heart, to the universe and beyond. Sleep then comes easily.

A new day dawns and I still can't seem to be at the Center enough. I'm happy to take charge of the coffee station for Rev. Jim Lockard's evening workshop. It's his first class at the Center since moving to California and I'm excited to see him again.

The evening is an amazing mix of different subjects including spiral dynamics. As Rev. Jim talks about Ken Wilber's work, Robert A. Monroe's books, which also discuss the increasing consciousness of life, come to mind. While Wilber uses quadrants of thirteen to describe development, Monroe uses circles to note seven levels of plant, animal, and human life. Monroe describes circles that never stop beyond the ones dealing with physical matter.

Walter Starcke tells us the circle is a significant symbol, all-inclusive and infinite, representing the feminine principle, the womb of life. It's really a "spiral" an ever-ascending evolution, which eventually frees us from the laws of distress and limitation. Once free, time is erased for we realize we've always been one life living itself.

Human physical life is addictive but we have a choice of going higher or staying within human form for another reincarnation when we reach a certain level. I'm at the point where I can surpass reincarnation and move on to the spiritual realm where much of the real work is done.

Rev. Jim now reminds us life circumstances prompt change. Dissatisfaction precedes all change. At times, it's hard to understand his lingo but I find it fascinating when talk of spiral dynamics extends to worldviews, objectives, goals, and missions. At this moment, I understand why communication with my husband, family, and friends is increasingly difficult. I've changed the way I look at things, and in the course of doing that, my mindset and values changed. Since everything is energy, our energies no longer attract one another.

My mind strays to reflect on years of experience. Between fleeting moments of safety and harmony, life as I knew it in younger years was a constant struggle to survive, totally instinctive and reactive to the world around me. The seemingly daily struggle from childhood to an early marriage at fifteen, divorce at nineteen, and another marriage at twenty-two made it easy to blame others instead of taking responsibility for my own actions.

Although there were periods of illusionary security and belonging, at twenty-six I finally realized there was more to life than what I'd experienced. The way I thought changed when my recently divorced friend Ester returned to school to follow her dream of nursing. It was time to test possibilities, once again, as I initiated another divorce and period of growth. I knew there were risks but was ready to explore new options knowing life could be better.

The following years were a mix of ecstasy and agony as I got my equivalency diploma, enrolled in community college, and dared to dream. Dreams became reality when a French friend opened a bakery in Florida. She soon offered me a new life in a city with one of the few colleges that offered the next degree I sought.

I climbed the ladder of consciousness haltingly, but willingly, and subsequently changed my dream to include a companion. Now after eighteen years of marriage, it's time to climb the ladder once again for I no longer 'fit' in my current living environment. Fully aware of the One in which we live, and move, and have our BEing in, the times I think of all people as equal and without fault expands.

Rev. Lockard jars me back to present time.

"People have a higher reject rate for the level you just left."

Confused, I try hard to understand the current discussion.

"More than one level apart and you have a hard time having a conversation with them."

67

I suddenly realize that's what happened to James and me for we can no longer stand to be in the same room. My family ignores me as well for we no longer relate. They can't understand why I don't complain about my health or discuss the woes of others and I can't understand why they don't realize we live in an illusion of our own making.

Our consciousness is limited for the brain can only record the strongest of signals at a time. Yet, this physical world is one dimension of many and we are multidimensional beings. Experiencing life as a human is just one species of many we are privileged to experience. Fortunately, we can never be separated from our spiritual energy for it's in our memory.

Robert Monroe describes the same concept Rev. Lockard discusses but in different terms. He speaks of eventually raising one's vibrational rate making it possible to leave this realm of existence. I plan to help others stuck in the illusion from the Otherside but see there seems to be divisions there as well. Entities on higher vibrational levels can return to assist those on lower levels but the emotional astral level of existence can be tricky. According to Monroe, if a vibrational rate is vastly different from yours it's unlikely you'll get direct guidance but you may be able to get some ideas.

As souls we invented a dimension with various planes of existence, each having levels we must experience. I believe we live simultaneous lives on other realms of existence and can change what happens in all of them by what occurs in any of them. A popular horror movie where a man went into the dreams of children to help them overcome fears comes to mind. We can change our nightmares into good dreams by consciously recognizing our ability to 'call the shots' shaping our own reality.

This morning's dream started with me sitting among friends in a huge arena packed with people getting ready to watch a show. As the crowd settled in, an angry man many rows in front of us forcefully pushed the shoulder of a woman he was facing, as if to shove her off her seat so she'd tumble down the arena stairs. I got the impression she was his wife, saw her unconcerned face, and noticed she wore a baby blue, scoop-necked top.

I gasped loudly along with several people. We got up and walked away drawing attention to the man. Numerous members of the audience followed our lead. It was a clever, stunning message that his behavior was not appropriate as we silently left the amphitheater.

Putting thoughts aside, I concentrate on the fourth handout, which offers areas to address for integral spirituality. I joyfully check everything in the "Shadow" area happy to be releasing my demons through therapy, dream work, music, and animals. Now it's time to work on the core area of body and build relationships of like mind. I believe I'm ready.

The next day passes quickly. Demonstrations are much more frequent than ever before. At least twenty butterflies fly gently by, or peek past the corner of my white light room, as I sit and meditate, say blessings, and treatments.

The new video project continues. As each videotape fills, I transfer its contents through the movie maker box originally bought to transfer family videos from VCR tapes onto DVD. Using my laptop, video camera, the movie maker box, and TV hookup, I transfer each tape onto DVD and into computer mpg files. It takes a very, very, long, time.

I'm blessed with another demonstration while checking the second DVD. It takes less time to check DVDs if I set the playback control to a faster rate. This time the DVD stops on a picture of Grandma and Grandpa taken on their anniversary. I push several keys to get it unstuck but nothing helps. Looking at the date of the picture, March 22, 1969, I note today would have been their anniversary. I touch each of their images and wish them a happy anniversary. The DVD begins to play normally.

Rebecca wants me to document verifiable demonstrations. She says that maybe she'll believe when I reach sixty to eighty percent. She's using my car while hers is being fixed again and called earlier to update me. When I told her about finding the Karen Drucker CD for a dollar, by following the voice in my head, she laughed, and then got upset. I decided to take Daniel's advice. Last night he reminded me to ease up on talking to Rebecca about demonstrations because, "she is going through a hard time right now." I'd forgotten but will try to remember in the future. Daniel told me other things as well.

Frankly, I think God uses Daniel's voice and mannerisms to reach me because his voice is the one I react to the most. The motion light in James' den comes on every few days or so and I just sit down on the stair leading to the room. I concentrate and write down what I hear but often forget to look at my notes.

Videotaping family photos is taking much more time than expected for an urge to discuss life in the past seems unavoidable. I'm oddly affected with memories of a trip to the Detroit Race Course while taping the third video. Remembering the day my French friend Tattie and I took seven-year-old Daniel to see Evel Kneival, jump and fail miserably, shakes me up. Shortly after discussing the race photos, I suddenly feel ill and pause to rest.

"Living as I do is kind of like being a Star Trek person," I note hours later while training the camera on color photos. "When there's a disturbance in the force you feel it. It makes you feel a little woozy, as if you have the flu and you're going to throw up, so you lie down. Sometimes you lie down for a long time and sometimes you just need to rest a bit. So think what you may. That's my story and I'm sticking to it."

I continue to hear *hurry, hurry, hurry,* while taping, but have no idea why. It's as if I'm on some kind of schedule. Later I note, "I was raised to be a housewife and loved to cook, bake and crochet. I've always documented my life thinking that I'd write a book someday. Maybe I will and maybe I won't. I know there's no Daniel, there's no me, and we are all spirits. But Rebecca doesn't want to hear it so I'll keep quiet."

Videoing one tape and putting it on DVD now takes a total of six to eight hours, depending on how stubborn I am about trying to do it my way instead of Daniel's spirit's way. The increasing energy around me is noticeable while playing the next DVD. Pictures are not coming through as they are in the photo album and the sound is weird. Sometimes it's muted. Occasional orbs, smoky mist, and white, blue, red, and yellow/gold energy enhance photos.

Perhaps my energy field is increasing so I must video all the pictures quickly. The project is taking much more time and effort than expected but since I talk and play music CDs or cassettes, which Daniel guides me to play; it does take longer to do. I've come to realize that I must place the computer away from energy sources, my room, and myself when I record the DVDs, because if I don't, the transfer and DVD recording process is often interrupted.

Spiritual conscious evolution, awakening of the 'memory' now plays much more of a role in my life than ever before. I'm grateful for leaders like Barbara Marx Hubbard and those at the

Center. The desire to be more, know more, and find my life purpose is strong. Inner guidance, motivation, and intuition increases daily.

I'm pleased with my evolutionary progress, and Rebecca and Samuel's progress of being more self-sufficient. There's just too much to relate and I feel my time is short. I may need to forget about some of the human stuff I hope to do before I pass. We must all find our own truth. If we're lucky, we have increased intuition to follow clues and learn faster... Love is the key!

As if writing to family I note, "I love you all. I will never die as no one does. It's just a graduation, a celebration of changing from one energy form to another. I expect to be back in human form right before the 'end times' to help gather the souls before the rapture. I trust you all will be with me in whatever form we take on."

A quote from *The Heart of Awareness: A Translation of the Ashtavakra Gita* comforts me as I lie down to sleep.

"Have faith, my child, have faith.

Do not be bewildered.

For you are beyond all things, the heart of all knowing.

You are the Self. You are God."

:-)

Chapter Ten

Inching Toward Spiritual Life

"...the veils between the dimensions are extremely thin, and those of the spirit world who love and support us are meeting us in our dreams and meditations, offering encouragement and guidance at this crucial moment in our evolution."
Christine Page – Spiritual Alchemy

Days and nights merge into a never-ending collage of communication. One message suddenly echoes though my brain.

Bathe three times.

I've received enough inspiring messages from this unidentified voice to know its validity. Right after James leaves for work, I take my first bath scrubbing quickly, feeling like a burglar. We're under water restrictions again and my last shower was less than six hours ago. A urine-like smell soon reminds me of dying hospital patients. Yet, a feeling of being born anew envelops me while smelling the repugnant aroma of ammonia.

Six hours later the distasteful smell returns when scrubbing quickly to finish before James returns from work. Prayers, meditation, and treatments fill the day until it's time for the third bath in twenty-four hours. I'm still repulsed by the smell as I scrub my body once again after James is fast asleep.

Days are filled with prayers, treatments, mediations, and self-study between emails to old colleagues asking if they're interested in binders full of local meeting minutes. I'm no longer inclined to keep reams of facts on nutritional needs, outcomes, funding, and other issues discussed during nine years of Ryan White volunteer positions. No one seems interested in the data.

Five new treatments enhance my collection after finishing the next day's ritual. [33-37] Energy flows while adding links to Daniels website before moving to the living room with another photo album. It's a challenge to stand while taping so I sit comfortably on the loveseat. A tiny white orb sits in the middle of

Tattie's forehead as Daniel's essence sends her love. Orbs of white or magenta appear near other photos.

The single multicolored kitten Wiley gave birth to days before offers an opportunity to break as I wander outside to search for it. It's nowhere in sight so I return to finish the video before happily walking to the Center.

Rev. Dr. Charles Geddes has returned to offer several workshops. I'm thrilled when he talks of memory banks, sharing memories of being somewhere else before birth on earth, somewhere else; a place he knows is home. Talk of living in the present and consciously changing old patterns and dramas fascinates me.

The next day's random reading from *The Science of Mind* again reminds me, "...we are to be fed, clothed, and supplied in every need, straight from the center and Source of all." It's a very welcome thought for I'm feeling a bit restricted.

Dr. Geddes second class on authentic spirituality, divine origin, and divine outcome lifts my mood hours later. I'm awestruck over the things I continue to see and hear. Holmes accurately mirrors the song in my heart on page 367 of *The Science of Mind*.

"Sweet song of the Silence, forever singing in my heart!

Words cannot express, the tongue cannot tell;

Only the heart knows the songs which were never sung, the music which was never written.

I have heard that great Harmony and felt that great Presence.

I have listened to the Silence; and in the deep places of Life, I have stood naked and receptive to Thy songs and they have entered my soul.

I am lost in the mighty depths of Thy inner calm and peace."

It's been a while since any of my electronics malfunctioned but I'm happy to note when they do. As I begin to listen to Karen Drucker's new song "Power of Women" the Windows Media Player repeatedly plays the word "power" until I notice.

"Sit back and take a break," the voice in my brain says.

I thank the spirit of my last-born son even realizing that it's all just me. The player sticks on the word peace, repeating it several times, before playing normally again. A feeling of peace surrounds me as I sit in my new, brown Lazy Boy with closed eyes.

As a woman of power, I'll continue to help humanity recognize our spiritual magnificence. We are much more powerful than we could ever realize. I'm fully convinced this is an illusion and even more fired up to announce that there's much more here than we can experience with our limited five senses. Even though it isn't needed to convince me, the song plays several more times without sticking on a word.

Tints of blue and pink adorn my hand while videoing the sixth photo album. Again, it seems like the project will take forever to complete for now I've videoed pictures out of chronological order. Time passes quickly moving from the project to treatments and meditation.

A total eclipse of the sun occurs in parts of Brazil, Africa, Turkey, central Asia, and Mongolia on Wednesday, March 29 as Rev. Geddes discusses the art of non-attachment and divine appointment. It's time to fulfill my divine appointment and intuition tells me he will soon be nearby to help.

I still fleetingly feel my time on earth is ending. A feeling of completion prompts me to design my obituary the next afternoon. It's a long piece as ego leads the way. I note a quiet passing, my birthplace, family members, current and past endeavors, and memorial service details ending with final wishes. "Empower children and nurture them in positive ways for they are the future of humanity."

The usual rituals complete before designing a new treatment for diabetes. [38] Time then slips away as I backtrack to videotape missed photos. It's after midnight when the DVD is finally finished.

Although James is fishing, I'm never alone. Magenta colored orbs now sporadically flow past my line of vision. "Hold On To Love" plays softly in the background while I check the newly made DVD. Photos of Tattie and her beautiful daughters flash by. The photos remind me of seeing Tattie and her oldest girl at Daniel's wake. Recognition of our eternal love for one another immediately fills my brain.

I've periodically asked for friends of like mind since Christmas Eve last year, and once again read, "My Vibration Attracts Friends to Me." It's within the pages of *The Science of Mind*. Although I'm happy to have Sylvia as a friend, our friendship now seems more distant so I'm looking forward to more friends of like mind.

74

Recent finds in Egypt intrigue me while weeding through the day's email. Archeologists discovered the "Lost City" of Heracleion and revealed treasures of a sunken Egyptian port. The water discovery really interests me so I investigate Egyptology Resources via website links. A twinge of excitement fills my gut upon noting Heracleion was surpassed in importance by Alexandria.

After designing more treatments, [39, 40] I replay the ninth DVD. There's no sound for the first seventy minutes and then there's the faint sound of my voice, for a minute, before it leaves again. The sound comes on abruptly as Daniel's old tape-recorded messages from Arizona play in the background.

Daniel speaks of attempts to stay drug-free and search for a fulfilling job as he again lives with the first love of his life at twenty-years-old. Their relationship blossomed and waned many times since he met her at age seventeen. Days later, he notes his stuff sits in a locked storage room. Now he's trying to raise money by selling his beloved motorcycle.

A multitude of difficulties wears him down and he discusses them in detail. The old van, bought from James for $200, is falling apart. He's lost all of his keys, including the vans, so now he's hot-wiring it. He's tired all the time. Since money is a problem, he's back to staying at Alfred's house, without his first love.

"I really need to get it together," he says as he admits going to a new, drug-free class.

It's clear he's struggling to be on his own.

"Life's a real bitch right now," Daniel reports with dismay. "Everyone has to make their own choice. I have to choose my own path and what I want to do. Please don't stop sending me tapes because they keep me going."

Daniel discusses the subconscious and the conscious mind. I'm amazed to hear he's reading a lot about astrology and the twelfth planet, the *Bible*, and the "spiritual light."

"I'm weirding out Mom," he confides filled with emotion, "but don't worry it's just a stage I'm going through. I know things are going to be okay. You know," he continues sounding happier, "it would be great to go to the bar with my mom and to the Keys."

I fondly recall the night his wish was fulfilled. After accepting a roundtrip airline ticket to visit while James and I married for a second time, this time in a Catholic Church, Daniel decided to return to Florida months later.

Work seemed easy to get as he honed construction skills. By the following year, he enjoyed weekends by barhopping with friends. When a new disco bar opened and held a contest, he won the opportunity to realize his forgotten wish. We had a grand time that night.

Pleased, knowing Daniel reaped the treasure of his emotion-filled thought to spend time with me in a bar, I trust his soul has moved on to higher endeavors. I smile, remembering, as he talks about going to school to be an electrical engineer. The tape begins to act erratically.

"I don't know what's wrong with this tape Mom," he says with concern, "but I know it will be okay when you listen to it."

I take a break, and as my stomach growls, reflect on past eating habits while designing a treatment for stomach and bowel trouble. [41] Emmanuel notes ingrained habits may be difficult to break, but not impossible. Daniel's essence guides me to focus wholly on eating during mealtimes so old eating habits are gone. I'm no longer standing or moving around in a rush eating while working, reading, or watching TV. I bless my food now, and give thanks for it, before sitting down to eat, slowly savoring every delicious bite. Digestion and assimilation occurs without bowel distress.

Checking email, I read the daily Beliefnet Buddhist Wisdom message, a quote from Dhammapada:

"All that we are is the result of our thoughts; it is founded on our thoughts and made up of our thoughts. With our thoughts we make the world. If you speak or act with a harmful thought, trouble will follow you as the wheel follows the ox that draws the cart. All that we are is the result of our thoughts; it is founded on our thoughts and made up of our thoughts. With our thoughts we make the world. If you speak or act with a harmonious thought, happiness will follow you as your own shadow, never leaving you."

NASA Science News for the previous week notes cosmic rays hitting human chromosomes can damage "telomeres" and cause premature symptoms of aging. The moon eclipsed the sun, a single star, but on Saturday, April 1, the moon is going to eclipse an entire star cluster – the Pleiades. I start looking for the slender crescent moon, among the stars of the Pleiades, as soon as the sun sets.

The electronic equipment malfunctions when I continue my video project working on the tenth DVD. I'm now accustomed to dealing with it but mention the ways of Spirit for those that watch the movie later.

"Sometimes when your vibrational energy is too high electronics don't work well. They might just refuse to work altogether or you might see a bunch of fuzzy stuff in the pictures. So, just be aware of that. And if you're seeing this now, and you're hearing this now, then you were meant to."

The stereo system emits only a high-pitched squeal minutes later as I try to play an old audio tape of Daniel talking. Blue orbs appear as I discuss listening to Deepak Chopra and the video camera speeds up, several times, while I talk. I know Daniel's essence is affecting it as I train the camera on his picture and the sound of my voice cuts out.

I'm still caught up in limitation noting a lack of money. For the first time in many years, I refused to reserve the annual Keys cabins. "I let go of that duty because I have no money," I report. My savings account is drained and the money from years of back child support is gone. There's only a few hundred dollars left from my cashed-in retirement account for tithing.

Other things grab my attention after setting the camcorder aside. The clutter around the house doesn't bother me as long as I stay in my room but I'm annoyed that most of the things I've held on to for decades are gone. The china cabinet is the only thing left from Michigan. I don't recognize the losses as gifts that help me to more easily move on and further evolve.

Pushing thoughts aside, I write Rachel a short letter thanking her for the wonderful job she's doing raising Abigail. I have no way of knowing what's going on in their world but I praise her for teaching Abigail the traits of love, compassion, and strength of character.

Today's self-study project urges me to design two treatments before logging onto the Internet. [42, 43] Space Weather News notes a sudden increase in solar activity as the biggest sunspots of the year cross the solar disk. One group is longer than ten earth diameters and poses a threat for solar flares. There's also a large and complex prominence dancing along the sun's limb.

It's April 4, 2006, the second anniversary of Daniel's passing, as I video the eleventh tape of family photo albums.

Depression overwhelms me while recording the blank photo album page signifying an empty Christmas in 1988. It's the first year my home is not full of celebrating family. "That's how my life looks," I note sadly, "empty without SOM."

Reminding myself to remain with inspiring people, I set the project aside and head to my first SOM 103 class. It opens the door to more friends of like mind for new people join the group. Dr. Bump's assignment to meditate daily is already my pleasure to do.

Daniel's essence surrounds me the next day while designing a treatment for weather conditions. [44]

"Remember Mom, storms will be more frequent now and stronger too."

I read the words of Ernest Holmes, with increased interest, recalling weather is a manifestation of Pure Spirit, variations of the One Life, in which we live, and move, and have all BEing in. It's a much-welcomed concept that I greet with joy.

Ruth and I still walk twice a week but today she cancels thinking she has the flu. I too feel odd and sleep a good part of the day feeling as if something different flows through my blood.

Compelled to continue my photo album videos later in the day, I express gratitude for the role James plays. I'm very aware that without him it's highly unlikely there would be an Abigail or Samuel. The thought of letting my children go off on their own, especially at such a young age, as I did, would never have crossed my mind without the distraction of someone to fill the void they left.

The telephone continues to ring as I dwell on the past. There will soon be elections in our area and it seems to ring constantly with calls to vote. I stop to answer it. This time it's the Republican Party asking for my opinion on abortion.

"What do you think about a woman's right to choose," the caller asks boldly.

I'm immediately angry remembering how I asked Rebecca to have an abortion so she could continue her violin lessons and embark on an exciting career. It's outrageous that soon woman who have been raped, or choose to abort a fetus with birth defects, may not have the opportunity to do so. After giving the caller a 'piece of my mind,' I viciously hang up the telephone.

"Okay," I say out loud, "so, let's take a deep breath as Rev. Bump would say." I pick up the video camera and focus on pictures taken in the Florida Keys to calm down. "Let's pretend we're in the Keys and every day we snorkel happily in the water."

A spontaneous prayer treatment flows from the depths of my being. "Every day we watch the sunset and there are no obstructions to our rights as humans for we are one with *It*. We are in complete health, spirits taking turns in different bodies. We always have the right to choose and are positive, kind and thankful, filled with love, peace, and harmony for all living things.

"We are a part of all living things. God is in us, and we are in God, for we are One, each and every one of us. And so I thankfully send these words into the Universal Consciousness knowing that we shall forevermore be in harmony with the One. And So It Is."

The videotape abruptly ends at the end of my prayer. Feeling better, I design a treatment about food and retire for the day. [45]

TV commentators report the next day's world news as I video in the living room. I'm soon prompted to listen to Daniel's old Billy Joel CDs instead and do so gladly. "Big Shot" plays in the background while I focus on Daniel's twenty-fourth birthday gala. The photos show us at a popular new disco celebrating his good fortune at having won a free birthday party.

The wish he voiced on a cassette tape and mailed to me three years before from Arizona has come true. He's having a drink at a bar with his mother. It's much more than he wished for because everyone in the family is there with us dancing and drinking for free. We dance and laugh with glee while blindly grabbing balloons that drop from the ceiling to look for ones with money.

"We all have the same power," I note calmly while slowly videoing the bar scenes. "It's just that some of us don't acknowledge and use it." I'm not sure Daniel knew he had the power as I continue taping and talking of evolution. "If you can't give up everything you got, and let go of your fear, then evolution doesn't occur."

I quickly recall Daniel's cross-country trip back to Florida. His vehicle broke down in Texas a few miles away from a dear friend, we had not seen in many years. He had no idea Beth lived nearby until he called me and I arranged for her to rescue him. His saga ended when he left the majority of his belongings behind after Beth loaned him money for airfare home.

Daniel still tells me what music to play the next morning as I video family photos from the early '90s. Pictures of my thin frame at ninety-nine pounds, after being diagnosed with irritable bowel syndrome, cause no emotion but the spring of '93 brings a rush of unexpected joy. "Take it to the Limit" plays in the background as the video records photos of my friends and me in Las Vegas attending Siegfried and Roy for $100 a ticket.

I wish to be in Vegas once again as the song ends amid a ringing telephone. Samuel wants to know when I'll be over to visit for Rebecca no longer asks me to pick him up from school. It's clear he misses me.

"We're having Chinese food," he tells me excitedly. "Why don't you come over for dinner?"

Rebecca asks me as well so I take a break from my project for dinner and a movie. Yet, it's hard to avoid conflict for everything I say bothers her. Both our roofs are still leaking and the dryer at her house broke months ago. Rebecca doesn't want to hear about the power of thought when I remind her of my many manifestations. I thank my hosts and depart when the movie ends.

The car seems to have a mind of its own as I drive past the usual turn leading off Sunrise Blvd. *A Course In Miracles* is on my mind and soon I find myself at Barnes and Noble. Cash still seems an issue but I enter the store and climb the stairs without asking where the textbook may be.

After easily finding the book, I turn from the bookcase to leave but find myself standing in front of another even larger case of books. My attention moves to the left even as I notice the shelves house bibles. I've avoided the *Bible* like the plague since my early college years, yet something tells me to pick one up.

My arm reaches out for the *New International Version Archaeological Study Bible* (study bible), a very heavy book with more than 1,300 pages. When it opens in my hands to a random page on ritual purity and bathing rituals of ancient times, my heart begins to race. These are the times that Bathsheba lived I silently tell myself. The cashier smiles when I whip out my charge card to buy both books.

Within minutes I'm home reading the cultural and historical notes on page 456. It's within the confines of 2 Samuel 11:12 where the author discusses King David's decision to send Uriah,

Bathsheba's husband back to battle. Goose bumps form on my arms while reading of ritual purity, achieved by bathing in ancient times.

I feel the disgust of Bathsheba and realize she bathed seeking to purify herself from defilement after her time with David. The goose bumps move down my thighs upon discovering that "priests were instructed to bathe three times daily to remove physical pollution and attain a spiritual life." There's no doubt that a loving unseen force leads me.

:-)

Chapter Eleven

Loving Connections

"I have never met a person whose greatest need was anything other than real, unconditional love. You can find it in a simple act of kindness toward someone who needs help. There is no mistaking love. You feel it in your heart. It is the common fiber of life, the flame that heals our soul, energizes our spirit, and supplies passion to our lives. It is our connection to God and to each other."
Elizabeth Kubler-Ross

Dying comet 73P/Schwassmann-Wachmann 3 (73P) continues to break apart as astronomers track fragments approaching earth for a harmless, but beautiful, close encounter in May. The walk to class doesn't reveal any fragments but I enjoy it anyway.

Being with people of like-mind feels great as I set snacks out during the break. Roberta slides up to my side and asks if I've tried Detox tea.

"It's great to get toxins out of your body," she reports, handing me a small box before slowly walking away.

James sits in front of the TV listening to the news when I arrive home to make myself a cup of Detox tea before heading to my room. The tea tastes great so I decide to drink it once a day. Usual blessings and treatments flow before designing new ones for rheumatism and intemperance. [46, 47] Sleep comes easily.

In the morning, I begin to video photo albums. The DVD/CD player refuses to work. Daniel tells me to play a certain CD but I try three others instead. The player finally works when I put in the one Daniel suggests. Music for each picture serves to note the mood of the time it's taken.

As the sun begins to set, I stop the video project to walk to the Center for the *Celestine Prophecy* movie. It excites me to set up tables of snacks, and prepare coffee, for we expect lots of people. I'm pleased to hug many new friends while we chat before and after the show. The movie is just as good as the book.

It's hard going back to the quiet and seemingly negative atmosphere of James' house. I rush through the den, dining room, kitchen, and hall, to reach my white light room. The candle still burns brightly. I gladly close the door before lying down to read more of *The Science of Mind*.

Rebecca telephones later the next day as I videotape the seventeenth video. Her car broke down again and she needs a ride. Keeping thoughts to myself, I let her use my car.

"When you get to eighty percent in your demonstrations, let me know," she announces before driving into the dusk.

Daniel is still talking to me as I enter the house ready to continue my project.

"No more talking Mom," he says. "Play the cassette tapes instead."

I intuitively know he means "The Camino" on audio by Shirley MacLaine, recently found at the thrift store for ten percent of its original cost. As Shirley notes Spirit is a subtle and non-visible energy, a higher reality that vibrates at a higher frequency than the physical dimension, I smile broadly.

MacLaine speaks of giving up old values. Since I'll listen to the tapes again while driving, I don't pay much attention. It's no news to me when she announces that nothing happens by accident.

Today, I'm reminded once again, there are no accidents. Most possessions were left behind in 2007, without a second thought, including the carefully taped family photo albums. As fate would have it, family brought many things to my new home in 2008.

Intuition prompted me to unpack a box after completing my first book. One photo album sat amid various keepsakes. A picture of three-year-old Samuel fell to the floor when I lifted it out of the box. Something guided me to design a new website and use it as the logo. Samuel held two playing cards with the numbers three and four. He wore his Original Baby outfit. When he held the cards for me to see in 1996, I didn't know the numbers three and four were prompts to wake-up.

Among other things, the number three represents the Holy Trinity, the number of the Holy Spirit associated to the triangle, and a favorable number associated with birth. The number four refers to creation. It represents the union of the Trinity into One and symbolizes the family, considered as another image of the number one. Symbolically, the square or the cross represents four. It's the symbol of totality and considered by the initiates as the root of all things.

You'll see a lot of four's if you don't pay attention to the three's you see. Daniel's transition date of 4/4/04 did the trick for me. The number 444 holds great symbolism for it represents the first divine woman. It's the call to awaken to our true being. Drunvalo Melchizedek notes three or more of the same number enhances the energies of whatever level we're on at the time we see them. The Resurrection number is 444 or 4444.

Days, I decide, will no longer fill with medication schedules and meal restrictions. Several months of prescribed drugs sit in my dresser for I've weaned myself off many of them. Yet, I still buy prescribed drugs thinking it may be good to have them, just in case.

Affirming the perfect health of my bladder again, I mentally renounce the need for Elmiron and Nortryptline. I also decide there's no need for hormones, creams, ointments, or Valium for gynecological health. My mental treatment continues noting a healthy stomach lining so there's no need for Prevacid. Two doses of Celebrex, which cause a wealth of side effects, are no longer necessary either, for spine and joints are perfect. My blood pressure and sinuses are just what the doctor ordered and the thyroid is functioning normally. And finally, there's no need to take the skin ointments prescribed by dermatologists.

The power of God within helps me to heal. Since I no longer need these unnatural substances for perfect body functioning, I can also forgo the NAC, because my liver no longer works overtime to rid itself of them. The antioxidants, B-complex, and multi-minerals will stay in their bottle as well for I'm tired of taking pills. As another way to cement the new groove of thought, I remove the insurance card and family pictures from my wallet. Reliving the past is no longer an option.

A quick trip to my favorite thrift store reaps a paperback book with exercises designed for the bands sitting quietly on my bookshelf for ages. Although it seems silly, I start working with the bands to strengthen my arms, back, legs, and stomach.

Dietary habits begin to change as I continue drinking the Detox tea, incorporating cinnamon. I'm led to purchase Daily Detox All Natural Tea from the health food store when the tea from Roberta is gone. It's not the exact tea so lovingly offered but has the same ingredients so I drink it twice a day. I give up the daily soda but it's tough to change my life-long habit of morning coffee.

As I dwell on the fire in my bladder, it occurs to me everything the body absorbs, including the sun on my skin, affects health in some way. It seems prudent to stop using substances such as bug spray, sunscreen and deodorant, and swimming in pools with chlorine. I don't know if it will make a difference in the dis-ease showing up as interstitial cystitis but it can't hurt. Since I've stopped taking the medications, it may even help.

Later in the day, it's time to take a break after making the nineteenth DVD of family albums. Wonder fills me upon opening *The Science of Mind* to page 512. In less than three months, I've opened the book, randomly three times, and pointed to "O Soul of Mine, Look Out and See."

"O Soul of mine, look out and see; look up and know Thy freedom. Be not cast down nor dismayed; be uplifted within me and exult, for Thy salvation has come. Behold the wonders of the Great Whole and the marvels of the Universe. Look out and see Thy good. It is not afar off, but is at hand. Prepare Thyself to accept and believe; to know and live. Let Life enter and live through Thee, Soul of mine, and rejoice that Thou hast vision so fair and so complete. Rejoice that the Perfect Whole is so completely reflected through Thee. My light has come."

The Camino continues to play after I capture the last family photo. "This is the last task I've been given to do," I report to the air around me scanning the room for more things to tape. "The butterflies I see everyday have increased, and maybe, if I'm lucky I'll get to go Home soon."

I'm actively searching for things to video until the audiotape ends. At this point, I slowly scan pictures from inside the file cabinet, dresser, and wall above the door, before moving on to things on my computer desk. The electronic Furby sits there with its open eyes. MacLaine notes increased love for technology and individuality, instead of Unity, causes disharmony. I begin to pay attention to her words.

She explains a soul mate is the reflection of one's own self. As she discusses relationships, I'm heartened to believe Daniel is my soul mate, identical in vibration and oscillation. I believe we always search for a reunion in different lives to love and support each other's spiritual growth. I'm also convinced that James is my twin mate here to help me serve humanity. Although he does not appear to be aware of his vital role, we serve each other's journeys back to One.

The video records Daniel's memorial posters, the smiley-face blackboard, artwork, and a poster of my adult life from fifteen to thirty-four made during college classes. Photos hanging on the walls throughout the house are videoed as well. All these items will soon be left behind but I don't know that. When I reach the collage of Abigail to age one, I play the microcassette of her talking as an infant with Papa. The videotape finally ends.

A candle still burns when I leave my room closing the door behind me to walk to class. The coordinator for Tuesday evening's 12-step program enters the kitchen as I make coffee. Our greeting hug fills me with a loving desire to share. I happily announce my commitment to volunteer at the convention center.

When he voices his tainted opinion of the speaker, I quickly realize it's an opinion based on the past. I silently recall Daniel's message to love others as I loved him and wonder if that's possible. *A Course In Miracles* notes we cannot enter into real relationships unless we love everyone equally. It's much easier to do when living in the Now moment.

Later in the evening, Dr. Bump again discusses the steps of treatment that help to enrich our lives. It doesn't take long to decide on the life condition I wish to experience differently. Our pod grouping during workshop period helps to clarify thoughts. It's time to end the pain I insist on feeling when reacting to other peoples words and actions.

Misunderstandings must remain in the past and be quickly forgotten recognizing the Unity of all life. I must step up my efforts to see God in everyone. It's for the greater good that I continually recognize the ever-present Oneness. I believe I'm ahead of the class and am anxious to complete homework for the next week building on the affirmation repeated constantly when with family. From this day forward, I'll remain positive and calm under all circumstances.

Back home, I complete a treatment for tranquility and no reaction to outside forces within minutes. [48] It's easy to do so I design one for supply and peace of mind as well. [49, 50]

Days before Easter the mail carrier brings a surprise from Abigail. It's a picture of a bunny colored with many different markers. The dark color of purple over the bunny's eyes, nose, and half of his mouth makes it impossible to see them clearly. I notice the gift was mailed on the second anniversary of Daniel's transition and silently thank Rachel for sending it. Abigail now knows how to write her first name.

Easter arrives and once again, the family celebrates at Rebecca's house. I want to stay in the serenity of my positive energy-filled room but know she spent a lot of time and money to make sure everyone forgets the past and has a good holiday. I've made the sweet potato dish everybody raves about at Christmas, as a contribution to dinner, and look forward to seeing family.

James arrives with his camera shortly after me and begins to take pictures. I notice his picture taking habits are much different from mine as he shoots multiple photos of the cat, the dog, parrots roosting, and a raccoon hanging out in a tree hole.

Rebecca makes us all participate in lawn games. As we race in teams across the yard holding an egg on a spoon, I have to admit, it's fun to act like a kid while we compete against Samuel and his best friend. I'm grateful to celebrate Easter with family and make a mental note to thank Rebecca again, in an email, for her efforts to help us have a joyous and pleasant Easter.

Although family thinks three to five days a week at the Center is too much, sometimes it's not enough. I happily leave after eating to attend the Sunday night service.

Listening to Rev. Rance, excitedly talk about James Allen's work in the early 1900's, inspires me. Allen's New Thought book, *As a Man Thinketh* documents the result of meditation and experience. I'm surprised to learn James Allen influenced many people by noting man is literally the complete sum of his thoughts before passing at age forty-eight in 1912.

Back in my room, I'm still trying to document the transformation within. Nothing out of the ordinary shows up in photos, not even orbs. Pictures of my energy-filled space fail to show the power I feel pulsating around and within the confines of my skin.

Depressed after reading Bin Laden warnings and Nostradamus' Quatrains online, I decide to change my viewpoint and learn more about Rev. Geddes. The SpirituallyConnected.com Web page reveals information on the church he's at in Montebello, CA. I like what I read:

"We believe there is a body of knowledge about spiritual laws which operates in the Universe as Cause and Effect. We teach that, "It is done unto you as you believe." Our thinking and our expectations create our reality. It is in studying and applying spiritual laws that we can change our unconscious beliefs and create improved conditions in our lives."

Something tells me Rev. Geddes will soon live in Fort Lauderdale. I relish the thought knowing the Center is still looking for someone to fill the spot Rev. Lockard left.

:-)

Chapter Twelve

Divine Intervention

"All the cosmos is a single substance of which we are a part. God is not an external manifestation, but everything that is."
Spinoza

D r. Bump talks about the reticular formation in class reminding me it's a forgotten subject from community college days. I don't consider myself ruled by logic for I'm led by intuition and ruled by emotion. Now I pay attention to what's said about that part of the brain, which acts as a switchboard, filtering out things that do not match our beliefs.

It's clear I need to change. Although bodies come and go, like clothes, I believe physical form holds memories of lives lived long ago. My body needs to rid itself of unconscious stress felt when considering physical circumstances seeming to surround me. If I'm to live a life of love, health, abundance, and prosperity, I must change the electrical impulses that stimulate stored memory. Increasing the amount of time spent in visualization and meditation makes this possible. Intuition informs me belief systems must change. It's time to focus on more positive and life-affirming thoughts so Spirit can act through me.

Spirit acts through all life forms by the Law of Attraction. Learning how this law works seems necessary as I pore over class materials. The Law of Attraction is always drawing our deepest desires so we become what we imagine. Visioning a better world enriches all life.

I'm willing to more consciously direct energy even though it's hard to believe I've invited all past events. Yet, divine intervention continues to keep me alive. Failed suicide attempts and five car accidents without a scratch, three when my life passed before my eyes, leads me to believe my purpose here is incomplete.

Divine intervention guided my footsteps along the path of life many times. The first recognized pivotal instance occurred in 1967 shortly after Daniel's birth. Working at Big Boys as a waitress, on the dreaded midnight shift, afforded me time with Daniel during most of his waking hours. He slept through most of the night before three-months of age so it was easier to leave him with his father as I worked to support us.

The bus boy began to take most of my tips after a few weeks. A short, stocky woman came in and sat down at the counter as I contemplated how to address the issue. She smiled broadly, ordered a cup of coffee, and began a friendly conversation. I liked her immediately. It was as if I'd known her for years.

Jezebel offered me a job as a pantry girl in her family's French restaurant, with a salary of $150 a week. I gladly accepted for it was almost twice my current salary. We immediately began a relationship spanning more than forty years. Even though I later learned she offered me the job due to my husband's indiscretion with her teenage daughters, I believe our relationship was predestined. Her wonderful family remained a huge part of our lives right up until Daniel made his transition. If I hadn't accepted Jezebel's unexpected offer our life would have been very different.

Shortly after I started working at LeBordeau, I had the occasion to experience yet another case of divine intervention. Peter and I had a tumultuous relationship with many breakups over the course of less than four years. After a heated argument, Peter took Daniel while I worked and disappeared. I had no idea where they were and no one seemed able to help.

Desperate and missing Daniel dearly, I gave my power away and felt there was nowhere to turn. A wave of utter despair and abandonment overtook me standing amid hand washed cloth diapers hung to dry two days before in the kitchen.

I decided to "take Sominex and sleep," to commit suicide. It was a drastic thought but I couldn't bear the idea of living without the son I'd brought into the world to love and always love me. I bought a bottle of sleeping pills and a bottle of over-the-counter tranquilizers. I don't know if it was my real intention to kill myself but I began to take the colorful pills as soon as I got home.

Peter walked into the house with his friend McKinnon just as I began to take the last handful of pills. The observant McKinnon noticed me in the dark kitchen clinging to the sink. I tried to struggle as he picked me up. McKinnon flung me over one of his broad shoulders while instructing Peter to drive us to the hospital. McKinnon was a big guy, bigger than Peter, who stopped complaining and drove. I remember McKinnon imploring him to drive faster.

At one point I died. I know this because someone sent me back. I've never felt so at Home, so loved, so at peace, as when I went to Source. As I walked through a beautiful field of colorful flowers towards the brilliant white light, I wanted nothing but to be there forever. I assumed God was the tall being of luminous white light who spoke words I'll never forget.

It's not your time. You must go back.

McKinnon slapped me hard in the face and that last word "back" rang in my ears.

The rest, as they say, is history. McKinnon carried me into the emergency room where they immediately saw the seriousness of the situation. I can say, with all honesty, getting your stomach pumped is not a pleasant experience at all. It's particularly hard when they knowingly teach you a lesson. It was an experience, a lesson in the sanctity of life. We are here for a specific purpose, and obviously, mine was not yet met.

Divine intervention always works in our favor. Sometimes we don't always have the information needed to make an educated decision. Experience is the best teacher. Holmes notes all experiences help us learn the lesson of life so we can return to the Godhead as freed souls. We enter the paradise of contentment when the experience is complete and the lesson learned. I swore days later, with Daniel safely in my arms, that no one would ever come between us again.

Less than two years later in 1969, the grace of God saved both Daniel and me. It was dark as we drove quickly down Southfield Freeway after a confrontation with Peter. Car lights shone like a beacon through the rain as I wiped tears and followed the car in front of me.

I blindly followed when the car turned off at an exit. After realizing it was not my exit, I swerved back on the freeway still driving at sixty miles an hour. The threadbare, car tires slipped on the pavement and the car began to spin. It spun around in the middle of the freeway, three times, as key life events quickly passed through my mind. I let go of the steering wheel in my panic and looked back at Daniel still sleeping soundly in the back seat. A soft voice spoke inside my head.

Take the wheel. It's not your time.

The car seemed to magically stop, crosswise directly in the middle of the six lane freeway, when I grabbed the steering wheel. People ran to us from several different areas. It was a miracle we weren't hit because there were no barriers separating the north and south lanes. All the cars just stopped before impact, some of them within inches of my own. I thanked God for his help and for the fact that Daniel slept through it as I shakily drove home.

Nine years later, another angel, my neighbor Dawson, stepped in to ensure I'd stay alive. It was a rough year for the kids and me as we adjusted to life without my second husband Saul. I'd sent the kids to Ruth and Naomi's for winter break while I tried to piece together the puzzle of my life. After visiting a childhood friend of Ruth's in the county mental institution, I chose to heal myself.

It didn't look like I was doing a good job. I seemed lost in the late 1970's while working at a piano bar called the Sing Along. Yet, coworkers who really cared surrounded me. My boss allowed me to work when I could and the head waitress always covered for me if I messed up. I didn't realize just how fortunate I was. Everything seemed upside down, as I sat in the foyer writing in a pocket-sized journal.

"I am always on time," I wrote as other servers took care of the customers. "I'm considerate. I'm levelheaded and competent. I have a strong sense of values. I have morals. I am a very organized person and find it depressing that nothing is organized anymore. I get everything organized then I get a job and a week later it's worse than it was before."

My thoughts spiraled into a sea of doubt as the pen moved furiously across the small note pad.

"I've been trying to read the first volume of Shakespeare for almost two years now. I read the daily paper, "Redbook," "Family Circle," "Women's Day," and still try to catch up by reading a book a month. I'm way behind. My dresser is a mess. The kitchen floor needs to be scoured and waxed. Walls need to be scrubbed and painted. Woodwork needs to be cleaned, my cars rust repaired. I could go on and on. I can't do it all; so many things are out of my reach.

"I've got to keep thinking but then isn't that what got me like this in the first place? The constant ringing in my head is unbearable. I used to be so capable. I could do three things at once and have my mind on the next three. Maybe I did too much… I can't control everything and I want to. I have always been in complete control. Now, ZAP, nothing! I will fight this thing. I can do it. I don't want to be like this. Once I get back I'll never allow myself to become this way again."

I prayed that no one else had to experience what I was going though for it was a state of pure hell. I wanted so badly to scream, "Please help me. I'm dying." Eventually I realized that whatever happened in the past made no difference now; it's gone. A strong urge to "get back" filled sleepless nights. I knew, somehow I'd be a much stronger person for the experience.

One night, I left work despondent to find the furnace out again. It had gone out on the first day of January but the gasman said he couldn't do anything. Saul then answered my request and did something to relight the flame. Trudging down the stairs to the basement before crawling into bed was a must. Throughout the night, I played with the switch and touched the battery Saul rigged to relight the furnace flame.

When daylight came, I realized it was my day off as I sniffed gas fumes in the air. It didn't seem important to get out of bed for I was drowsy and not thinking clearly. Loud pounding woke me some time later but I ignored it and fell back asleep. Minutes later, my younger neighbor Dawson was at my bedside yelling. Before I had time to reply he lifted me up and carried me out the front door to safety.

Currently, in the illusion of my white light room, I help others. Pleas for assistance from far away countries such as Nairobi, Kenya continue to land in my email box. I forward them to colleagues still working in the field of hiv/aids. One night, soon, in the wee hours of the morning, or perhaps as the sun begins to rise; my heart will burst with joy. I'll be Home once again to rest and recuperate from the rigors of living a life full of changes, challenges, and lessons.

I am free now but must wait for the appropriate time to pass so I can help humanity from the other side of life. I'll be that unformed matter that swirls and jumps as you look in front of your face. I'll be that shining spark of flame that escapes out from the fire you poke with your bonfire stick. And I will be one of the many, many, sparks that fly off your sparkler on the Fourth of July.

Be happy for me and for yourself for I will never leave you. I will always remain a part of all living things. I am perfect love, perfect peace, perfect harmony, consciously aware of my destiny throughout all time and space. Have a few good bouts of crying, if you must, but be aware that you are crying only for yourself. Celebrate my new form, my new life, and celebrate your growth as you continue to learn with me by your side. Love never dies. Energy **cannot** be destroyed, remember?

As I sit studying in my room, it occurs to me that heart disease runs rampant on father's side of the family. Dad's mother and several uncles died of heart attacks in their early sixties. I too will die in the middle of the night from a quick, painless heart attack while sleeping.

Some note dis-ease of the body, which originates above the physical plane, is the result of a conflict between our spiritual and mortal selves. Our souls bring us back to the path of Truth and Light this way. I recall a serious one-way conversation with James in December of 2004 when I told him it was time for me to be true to my soul. The memory of that night sticks with me now because the words flowed from within the depths of my soul as I stood back and allowed Spirit to work through me.

I rise on June 18, 2009 to hear, "The form that represents us is just one of many forms our soul takes on to help us realize we are not really a form at all. We are as formless as our Creator."

:-)

Chapter Thirteen

Turning Point

"Mind is the Master power that moulds and makes,
And Man is Mind, and evermore he takes
The tool of Thought, and, shaping what he wills,
Brings forth a thousand joys, a thousand ills: –
He thinks in secret, and it comes to pass:
Environment is but his looking glass."
James Allen – As a Man Thinketh

A sense of wholeness fully envelopes me Wednesday evening while listening to Ester Nicholson, background vocalist for stars such as Bette Midler and Rod Stewart. Songs from her first CD, "Child Above the Sun," complement Rev. Jean's inspiring message. She greatly improves the Center's service and I'm grateful to attend.

Everything changes with the dawn as I lie on the futon, feeling pain, again wondering, "When can I return Home?" Classes and spiritual reading highlight a vital point in healing. It's necessary to give oneself to the service of God in order to be completely cured. I'm not sure if I'm ready to let God's Will be done through me so I fall back asleep.

It's not your time, rings loudly in my ears minutes later.

Even knowing I'm limited only by thoughts, the idea makes me angry. I adamantly shout out loud.

"Well, dam it; if I have to live I'm going to be perfectly healthy. I am sick and tired of being sick and tired."

Something within prompts me to devote my life to God. Ego angrily responds as I passionately shout out to the empty house.

"I will dedicate my life to God, but by God, I'm going to live the rest of my life healthy, wealthy, and happy. I will no longer be limited in any way."

My heart pounds as I yank open *The Science of Mind* to study.

Anger is power. In <u>Beyond the Indigo Children</u>, P.M.H. Atwater notes a link between anger and healing. If we're truly *motivated, truly angry, we can overcome most illnesses and repair damage caused by nearly all injuries. The power of anger pushes or inspires us, to move, getting things done quickly and with less effort. Committing that energy to the greater good, in service to others, transmutes the power of anger into healing energy that warms, uplifts, and makes whole. Suffering ceases and the body becomes pure after ego serves its purpose of burning out the useless and impure.*

Karen Drucker's "Hold on to Love" plays in the background while I reformat old records into mpg files to make a compilation CD. After completing the task, I search the closet for something to wear to Jody Ebling's one-woman show, "Broadway Baby."

Plastic bags, filled with clothes the previous month, line the floor. I recall storing them with the belief that I'd soon be freed from physicality. Many articles of clothing no longer fit for I lost more weight. Others have not fit for decades. Although I had no idea why, it seemed wise to store them noting their origin as made in the U.S.

Heaven is a state of consciousness as I set up beverages and snacks ninety minutes before the Center's Saturday night performance. Jody is captivating and my heart swells as her voice soars on stage. I'm truly in Heaven among friends of like mind knowing that tomorrow will be the same when I volunteer again.

The next day at the Broward County Convention Center, I'm filled with excitement while working in the "will call" ticket booth. Wayne Dyer promotes his new book *Inspiration: Your Ultimate Calling* and I'm thrilled to attend. There's just enough time to nap before the evening's service when I return home.

Rev. Rance talks about his father as I relate to every word. He confirms my thoughts. Dad never meant for his actions to hurt me. He was just doing the best he could with the education and awareness that he possessed. When the service ends, I silently thank Dad before breaking down the refreshment center.

The worksheet from last Tuesday's class helps me complete this week's assignment. It's a Spiritual Mind Treatment designed to ease my current conditions of bladder and bowel pain, headaches, blurred vision, and skin disturbances. Although the prayer completely ignores the conditions, I know it's perfect, for it's a treatment for conscious evolution. [51]

Study keeps me centered in Christ Consciousness. Spiritual blindness and ignorance lifts daily. There's no longer an urge to reinforce false notions. At one point, I find myself literally blind. It's a new experience to sit with eyes flooded by tears. I panic for a fleeting moment and claw at my eyes wiping the fluid away while trying to see. Stillness envelops the room when I suddenly realize it's part of the process, the process of coming Home.

The next morning I'm drawn to photograph the rising sun. Nothing looks different from any other dawn. Space Weather updates note more than thirty fragments of dying comet 73P. Venus and the crescent moon are beautifully close together before sunrise in the eastern horizon. I forward the Space Weather update to Rebecca with a question. Do these events affect humans?

Negativity clouds the area whenever James is near so I continue to avoid him by remaining in my sunlit room. I limit charge card expenses to bare necessities remaining thankful he pays the bills. Since he seems dissatisfied with my new path, I don't ask for money but count on providing the Center with services to continue lessons.

Walking joyfully to class, I extend the trip by an extra two blocks. Positive energy surrounds me while setting up the coffee station. It feels good to tithe more by tossing money into the teen center and coffee station baskets. Yet, I'm fearful that when my stash is gone I'll be unable to replenish it. It's the first time in my adult life that I don't control the finances in the house where I live and it's scary.

The Law of Attraction demands that we pay attention to our thoughts. I've spent my life repeating limiting thoughts, over and over again, without even realizing it. Tonight's class is again about the Law of Attraction, visioning a better world, and the power of tithing. While sitting at a back table in class, it's clear I need to be more conscious of beliefs and self-talk.

Rev. Geddes is still in town conducting class for Rev. Bump. A sense of ease fills the room when he asks us to refer to him as Charles. His viewpoints prompt me to see the world differently. I've never considered the possibility that people who do bad things are just showing us their pain. We're all looking for love in our own way. My consciousness of forgiveness, I now know, must expand.

Charles moves on to talk about prosperity. The idea that wealth is a habit, just like everything else, prompts me to consider more life-affirming changes. I'm intrigued by the notion that money is Spirit in action. Tithing is an act of faith that acts as a magnet for more abundance and prosperity. It's helpful to know our mind accepts the ability to give as a signal that there's always enough to share. The Law of Heaven relates that giving and receiving are the same, and the Law of Extension produces abundance.

I adore Charles and wish he'd teach more classes. His way of teaching is mind-expanding, to the max, when he goes between channeling and teaching as a human. My heart sings in union with the One as he channels God's words.

"The intention in this life is to get a break from human life after this one," Charles tells us intently. His eyes close as he stands before us. It's clear he's listening to something we can't hear.

"We are not alone," he begins again in earnest. "Allow the energy to commune with you. We play a role in the earth's evolution. Energy fields shift belief systems and you can help to make the shift. There are many mansions in the Infinite Reality that is the Eternal, the defining of God. Everything is perception. As life forms, the Light dispels the darkness. Healed misperceptions dissolve in the Light. Be mindful, Light dispels darkness. Our purpose is to dispel darkness and be free. Ignorance results in pain and suffering from misperceptions. Remember, the Truth, the Light, the Originating Substance."

He stands there silently and as tears flow from his face I realize he is literally blind, just like I was in the seclusion of my room. After a few moments, he clumsily wipes the tears from his eyes with the back of his hand, shakes his head very slowly, and smiles. "I think that will be all for tonight," he announces before bowing his head in silence.

I sit spellbound knowing that what we just witnessed is the 'real thing'. We are blessed to have him with us and I'm thrilled that he's stepped in to teach the week's lesson for Rev. Bump.

It's my practice to write down parts of *The Science of Mind* onto a small legal pad at home and later add insights received during class. As I look at notes while Charles channeled the words of God, I notice the writing stops on page 296. I'm stunned to read that the ones to whom we are most strongly attracted "are the ones from whom we receive 'that something,' which emanates from within. It is the inner recognition of Reality."

Yes! Charles will offer 'real answers' to questions. I've just begun to study *A Course In Miracles* but don't yet know that it's normal for Course students to see periodic jagged flashes of light.

Reviewing the night's lesson back home, I know all is well, despite physical appearances. We truly are spirits in a human world. Yes, if Charles can, I too can love everyone as Daniel told me I must. I will refuse to be misunderstood and I'll ignore the negative side of everyone. I know Love is the greatest healing power on earth, the reason for our being. My thoughts will now focus more fully on what I want in life, for that is what returns to me.

I'm determined to see things differently, knowing I'll see what I desire, for the world is merely an effect and I can change its cause. According to the Law of Cause and Effect, what we persist in recognizing will be held in place. It's time to neutralize unwanted conditions by embodying the perfect principle of Spirit and refusing to recognize anything else. Today, I tweak, and add, an affirmation from page 305 of *The Science of Mind* to my daily routine.

"Today the possibilities of my experience are unlimited. The Spirit flows through me, inspiring me and sustaining that inspiration. I have divinely sustained ability and talent and I am busy using them."

I know the affirmation will serve me well, yet ego rears its ugly head recalling thoughts of a third "failed marriage." It appears I'm right back where I was thirty-seven years ago, trying to figure out what went wrong. A poem written for my first husband at 17-years-old surfaces as it did during my second divorce.

The things we do and say were all said yesterday.
And though you come and go, surely you must know, I grew.
Why didn't you?
There always comes a time when we look inside our mind
and find a place to grow.
I know I grew.
Why didn't you?
So it's all said and done.
One day we were just one but I grew.
Why didn't you?

It now occurs to me my marriages were a tool just like the birth of Daniel. Each physical being I chose to make me feel whole chose as a soul to help me recognize my Divine Power. We are One, without having to cling to another. *We are One living in a state of grace through the power of God.*

Monroe notes this Oneness so eloquently on page 60 of his book *Far Journeys*. To quote just a bit:

"I am the very breath you breathe. We are one in the Father. Do not despair, I will never leave thee nor forsake thee, nor can you truly forsake me, for we are one. Let the old way be gone. It must die and its ashes be blown to the four corners of the earth. The new is emerging but you must change your perception."

Today my perception is vastly different from the days when I unconsciously replicated relationships filled with physical and mental abuse to spur me into ascension. Slowly taking back the power I gave to others helps me become responsible for myself.

By late April, I'm positive that solar activities affect us but I'm not sure how. The sky sporadically draws me to the east windows in the early morning. I'm compelled to take a picture shortly before 5:00 AM. Physical evidence again fails to reveal anything out of the ordinary.

After checking satellite information on sunspots and flares, I email a disbelieving Rebecca for she continues to deny there's anything different in the space around us. "So," I type quickly, "are you paying attention yet?" I attach several pages of information from "What's Up in Space" noting dying comet 73P and Sunspot 875 crackling with solar flares.

My new friend Leah offers a collection of spiritual books after cleaning out her spare room. It's a blessing to pore through Catherine Ponder's *The Prosperity Secrets of the Ages*. Ponder notes we can have everything if we know the power within and dare to use it. I know I'm reading the right book at the right time after reviewing a phrase in the introduction.

"Your success power is released through your mental attitudes and your emotional reactions toward life. You become what you think. Think straight and life becomes straight for you. It's as simple as that."

When at the 99 Cent store, I find a rack with play money and buy two packages. I take out the $100 bills for myself and give the remaining bills to Samuel and Rebecca. Every day I joyfully count the $100 bills pretending they're real.

"I Control My Mental Household" on page 543 of *The Science of Mind* reminds me there are no coincidences. This is the third time I've randomly chosen to read this particular passage in the past four weeks. It's no accident for I've been actively changing the way I think and speak.

Daily practices make it easier to turn away from negative experience. I now recognize limitation and poverty are the results of restricted thinking. I've lived in some fairly dire circumstances and don't want to ever go back to feeling poverty again. Yet, the thought of spending my small stash leaves me in a state quite near panic. I raid the stash to comply when Rev. Peck talks about keeping a $100 bill in your wallet, even if you have to borrow it, to help create a feeling of prosperity.

Money is God's energy in action Rev. Peck tells us during Wednesday evening's service. We feel restricted upon sensing separation from Spirit. Realizing we are one with our Creator changes the currents of causation and brings happier experiences into our life. I secretly tuck a $5 bill into an envelope before putting it into the donation basket. Happy to contribute, I move away from my place at the audio station to circulate the basket.

Completing the next night's homework, hours later in my energy-filled room, I vow once again to pay more attention to thoughts and spoken words. Designing a treatment for abundance, (52) I start with an affirmation easily repeated either out loud or silently. "Substance always manifests whatever I need before a need arises." At this instant, I make a decision to distinguish the difference between self-talk and God-talk and choose to add a few more dollars into the weekly donation basket on Wednesdays and Sundays.

I'm guided during self-study to design a "Wake Up to Life" treatment (53) after watching satellite TV news from around the world. It seems important that everyone know we are part of the Cosmic no matter what we call *It*.

Ego is still trying to prove how reliable it is at predicting future events as I forward emails of bird flu in Key West. "So, have I hit eighty percent yet?" I ask Rebecca. I also forward information that might be of value to friends "in the trenches" even though I've ended all volunteer commitments related to nutrition and hiv.

In shark contrast, as spiritual growth continues to open new ways to express myself, I offer online friends information on Spiritual Mind Treatments. Treatments, I note, are structured prayers, and when said by those who embody the principles of our Creator, can be very powerful. Spirit, Allah (or whatever name you may call your God) is everywhere, and in all of us, ever changing. Treatments on weather conditions, food, and waking up to Life are easily shared. I know they will help people to increase their spiritual growth and decrease the upset in this world.

I'm greatly encouraged and feeling blessed to be in a new family when an electronic greeting card arrives from Rev. Haggerty. Other email holds greetings from old friends who wonder why I no longer participate in the field of hiv/aids. Before blessing them with Love and Light, I tell them they're missed but my higher calling gets top billing.

Dr. Bump again mentions the Center's trip to Greece at the end of class five on abundance and prosperity. It sounds like a once in a lifetime, 13-day, dream come true to wander through places such as Athens, Olympia, Delphi, Mykonos and Turkey.

I've wanted to go to Greece ever since watching *The Tempest* directed by John Cassavetes but it's impossible to envision myself there for several reasons. I can't imagine not knowing when I'll be able to use a bathroom and even getting small change from James is difficult. The money tucked away is not nearly enough for a trip costing several thousand dollars.

The coffee maker breaks the next morning, but instead of recognizing it as a sign to stop drinking coffee, I strain hot water through paper towels. The glass pot broke months ago but I quickly replaced it with a metal one. I couldn't give up my daily pot of coffee despite gastritis. James returns after a visit with his sister days later to present me with one of several coffee makers stored in her garage. I gladly send Delilah a thank you card happy to have meandered upon Gratefulness.org.

On the last day of April, a waking thought fills me with curiosity. *Military will be stationed at Holy Cross in the future.* I wonder why anyone would station military at any hospital. It seems highly unlikely that the nuns worked with in the past would put up with such nonsense.

The last time I visited someone at Holy Cross Hospital there was indeed a guard dressed in what appeared to be a military outfit stationed near the door. I'm surprised to note security measures, including guards, now at all the hospitals I've been to lately. The grace of God often helps to assure that guards avoid me.

:-)

Chapter Fourteen

Revisiting the Past

"To expose the soul requires letting go of control, breaking habits,
allowing feelings to flow, and not hiding from emotions."
Dennis William Hauck – The Emerald Tablet: Alchemy for Personal
Transformation

Atmosphere changes are hard to document but shortly after dawn I try again in May. Photographs fail to reveal anything extraordinary. Daniel's voice enters my brain at eight o'clock while staring at the east windows.

"Take the shot Mom," he quietly advises.

I quickly grab my camera to take a picture looking directly into the sun as it shines through the screen and window. The results are hard to describe. It looks like a series of blue circles emanating from the center of the sun. A vertical line of magenta colored orbs gushes from the middle. Other orbs appear near them. Overjoyed to, finally, have proof something extraordinary is indeed occurring, I quickly transfer the picture to my hard drive.

Perceptions build on the basis of experience. It's impossible to see what we do not believe but I believe in the unseen. *A Course In Miracles* quote, about accepting God's Will as one's own, comes to mind. *When the light comes and you have said, "God's Will is mine," you will see such beauty that you will know it is not of you.*

Daniel's essence again advises me to "take the shot" shortly after seven o'clock the next morning. I don't need to be told again. These results are even more majestic than yesterdays. A comforting feeling of love and community envelopes me as brilliant, blinding sunshine fills the room. Numerous orbs of different colors, shapes, and densities stream forth, amid beams of multicolored lights. What joy to grab my sunglasses, completely spellbound, to sit on the futon and stare!

I invite the unseen to reveal itself and am overjoyed to have physical proof that you see what you expect. Pictures taken later during the month reveal magnificent orbs as well. The feeling of unseen forces is unmistakable. It's even more extraordinary than feeling Daniel's essence. Yet, I try to explain the phenomena away by telling myself orbs appear due to a small stained glass trinket of the sun hanging in the other east window.

Later, the words of Ernest Holmes demand attention while reading the days homework. "If you have possessions which possess you, it is better for you to lose them that you may understand their temporary, fleeting form." A chill passes though me at the thought of losing the home I remodeled and poured my heart into for nearly eighteen years.

Your Psychic Pathway by Sonia Choquette plays in the background as I scan email while silently thanking Leah for cleaning out her bookcase. It's interesting to note that along with drugs and alcohol, certain foods, and chemicals, manifest disharmony in the body.

Sonia's voice vibrates through the room as I view space weather reports of the Aquarid Meteor Shower. It's a stream of dust from Halley's Comet earth is about to pass through. The biggest meteor fragment of dying comet 73P will glide by the Ring Nebula in Lyra in a few days.

The speakers shake with Sonia's voice while I contemplate more changes in personal habits. God's Voice speaks to us through thoughts and inspirations that circulate in the airways but I've blocked communication for a very, long, time. Yet, there's a part of my mind where truth abides, and it's in constant communication with God. I need to rediscover that part of the Godhead, which is really the only part there is.

It's time to forge the energy of my physical host so it vibrates at a higher octave. Purifying the physical form to reach higher levels of consciousness is vital. Besides insuring the health of my bladder and liver, I must retune the vibration of my entire form. Drinking and eating habits must change. I decide to drink only spring water whenever possible for its higher vibration. Although I'm not ready to stop eating ice cream and brownies, I vow to eat more fruits and vegetables. Everything I consume, put on my skin, or bathe in, must be reconsidered.

My small mind switches gears quickly after an email link leads to world news. Reports fill me with fear and dread so I stop reading. Another project begins as I extract certain pictures from photo album videos to make a new show. I carefully review every record in my collection to match songs with pictures. The plastic laptop microphone records music coming from the living room stereo and makes it easy to convert music to mpg files, which I later add to video. The time-consuming project will continue through hot, summer months.

Playing records not heard in years improves my mood while singing and remembering past times. As Marmalade sings "Reflections of My Life," I take a trip down memory lane remembering life as a pre-teen.

Dad wasn't real good at paying bills on time and we went without the basic necessities of life on many occasions. Our family suffered greatly for pride consumed him and he refused offers of help from social service agencies. Dad dropped out of school in the sixth grade, tried hard not to let anyone know he couldn't read, and barely knew how to write his own name. I completed many job applications for him wondering if he'd ever find steady employment. Sporadic blue-collar work offered low pay, no benefits, and no future for advancement.

Memories now fill me with warmth knowing I'd chosen this old soul to offer the chances needed to evolve. Even though those days are long gone, lessons and learned character traits remain to carry me through the years. Without the plethora of opportunities Dad offered, I would not have become self-reliant and strong, yet unafraid to ask for help when I really needed it.

I smile and start homework realizing that over the last sixty-five days I've designed thirty-four treatments that have not been part of the usual homework. I must design two treatments for class five today. One is a treatment for my classmate to help him lessen habitual emotional reactions to outside forces. [54] The other on abundance and prosperity is already done. I'm happy to have progressed in spiritual studies as the day ends.

It's taken me a long time to recognize that nothing happens by chance. Whether I immediately realize it, or not, everything occurs for a reason. Classes served to group me with people who acted as mirrors, always seeking treatments that I needed myself.

When the next morning's ritual is complete, I again play old records recording them into the laptop. Ego tells me impending storms will rip open the leaking roof and carry everything away. I don't realize this divinely guided task improves mood and raises my vibration.

Recording while singing the Carole King hit, "Goodbye Don't Mean I'm Gone," I add a message for family.

"I'll talk to you later maybe in your dreams. You know my love is always there for the taking, just call my name. Goodbye don't mean I'm gone. Goodbye don't mean I'm gone, because I'm **not**. You just got to practice, really hard, and then you'll be able to see me. The substance and the matter of the universe are all around you. Concentrate; think of me, you'll see if you want it to be. That's my advice for the day."

Now I recall the days when Ruth and I were close as pre-teens, lying in a huge field of grass in the middle of the projects, sorting out shapes in clouds. A formation took shape high above us in early October 1963. As I watched the clouds filled with wonder, a funeral procession appeared.

It was a long procession of many horse-drawn black carriages like people used years ago. A large group of mourners dressed in black, from head to toe, followed the carriages on foot. Looking at the many women wearing long black dresses I asked Ruth if she saw what I saw. Her face told me what I needed to know well before she finally replied with a stunned yes. It's a day I will never forget for Ruth and I experienced another phenomenon before dropping off to sleep several nights later on October 7, 1963. A vision of Grandma Olive appeared next to our bed.

"I have to go now girls," she said. And then she was gone.

The telephone rang minutes later as we quietly cried. Daddy's heavy step on the stairs filled the air as he trudged up to give us the news. I'll never forget the look of shock on his face when we told him Grandma just told us goodbye.

Right now, it's great fun singing along to favorite songs from the past. I sing and dance remembering my pantomime of Kathy Linden's "Heartaches at Sweet Sixteen," during my first and last high school drama class. Filled with happiness, I remember the melancholy singing "O-o-h Child" by the Five Stairsteps, to Daniel as he sat watching me wash dishes at the French restaurant less than two years later.

"This life we got everybody together," I now remark with a knowing at the end of the song. "We got it all undone."

As I type, beginning to feel a twinge of loss, I recall the words heard sometime last year.

"Have faith, keep your faith. God's Will is done by you."

The new laptop computer just wasn't collaborating and I knew Daniel's essence was with me. He told me to be careful of what I say, and to take care of myself, for soon it would be strenuous times. I questioned him, noting how I thought it was supposed to go easily for me now. The reply came quickly.

"Others will have strenuous times and you will help them."
"I want to go Home," I replied with great sadness.

The words I heard next were not new to me.

"You have to finish your contract. You know you have to stay. You need to quit complaining. You need to live with joy and abundance just like Charles told you to do. Understand?"
"Yes," I said thankful for the connection with Daniel that seems much less frequent now. "Yes, I understand."

Still wrapped up in the past, I continue my project a few days later. Even though it hurts, I force myself to sing along to Barbra Streisand's "Sing," remembering the many times I sang it to Daniel. His presence fills the air lifting my mood. I'm instantly delighted to play Carole King's "In the Name of Love," remembering the essence of my departed father while recording it for my own memorial CD, months before Daniel passed. Yes, our spirits live on way past the time of physical death!

I'm on a mission deciding to name my new video project Nana's Legacy. Clearly, the endeavor is going to result in much more than one two-hour movie. The project keeps me occupied as each song documents a phase in my life. I remain blissfully unaware that ego is having its way with me, pulling me deeper into the illusion.

It's time to teach esoterically by being a different kind of role model than the one my family knows. Playing back the first DVD I hear the craziness within me acting out as I talk through "Born to Be Wild" by Steppenwolf.

"We are born again, and again, and again," I announce with great excitement. "Learn your lessons now and you won't have to be born again."

I continue to note the past, insisting on linear time, still trying to predict the future.

We are reborn, Emmanuel tells us, whenever we allow a new concept to enter our awareness for everything shifts, and rearranges itself, to allow for infusion of the new. Just one new thought or experience makes us different than we were the moment before.

Watching the videos now, it's plain to see how one would think I was crazy, as they listen to the music and my occasional talk. Yet, the changing field within each still photo is clearly visible. Varied hues of blue, reddish-pink, and fleeting yellow continue to amaze, for the photos are black and white.

I still feel the Love that surrounded me when I videoed those photos. Although certain still photos are merged with music, I don't discuss the people in them. It seems that whenever I do talk, I'm noting the Presence and our Oneness with __It__. All I can surmise now is that I was ridding myself of the past the only way I knew how, to dwell on it and bring up the pain, the hopelessness, and the fleeting moments of fun and love, without commiseration.

Memory of another dream fills my brain the next morning. I'm driving with Rebecca, and I think a child, knowing cars were blown up on the freeway the previous day. It wasn't reported on the news. White mushroom clouds appear far ahead in the distance interrupting our conversation. Plumes of black smoke fill the air miles away. Many people stop their cars, get out, and began to run towards us. We follow their lead to run back the way we came.

Car keys and something else drop from my hands but I keep running. The location changes and now I'm barefoot in a hospital realizing I kicked my shoes off to run faster. Two girls who work at the hospital are standing in front of the curtain to where I am. I listen as one of them admits she's never taken care of a patient before. The other girl tells her she will have to start seeing patients, whether she's ready to or not. There are just too many people to care for and they need her help.

I get up and sneak sideways through another curtained section deciding to leave the hospital. Before leaving, I tell a nurse I've lost my shoes and describe them as blue. If anyone finds them, I say, save them for I'll be back. She snickers as if to say, "Sure, you will, not!"

The phone rings. I'm now fully awake assuring the caller it's okay that they dialed a wrong number. I reach for my laptop after hanging up the receiver to document the dream quickly, which I think is a glimpse into a future life.

I've allowed everyone to distance themselves from me but SOM members. Rebecca and Samuel call once or twice a month and I go see a movie at their home when they do. James seems more peaceful toward me and now does his own food shopping. Still, alas, no cleaning. I stay in my room when he's here. There's a strong sense that I need to sign something before I'm renewed into a greater energy form. Maybe this is it, *SAM*.

I'll be going to help from the Otherside soon, but have agreed to return to earth with the rest of my spirit group before the end of the days to try and bring more people to Light. There are no "wrong numbers" and the phone rang so I could write all this down.

It's been at least a month, maybe three or more, since I've had dreams such as this. I'm close to my intention. Before going back to sleep after sunrise treatments, I ask for clarity of where I am on the path. The random page I choose is perfect as my finger points to "The Dawn has Come," a meditation on page 532 of *The Science of Mind*. I do feel renewed in strength knowing Good, and I know my light has come.

I see and intuitively know so much that I dare not discuss. There will be hard years ahead and that is all I can say. Maybe four times forty for I got this in my head about six months ago.

Upon waking, ego pulls me further down the rabbit's hole as I respond to Act For Change email petitions on a variety of political issues. Shifting gears quickly, I video Nana's Legacy number two, while singing to "Simple Things" by Carole King. I know the secret to living is Life and Love.

The photos on my computer have fleeting specks of yellow and blue that were not there when I scanned them into the laptop using the printer/scanner. I'm filled with joy to think Stuff of Matter is changing the room's atmosphere. Carole King sings "In the Name of Love" as I begin to speak for those who may listen in the future. "We never," I report with conviction, "die. We just change our energy so know this and you'll be totally free."

"Born to be Alive" plays while pictures of a newborn Rebecca splash across the screen. Alice Cooper's "Love it to Death" then blasts loudly as I realize Daniel and I have always known our destiny. "We still got a long way to go," drones Cooper while pictures from the mid-seventies flash by. I've been singing for more than thirty minutes now and am seeing touches of magenta and less yellow in pictures.

The next morning upon waking, I hear, and see behind closed eyes, the shadow of someone mourning the loss of their unborn baby. I hope it's not Lydia.

We make many choices, and bargain as souls, before coming into physicality. We always help one another to learn and teach lessons through a variety of experiences. One soul may need to learn the sanctity of life, while another agrees to help with that lesson, by inhabiting the human form for a short period. As noted in the workbook for A Course In Miracles, "The world you see has nothing to do with reality. It is of your own making, and it does not exist." We are spirits in human form having a physical experience on earth.

I rise and reach for *A Course In Miracles* reading several pages of the student text before concentrating on the day's lesson. The lessons so match current thoughts. Yes, I see a real world as I look to my real thoughts as my guide for seeing. I know this is a schoolroom of illusion and sometimes I'm graced with glimpses of the unseen Cosmic behind closed eyes.

Nights fill, waking repeatedly, as I maintain a lit candle on the computer desk. Days are spent between SOM studies, video projects, and naps. Today's Democracy Now grabs my attention, as I stand dumbfounded in front of the TV. AT&T, Verizon, and BellSouth are helping the U.S. Government to spy on millions of Americans by allowing the NSA to collect phone call records secretly. I turn the show off deciding to take my usual nap.

Rebecca phones to see if I've changed my mind about going with the family to the Keys. "I'm staying home this year," I tell her without disclosing the reasons. This decision is a necessary distancing, to make it easier on the family, because surely I'll soon get to go Home for a while. It's clear Rebecca is upset when she abruptly ends the call. She thinks I'll be alone when James leaves to join them in a few hours. Thoughts of having the house to share solely with spirit friends are exciting. James and I now have vastly different preferences in almost everything and air temperature is a huge issue for me. This week they'll be no need to sneak into the hall to adjust the air conditioning while he sleeps.

The tape cassette malfunctions as I listen to Liza Minella at 1:56 AM. It's the first time a cassette keeps repeating the same words, "friend is Gus who's like us, old friend. You learn stuff from old people." I sense Daniel and soon the cassette plays normally. The motion light in the den comes on.

"Time for bed Mom," he says in my brain.

James is gone when I wake at sunrise on Mother's Day, the third one without Daniel. Peace fills me upon remembering wonderful dreams. A rainbow appears on one-third of the ceiling to let me know I'm not alone as I repeat the usual meditation. The tape cassette player switches back and forth when I turn it on. This time I don't get a clear message so I leave it on and walk to church.

When I return three hours later, it's clicking away as if someone presses the stop and play button repeatedly. I sit and try to communicate. The cassette player either slows down or speeds up, clicking more often, as I think of Rachel. I promptly call to wish her a happy Mother's Day and spurt out a message for the machine.

Intuition now tells me there's a spirit stuck on earth that needs my help. It's easy to release the spirit proclaiming its freedom to travel. I let it know only Love, Light, and All the Good There Is fills the house. Rebecca then calls to wish me a happy Mother's Day. She again asks if I'm coming to the Keys and sounds upset but resigned when I again note my plan to stay home.

I don't feel guilty about not going at all. Holmes notes the expression of more life, happiness, and peace, without harm to another, is the criterion as to what is right or wrong. Expressing more life seemingly alone in an energy-filled room makes me happy. A hot bed of drama no longer serves higher good.

:-)

Chapter Fifteen

Friends and Family

*"There is only One. Everything that seems to indicate otherwise is
merely an illusion of duality."*
Helen Brungardt-Pope – For the Aspiring Mystic

Sylvia calls to request a ride to her Wednesday physical therapy
appointment. She's not feeling well and the bus is too much work. I
tell her to call me Wednesday morning at eleven o'clock. If I'm
here, I'll take her. She seems to understand my indirect answer
knowing I believe it may soon be time to go Home.

The Internet offers an avenue to share a new treatment on
food safety and security in the afternoon. Weather reports tell us
storms are increasing across the country so I also upload the
Weather Conditions Treatment. I repeated the same prayer
throughout the ravages of Hurricane Wilma and remained safe. My
goal now is to give people hope and faith in the beauty of nature,
while remaining calm and safe during changing environments.

Email holds a notice from the U. S. Patent and Trademark
Office. They denied my small business trademark application. It's
another message from the Universe that my mission changed.

Space weather offers updates on Venus, the crescent moon,
and comets of interest. As earth passes through the dusty tail of
Comet Thatcher, and another comet splitting in two, the Lyrid
Meteor Shower appears. Astronomers continue to monitor more
than thirty fragments of dying comet 73P for a close encounter in
mid-May.

As I continue to work on the draft of this book, sometimes I
use my new laptop, and speak into a microphone. Today, while
looking at the computer screen to review what I already said the
words, "up up up two find that a bit and and it is" suddenly
appeared as if I'd said the words. Since I was reading, and not
talking, the words immediately got my attention.

I knew they came from an unseen force to make me get up. I
had to get out and exercise. I pushed the thought out of my mind

several times thinking I'd walked enough in the store today. Yet, Spirit has a mind of its own, and I must listen. I'm glad I did, for I saw a beautiful sunset and said hello to a few neighbors. I am beginning to like being a puppet on a string to that unseen force of Spirit.

Truth is the absence of illusion and can only be experienced. I'm getting accustomed to the notion that my will and the Will of God are one. Doing God's Will is much more second nature to me since I angrily resigned myself to living a life of health and abundance. The anger is gone and wonders increase.

Jesus tells us we have the power to work miracles but we must be ready and willing to perform them when opportunities arrive. I'm ready to accept guidance from within, certain God's Voice will direct me very specifically, just as it notes in *A Course In Miracles*. Soon I'll begin to erase limitations through new understanding. I'm ecstatic to know God will guide me to specific people, or certain people will come to me for help. I'll be told all I need to know as God speaks through me. Readiness to perform miracles advances daily as I consciously listen to God's Voice. But how long will it take my ego to stop interfering and get out of the way? *The Science of Mind* daily random reading on page 369 is immensely encouraging.

"Be still, O Soul, and *know*. Look unto the One and be illumined.

Rejoice and be glad, for thy Spirit lights the way.

Lift up thine eyes and behold Him, for He is fair to look upon.

Listen for His voice, for He will tell thee of marvelous things.

Receive Him, for in His presence there is peace.

Embrace Him, for He is thy Lover.

Let Him tarry with thee, that thou mayest not be lonely.

Take council from Him, for He is wise.

Learn from Him, for he knows.

Be still in His presence and rejoice in His Love forevermore."

Sylvia calls and I'm on my way. It's a beautiful, sunny day as I drive listening to Shirley MacLaine talk of *The Camino*. I'm glad to have a friend that gets me out of the house to see it. Sylvia stands outside the complex door with Emilytine. She smiles broadly when I pull up to the curb. The sweat on her brow tells me she's been there for several minutes so I'm glad to share my air-conditioned car.

"I'm sorry I don't have any money for gas," Sylvia says as soon as she settles into the front seat. "What's playing on the radio?"

"Don't worry about the gas," I reply with a broad grin. "I've got my trusty Visa card. I hand her the cardboard box sitting between us to finish my reply. "It's Shirley MacLaine talking about her soul-searching trek."

Emilytine draws back in her seat as she shakes her broad head slowly from side to side.

"I'd love to listen to all these tapes," Sylvia informs me with glee. "Can I borrow them?"

Emilytine mutters something from the back seat but I can't make it out. When Sylvia tries to hand her the cardboard box, she pushes it away.

"Sure," I reply ignoring Emilytine while stopping for a red light. I reach under my seat and hand Sylvia a book as well. "Here's the book you wanted to borrow."

Sylvia takes *The Tibetan Book of Living and Dying* and quietly looks at it as we motor down the busy road.

"I'll read this after Emilytine goes back to Jamaica," she says minutes later taking a glance at her now quiet daughter sitting in the middle of the back seat.

As Sylvia goes through her exercises with the physical therapist, I search for Mary. Two hours later, I motor slowly back to my room after promising to drive Sylvia to the rest of her appointments.

This month the mysterious is much appreciated when making its self known. The more I focus on something the more it appears. Homework requires that we notice beauty everywhere. God's splendor is evident outside the east windows in my brilliantly sunlit room. Although a high hedge of lovely bushes blocks the view of the neighbor's house it still allows me a glimpse of the rising sun.

My senses increasingly detect normally unseen energy everywhere. It's more apparent in sunrise photos and in the videos of my new project. I decide to use the orb pictures for a class final.

This rarely seen view of the typically undetected world, which never stops moving, must be shared.

Orb pictures are the closest thing I have to show others the splendor of Mind. *A Course In Miracles* tells us space and time are merely beliefs. Time is just the measure of an experience, and space is not apart from, but in Mind. We are part of Him and nothing else exists but using our free will. We've elected to be in time rather than eternity. The body neither lives nor dies and our seeming separation from God is just a failure in communication. Only the Mind that is everywhere, and in everything, is real and shared.

What a relief to know that Jesus believed, as I, in a Universal Spirit, an Intelligence he consciously talked with and received replies from. I'm not cuckoo like my family says! It's time to stop talking with relatives on the telephone for we often gossip about others instead of concentrating on ourselves. More time must be spent connecting with God through meditation.

Our thoughts have great power. When we fail to share a thought system, we weaken it. Jesus tells us in *A Course In Miracles*, when you meet anyone, remember it's a holy encounter and as you see him, you'll see yourself. As you treat him, you'll treat yourself and as you think of him, you'll think of yourself. And in him, you will find yourself or lose yourself. I vow to concentrate more on seeing others, and myself, as the perfection of God.

The Science of Mind calls to me from its roost on top of the small gray file cabinet that acts as a nightstand. When I open my eyes after pointing to a random place in the book, I'm ecstatic to see it's the third time, in less than six months, that I've chosen to meditate on "I Have Known, Always" on page 533. Yes, I have always known the Truth. My Higher Self happily listens to God's Voice knowing all is well.

Sometimes I'm tested but seem to pass the tests. As long as I follow Divine direction, and I often do, my life is perfect. I am perfect, whole, complete, disease-free, and full of conscious, joyous gratefulness. My goal will be met with Divine Timing!

Two days later, after repeating the usual treatments, I leave the house quickly to make the three hour round trip to physical therapy with Sylvia. This time Emilytine waits for her at home. I'm so very grateful to have someone of like-mind to share mystical experiences with and return home happier than when I left.

Things improve as more friends of like-mind appear. Today's email holds a card from Rev. Peck acknowledging my service to the Center. I'm overwhelmed with joy to receive it. My mentor is on her way to serve a community in North Carolina for the summer.

An old colleague's latest book is now available so I gladly spread his news on the weekly business update before logging off the Internet to meditate. It's almost time to see Samuel in his school play. I don't want to miss a minute of it but need to center myself fully before meeting family.

My tall grandson has the lead role in Oliver Twist. The cast begins their round trip through the area as I enter the room. Samuel wears a baggy, long, brown shirt with too short gray pants, and red suspenders, while everyone else is dressed in white t-shirts and jeans. He smiles, and waves happily while still singing, as they pass and make their way through the crowded room back to the stage.

It's a standing-room only event. The crowd allows me to weave through to the sidelines on the right where a glimpse of the stage is best. I quickly spot Rebecca on the left side of the room and zigzag my way to her while videoing.

My heart swells with pride as a short, child actor pulls Oliver past us and around the room by his ear. I laugh with glee watching Samuel allow him to tug his ear as they parade back to the stage before the first act ends.

When the heavy, dark blue curtains close I turn my attention to Rebecca. She begins to complain about her health after I ask how she is. The anger within is apparent as I talk about doing a treatment for her. Rebecca still doesn't want to believe in my new way of life. She's using anger to hide her fear of change.

Ruth pops up near the stage and passes by the front row to join us. She jokingly pretends to pick her nose when I ask if she's part of the show. As we watch Oliver sold for three guineas, and pushed onto the cold floor to sleep, my heart goes out to that part of me releasing thoughts of bondage. I lovingly look on as Samuel sweetly sings, "Where is Love?"

James arrives from work as Samuel's voice breaks, like an adolescent boy with changing vocal cords. My heart soars when he smiles after the song while the audience claps and hoots. I'm proud beyond belief to watch the show and sad when it ends. My family quickly heads to the exit ahead of the crowd while I linger inside.

As the audience files out the door, and clean up begins, one of the adult cast members sings Frank Sinatra songs. My video camera records the action.

"Are you coming with us to dinner Samantha?" Ruth asks from the doorway.

I nod yes and begin to follow her slowly still giggling as the man clowns around on stage. Everyone heads for their cars while the video camera records spirit orbs. There's a spring in my step knowing that one day I too will be a guiding spirit.

"Thank you," I say to the wind sensing their presence. "You're so good to me. The family, they won't see this video for years, but I can see it right now."

James cringes but remains silent when I charge everyone's dinner to my Visa card. I'm thankful to spend time with the family even though we are distanced in thought. No one seems to value my new beliefs. Yet, I'm still locked in the energy of limitation wondering how I'll live without them in the future.

The day's video plays quietly back in the energy of my light filled room. Diamond shaped orbs of various colors, along with a dense white spot of light, which seems to come from the sun, amaze me. A short conversation with James soon prompts a message from the unseen. The answer to his question comes on the brink of sleep.

New souls are being born now because there are just too many jaded souls on earth.

It feels good to have a friend of like mind the next morning. Sylvia and Emilytine are ready when I arrive to transport them to the rehabilitation center.

"Turn here at the next corner," Sylvia announces with a broad smile as we drive through light traffic, "for we need to stop at the bank."

"How much should I withdraw?" Emilytine asks her mom as she opens the car door.

"Take out $50," Sylvia replies turning towards me. "You know I really like that MacLaine audio book but have not had much time to hear it. Emilytine doesn't believe in such things."

I smile and nod as we trade stories of family differences until Emilytine returns to hand her mom the money.

"This is for you," Sylvia says turning to hand me the $50. "It's to pay for all the gas you used to get me back and forth to the hospital and rehab," she adds thrusting crisp bills into my hand.

My response flows from the heart.

"I can't accept this. It's just too much and really not necessary."

"Momma," Emilytine remarks from the back seat, "that's almost every penny in your bank account."

"Sam is a good friend and I must pay my own way," Sylvia announces with dignity. "And that is the end of the matter."

Emilytine looks on with dismay as I thank her mom and shove the money in my pocket before backing out of the bank lot. It's the most cash I've seen in months and much appreciated for getting cash from James seems impossible.

Sylvia's visit with the physical therapist is short. We're soon on our way back to her place as she talks of Jamaica. Emilytine convinced her it's time to go back home for a visit but there are no plans to get there yet. I leave them at the entrance after hearty hugs goodbye.

:-)

Chapter Sixteen

Soul Lessons

"In truth, all you are and all I am is thoughts and feelings, yet all thoughts are from just One Mind; and all feelings are in just One Thing. Therefore, your consciousness is both a part and the whole."
Dennis William Hauck – The Emerald Tablet: Alchemy for Personal Transformation

It occurs to me I may never see Sylvia again while walking at a small park later in the day. I shrug off the thought and return to the house on 47th Drive to continue Nana's Legacy. Daniel chooses the music once again prompting me to recall darker days of cocaine and alcohol in 1978. As Alice Cooper sings "Welcome to My Nightmare," I fondly recall the days we loudly sang along not realizing the truth of Cooper's words.

"We sweat and laugh and scream here cause life is just a dream here."

Making the DVD tires me so I take a short nap. I'm prompted to investigate another past life upon waking. Minutes later, I lie quietly on the black futon listening to my recorded voice recite Dr. Weiss's words from the back of *Through Time into Healing.*

It's now 1583. I am Joseph, a young black man with hairy arms who works in a shipyard. Reddish looking sandals adorn my feet. Short, dark pants and a blue shirt that looks too small cover my large frame. I have a big, round face. My nose looks flat and is shadowed under a small, black cap. Another black man walks up to me.

"The boss man says it's time to get back to work," he announces with authority.

I see the rich boss's daughter walking down the gangplank of a ship nearby and now sense she is Rebecca in my current life. She's a young white girl wearing white clothes. Her pantaloons flutter in the light wind. The pictures in my mind change. At this point, I'm charged with her death and hanged. I don't see how she dies but know I'm responsible.

When I ask what the life lessons were, I hear there were two. No man can be my boss because I am my own boss and everyone has to answer to God for all they do. I sit up and open my eyes still worried. Rebecca and I have never been as chummy as Daniel and me. Yet I know, for this life the three of us made a pact to forget what happened in the past. Our goal is to learn there's no limitation, no bondage in any form. I regress myself now, to our first life together, to see if there's something else to know.

A white beam from above covers me in golden light. As I walk down the stairs, I look a bit older than twenty years old, dressed in a white robe with gold trim. The door I arrive at is wooden and covered with green vines. On the other side of the door, I am a six-year-old white girl named Elena living before the Common Era (B.C.). One of many birds answers my questions.

I'm nude, of a normal weight, walking barefoot in a lush, garden-like setting. It looks like a non-threatening tropical jungle with lots of vines, small, unidentified trees, flowers, and various fruit trees.

The images change. Now I'm older. An even older, gruff looking woman, with wrinkles in her skin, stands nearby. She wears a brown, sack-like cover to hide her body because she's no longer pleasing to her husband. The cover reaches just above her ankles. Something like sandals adorn her feet. They have a twine/cord-like material just to protect them from the earth. The woman has olive-colored skin, brown eyes, and shoulder-length, messed up, brown hair, which she cuts herself.

"Go see the master," she commands while prodding me with a stick of brown wood from a tree limb.

I don't want to go knowing he will abuse me again the same way he used to abuse her when she was pretty. The woman is Rebecca in another incarnation. She birthed children but they were all stillborn. Now she buys youngsters for the master to use from a slave trader, in a nearby town called Bethel. They help with her duties of keeping up the house and land. The plot of land is not unusually large but normal for that time. It is outside of Sodom and Gomorrah.

I have no idea where these places are or even if they are near one another. Although religious studies at a young age taught me about what happened in Sodom and Gomorrah, I still do not know exactly where it is, or was.

As I continue refining the draft of this book, something prompts me to pull out my copy of the study bible. A picture of one road seemed familiar when I scanned the book more than three years ago. It's truly divine intervention that I have copies of the book, and the computer disk, for I gave the book away and left the copies behind when I left the house on 47th Drive.

An article on Bethel grabs my attention as awareness fills my brain. Yes! I have written of this town without knowing it existed. I pore over the book filled with wonder and look up the maps on disk knowing it's a sign to document the experience here.

According to page 59 of the study bible, the holy site of Bethel played an important role in the lives of Abraham, Jacob/Israel, and Israelite history. I'm certain it played an important role in my soul's evolution as well.

Most biblical scholars place the town of Bethel near Jerusalem within the area now referred to as the West Bank. Sodom and Gomorrah appears to have been southeast of Bethel. According to the maps in the study bible, both appear to be in the vicinity of Canaan, an area controlled by ancient Israel.

A boy comes out as I approach the place where the master is. He has blonde hair and blue eyes like me and looks about 12-years-old. Unclothed and bleeding about the face, he senses my fear and tries to comfort me.

"He has taken his anger out on me and will not be so hard on you," he says holding me close. "I'll wait for you here."

The house is the color of brown mud made of adobe, some type of concrete or smooth stone, with a flat roof. It has two rooms. The master now stands before me. He is an ugly looking man, overweight and in his 60's.

"I have branded the boy," he says, "so all will know he is mine and now I will brand you."

I cry and try to go outside without success. The scene that follows is not pleasant and as a result, my life is over. The master calls for his wife who protests when she learns I am gone. Her husband treats her badly until she timidly makes his soup and serves it to him with bread and wine. As he eats, she follows his instructions to "secure the boy."

121

The boy is still crouched down at the base of the first olive tree outside the house. He's crying for he knows I'm gone. The old woman leaves the house, secures him to the tree with a rope-like cord, and goes back inside.

"It is done," she tells her master.

"Take him with you to the market tomorrow morning," he tells her. "Pick out two girls for I may tire of one soon."

She quietly cleans his mess as he lays his drunken head on the table. He sleeps there all night while she goes to rest her tired body in the other room that has only straw on the floor.

In the morning, the master gives her what I think are shekels to buy two new girls. The old woman has already untied the boy and given him some bread and soup left from the master's dinner. She decides to flee because she knows it will all continue if she does not. She takes the coins from the master as he instructs her and then speaks gruffly to the boy as they leave the property to go to the market.

The old woman tells the boy of her plan to flee when they arrive. They begin to run through the market past the merchants. No one follows them but someone does tell the master later they were running. It is by then too late for the master to find them. I don't know who "the master" is in this life and I don't want to know so I don't ask.

The old woman and boy, Rebecca and Daniel in my current life, flee to an area outside of Sodom and Gomorrah. They live in one room where Daniel cares for Rebecca until she passes of old age. He's about 40-years-old by then and places her in the fire as he has seen his master do with others. It's all he knows to do. I stop the regression before asking what my lessons for that life were for I cannot know more for now.

Suddenly, I remember this regression relates to the one I did days before New Year's Eve. Notes remind me this was the first life lived with both Rebecca and Daniel. Daniel and I shared the same life lessons. We were to know that pain and suffering teaches compassion and that we do not always have control over our life, due to environmental and age issues. Since I died so young in this first life, it is now my turn to mourn the loss of Daniel as he mourned for me so many thousands of years ago.

My journal notes the place where we lived was Nubia. I have no idea where it is or was. Children were born to serve the master of the house during the time of this life. The master who tormented us is Daniel's father in our current life.

At this instant, I know the physical aliments we have are from many lives of abuse. It's time to rid ourselves of these aliments. SOM will show the way to Rebecca and the others from this side when it's time for me to guide them from the Otherside. It's my destiny to do so and I'll do it humbly, gratefully, and joyfully.

Two days later, another odd wakening thought fills my brain.

Whatever to one, is from 3 1 6 1?

The numbers are spaced apart. With a clear mind, I turn on the recorder, lie back on the black futon, and listen to the soothing tone of my own voice. A woman's image soon appears behind closed eyes. She's white, with a shapely figure, has long, black, wavy hair, and wears delicate string sandals. Several golden bracelets enhance arms, which are much thinner than mine are. Gold rings adorn fingers and a gold heavy necklace hangs around her neck. The necklace is thick and shaped to point down. It reminds me of the style of necklaces worn in Egyptian days.

The woman's dress is a beautiful, flowing vision of many bright colors that appear to be several layers, of different colored thin cloth, such as silk. I realize, with great excitement, that she is I, twirling around inside a palace dancing. Other people watch as they sit on the marble floor. I'm happy and carefree while dancing gracefully before them. I stop dancing and ask what appears to be a handmaiden for the date.

She replies, "Why it's 3 1 61, you know that my lady."

"Why did you call me my lady?"

She looks at me in surprise and smiles broadly.

"Because you are the lady of the house."

"Then why am I dancing?"

"Because you like to dance," she says grinning while turning away.

I think she has brown hair, and try to visualize her again, but instantly hear it's not important who she is, or what she looks like. Now I notice some kind of black makeup around my eyes.

"Who am I?" I ask.

"Cleo," she answers in a matter-of-fact voice.

"Cleo who?"

"Cleopatra," the handmaiden announces somewhat astonished that I've asked.

I begin to deny what she said but then remember I agreed before the session to accept what I hear.

The handmaiden informs me, "Anthony loves to watch you dance. He says you are an angel and float like a breeze."

I take a break to write down what occurred before finishing the regression. After I write it out in longhand on my steno pad, I lay back down. Within minutes, I see myself walking over to Anthony.

"Who are you, really, in spirit?" I calmly ask.

"Daniel, your soul mate," he replies.

"Why are we here?"

"We are peacekeepers."

"What do you mean?"

Daniel tells me there was too much war on earth and we were sent to bring peace to the land. When I ask him what we are going to do, he tells me we'll feast, drink, and then make love. I continue asking questions even when he holds a golden goblet up to my lips.

"What will happen to us in the future?"

"Do you really want to know?"

"Yes."

"All you need to know is we are slain. We are separated and slain."

I am in awe of what I'm hearing and stop again to write it down so I'll never forget. Anthony's words fill my head after I settle back down and close my eyes.

"We were killed because other people wanted the power."

I hear it does not matter who they were.

"The only way they could get the power was to kill us."

I ask who in my current life is in this past one. The answer surprises me. It's Terry, Alfred, Naomi, Rebecca, Ruth, Samuel, Abigail, Rachel, Joy, Aunt Lois, Aunt Deborah, Zephaniah, Martha, and others. I stop again to write down all the names in wonder. I've already sensed many times that this current life is the life where we, perhaps Daniel and I, put everything together and try to make it "right." This life includes everyone I have ever known in past lives.

Daniel now notes the lessons for this past life.

"We were honing our skills learning to be true peace keepers. We learned that abundance and prosperity in material things is not the best way to God."

I ask for examples of other lessons but Daniel brushes off the question.

"Mom, we learned a lot of lessons but those were the most important. You don't need to know the other ones."

I stop the regression and sit up to write sensing Daniel only has a limited time to be with me. Perhaps his spirit is more available as his soul's new human form sleeps. I have learned to follow the clues, the words in my head, especially Daniels when I have the slightest hesitation to believe and do as I hear. He sometimes causes me to laugh with joy, go out in the yard, and play where I talk with the critters, birds, etc.

In the summer of 2007, I'll ask psychic/medium Sally Baldwin about the Cleopatra life regression. She'll verify I was there but tell me my soul was not in the human form of Cleopatra. Experience gleaned over the following years helps me understand the memory of this past life.

Before I expand on this, I'd like to note that as humans, and as souls, we put too many layers between Source and ourselves. Although we are here on earth in physical form, our true reality is formless. That consciousness is still merged with the Godhead, Source, Cosmic, God. Whatever you care to name It; It has no name, no boundaries, no form. It is unerringly perfect and unchangeable. Yet, on earth, humans often relate to separate entities.

Now, based on the teachings of Michael, we are fragments, individual parts of total consciousness, striving to know more about itself through the game of separation. As fragments, we joined to form entities of about 1,000 fragments who share their consciousness and experiences. As humans, we live on the Physical Plane, one of seven planes of existence, at various times.

It's clear to me the fragment that experienced being Cleopatra is within the same entity as my fragment. And because I still think as a human, it's natural for Anthony to be the essence of my last-born son.

:-)

Chapter Seventeen

The Unseen Becomes More Real

"It is not space, time, matter, and energy that are the fundamental reality; instead, consciousness is the fundamental reality, out of which space, time, matter, and energy emerge."
Peter Russell – The Global Brain Awakens

A presence fills the area in late May as morning treatments flow from head to lips. Senses move to the wind chime above while focusing the camera. The photo reveals a large, transparent, white orb close to the chime. What looks like a wormhole sits nearby.

Sylvia doesn't answer the telephone when I call to report the phenomenon so I figure she left with Emilytine to visit Jamaica. Unseen forces are always with me even though I feel physically alone. *A Course In Miracles* notes, "As you perceive the holy companions who travel with you, you will realize that there is no journey, but only an awakening."

I rise at sunrise several days later to repeat the usual treatments. Something prompts me to take a picture of the sun. A sudden urge to walk stops me from checking the result in the camera's display. It's a clear day so I quickly leave for a local park. The railroad gates suddenly block my way at the tracks.

A dark blue service truck sits idling in front of the car as I watch the usual three orbs through the car's windshield. They all seem to come from the sun. The bright white solid one is nearer to it while the others are lower, drifting more to the left.

These transparent orbs do a good job of convincing me they're real as I wait for the train to pass. They shift gracefully and touch each other to make the sign of infinity like an eight. I sit spellbound as they move apart, just a bit,

leaving a space so I can see small Stuff of Matter (minuscule dot's – some solid, some transparent) move from the top orb to the bottom one. Substance begins to flow from the bottom orb up to the top one as the train speeds away.

The blue truck now moves ahead making it difficult to see the orbs clearly. Spirit tells me to write about it as my car moves forward. Spirit wants everyone to know, **yes, we are One**. We connect together like the ocean.

Arriving at the park, I walk quickly, anxious to document how the orbs moved and flowed into one another. Yet, upon returning to my room, Spirit tells me to put the picture taken near sunrise on the computer with the others. The pictures will help to convince people (I suppose relatives) that there really is more to life than what we think.

The printer has a Smart Media slot making it easy to move digital photos from camera to laptop. I don't usually turn it on and am surprised to note the display. It says 12-13-2006, 1:23 PM. Today is 6-2-2006 and it's 9:03 AM. It's the third time I've noticed an error in dates on the printer.

Minutes later, I finally see the picture taken earlier in the day. It shows a blue stream of light streaking across the room among several multicolored orbs. Two orbs are a nurturing green inside but ringed with what I refer to as fuscia, commonly known as magenta. A couple of solid magenta colored orbs are in the photo as well.

In Edgar Cayce on The Power of Color, Stones, and Crystals Dan Campbell notes, "red, green, and blue are symbolic of: Spirit prompting us to awaken our souls to their purpose."

A Course In Miracles tells us, "Only the creations of light are real." I know humans exist in a universal bowl of soup for the undifferentiated substance, Stuff of Matter, flows all over. It's way cool to see how we are connected. Yet, there's a sense of running against the wind as Nana's Legacy continues. Although nothing like being the sole breadwinner after two divorces, without a high school diploma, I still allow myself, occasionally, to feel totally alone.

While recounting the experience of poring over family photos, it occurs to me that it was, and still is, part of a desensitizing project meant to disassociate myself from physical reality. Emotion felt in the past is gone while watching videos now to write this book. Very few affect me. When they do cause a spark of emotion, I promptly remind myself this is a dream world. We live in an illusion of our own making but can eventually change it to our liking.

I again ask to see a future life before falling asleep. Upon waking, I recall seeing Terry and Sarah, with Samuel sitting in front of her, as she holds him. Samuel was smaller than he is now. They were all watching something as they sat on the floor; something like TV, but I sense different in some way...

There's just too much to relate. I must finish my task, or at least keep trying to finish, helping people to understand how things are. Nana's Legacy consists of frames lifted from videos of pictures in family photo albums. After filmed with my camcorder and put onto DVD, certain pictures were then captured from the DVD for a new video.

At this moment in time, I know why Spirit guided me to do this. Changing colors in this new video show the ever-changing substance flowing around me during filming. The Substance and Matter of the Universe (magenta for Love, blue for new Life, white for pure Spirit, et cetera), forms before me as I'm directed yet more in the choosing and finishing of this project.

Daniel and I agreed to come back in human form one last time, right before the very end, when the rest of you who agreed will be there too. I see upon waking from a nap some of our family and friends. There's Daniel and his pal Bruzer, Sarah, and Terry but I can't remember the others. The days near the end appear gruesome and I cannot speak of them. You must find your own way, the path yourself. But until I return for the last time in physical form, I will guide you if you wish.

As I work on the draft of this third book, I'm reminded to note that future events change rapidly with thoughts and actions. Things intuitively sensed and seen related to the future may alter due to positive thoughts and deeds.

There are many groups working all over the world to make this a more nurturing place to exist. I am often astounded at the sheer number of us who congregate regularly to merge positive waves of love, wholeness, and prosperity into the earth and its inhabitants. We have all the support we need for the ultimate evolution of humanity, a belief in the wholeness of One.

I currently believe everything physical and even thoughts are illusion. As humans, we designed multiple layers to place between Source and ourselves. But in reality, there are no layers. In reality, we are unique parts of One, just as a drop of water that flows to the beach is still a part of the vast ocean. We live, move and have all being within a Universal God Soup. There is nothing, absolutely nothing, outside of that soup, Love, which is Source. There is no outside; nothing that reeks of duality exists.

It gets confusing on earth because free unique will reigns here making it appear that we're separate. More people each day realize this is not the case. However, as we do seem to be on earth, it seems necessary to play the game of life. Since we think differently, there's always another opinion, another experience, another way to live.

There have been many times when I've asked to wake up in a reality more advanced than the one I go to sleep in. There have also been times when I've agreed with those who say nothing more needs to be done, because everything has already been done. I now believe, as so many others, we've changed the "rules" of the game by rewriting the script. The only thing 'set in stone' is our return to One. That appears to be happening sooner for some people than others.

Over the past five years, I've learned that what I believe in eventually comes to pass. Meditation is vital to stay in tune with Source. Positive thoughts continue to reap positive experiences and an attitude of gratefulness and joy is the most nurturing tool in my arsenal of weapons against the negativism of duality.

Words come to me often, both in pieces and sentences. Some of them I'm not to relate but I can write, *They will be given the chance to sip from the well once more.* Humanity will be given one more opportunity to turn to Source. I can't stay much longer. For me, it's both a truth and a sense, an increase in visions and demonstrations. For the sake of the Whole All of us, please search for the clues I have left and follow them. I can say no more but I will **never** leave any of you who wish to be Whole again.

I begin the fifth legacy series DVD as if in a daze. By now, I'm consciously aware of spirits surrounding me and leave open bottles of water around the room to fill with good energy. After a day, I place caps back on the bottles to distribute to family to help them evolve.

I've now stopped taking all medications and feel better than I have in years while singing along to "I Am the Walrus" by John Lennon and Paul McCartney.

"I am he, as you are he, as you are me, and we are all together."

Something compels me to share my progress letting everyone know it's possible to change his or her life as well. "I don't take any medication," I happily announce to the physically empty room. "I don't have any conditions because Spirit carries me. I live in the path and when you live in the path that's what happens."

"I am meant to show the way to you, the way Daniel showed the way to me. I have to do it fast because there isn't much more time for me here. But I will always be with you. I am one part of the whole right in the middle of the soup. The way is to share, not be one person all alone. You've got to share."

"It burst from the pure joy of it all," I report later, thinking of when I will pass from a heart defect in the middle of the night, while asleep. They tell me to nap because I get too excited seeing Spirit all around me. It's a physical heart but I know I am a spirit and it's not mine."

"I will always be here for you. If you don't want me to be around, I'll go away. But I'll return, just like the Avon lady who comes once a month, to see if you've changed your mind."

The music changes once again as other pictures splash across the computer screen. Bob Seger sings "In Your Time," noting the events of a changing world, while I tell listeners to plan for their next life. "There are many of us," I announce happily. "Perhaps you're one; if so, you'll know at the right time for you."

Carole King sweetly sings "Bitter with the Sweet" as I break in to announce that no, we do not have to take the bitter with the sweet. "Follow the path. I'll light it for you all the way. Remember, we live many lives. How many more lives you have now are up to you."

I sound like a crazed woman singing along to "All You Need Is Love" as I note, "The more you sing the more spirits fly. I see them right now. They're all different colors. Love is all you need. We love you, ya, ya, ya. The whole pot of soup is here. Open your eyes and see It. Just open your mind. Wake-up in this life and beat the rush. Please, don't be long. The world is changing too fast. Please don't be long."

"Strawberry Fields Forever" plays softly in the background.

"...you and I know it's a dream and nothing is real on earth."

I continue my message.

"Just tune in and change the channel and you'll see it. You only gain in trying. Change your thinking and that will change your life. Don't forget it's a process and it takes time. It's taken me more than two years to get here, so start changing now."

When the DVD is finished, I lie down to nap before continuing the day.

The night sky captures my attention upon waking. Email alerts from NASA explain why. No one knows exactly what will happen when the two biggest storms in the solar system "go bump in the night" but I'm certain the event will affect humanity. One storm is the Great Red Spot, twice as wide as earth, and spinning around Jupiter for hundreds of years with winds blowing at 350 m.p.h. The second storm known as Oval BA, or "Red Jr.," is a youngster of a storm only six years old, and half the size of the first, but blows just as hard. Scientists estimate their closest approach on the Fourth of July.

Ego pulls me back as I try unsuccessfully to log onto Daniel's website control panel. There's a massive spam issue with the guest book and I cannot figure out how to delete disgusting entries. As usual, the website host finds a way to help but it's necessary to delete the guest book. The Universe is again trying to tell me to let go of the illusion and stop clinging to earthy forms. With gratitude for all blessings, and especially for the ability to write longhand again, I continue to watch the evening unfold.

:-)

Chapter Eighteen

We Are One

"One Presence is the Truth and the Reality that unites all things."
Helen Brungardt-Pope – For the Aspiring Mystic

Upon waking to recall Princess Rebecca is now thirty-two, I silently wish her a happy birthday. She picks up the phone when I call but is steadfast to skip a celebration dinner ending our conversation quickly. Rebecca still misses Daniel. Today the thought overwhelms her.

Although I miss her, all is as it should be as *The Science of Mind* opens for today's random reading. My finger lands on page 535, "Sorrow Flees from Me." Gratefulness comes to recall nothing is lost or gone.

Dreams were rampant last night but I remember only one, probably of another life. I currently believe we live several lives, as different personalities, at the same time. There's one more life to go before staying in the afterlife to help all towards Light until the very final days of earth.

Ruth was with me in the dream. Our grandparents died and left us a bunch of old money hidden in aged newspapers. I vividly recall a dilapidated garage where it was carefully stored in the dark, attic rafters.

We had to find a place to exchange the currency so the government wouldn't know it came from us. Places like pawnshops seemed reasonable since we couldn't take it to the bank. I woke up at that point in the dream to look at a rainbow ceiling. I am the pot at the end of the rainbow. A smile :-) is in the middle!

Day fills with prayer and study. I begin Nana's Legacy, DVD number six, well after midnight for tonight sleep is elusive. Lines from a long ago forgotten song play in the background as I tell listeners to read between the lines and think for themselves. Photo stills, lifted from the family history video, note my small family's move from Michigan to Florida.

Fond memories of singing my heart out to Barbra Streisand's "Everything" while viewing pictures of my community college graduation in 1982 come. It doesn't take long to realize, I indeed got another chance to turn the tide to become a better person.

Daniel's voice rings in my brain while again telling everyone, I'll always be there for them. Rebecca, still angry with her brother for seeming to depart, continues to ignore his subtle ways of communication. If she's not receptive when I transition, I'll check back until she is.

"Have a seat Mom," Daniel says as too much singing causes me to flush the next day.

Overjoyed by his essence, I sit on the futon that is now my only bed. *The Science of Mind* beckons. Feeling grateful, I open it to a random page in the back and point to the word Heaven. It's clear to see I'm there for Heaven is a state of happiness. I hug the book and smile before logging on to view email.

Space Weather News notes another wave of electric-blue, noctilucent clouds swept across northern Europe. These mysterious clouds have been sighted in recent years as far south as Colorado and Utah after sunset. Mercury appears as a bright pink "star" beaming through the glow of sunset, and new sunspots have emerged. One is large and the other is growing with wild abandon. The news is unexplainably comforting as I log off to nap.

The ringing telephone jars me awake. I rise quickly to clear the air of its piercing wavelength. Rebecca sounds upset as she asks how I am.

I cut to the chase to ask, "What's going on with you?"

"Samuel has been kicked out of summer camp for roughing up another kid," she announces with great emotion. "The kid called him fat and wouldn't stop when Samuel asked him nicely."

"I'm sorry to hear that," I reply picking up my textbook to look for something on anger management.

Rebecca continues in a low voice as if to make sure she's not overheard. "The thing is Mom; he needs to do community service now. Can he do it at your church?"

My heart soars despite the seriousness of the situation. I've been hoping for an opportunity to introduce Samuel to the Center.

"I'll see what I can do and phone you back," I calmly reply. "Don't worry. I have a feeling this is going to work out."

"I hope so Mom because this is a nightmare and I don't know what else to do," responds Rebecca before thanking me and ending our call.

After finalizing plans with Rev. Haggerty to bring him the next day, I begin to design a treatment for Samuel. I haven't seen him as much as before and have no idea what's going on in his life. Yet, I sense a great disturbance best addressed by aligning him with Source. My fingers fly over the keyboard after reading parts of *The Science of Mind*. Samuel's treatment is soon complete. [55] I decide to say it for him every day until positive changes occur. It's been a long day and now I'm ready for bed.

Samuel is ready to go on Saturday when I arrive. He's upset with himself and cries on the way to the Center knowing he acted inappropriately. I'm glad to be more involved and try my best to help him understand violence is never the answer. I don't think he knows that spoken words can reflect how we feel about ourselves.

Rev. Haggerty is kind and understanding as she talks to him about the work he'll do. Since there's office work today, I stick around and help while Samuel settles in. By the time we go, I'm grateful to have the opportunity to visit, twice a week, upon picking him up for future community service stints.

As we open the door to his house, I decide to keep my promise and deliver a message from Daniel. Several months ago, Samuel found two unusual rocks near his house. Each rock is about the same size and appears very old with different gradients. One is ruby-red while the other is jade green. I didn't think about their color when he showed them to me. Since I was not as progressed spiritually as I am now, I did not give it much thought. I did sense they were special and perhaps sent from above. Now Daniel wants me to tell Samuel about the stones.

"So are you taking good care of the unusual rocks you found near the house Samuel?" I ask quietly.

"The green rock is probably somewhere at school," Samuel notes still zealously playing his video game.

"Uncle Daniel says he made it possible for you to find them. The red one represents love while the jade green one represents protection. It's important to keep both rocks close to you."

Samuel looks up and immediately begins to cry. It's clear he does not want to be reminded of the illusionary loss of Daniel.

"It's important to get the green one from school and keep them both with you Samuel."

He continues to cry while telling me to shut up or leave. I stop talking, reach out to hug him, and quickly apologize. Daniel's spirit fills the room as we cling to one another crying softly together.

James is home when I return to the house on 47th Drive. We are now resigned to living in separate bedrooms, usually ignoring one another. I skirt though the house to the safety of my room. There's a strong sense that our marriage is over but it's not time for me to move on. In the safety of my white light room, I continually treat for God's Will not really knowing what that is. Money still seems hard to get but I've found that if I limit credit card charges below $200 a month, James pays for food, gas, and incidentals charged at the 99 Cent store.

I'm beginning to believe that supply comes from one's own giving. My stash is dwindling down as I continue to secretly tithe at the Center but I have faith that soon Dad's lawsuit will be final. Terry calls Aaron for updates every week and each time says the lawyer insists the insurance company will settle any day now. Although I plan to give whatever I get to Rebecca and Samuel, something tells me I must keep it for myself.

Tonight marks the beginning of SOM 104 "Principles of Successful Living." How great it is to breathe fresh air while walking to class! Ready to continue spiritual growth, I once again volunteer to set up the coffee station in return for free classes. Honestly, I'd do it anyway because it gets me out of the negative atmosphere of the house. Being in the company of people who think as I, knowing we all have a purpose, even if we don't work outside the home, is much more enjoyable.

Before class, I buy my first copy of *Creative Thought* to meditate on different inspiring treatments. I hungrily read through the booklet deciding to concentrate on Dr. Jay Scott Neale's "Prosperity Is My Way." As Dr. Bump later discusses subjective and invisible cause and effect, I realize why I've always been what most people would call "poor." I've accepted the consciousness of limitation from lifetimes of poverty.

There's an unlimited unified energy but individual souls separated from the higher vibration in the process of creating various life forms. Focusing on creations, we became trapped in the physical and lost our connection with unlimited Source. This led to the concepts of duality and karma, cause and effect, as a means to eventually eliminate the artificial concepts of good and evil.

Holmes and others note karma is the Law of Cause and Effect. It's the neutral, compassionate dynamic through which we learn to create responsibly. When we choose the cause, that choice includes our choice of an effect. Things that we set in motion through the law ultimately return to us.

Karmic Law works through the Medium of the World-Soul and is the result of how humans use their mentality. This mental tendency is both individual and Universal. Soul contains a record of our inherited tendencies and everything that has ever happened to us. Although these memories represent the subjective tendency of our life, we can change this predisposition with constant effort and a determined persistency of purpose.

It's time to erase erroneous beliefs and soar above the law of averages into the higher law of Spiritual Individualism. I can do it for I've already made a difference in the families power play games. Family calls discussing their poor state of health have dwindled for they know I no longer feed the pity me routine. Since most of my health issues disappeared, they know I'll only tell them to work on themselves instead of wasting precious energy complaining.

I've stopped practicing or relating to the ploys of intimidation or interrogation as well and get my energy from Source, the power flowing through us all. This coherent energy is our creation, which displays the reality of the whole as far greater than the sum of *Its* parts.

Past the initial discomfort of these changes, I'm more conscious of how I think and act. The vast amount of time spent alone on healing and studies are well deserved and necessary. Addressing self-talk and being in the moment seems easy. Days and nights are unconsciously directed by Cosmic forces.

Samuel's voice wakes me shortly after 4:00 AM. Of course, he's home in his own bed but I know he's upset, dreaming about what I said yesterday. I talk to him in mind as I have done many times with Abigail (who has now started to come to me in mind on her own). It's a short conversation but enough to connect.

Today starts a routine of six treatments, said before sunrise, when I always repeat the "World Healing Meditation." Samuel's treatment is first then I'm deliriously happy to repeat the Treatment for Continued Peace, Inner Sight, and Clarity. I've said it every day for nearly two months but recently revised it because of a piece of mail that mistakenly arrived in my Post Office box.

Although addressed to someone else, the religious material seemed meant for me so I glanced at the cover before placing it in the "oops slot." Jesus' words, said during the crucifixion, stood out.

"Father, I commend my spirit to thee."

Ready to serve in the way contracted to as a soul, I add it to my treatment and now repeat it twice a day.

Later, I'm stunned to read, "Nothing can prevail against a Son of God who commends his spirit into the Hands of his Father. By doing this, the mind awakens from its sleep and remembers its Creator. All sense of separation disappears."

Another book notes that when we return to earth we agree to forget who we really are. This makes it more difficult to progress spiritually. One of the reasons I designed the clarity treatment was to insure that I'd never forget the nature of my True Being, or the lessons and experiences obtained in past or perhaps future lives. Yet, if I return to earth in a different body, it will be the last time.

Cayce notes although we take on various forms in different dimensions, we are "as light, a ray that does not end, lives on and on, until it becomes one in essence with the source of light."

In her book Spiritual Alchemy, Dr. Christine Page tells us the primary essence of our soul is pure white light seen when the soul's consciousness is fully expressed. This vibrating energy source, also known as consciousness, contains the colors of the rainbow, each vibrating at its own frequency, and collectively radiating at the vibration of white light. The light "is a synthesis of the wisdom gained from previous lives, the energetic union with other sentient beings, the vibratory blueprint of lives still be to experienced and the eternal connection to universal consciousness."

Jesus lifted his consciousness to the vibration of pure light demonstrating our next stage of life with powers over the material world through crucifixion. He knew he could reassemble the body as it was nailed to the cross because all matter is spirit or energy and when lifted to the speed of light becomes light.

In her book For the Aspiring Mystic, Helen Brungardt-Pope declares: "In Christianity, going to the cross represents, among other things, crossing out the belief in two powers. We overcome the appearance of duality. The aspiring mystic is eventually resurrected or lifted out of all illusion of duality."

The only message of the crucifixion is that we are not of the earth. Our essence is divine and we can overcome the cross for the physical body, time, and space are not the ultimate reality. The words Jesus spoke while on the cross were mistranslated. According to Spalding, they were actually, "My God, my God. Thou hast never forsaken me or any of Thy children, for Thy children can come to Thee as I have come. They can see my life as I have lived my life. Thus, by living that life, they do incorporate the Christ and become One with Thee, God my Father."

Consciousness can transform the material world, heal, and manifest anything man can imagine. Starcke notes, "There wasn't any God outside of Jesus that raised him up. It was Jesus' own consciousness that did it. The crucifixion was "a stage in the creative and divine process" showing that we too can resurrect ascending to the awareness of Mind. Starcke continues, "What we must realize today is that what is happening to us is our second life, the Second Coming of Christ – first objectively as Jesus and now subjectively as universal consciousness."

I repeat "Treatment for Perfect Physical Health" before others, while consciously merging with the Oneness of Life. After a short pause to feel the Wholeness within, my ritual continues by repeating a prayer for stability and conscious life with my grandchildren in mind.

The fifth treatment, for a drug-free body, is for Amos while the next one is for the children of earth. I end the morning's routine with a treatment for health, peace of mind, and unity with God, keeping in mind Rebecca and Ruth. Designed in October 2005, it's a structured prayer that I've revised several times.

The seventh DVD of my latest project begins by noting I'm not the one who picks the pictures. Daniel is trying to show me something for the pictures seem to choose themselves. Perhaps he's showing me how the Stuff of Matter creates an ever-changing vista of substance. Photos seem to change before my eyes, as dabs of blue or magenta suddenly appear, disappear, and reappear.

I continue with words of advice as Jimi Hendricks "Experience" ends.

"What you have is what you chose. Think again before you think, hmmm, what do I want? Think about what will happen if you get what you want. Think about how it will change your life and decide if you really want it.

"This is a blue-light special and there's only a few minutes left, in comparative time, so come to God." The DVD ends as I'm clapping vigorously after letting everyone know, "This is the life. We are getting out after this life!"

Today I saw 11:13 as I closed my eyes before resting after my treatment/meditation time. Soon, something said, "Arise" for there was something I needed to see. It was on Link TV, of course, Democracy Now. I turned on the TV and noted the time, exactly 11:13 AM.

Sara Richardson, mother of a female soldier repeatedly raped and mistreated by her own sergeant and male soldiers, talked about her daughter's dilemma. Her daughter finally refused to return to duty and got a lawyer. The federal government – military – came to her mother's home at 10:30 PM, arrested her and took her back to Iraq to be under the command of the same sergeant who abused her.

I start to react but know I must not cry. Earthly outcomes are not my concern now. I saw the TV show only to verify that, yes, the need for more of us that live the Truth are needed badly on the Otherside to help people here on earth, the way Daniel helped me. I now bless Sara and Amy Goodman, the show's moderator, before doing a treatment for them remembering to say it in present tense.

I'm humbled and pleased to do it. It's a blessing and the greatest gift any human can ever give. I have loved and given all my life and get to do so on the Otherside until near the very end. It's occasionally a kind of scary thought but after all I've seen and been through, all I've been led and guided to do, I know all is well, as it should be. I am not afraid. I await Divine Timing, Divine Law to take its course.

Rapidly changing gears, I check email and note the message from Beliefnet Buddhist Wisdom. Thich Nhat Hanh tells us:

"Feelings, whether of compassion or irritation, should be welcomed, recognized, and treated on an absolutely equal basis; because both are ourselves... Nothing should be treated more carefully than anything else."

:-)

139

Chapter Nineteen

Messages

"...everything exists in this Universe as energy vibrating at various speeds and that heightened consciousness comes from being able to appreciate our own energetic nature and use the mind and breath to move through the various dimensions."
Christine Page – Spiritual Alchemy

A*von, you shall do exactly as I say. Do you understand?*

A white collar highlights the neck of a big, white man dressed in black. He's sitting very close to me and speaking harshly. It's past sunrise as I wake from the dream. This is another past life but there's no need to investigate. It's vital to rest more each day for, I hear, *a great change is taking place within you.*

The business is much less important than ever before. More of the fruitless hiv nutrition work is set aside while I agree to rest. Bedtime is two hours earlier, now at 1:00 AM. I'm guided to work on getting to bed at midnight. Many, many, wonderful demonstrations and verifications, of my path as Truth, have occurred but I cannot speak of them.

I've become accustomed to waking with words in my head. *Rise and meet the day*, or *Today is a day of atonement*, are just two of many such thoughts. Today I hear to rise earlier than usual and start washing bedclothes. I rise quickly from the futon gathering bedspread and pillowcases.

The power of constant thoughts, about butterflies and caterpillars, comes in unexpected ways. A caterpillar sits outside near the place where the others were when I open the door to go out to the laundry room. I bless it before announcing I'll bring it in if it remains in the same place. A huge, yellow butterfly glides swiftly past my vision.

After loading the washer, I move back to the caterpillar and ask if it wants to come in. It replies yes and crawls onto my outstretched palm. Numerous caterpillars sit in plastic cups on the shelf already so I get a new cup from the kitchen.

"Do you want to go into the cup?" I ask setting it down.

The caterpillar crawls into the cup, while I fix myself a cup of detox tea and grab a handful of dried fruit tidbits. Another butterfly, this one bright orange and black, drifts past window as I slowly savor the snack while reading.

When the large cup is empty, I pick up another load of dirty clothes. It occurs to me to look down at the floor while opening the door to the laundry room. Another caterpillar sits in my path. This one is larger, and more beautiful, than the one brought in earlier. I bless it, thank it, and caution it to move away from the path of the door. Of course, it lets me know it too wants entrance to my room. I envision all the caterpillars building cocoons and flying about the house as butterflies to convince James there's magic in the air.

"I'll load the clothes into the dryer and when I come to take them out bring you in, if you're in front of the dryer," I announce.

Later, when transferring more laundry from washer to dryer, I note with surprise that the second caterpillar crawled to the spot mentioned. The caterpillar's positive response when I ask if it wants to come in delights me. "I'll take you in if you stay where you are," I say, taking the warm bedspread and pillowcases inside the house.

The caterpillar soon crawls willingly upon my hand when I lay it down on warm cement. It's more than an inch long, green, with orange stripes, and black markings. I tell it how beautiful it is and watch it filled with wonder as we walk to my room. I think it lays an egg in my hand. Filled with love, I place the caterpillar and its egg on a paper towel near the first one.

Suddenly tired, I lie down for a quick nap. Certain words revive me on the brink of sleep. It's a message for Amos that I quickly write down before forgetting. Even though I have no idea where he is, I must quickly deliver the message. Not accustomed to leaving the house at such an early time, filled with faith, I choose to deliver the message even though it's only 7:30 AM.

Take two bottles of water from the freezer, the voice inside my brain kindly advises.

I smile remembering six bottles of water, already blessed with love and good, and pull two out of the freezer for Amos.

Family rumors fill my brain while driving. Terry's last report places Amos living with a girlfriend in a trailer park, while Ruth reports he's back on the streets. I'm divinely upheld and no harm can come to me. It's wonderful to be free of fear and worry while making my way toward the unknown. Intuition tells me Amos is at his old job. There's no doubt I'm led to the correct spot for there are no stops or delays. All five traffic lights are green as I pass through intersections. The tire shop sits before me after ten minutes.

Amos is nowhere in sight when I pull into the wide drive. Two dark skinned men, standing next to a small stand by the garage doors, watch as I boldly approach.

"Is Amos here?" I ask addressing the largest man.

"He hasn't worked here for a long time," the man replies with a smile revealing two gold teeth. "Can I get someone else to help you?"

"No, thank you," I answer playing with the keys in my hand nervously. "He's my brother. He used to be the manager here. I have to see him. Do you know where he is?"

The two men look at one another shaking their heads. I stare at them with disbelief until one man's head stops shaking, and moves ever so slightly to the left, as if a thought just occurred.

"Oh, you mean the manager who was fired?"

The men look at each other with a knowing look when I answer yes.

"That's where he lives," the new manager says pointing to an old, red storage container in the back of the building.

He smiles and leads the way.

"There," he says pointing to a boxcar-shaped abandoned commercial truck.

I thank him pleased to know Amos is there but disappointed to see he now lives under such deplorable circumstances. The new manager quickly walks back around the corner.

A crack about two inches wide separates the back door and side of the rig. I slip my finger into the crack and try to pull the door open but it seems secured. Peering into the darkness beyond the crack, I call out.

"Amos, are you in there?"

There's no reply as I pick up a rock to pound on the steel door.

"Who is it?" Amos finally calls out loudly.

"It's me, your sister Sam."

Within seconds, I hear him slide something across the door to open it. It's clear Amos was sleeping. He motions me to come

142

inside when the opening is wide enough to allow entry before placing a tire iron back into position to secure the door behind me.

"Hey, Jo, Jo mama, how ya doing?" he asks quietly.

The smell of used oil saturates the air. Sunlight peeks through cracks in the container as I try not to look appalled. The space is dark, gloomy, and full of clothes scattered about on top of oil drums. Amos sits on a dirty, brown couch in the far corner, while I began to explain why I'm there.

"I don't expect you to understand but here's a message for you."

I read the words quickly before handing him the piece of paper they're on. His family needs him but I'm not sure if it's his family in Florida, his girlfriend who both Sarah and I sense is with child, or his daughter back in Michigan.

After sitting next to him, I note Momma is scratching her face, ears, and neck again until they're raw. I know from my studies it's a sign of disharmony, a sign of her being ill at ease as she continues to ask if we've heard from him. When Amos admits with a hanged head that he has not seen her, I implore him to do so.

His head lifts when I discuss how my visit came about, how I had no idea that he was there. I just followed the words of God in my mind as I had so many times over the last six months. My brain silently hopes earlier Sunday School teachings will surface and he'll begin to 'see the light.'

I talk of my healing and the two butterflies God sent me earlier. He's surprised that I've cured myself and no longer take prescription drugs. Currently, I eat and drink anything but choose to avoid alcohol and caffeine. Amos is clearly stumped for now he can no longer use my medication use to try and make it all right for him to do the same with crack.

"I've got everything I need right here," he notes defensively. "My buddy, the car mechanic, lets me stay here free for cleaning up the shop at the end of the day. I've got a bed to sleep on, a lawn hose to shower with, and a TV with an electrical hookup from the shop. I come and go as I please and there's no one to fight with me."

Amos seems quite pleased to have found a way to live outside the constraints of society yet get what he needs. He goes on to note how he's never gotten along with family and then laments about how all the family does is fight. I don't remind him of all the times we got along and took care of him. He acts like the old Amos, very polite and caring. Although he's again thin, at about 120 pounds on his 5 foot 6 inch frame, it doesn't seem that he's using drugs. I don't detect the smell of crack.

I stand to leave after talking with him for about fifteen minutes. He pulls a shirt off of a greasy drum of used oil and covers his emaciated sun-browned body to walk me to the car. The shirt is white with a blue horizontal stripe across the chest and back, yet I don't notice if it's dirty or clean. I'm at my limit of noticing details.

We talk for a few minutes at the door of my car before I reach in to pull the water bottles out. I pick up the two frozen bottles of water, and grab two bottles of water with electrolytes that I usually give to street people, from the backseat.

Amos appears genuinely happy to get the water and I half wish I'd brought him food as well. Yet, I know that was not in God's plan, for if it had been I would have been guided to bring food. I'm surprised as he kisses me goodbye, three times, just as Daniel did the last time I saw him.

Happiness abounds while driving back to 47th Drive. I've successfully accomplished another God-driven task.

As I enter my room, I spot a caterpillar on the floor facing the east window. I pick it up and place it on the bookshelf. Bending down to sit on the futon to read, I spot another caterpillar facing the north window. Utterly spellbound, I fall down on my knees thanking God for such a grand demonstration.

"Change your thinking it really changes your life," I later remark with excitement as Nana's Legacy DVD number eight begins. "I'm having a ball and am in Heaven. If you could only see what I see, wow! Break the chains. I'd recommend it to anyone. I am so consciously, joyously grateful, for I've found the magic and you can too. The light is inside of you in the very center."

Days and nights are heavenly as the awareness of Oneness increases. Every second of the night, I live another life when my body rests. Most of the music I play now notes something is "out there," something we can't physically see. As I turn the page of the photo album, while videoing family history movies, a photo of my hand moves across the screen in slow motion. Splotches of blue and magenta appear and disappear as the hand moves in and out of sight.

"Nothing's going to stand in my way," I announce. "I shall always meet my true destiny." The video ends abruptly after I repeat, "It is a glorious day."

"That's it for today Mom," Daniel says softly in my brain.

Leaving to pick up Samuel for his community service work, I'm much more satisfied and at peace, noticing the difference between Reality, and this illusion in which we live. Evening class is increasingly helpful as we discuss the meaning of consciousness in small workshops.

The video project continues. My struggle with ego persists as "Some Days You Just Can't Win," by Ultimate Spinach, plays in the background. Panda antivirus software, purchased with such high hopes of computer protection, expires in fifteen days. I'm not sure it will be renewed. I'm beginning to get the impression that it too is deleting files without my permission just like Norton Antivirus. As "Dog and Butterfly" plays softly in the background of Nana's Legacy number nine, I sing along adding words of wisdom.

"We can all fly. You've got light inside of you. You've got to let the light grow. Let the light flow. Love, Light, All the Good There Is. It's always waiting for you, and you can make your dreams come true, and be a butterfly, and fly everywhere you wish. For what you wish for is what you get."

As the record album plays softly, I continue to speak.

"It's important that you know why I did this. I started it way back in January without realizing what I was doing. I've come to follow the guidance received for I've learned it's true. Whenever I've doubted, I've learned that my doubts were unwarranted, that the guidance is true, so I follow it. I very, very, very, rarely do not follow it. I heard back in January, that storms would be rough and assumed them storms here in this area of the United States. Intuition led me to videotape all the photo albums.

"And so I laboriously videotaped, sometimes in my room, and sometimes in the living room. Sometimes I used the white light or the yellow light in the living room to try and make sure I had enough light. In the beginning, sometimes I used the light in the video camera. As time went on, I stopped using the light in the video camera and came into this room, my room, the room filled with all the Love and All the Good There Is. I've also filled the house and the property, and the houses on either side, and the lands on either side, with all the Love and All the Good There Is.

"I've learned that Love is the color of magenta, kind of a pinkish-reddish color. Blue is the color of new life, and I'm sure, if you wish, you can check this; as far as orbs go these will be the colors. In any event, it took me quite a while to videotape photo albums, for as I videotaped, I played music or talked. When done, I wrapped each photo album carefully in large Ziploc bags before storing it in a large plastic bin.

"I transferred each videotape onto my computer using a program bought a couple of years ago for family movies. And then I put each one in segments onto DVDs before storing one of each DVD at Rebecca's and one here. If I had an extra, I put it away for Ruth. I thought that was the end of my project.

"But then I heard something else say that it was important for me to do my legacy, or perhaps it was just me that thought that. I don't know now. It's not important anymore. In any event, I decided to lift certain pictures from videotapes placed on DVD's. I did not use the original pictures because they were packed away.

"So, taking the videotape of pictures from albums on DVDs and computer mpeg files, I put them into the Video Studio 7 computer software program to start the Nana Legacy project. I noticed that certain pictures seemed to change as the movie played but I didn't pay attention to them in the beginning.

"I called the project Nana's Legacy because I wanted everyone to know why I'd chosen the path I'm on, because I've always known the nature of my True BEing. I might not have stayed on the path all the time, but I've always known, and always been about love and giving.

"It was a few legacy DVDs ago, maybe six, and this is number nine, that I started to realize that colors within a single picture changed. I could take one picture and break it down into several frames. Each frame was different, particularly when I started videotaping here in this room, my white light room.

"Some frames, as you'll see, if you look at them closely, are much different than the ones before. I don't edit them anymore. I stopped editing them around DVD number six or seven. It's clear to see that magenta and blue tint the background of photo paper. Some pictures show the movement of power. I believe that Spirit guided me, to show the movement of power from one person to another, to illustrate how something invisible is all around us.

"It's in this room and I see it. I've seen it for quite a while. Perhaps that is why I started this series. I didn't know it then. Yet, I know it now and now you know it as well. So when you look at each picture, see if you can find the faces, the colors, and the mist.

146

There were parts that I played back during the movie, to get pictures and take frames, where there was static, no music, or talking. Those times really showed mist and the flow of blue or magenta, sometimes gold. I'm not sure but the gold may have come from the yellow light used in the beginning of the series.

"In any event, if you look the pictures over carefully, you will see that there is a tinge of blue and a tinge of magenta, and that there are faces, and around peoples faces there are orb's that change with each frame. It is a wondrous thing. I didn't know what I was taping and therefore I guess that's why I captured it because when you go to capture it, it's not there.

"I wasn't trying to capture it. I was just trying to extract one single picture off of an mpeg file or DVD video. Yet, as I videotaped the pictures previously, these things were in the room and they showed up on video. It is an amazing thing and that is my reason for doing this legacy. I guess it wasn't about my path after all. I guess it's about everyone's legacy. Well, I know it is."

I stop talking as Ultimate Spinach begins to play one of my favorite songs from the '70's hippie days when music was my drug of choice.

Many scientific experiments show that intentions affect results. Different intentions produce different effects. Unexpected results occur when we don't focus on the process or the results. It's only now, three years later, that I truly realize the video captured Stuff of Matter as it swirled throughout my room, while I continually blessed it, and everything in and around it, with Light, Love, and Good.

The undifferentiated Stuff of Matter then began to change colors that affected the white photo album pages and white frames of photos during the process of videoing. This was more apparent in many of the photo stills lifted from videos. Thoughts and spoken words do indeed manifest into differentiated Stuff of Matter.

I rise the next day upon hearing *the time is coming*. Thinking the message may mean it's time for my physical body to be laid to rest finally; I design a final arrangement plan, obituary, and last will and testament.

Ego leads the way while noting the particulars of my physical host. I then request cremation before a simple memorial service at the Center and a celebration of life and graduation party

147

later. Pay it forward, I ask, by sending peace, love, and harmony to all living things in lieu of flowers, or donate money for my grandchildren's higher education. Remembering messages from the unseen, I add a note of caution. "It should **not** be kept in any financial institution or in U.S. government funds."

The Treatment of the week, "Spirit is Risen In Me" by Rev. Jim Lockard, found in the Center's email, seems most appropriate for my state of mind:

"I awaken to the reality of Spirit within me. One Power, One Mind, One Heart, expressing in perfection and joy. I AM that One. There is nothing else that I could be. I settle into the joy of knowing this Truth. In quiet expectation, I anticipate the next revelation of Spirit as me…"

As I work on the book listening to uplifting music, the CD player stops between songs.

"Don't be sad Mom," I hear in my head.

I hold back tears while silently replying. "I am acting sad aren't I?"

I've been home for almost three hours now having spent less than that at Ruth's with the family. Fireworks are starting now. Although I enjoyed seeing Ruth, Rebecca, Samuel, and his buddy, Momma, Terry, Rachel, and Abigail it seemed like I was alone.

"Remember, this is just an illusion, a dream world Mom. You can make it what you want to. You can choose to be happy or you can choose to be sad," Daniel's essence notes.

"I know but it just seems so real," I answer, knowing what I'm hearing is true. "I choose to be happy and enjoy my time here."

As the sun continues to set, I watch a funny movie on the back porch using my laptop and headphones. The movie quickly transports my mind. It's nearly midnight when I shower before bedtime.

Sleep is difficult. I find myself on the Internet at one o'clock in the morning. Two friends sent messages of love. Charles sends a message in bold type font, twenty times its normal size. "THE MOST GIANT QUANTUM HUG YOU CAN POSSIBLY IMAGINE!!!!" Sara from Michigan sends a series of funny cartoons that make me laugh out loud before finally feeling the tiredness of the day.

I wake after 9:00 AM unable to sleep more and lie there thinking about my day. I know I'll write more, that's a given, but what else can I fill my seemingly lonely day with. There's one more plant to repot and I begin to think of a planter from decades ago with a kitten face on it. I rise and find it in the china hutch that Daniel made me years ago. Due to many circumstances, it's a miracle to have it.

The ceramic piece looks much too fragile and precious to use as a planter. My eyes are drawn to a present from Daniel received in the 1990's as I put it back on the top shelf. The sunshine pillow is still in its box sitting next to the ceramic angel that says "Hope." Abigail gave me the angel last Christmas. I pick the box up and lift the pillow out stroking the "You Are My Sunshine" lettering, amid the puffy cloud and smiling sun.

A thought flashes through my mind. There's a message somewhere that I've never seen before. Reaching to the bottom of the box, I find a slip of paper from a fortune cookie with a quote from Eleanor Roosevelt.

"The future belongs to those who believe in the beauty of their dreams."

It occurs to me that Spirit's clues are subtle but now I'm paying attention. Placing the paper back, I squeeze the pillow thinking of Daniel and notice the still attached tag. "It's just a manufacture tag with information," I think, even as I'm drawn to open the flap. Daniel's beautiful penmanship proves me wrong.

"I still remember when I was a child you used to sing me this song."

My heart melts reading the message. I finally allow myself to cry, once again, for the son I know I never really had.

"I can cry now, can't I?" I ask the air around me. "It's been a long time."

For a few moments, I cry like a mother who lost her child, even knowing his essence led me to find the treasure at this time to boost my faith in the mission our souls agreed to.

"Mom, you're never really alone," Daniel's voice rings in my ear. "You know that we are always with you and you know this is a dream world."

"I want to come Home," I silently repeat while walking to the kitchen window, even as I smile thinking, Daniel is already there.

"A few more years Mom."

"That's right. I have to wake up as many parts of me that I can. We are all parts of God and no one can truly go Home to stay without the others. I know I will continue to receive the love and support that I need to finish my work and I'm grateful."

"Go outside in the sun even if you don't leave the porch Mom. Go outside."

I wipe tears from my face, walk back to the room where the china hutch stands, and put the pillow back in its box before opening the sliding glass door. The sweet song of birds at the bird feeder surrounds me. My mood begins to change as I stand in the sun. I know Spirit guides me. Comfort and encouragement will continue to come when I mistakenly think I need them.

:-)

Chapter Twenty

Journaling

*"Now in the fifth root race of the **Aryan Era** we're moving back to the source, using the very inner consciousness that created individualization to now remember and re-establish unity."*
Christine Page – Spiritual Alchemy

It's July 5, 2006 as Nana's Legacy number ten begins with a reminder.

"At this point I'm told to remind the viewer these are pictures and not really a video. I videoed family photos after filling the house with Love and All the Good There Is. My hand may have moved the camera as I filmed but that does not account for the change in colors. That does not account for the faces, and the orbs that are above the faces, and on the bodies of the people within pictures. Now, I am consciously extracting stills that display the substance and matter of the universe that wandered around each picture as I videoed. They are still just pictures. These frames are particularly interesting because there are so many of them yet, each is different.

"Notice the colors in each and the orbs in each," I announce while choosing frames of a single picture taken on Daniel's seventeenth birthday. They are paced rather quickly, at only three seconds each frame, because there are so many. The spirit known as this person never was, as you are not, nor ever will be again. And so it chooses not to be recognized as a person but Spirit showing you what is in the universe. Samuel is right. We live in a matrix and it is up to us to open the door for ourselves. Namaste."

"If you could only see the world I see, you would never doubt me," I announce later as the eleventh DVD in the series ends.

The laptop computer starts acting oddly. As previous projects, I'm to stop but don't know why. It takes two weeks to complete the last DVD. Nana's Legacy series ends on the last day of 1988 with a photo of Rebecca holding her precious cat Batman, while "Hold On" by Kansas plays in the background.

A few hours remain before class so I scan the bookcase for an easy read. *Prosperity Mind: How to Harness the Power of Thought* by Randy Gage captures my attention. Before the short drive to class, I read this part of a five-book series blessing Leah for giving it to me.

Rev. Ernie Chu is the guest instructor on this hot July night as we discuss the Law of Attraction. I'm so grateful for the handouts that help us mold our new life. I choose to change so many things that it sometimes seems impossible, but I know it is not.

I'm grateful to change what I attract by changing what I am. My gratefulness log includes many things, which I'm certain are just on the horizon. [56] I'll review it morning and night knowing the Law of Attraction works!

As I review the gratefulness log of 2006, it's clear I've realized all the things I was grateful for then. I am ever so grateful for the abundance and prosperity that allows me to have everything I need, before I need it, and to travel, and share my abundance and prosperity, with all of humanity for the greater good of all!

Although I don't document specifics, by the next morning, I've gained knowledge from a life regression to learn about lessons needed for this life. I chose Momma to help me learn humility and for us both to give more to the greater good. Dad helped me learn the lesson of having too much pride. Something tells me I need to work more on humility and gratitude for what I have. I also need to give more to myself before my special path reveals itself.

The month passes quickly as I continue SOM studies and treatments. Seeing Samuel during our twice a week drive to and from the Center fills me with gratitude. Upon waking one morning, I hear *Hurricane is Selma*. After a day of revelations, I type quickly into the computer with an increased urge to document life.

"I've learned since April 4, 2004 to trust in the unknown so my journal work will be seen, if it's meant to be. Perhaps, it may even grow into the long anticipated book started in my early teens.

"Stuff is happening at a much faster pace than ever before. I've hesitated to document experiences over the past two-plus years for I'm not sure the happenings should be told to others. If they are, the way will become clear. Things meant to be seen or heard are, and if not, disappear, or the mode they are documented in does not work. For instance, my camcorder no longer works and the digital camera no longer displays pictures.

"There is no doubt that an unseen force guides me. So many times these past two-plus years, I've been prompted to do a project, or go somewhere, not knowing the real goal. The recent video projects are only one example. Without wanting to, I captured the very substance and matter of the universe, unformed stuff all over the place! I believe this stuff increased the more I actively filled the house with all the good and love there is. I had not even considered that this conscious act of making the house more livable for me might change the outcome of projects.

"There have been many times when a project refused to flow and the new computer froze up, the program I was working with just stopped. And yet, the computer always works unerringly when I do something I'm guided to do. I often thought it strange but now am firm in my belief that God directs me. I am consciously, joyfully grateful for this knowledge.

"Too much has happened to relate but I will say I am spreading the news of "Hurricane Selma." I don't know if the name Selma is on the list for this year but telephoned Rebecca to ask her to check. She relishes the thought of saying, 'nana, nana, boo, boo, you were wrong.' We will see. If it is on the list, I will continue to spread the word for people to prepare. I'm told there will be several hurricanes and Selma will be devastating. I assume it means to Fort Lauderdale, but again, I could be wrong."

The National Hurricane Center notes Selma as an Eastern North Pacific name for the year 2011. Although I cannot predict the future, I must also note that many times spirit guides alerted me to upcoming conditions. However, we have the power to change the future with collective thought.

I end the journal entry and turn my attention to email news of a solar eruption. Space Weather News reports a magnetic filament snapped on the sun resulting in an explosion that hurled a CME into space and sent beautiful waves of energy surging through the sun's atmosphere. I still don't know what a CME is but sense great change, reflected in the planets above earth. Scientists suspect the outskirts of the CME may cause a mild geomagnetic storm. I believe these storms affect me in a peculiar way.

Research shows solar activity affects humanity. We are magnetic beings and feel electric currents because they change our magnetism. Sensitive humans recognize magnetic fluxuations within earth's magnetic field both emotionally and physically. Geomagnetic activity disrupts electrical power, causes auroras, affects sleep patterns, thoughts, dreams, cardiovascular health, and increases paranormal experiences.

As earth's magnetics change, so do our bodies. Previously, changes in geomagnetic activity wiped out the species on earth but this time the earth will not end. Changes occurring now help Mother Earth to transform into the New Earth. The earth's decreasing gravitational field is also a contributing factor to human enlightenment. We are evolving energetically, becoming more Christ conscious, knowing we have the ability to move between worlds.

We must continue to mold a new reality. Ascension is only increased awareness of what really is. There have been at least four, including Lemuria and Atlantis, and possibly two more great civilizations, which progressed to a high conception and vanished. We are at the end of another 26,000-year cycle. But we changed the game, shifted reality to a state of awakening for all.

During this Great Shift, humans are mortals, moving quickly toward immortality to a New World, which is a fusion of polarities where there is no light and dark. It's a world of non-local reality where we communicate telepathically. Because there's no separation, we will feel everything and therefore negative behaviors will end.

In The Twelve Powers of Man, Charles Fillmore notes Jesus was the first human to transform by gradual refinement. Our civilization will follow his example and blend into the next race without going back as others have done. Much talk as I write this book focuses on the assistance we are getting from unseen forces to help us step up this evolution.

Only crystalline substances can exist on higher dimensional levels. Karen Bishop notes in The Ascension Primer that solar flares bring in very strong blasts of higher crystalline energy, the new structure for our bodies. Crystal makes it possible to resonate to a higher level of divine consciousness. This fiber creates a new internal foundation and is necessary to help us adapt to the New Earth.

Surges of crystalline energy are the most forceful, dramatic, and powerful forms of energy shifts, creating the most immediate change within us, pushing the older and denser energies out. These phenomenal energy surges can cause symptoms such as insomnia, anxiety, heart palpitations, severe bloating, and indigestion.

The geomagnetic field is increasingly unsettled with active conditions each time CME activity occurs. Anomalies in the earth's overall energetics and magnetism grids will continue to affect humanities electrical energy and electronics over the next few years. Currently in 2010, we are increasingly feeling the effects of solar active regions, experiencing unsettled levels in the geomagnetic field due to recurrent coronal holes. Solar active regions are growing in both white light area coverage and sunspot count.

There's so much to write about. Today, I get to write about butterflies. I've always loved the beauty and freedom of the butterfly. This past year I've learned to appreciate the caterpillar as well for it represents a state of transformation. I used to count the number of butterflies and caterpillars that came to me, but have now lost count, and see no reason to begin counting again. They are gifts from God to reward me, help me on my way and boost faith.

The beginning of my butterfly metamorphosis happened shortly after Daniel passed. His essence guided me to begin the arduous task of viewing family videos to find happy segments of him for a single VCR tape. I watched a certain family vacation video repeatedly. Something odd always occurred after watching it.

The video showed Daniel placing a big, plastic, palmetto bug in various places to startle family members. It was very funny. At one point, I even joined in the fun and tried, to no avail, to freak out Rebecca when she woke.

Each time after seeing the video segment, a large palmetto bug, much like the one in the video, confronted me. This happened sometimes within a few minutes of watching the video, to after I began to catch on, a few days later.

At first, I killed them with bug spray but soon sensed there was nothing to fear and I had to portray this in my actions. The palmettos were just coming to let me know Daniel's spirit was indeed still with me.

I finally began to talk to the creatures and tell them not to fear for I would set them free outside where they belonged. Over a period of about a year, or more, I freed numerous large, and then smaller, palmetto bugs. I eventually began to do it in front of James using a small tissue, instead of a large container or paper towel, to grasp them.

I began the Science of the Mind 101 series last year in late September. Things changed as I learned. A few months ago, I began to explain to Divine Mind that palmettos were not pleasing to my physical body's eye. I preferred to see butterflies instead. Almost immediately, I began to see a large number of butterflies, each day, through the windows facing east. They were varied in color and size, from the common type, to butterflies that were brilliant yellow, variations of orange and green, black and orange, black and yellow, or solid orange, black, or white.

The most amazing occurrence at that time was the morning I woke to find at least a dozen baby caterpillars in their cocoons clinging to the north bathroom window. They were either on the outside of the window, upon the inside of it, or on the screen inside the house. Each measured only about 1/16 of an inch. It happened in the only bathroom that I use and was an amazing demonstration.

I then got to the point where I began asking for a specific kind of butterfly. In time, I asked for a golden orange butterfly, with large yellow spots, and a black spot within each yellow spot. I finally spotted a tiny, baby butterfly fitting that description while led to observe the Center's grounds.

On that day, something guided me to leave earlier than necessary to volunteer as snack person for a movie. A bird hopped onto my car and told me to "come out and play" upon arriving. It was a glorious time lasting ten to fifteen minutes, as I circled the grounds looking at beautiful foliage, flowers and creatures. I saw numerous other beautiful, and some unexplainable things.

For instance, as I began to search for an unlocked door, the grass path leading to a normally unused door in the back suddenly brightened as I watched (like in the *Celestine Prophecy* movie). The door was unlocked. I also found a lost receipt for roofing supplies and gave it to one of the Reverends.

Butterflies continue to pass by my east and north windows. But they have not been as frequent since the rains began. However, caterpillars continue to seek me out. The first time I saw one was when I heard to "look out the door." I left my room and went to the only door that I use to enter and exit the house. A caterpillar sat securely on the wall directly in my line of vision. I blessed it as I have now become accustomed to blessing just about everything. I then asked the caterpillar if it had a message for me and distinctly heard it ask to come into my room.

I've lost count of the number of caterpillars coming to me over the past six or so months. For the first four months, I put fresh leafs and flower buds from the night blooming jasmine into a water bottle cap each time I brought a caterpillar into my room. The most notable butterfly occurrence happened when Spirit sent me to see Amos.

The butterflies and caterpillars continue to visit sporadically. Today I pulled a caterpillar out of the upright lampshade upon noticing it trying to free itself after I turned the lamp on minutes before...

It's interesting to note how being in a state of grace can utterly change one's perspective. This was a time where the body that I inhabit lived in a state of pure grace. Being in this state allowed me to not only communicate with nature but love unconditionally as well. Everything seemed perfect at this time, despite physical appearances.

At this moment, I realize this experience was an exercise in unconditional love. Samuel eventually told me, the creatures I so lovingly harbored were not caterpillars but millipedes. If I'd realized these creatures were not caterpillars I would have ignored their requests to enter the house. Yet, even when the creatures defecated in my hand, I looked at the occurrence as a gift from Source. How different the world will be when we all live in a state of grace!

:-)

Chapter Twenty-One

Ego's Drama Abounds

"Anger or hatred is like a fisherman's hook. It is very important for us to ensure that we are not caught by it."
Dalai Lama

Perfect weather graces us for Rev. Edwene Gaines Sunday morning talk on the secret of prosperity. Rev. Bump is at Asilomar and I've promised to make coffee for all three services. Rev. Gaines is a vibrant speaker. Her talk about permanent prosperity and ex-husbands is very enlightening. I leave the Center choosing to thank God more for James. Visioning him as a world famous fly-casting guide seems appropriate for he's still fishing.

After hours of study and meditation, I return to brew coffee for the evening service. Attendance increased despite a lack of advertising. A young bi-racial couple from Hollywood, Florida pleases me. They talk excitedly of seeing *The Secret* and their subsequent manifestation of a beach house. Now they feverishly treat for a new convertible and distribute copies of the movie.

SOM class is in recess but I fill time with other spiritual tasks. Safely back in my room, random textbook reading reminds me I'm not alone. A Divine Companion always travels with me.

Several days ago, I began to copy the study bible because Daniel told me to give it to Naomi for her birthday. It's such a wonderful guide. I hate to let it go but understand why Naomi should have it. She's outrageously devoted to daily *Bible* study, using the same book for many decades. The *Bible* is her only guide and she literally believes every word. The study bible will help to open her mind. It holds so much more information about the book we believed that God wrote.

An urge to join the Center's Greece trip increases while painstakingly copying photos of Greece and Turkey. Viewing the early history of Ephesus fills me with a knowing of being there. My brain cries for sleep whilst visualizing countless rides down the main marble street in a chariot.

Later upon waking after a dream, I remember *minister to the sick, the poor, the needy*. I pause to ask, "Why am I here at this time, in this place of history?"

To rectify, to make right, to undo, is the reply.

A smile graces my lips upon hearing words when I rise from the uncomfortable futon minutes later.

472 - Our armies are the armies of God. And we shall be strong again. You will not be here next year. Rise and meet the day.

The air fills with excitement for I'm closer to the greater authentic Truth. Pride and fear of inadequacy will never again inhibit the task of my soul.

Ego draws me back to the world of technology after hours of treatments and study. Email offers many subjects to focus on, from Sara's jokes, to MoveOn.org's query about their latest bumper sticker. I choose to concentrate on Beliefnet messages instead before leaving to get Samuel for his community service. It helps to stay connected with the outside world while playing a role in Samuel's life. He stops me whenever it sounds like I'll say something spiritual. But his increased knowledge of the Center delights me.

We stop by the house on 47th Drive so he can have a snack before helping with the Center's yard work. Eager to go, he's ready to leave before cleaning his plate. A butterfly cocoon sits in our path as we exit the house. It's very beautiful, hairy, and different from the others. I've prayed for this one. My mind is in a quandary remembering a much-repeated secret prayer to transition along with a beautiful cocoon.

Since Samuel is near, I don't carry it into the house but hurriedly pass by hoping it will stick around. I'm still looking at my baggage trying to determine if it should be left behind for emotions surface with thoughts of certain situations. Clearly, it's time to let go and let the water carry me knowing I'll arrive safely at the shore. The cocoon is not there when I return.

The fine art of lucid dreaming eludes me. Nights fill with strange messages that I usually fail to recall, despite best efforts. I cannot remember dreams. Yet, some wakening brain waves break through the veil of forgetfulness. A happy thought now wakes me.

As you light the way for others, I shall light the way for you.

I'm in seventh Heaven treating for wholeness and prosperity while studying *A Course In Miracles* and *The Science of Mind*, between periods of sleep. Morning passes quickly. Upon waking from an afternoon nap, more words come.

You shall learn the ways of the Lord. The Truth shall reveal its self to you.

Each day brings new words of encouragement.

The path is True and I shall guide you all the way fills my brain before the dawn of a new day.

More words enter my mind while drifting back to sleep. A blue jay sits perched on a tree branch as I open my eyes to hear the words. *Blessings be upon you now.* As the last word leaves my head, the bird slowly coasts from north to east, zips around the corner, and heads south past the east window.

Papers from a Michigan lawyer arrive via mail on August 1, 2006. The proposed settlement to finalize a lawsuit, against the entities that abruptly ended Dad's physical life, comes as a surprise. It arrives after sporadic words of progress, or lack thereof, coming from Terry who Aaron prefers to telephone.

"The lawyer's getting most of the money," Aaron informs me with great emotion when I telephone minutes after reading them. "Everyone else is getting $10K except me. The lawyer said I should get $70K."

"Will the grandchildren be included in the lawsuit?" I ask calmly.

"No," replies Aaron quickly, "because he didn't see them very much."

I pause to form words carefully so Aaron will understand that the traffic accident affected everyone in the family.

"Daniel and Rebecca were close to Dad for many years. When we moved here, he spent more time with Terry and Joel. And just because he hasn't seen Amos' daughter for many years, or never met Abigail, doesn't change things. They're his great grandchildren. Abigail especially should get something since Daniel is gone."

Aaron is speechless as static fills the telephone line.

"Why isn't the lawyer including the grandchildren in the settlement Aaron?" I ask forcefully.

"Well," Aaron replies sounding confused as his wife Matilda talks in the background, "write a letter to him if you want. He's going to court in two weeks. Here, Matilda will give you the address."

Matilda comes on the line to offer the lawyer's address. I thank her and write it down before ending our call. A strong desire to lead surfaces so I need to know if there's anything else to do. Ego takes control while recalling Dad's accident and the family's saga to see him before he passed. The act of remembering our Michigan trip, weeks before Thanksgiving four years earlier, pulls me down to a lower level of consciousness. It seems fitting that I'm up to my copying task of the study bible at the point of Paul's letters.

God will answer my prayer for guidance as he has so many times over the past two years. It seems timely that I've just finished listening to Sonia's Choquette's audio tape series, which discusses angels. Filled with confidence, I ask my Spiritual Guidance Angel to speak to the Spiritual Guidance Angels of those involved, for a just and honest settlement in the eyes of God. I go to bed after midnight confused, appalled, and disappointed, but don't sleep for long.

A reply comes in the wee hours of the night. Dad wants all of his heirs to share in this settlement. He could not provide for us adequately when he was here and now this opportunity offers a means to leave us with something of material value, even though he and I know that is not what matters most in human life.

After nearly four years, I've concluded that we each got the money to help us evolve. The settlement offered me an opportunity to experience and mange ever-increasing prosperity. Using the money, I broke free of limitation by traveling to experience new horizons and other ways of living. Although I cannot be certain, my sisters and brothers also had opportunities to turn their lives around by using the money wisely.

What matters is the legacy, the thought of caring, loving, wanting to assure those left behind that he indeed thinks of them. Although, like Daniel, Dad never was and never will be, it's somehow a comforting thought that perhaps, this may be another way for Dad to nourish his soul.

It could be difficult to form words addressing this settlement proposition without complaining or arguing, but God has given me a way, and that way is the truth. As I clarify what to say and who to say it to, I copy Philippians thankful the door is open and that I've stepped out into the Light of Truth.

Yes, we all know the Truth even though some of us may try to shove it under the carpet from time to time. Yet, Truth is just that,

161

Truth, unerring and unchangeable. I'm reminded of the Truth and have to speak it without embellishing or inserting my own words. As I copy the pages of the study bible, my eye catches certain phrases of text.

Philippians 2:1-4 notes those united with Christ increase God's joy "by being like-minded, having the same love, being one spirit and purpose... Each of you should look not only to your own interests, but also to the interests of others."

I'm pleased with myself for thinking of the grandchildren while reviewing the proposal. There was no interest in the money before hearing Dad's message of love. Now, as each relative calls in the heat of anger, I relate my own truths. I note ten percent of any portion assigned to me will go to the Center. Of course, if there are taxes to be paid that amount will go to James for he's now in control of our finances. The rest will go to Rebecca for her needs are greater than mine are. She has Samuel to care for and I know what it's like to raise children alone.

I inform Terry, Rebecca, and then Ruth, that money is the root of all evil and the more people get, the more they want. I want no part of it and prefer to remove it from my control or James' for that matter. After nineteen years of turning from my True Self, I now have earned the right to be free of the burdens placed upon myself. And I thank God for the knowledge of that freedom.

It's a bit difficult to speak to the family through the telephone in the hall. Controlling my ego is a challenge because the papers allocate much more for Aaron than for the rest of Dad's children, and clearly omit any mention of grandchildren. It's almost impossible to ignore the papers deceiving outline of spent funds, and complete omission of previous funds allocated to "the boys" from Dad's meager life insurance.

Addressing the fact that none of us, least of all Aaron, enjoyed a close relationship with Dad is out of the question. Like my sister, brother, and daughter, I'm in shock at the proposed settlement. As Rebecca, I feel nauseous and sick at heart, and as Ruth, I'm appalled and disappointed. Thank God, I'm not angry, enraged, or placing blame. Yet, while speaking, I note the need to let everyone "reap what they sow."

Today I reflect on the words in Ephesians 4:17-28, on "Children of Light."

"So I tell you this, and insist on it in the Lord, that you must no longer live as the Gentiles do, in the futility of their thinking..." "You were taught, with regard to your former way of life, to put off your old self, which is being corrupted by its deceitful desires; to be made new in the attitude of your minds; and to put on the new self, created to be like God in true righteousness and holiness.

"Therefore each of you must put off falsehood and speak truthfully to his neighbor, for we are all members of one body. In your anger do not sin. Do not let the sun go down while you are still angry, and do not give the devil a foothold..."

In Ephesians 4:29-32 the study bible notes:

"Do not let anything unwholesome come out of your mouths, but only what is helpful for building others up according to their needs, that it may benefit those who listen. And do not grieve the Holy Spirit of God, with whom you were sealed for the day of redemption. Get rid of all bitterness, rage and anger, brawling and slander, along with every form of malice. Be kind and compassionate to one another, forgiving each other, just as in Christ God forgave you."

Thank God, I chose my words carefully while speaking to the family. Now it's vital to help them through anger, rage, and bitterness before it overflows like a muddy canal in a rainy hurricane to blacken family bonds even more.

It must be difficult for Aaron to be the self-appointed "black sheep" of the family. He started to distance from society during teen years and always went out of his way to go against the norm. Surely, it was challenging, for everyone after I chose to leave, and with Aaron being the fifth of six kids, I'm betting he craved attention.

Finding his older wife was a blessing until a month after the wedding when doctors diagnosed a brain tumor. The heart attack suffered after surgery left her confined to a wheelchair so Aaron waited on her hand and foot learning unconditional love. There might be very little to look forward to in his mind. Sunday church attendance comes to mind while recalling Aaron's participation in plays as a young child. Does he still hold God in his heart?

As a reborn "Son of God," it's my duty to lead the way. I begin to compose a letter to the lawyer in my head while copying Ephesians 5:1-2.

"Be imitators of God, therefore, as dearly loved children and live a life of love, just as Christ loved us and gave himself up for us as a fragrant offering and sacrifice to God."

It's clearly time to branch out and practice imitating the ways of God more with my family. I now read Ephesians 5:5-13:

"...Let no one deceive you with empty words... For you were once darkness, but now you are light in the Lord.

"Live as children of light (for the fruit of the light consists in all goodness, righteousness and truth) and find out what pleases the Lord. Have nothing to do with the fruitless deeds of darkness, but rather expose them. For it is shameful even to mention what the disobedient do in secret. But everything exposed by the light becomes visible..."

It's a bit surprising these words are so close to what's going on for I do feel someone is trying to deceive us with the settlement proposition. I must find the perfect words without causing any more anger, rage, or bitterness. Looking back at Galatians, I note with wonder verses 6:1-8. Surely, the One guided my words yesterday. The passages read:

"Brothers, if someone is caught in a sin, you who are spiritual should restore him gently. But watch yourself, or you also may be tempted. Carry each other's burdens, and in this way you will fulfill the law of Christ.

"Each one should test his own actions. Then he can take pride in himself, without comparing himself to somebody else, for each one should carry his own load.... A man reaps what he sows. The one who sows to please his sinful nature, from that nature will reap destruction..."

How true the study bible's words are to me at this time, how real that I spoke and thought them as related to this dilemma. We mold our destiny through thoughts, words, and deeds. God will guide my words as I write the letter to the lawyer and I'll bring the Truth to everyone's attention so they can rectify errors or omissions on their own. A copy of the letter will go to the lawyer and to Aaron as well.

Although reared as a Southern Baptist and taught that the Bible is God's word, I no longer believe it. After careful consideration, and in light of experience gained through the years, I now know it's an account written by man. The Bible is based on

164

mortal man's subjective perception. In fact, several men, who may or may not have lived during the times they recorded, wrote it.

Furthermore, everything here is just illusion, something we make up with thought. We are much more powerful than one could ever imagine but have forgotten our true nature as perfect unerring fragments of consciousness. Many humans in America call that consciousness God, and use the <u>Bible</u> as a way to control and keep others "in line" with what's referred to as appropriate.

Life on earth is much easier having faith in the Oneness of all living things. Once we're fully aware that all is God, and God is One, we no longer require guidance from a source outside ourselves. The knowledge of our Oneness as perfect Love, unlimited in power and grace, offers a new perspective that nurtures all life.

My correspondence to the lawyer must be worded very carefully. I start typing it on my laptop at 5:00 AM. Sun breaks on the horizon and begins its ascent towards sky blue heavens as the printer comes to life. Daylight affords me the pleasure of reading the letter one last time before placing it into an envelope.

We all bear the brunt of not being able to see Dad, hear him, send him a card or letter, relive memories, or make new memories with him. And although no amount of money could ever replace him, I note all family members have a right to be included in the resolution of his untimely transition. I sign the letter knowing the lawyer will make equitable changes before he goes to court and then telephone Rebecca. She agrees to mail it from her job using a quicker route than usual.

Rebecca soon arrives. A bottle of wine, she sheepishly admits, consoled her during last night's depression. It often amazes me that she's so like her mother. But she'll be more successful than I at dealing with what the world offers. Now she's clearly disappointed to think I'll be the only one to address the unfairness of the proposed settlement. It sounds as if no one wants to delay the actual dispensing of the money. I try to reassure her all is well but she remains unconvinced.

"Call Ruth and tell her about the letter. Tell her if she wants to call me, do it later in the afternoon. I'm going back to sleep."

Rebecca leaves but I'm too filled with adrenaline to sleep. I rise after several minutes to say usual meditations and repeat beliefs of those who habitually attend the Center. It feels good to repeat my treatment for clarity of mind and increased spiritual growth as well.

How disappointing to not help now from the Otherside! It's obviously God's time schedule so I must make the most of my remaining time on earth. As usual, "The Golden Key" helps for I know it resides within every tissue, cell, organ, every atom of my being. Morning treatments boost my spirits before phoning Aaron.

Aaron answers the telephone immediately. When I ask how he is, he replies in one word.

"Hot."

It's also hot in Fort Lauderdale, I tell him, and we're getting ready for another rainstorm. He interrupts me defensively when I tell him to expect a copy of the letter.

"Dad would have wanted the grandkids included in the settlement because they were a big part of his life, especially in his later years," I admit. "So that's why I've written a letter."

We talk for several minutes. Each time Aaron tries to defend himself I interrupt to note I'm not blaming anyone, especially him. He doesn't seem surprised or angry about my decision but thinks the lawyer is taking too much money for himself. The lawyer figured Aaron bore the brunt of losing Dad's companionship since he was the only one who remained in Detroit near Dad.

"I love you Aaron," I reply. "It will all work out, don't worry."

"I love you too sis," he says before hanging up the telephone.

Weary, I try once again to fall asleep. This time I wake within a minute of dozing off with words from Daniel swimming in my brain.

"I gave him the $500 Mom."

I rise from the futon thanking Daniel for clearing my confusion. The figure noted in the settlement under Aaron's name as needing to be reimbursed puzzled me. Now, I remember. Daniel gave Aaron $500 without asking what we thought. He knew there would be expenses related to Dad's untimely death, and just wanted to help, knowing Aaron was broke.

Terry surprises me when I telephone by noting he's writing a letter as well. I remind him his son Joel, as Rebecca, and even Amos' and Daniel's daughter should be included in the settlement. The call ends with me being upset with myself for mentioning how none of us was really close to Dad.

Reading *A Course In Miracles* and a few mediations from *The Science of Mind* calms me. Ruth returns my call and agrees to write a letter to the lawyer as well. At this point, there are four letters responding to the unfairness of the proposed settlement. We agree to sit back and wait for the outcome.

I disappoint myself again by reminding Ruth of the costs involved during our week in Detroit after Dad's accident. The call ends after Ruth speaks of the insurance proceeds "the boys" got. It suddenly occurs to me I should have kept silent about past expenditures.

The day reaffirms my belief that I need more work 'walking the walk' if I am to 'talk the talk'. That is what God wants me to do. I must apply the Principle of Mind intelligently. It's time to make use of the information learned in class. The Law of Correspondence tells us the limit of our ability to demonstrate depends upon our ability to provide a mental equivalent of our desires. This is because the law works from the belief to the manifestation of what we desire. If I am to truly 'walk the walk', as I 'talk the talk', I must focus more on the Infinite Indwelling Spirit in which we all live, and move, and have our being in.

It's time to provide a greater mental equivalent, to abandon the past and think only of the Now, with love in my heart. I vow to work harder to change the dominant attitude within my little mind so I can grow within, beyond the duality of this world, focusing only on the unlimited wholeness and love of God.

As Ernest Holmes duly wrote, "Our lives are the result of our self-contemplations, and are peopled with the personifications of our thoughts and ideas." He adds, "Nothing is real to us unless we make it real."

Another message wakes me the next morning.

All things in time sayeth the Lord.

I rise with a smile to meet the day quietly repeating treatments and blessings before driving to Rebecca's house. She's out of town on business so Samuel and I get to visit for a few days.

The laptop computer continues to malfunction but Rebecca's desktop computer helps me slip out of the Now to take care of earthly business. I renew Daniel's website pleased after checking site statistics to see that people from many parts of the world visit.

Rebecca returns days later, just in time for me to see *The Secret* at the Center. This time, the crowd of people entering the sanctuary is much larger than previous movies. The film begins before I'm done setting up food and beverages. A good spot is waiting when I finally slip inside the darkened sanctuary.

Although I've never enjoyed movies that appear like documentaries, this one seems different so I try my best to pay attention. The man, who tells a story about moving into his dream house, unaware of the fact until his old vision board is unpacked, intrigues me.

A vision board begins to take shape upon arriving back in my room. I add lots of smiling mouths with full sets of beautiful teeth, pictures of a home in the Blue Ridge Mountains, other exotic locations, and words of inspiration, love, abundance, good, travel, and prosperity. "Awakening humanity to its spiritual magnificence," is my new mantra.

:-)

Chapter Twenty-Two

Unseen Forces

"We actively create our entire worlds by having faith and then living our faith."
Walter Starcke – It's All God

Words jerk me awake at 5:00 AM.

I am shaking up here on the Summit.

Fifty minutes later, I'm up again remembering people who worked with me at the Sing Along many years ago. Intuition tells me the bartender transitioned and now sends blessings of love. Sun sits below the horizon as my ever-present candle burns brightly. I doze off after repeating sunrise prayers but, as usual, rouse to wakefulness fifty minutes later.

What a joy it is to be in Costa Rica, I hear myself say, right before a hissing sound fills the air. The sound is like a steam engine hiss. I expect it's when the Second Body, as discussed in Robert Monroe's books, returns to the first.

Brilliant sun shines through the east window again prompting thoughts of outer space. Space Weather News notes a large and beautiful new sunspot emerging from the sun's eastern limb. The spot is growing fast and turning toward earth.

My wall clock notes 8:26 AM, but the printer displays the date and time as 1-1-1970, 10:45 AM. I was 19-years-old then. The details of my life at that time are vague. Right now, I feel restricted, cooped up in one space. It feels very uncomfortable to be in other areas of the house.

The day's random reading reminds me we are the life we live. I'm depressed over not being able to see Abigail but now push the thought aside and decide to be happy. All the toys she played with while here are still in the closet. It's time to donate them to my favorite charity. Minutes later, I'm out the door to drop them off at the thrift store where all proceeds go to feeding hiv-positive people.

Donating the toys makes me feel good as I leave the past behind before heading back to the house. The motion detector light is on when I open the den door. It's a signal that a message is forthcoming. I've gotten so many wonderful messages after noticing the light on that I no longer think it extraordinary.

The message comes in a clear string of short sentences as soon as I sit, open and receptive, in my usual position on the stair between the den and dining room.

Go whitherest thy may. You are healed. Thus sayeth the Lord.

Ecstatic to hear the words of God, I jump up in jubilation and give thanks for the healing. The Center's trip to Greece, less than a month away, enters my mind. Is it too late to sign up? Where will the money come from? What if there are storms? I don't need to be here but await a new sign and decide to speak with Dr. Bump during class.

It's time to start getting out more and not worry about things like bathrooms, pill schedules, heat, and other worries that keep me in limitation. Happy with life and ready to celebrate, I remember the SPIRIT group's field trip. Tonight they plan to experience the Bon Festival at Morikami Museum and Japanese Gardens. The Bon Festival is a traditional Japanese observance that signifies a time when spirits of deceased family members return for a brief visit. It's a tribute to our departed ancestors. Rev. Steve Hooks sounds happy to hear my voice when I telephone hoping to join the SPIRIT group.

"We'd love to have you join us Sam," he cheerfully announces. "There's room in my car."

It's been a very, long, time since I've allowed myself the pleasure of adventure. Elated, I hang up the telephone, knowing God will care for my needs.

The ride an hour later is smooth and soon we're amid a horde of colorful street fair booths. I pass each stall delighted to be out of the house feeling spirit friends.

As dark descends, a furry of activity near the water catches my attention. People run to and fro placing brown paper bags among lily pads. This time helps our ancestors depart to the Otherside. Farewell fires in the form of simple paper lanterns illuminate their journey.

Many ancestors come to mind while watching rows upon rows of candles burning in paper bags. I thank them for their gifts, and then thank them again, for soaring with me as I enter that spirit state right after falling asleep. They continue to prepare me for the best life that anyone can ever experience, the afterlife.

The evening is a success and I don't need to use the bathroom during the few hours we're there. It's a huge miracle in my mind. I tell Rev. Hooks about my message as we drive down the freeway on the short trip home.

"Spirit has a way of putting us where we need to be," he tells me when I ask about the Greece trip. "I know it's booked but that shouldn't stop you from calling to ask Dr. Bump if there's an opening."

I take it as a sign and make a note to telephone her on Sunday before going to the evening service. Doubts about going to Greece consume me as I wonder how I'll find the money to go. It's the first time I've been without some kind of cash hidden away for the secret stash is depleted.

Daniel's voice fills my brain, "Don't you remember Mom? You still have your tax-deferred annuity from the hospital and you can borrow on it."

The thought sparks a glimmer of hope as I recall the small tax-deferred annuity (TDA).

Sunday morning's treatment and study time fills me with joy. Shortly after the second service ends, I telephone Dr. Bump at the Center.

"The first of May was the last day to reserve," she confides with authority, "but you never know there might be an opening. I'll give you the number of the gal in charge of reservations."

With great excitement, I telephone the trip coordinator and learn that someone's roommate just canceled. The trip will cost $3,214. Doubts continue but I'm ready to put the charge on my trusty Visa credit card. I give the doubts to God feeling magic in the air. After telling her I'll call the next day, I open *The Science of Mind* knowing this is a turning point. I've experienced the healing and heard the words of God. It's time to test my faith further.

On Monday morning, I wake while lying on my left side. There's a strong urge to celebrate for it's been more than three years since I've been able to sleep in any position except for on my back. Daniel's spirit advises me to call James at exactly 10:00 AM. I'm to ask if he wants to go to Greece.

Filled with anticipation, I repeat morning blessings and prayers before reviewing the Greece itinerary downloaded from the

Internet. I'm too excited to eat so busy myself copying more pages from the study bible to keep busy until the time to call James arrives. He answers his cell phone on the second ring sounding surprised to hear from me. I rarely telephone him.

"My church is going to Greece next month and I'd like to go," I excitedly announce. "I've always wanted to go to Greece. Would you like to go with me?"

"I can't just take off work and go to Greece," he replies quickly. "And anyways there's no money to go. If you can find the money to pay for it you can go."

My mind is racing as he talks. After all I have been through, and am still going through, I deserve this trip, it says while my mouth stays closed. I don't mention the new found $7K in a TDA account from 1990.

"So, you don't want to go with me?" I ask James out loud.

"Again, you can go if you find the money to go," he repeats slowly, "but some of us have to work. I need to get back to work now."

"Well, okay then. I'll see you later."

The plans fall quickly into place despite all odds. A quick telephone call confirms I can borrow half the funds in my last retirement account for a small fee. The fee is minor considering that I only put $2K into the account and forgot it existed. At this point, I'm borrowing more than I put in, because life is short, and I don't expect to need the money for retirement. These are my twilight years and I plan to enjoy life at last.

The reservations are made quickly. Greece awaits me! I'm thrilled to be alive, grateful to be healed and beginning yet another life, which I estimate to be life number nine. It's the number of times I've leaped forward, broke the mold, and redefined life on earth.

My longest "life" in this body was from the ages of birth to fourteen, before I met Daniel's father. Being with Peter from age fifteen to eighteen, opened a whole new world, where I made my own rules. Life without him, raising Daniel on my own for several years, helped to break further out of the stifling family mold.

The next four years with Saul brought me back to the beginning. I finally became aware of the fact that, yes, there was something more to life than imagined. Separating from Rebecca's father marked the beginning of yet another life from age twenty-seven to twenty-nine where I fought inner demons that tried to keep me locked in a world of tradition. For the next two years, I bucked the system, broke tradition, and moved forward with efforts to increase education.

The following four years were a mixture of freedom, knowing life could indeed be more than imagined, and disappointment as family and friends disappeared. They prepared me for yet another new life with James, living under circumstances that exceeded all previous experiences, and expectations. Life began anew the day Daniel transitioned. He clued me in to the limitless possibilities of life beyond the veil of physical forms on earth.

As I write, it occurs to me another life has begun. Living on my own as a newly published author, this time without children to support or a traditional job, leads me to unknown territory once again. However, I have full faith the miracles that occurred to get me here will continue to get me where I am meant to be.

Although forms deceive and everything changes, it's comforting to know appearances can change with the concentrated power of thought. My mind is open to change. The Reality I seek is changeless for it transcends all form to be itself and cannot change.

It's unthinkable to stop repeating blessings and treatments for now they're a part of me. Knowing I'll have a roommate, I prepare for the Greece trip by burning a CD. The daily ritual, including treatments, "The Golden Key," and work lessons from *A Course In Miracles* are repeated into a microphone hooked up to my computer. A description of my vision board and the many things I'm thankful for (which are not yet physically evident) follow.

There's still room on the CD for a Mose Henry meditation offered by Rev. Irene DeGroot and spiritual music between tracks. I savor the thought of listening to favored Karen Drucker and Carole King songs in Greece. Hearing Carole King sing "In the Name of Love" – speeded up at the end – reminding me of Dad's invisible presence when I recorded it, always reaps a smile.

Pleased while listening to words from *A Course In Miracles*, I'm sure that what has been done though me enabled love to replace fear, laughter to replace tears and abundance to replace loss. I'm grateful to repeat throughout the day, "I forgive and am happy."

Days later, I'm astonished to barely pass the "SOM 104 Evaluative Exam." Answers come from quotes in the book, and although a few of mine would be acceptable, I cannot speedily match them with quotes. There is more work to be done before I'm satisfied with my spiritual progress.

Hours after falling asleep, I hear the song "Songbird" by Fleetwood Mac. I have not listened to it for a very, long, time. The Timex indigo watch bought several days ago for my trip to Greece notes it's 4:30 AM. *For you there'll be no more crying*, continues to resound as I drift back asleep. A friendly and informative voice speaks soon after.

It comes back and hangs out with you.

The Timex is missing from its perch on the file cabinet so I rise and turn on the printer to see what time it notes. The printer display shows 11:30 AM on 2-26-2007. I shake my head before starting the days study and soon find myself straying to check email on the Internet.

Ego succeeds in pulling me into the illusion as I take the time to answer a query from someone with a degree in dietetic technology trying to make a living. I'm surprised one of my letters from 1998 is still on the Internet. "Unfortunately," I note to my curious correspondent, "since licensure here in Florida, we must work 'under' the Registered Dietitian, so no, we cannot do private practice anymore..."

My trek into the land of ego continues while signing a multitude of petitions to stop wiretapping, presidential lawbreaking, and a variety of other issues. Moving on, I forward an empowering quote to Rebecca noting what we resist shall persist for it's a form of negative affirmation giving energy to what we do not want.

It's clearly time to ignore the circumstances that seem so apparent and create new mental thoughts expanding them to exactly what I want. Today I vow to look more steadfastly at life as I wish it to be, full of love, peace, joy, friends of like-mind, and more material wealth. The manifestation of thought will show up sooner or later. I refuse to let the opinions of others cause doubts and work more diligently on thinking affluently to demonstrate prosperity.

I AM the Christ in God, with access to the Intelligence of the Universe, giving *It* an outlet through pure inspiration and intuition, instead of the bitter experience of the past. My treatments provide the avenue through which changes occur. Listening to the CD prepared for my Greece trip serves to further expand consciousness and let Reality through.

The telephone jerks me awake from a nap. Ruth says she'll be out of town for a week of training for a new job.

"Is Naomi sharing the room with you?" I ask.

"No, she's starting a job working at the school cafeteria," says Ruth resigned to make the trip alone.

My mind fills with possibilities fighting egos limiting ways. This is an opportunity to expand horizons. Spirit prompts me to change circumstances for a change in environment, if only for a short time, can help fuel the imagination of other ways to live.

"So, do you think I could come with you and share the room?"

"Well, the company is paying for the room and it does have two beds so I don't see why not," replies Ruth matter-of-factly. "I don't know how much time I'll have to spend with you though for we're working long days."

I'm thrilled at the thought of getting out of the house and into a new environment. The thought of sleeping in a real bed sounds like a bonus.

"That's okay. I don't mind being alone and I promise to keep a low profile."

"Alright," Ruth replies amid background noise of moving traffic. "I'll pick you up in a few days. I'm on my way to the store."

The sun shines into my room as I thank God for this new opportunity. I've always thought the sun had special qualities, and that sunshine was more than what it seemed to be. It's why I named my beautiful newborn son *Sunshine Boy*. Daniel grew into my *Sunshine Man* and is now my *Sunshine Spirit*. I'm ever thankful to God for his continuing presence in this, my illusionary life.

The next morning, I reaffirm my belief in the exquisite wonder of the sun, noticing floating dust upon waking to the brilliance of golden yellow sunlight streaming in through east windows. Hair brushes over my face as I rise to a sitting position, and again, witness the real beauty of creation. Specks of twinkling star-shaped white matter float down pass my vision, throughout a cloud of dust. Twirling pieces of substance make their way effortlessly through floating Stuff of Matter as I gaze filled with wonder.

Brown strings of hair turn into striated strands of see-through taffy while I stare. Each piece holds multiple circles of rainbow colors, particularly noticeable where the strands of hair bend. I look in wonder for several minutes remembering an earlier instance of seeing my hair like this. The rainbow circles scatter haphazardly with some on top of others while other circles line up next to each other. It seems impossible for me to try to duplicate the way it appears.

After a few minutes, I begin to move my fingers slowly to experiment with the strands of hair. Each hair seemed to have at least thirty bands of substance running through it lengthwise. I suspect the strands are far more than what I see, even with what appears to be my current, greatly heightened, sense of vision.

I try to remove the rainbow colored orbs by sliding fingers through the hair but the orbs remain. The very substance of the universe drifts past strands of hair as I look at them in great astonishment. Of course, I've seen the substance and matter of the universe many times but still am amazed that YES; we live in a gigantic bowl of soup!

Two digital pictures of my hair do not reveal the majesty I see. There's no doubt I'll continue to try and document the wonders of the sun as I open a software program on the laptop to try.

Later, I think about how life becomes greater each day. The atoms swiftly flow by while a rainstorm swirls around the neighborhood. I'm going to Ocala with my sister in a few days and then on to Greece and Turkey next month!

Watching a toad climb on the north window, I realize, I've always had needs met, even if unrecognized at the moment. Many examples surface where answers, solutions, and blessings came from out of nowhere.

I remember standing in the middle of winter, in frigid cold next to my car in 1979, trying to figure out how I could have foolishly locked the keys inside. As I kicked the car, I thought about how unusual it was for me to do such a thing. Snow stood at least a foot deep and it didn't look like it would ever stop. Panic began as twilight signaled the end of daylight.

Ruth lived sixty miles away, in Stockbridge. There was no one else to count on and no telephone in sight as I began to cry. A stranger appeared, unlocked the door easily within minutes without any damage to the car, and quickly disappeared into darkness.

A rented house in Inkster, Michigan is yet another example of blessings from a stranger. Summer was quickly ending and I was beginning to panic. If I couldn't find a house to rent outside of

Detroit, the children would be bussed to inner city schools. Since they were still adjusting to life without Rebecca's father Saul, I didn't want to overload them with too much change.

Daniel was finishing his year at a school in Redford since the recent move to Detroit from our beautiful, red brick, safe haven. Both he, and sweet, seven-year-old Rebecca, would be forced to help the city change the ratio of ethnic groups attending schools within the Detroit school system.

We moved through so much turmoil during the past few years, since our separation from Saul, that I was determined to see my children in schools where they easily fit in. I could not bear the thought of them experiencing any more unnecessary changes to affect their quality of life.

Yet, I was going to community college and on Aid to Dependant Families, which meant our income was somewhat fixed. Of course, I did have a part time job at the piano bar but at $2.01 an hour, plus an erratic amount of tip money, we had little money to spare. Some weeks I made less than $20 in tips for four lunch shifts. I had to find a suitable home for us, in a good neighborhood, which did not bus the kids to inner city schools.

After feverishly searching for more than a month, I found a few possible houses. No one would accept the meager amount of money offered by welfare. I began either getting the newspaper after work or waking up in the wee hours of the morning to wait until carriers placed it in newsstands. Our new home appeared just as I was ready to lose hope and increase my Valium. The house was a dream come true and I never, in my wildest dreams, thought we could live so richly.

A general contractor sponsored us in a home closer to the community college. Helped many times himself, he decided to build a new home for a family just like ours. The thought of renting his house to a single, struggling mother trying to better her life and that of her kids gave him immense pleasure. I guess I never really appreciated the full extent of his gesture until now.

The brand new house had a bedroom for each of us, a huge back yard and things I never dreamed of like a dishwasher. When I told him about our life, and my plans to get an education and keep the kids out of inner city schools, he readily agreed to accept the paltry sum allowed by Aid to Dependant Families. He was such a wonderful man just 'paying it forward' and now I thank God even more for that angel who helped us on our way.

I now recall working sixteen hours a day in the early 1990's to get the hiv nutrition business running smoothly. It seemed like such a chore at times, as I'd wake during the night with a new idea to spur company growth. Those break through ideas increased newsletter sales so I could continue to educate people on hiv nutrition. At the time, it seemed natural to get these thoughts in the dead of night but now I realize unseen forces guided me. There's my friend Luke's spirit to thank and I'm certain many others as well.

The storm has passed. As I look out at bright sunlight covering trees, more orbs appear. They sparkle with the magenta color of love in the glow of the sun. Last night, the hedges under my window revealed several solid, twinkling, white lights. The effect lasted for less than five minutes but was enough to prompt me to thank God for my blessings. I see more things that are spectacular each day. Yes! Days will be full of ordinary miracles when I go on my adventure to Greece and Turkey.

:-)

Chapter Twenty-Three

Changing the Groove

"One needs to always think of this life in better terms of living."
SAM – Book of One :-) Volume 1

It seems like only hours since our telephone conversation when Ruth arrives to pick me up for the Ocala trip. Joy and hope overwhelms for this manifestation places me on the road to higher ground, in a new environment. I'm looking forward to our visit for it's been quite a while since we've spent time together without anyone else around. How wonderful to reconnect with her in a neutral place without the pressures of everyday life!

Ruth drives skillfully down the highway while I share the many changes in my life. There's so much to relate, but she allows me to talk it all out, making few comments throughout the five-hour drive. We're grateful there's very little delay, and just a bit of rain, as we check into the small Microtel Inn.

A grin covers Ruth's face after we quickly store our clothes away in polished wooden drawers. She opens her cell phone to call Rebecca. I laugh when she teases her about the cappuccino machine in the downstairs lobby. Rebecca loves cappuccino. Minutes later, we bypass the machine on our way out the door for dinner. One of my favorite restaurants is only a few miles up the road.

I'm reminded of Daniel and Rachel as we stroll on the restaurant's porch. Beautiful hardwood and reed rockers, which seat numerous people right up to the entrance, line our path. I recall the excitement in Daniel's voice as he showed James and me the rocker he and Rachel bought from a similar restaurant. He spoke with such reverence for the artistry of the chair.

The restaurant décor is delightful; the waitress friendly, delivering plentiful food quicker than I imagine it can be cooked. I thoroughly enjoy lemon pepper trout, dumplings, apples, green beans, and country biscuit. It's such a treat and clearly enjoyed by Ruth as well. We bring leftover biscuits and half of the spiced apples back to the hotel.

Ruth slips under sheets with a big smile ready for a good night's sleep. She seems so happy away from the hustle and bustle of the city for Ocala is a small town. My old digital camera gives the now familiar "wait a second" signal while trying to take her picture. I turn it off, back on, and snap the shot. Spirit orbs linger above her head.

What a pleasure to rest upon a real mattress! Ruth drifts off to sleep while I slip headphones on to complete the nightly ritual without distracting her. I'm thankful for the guidance that helped me make the CD. My sister's mild snoring doesn't bother me at all.

God continues to repair my body's balance. As usual, I wake every fifty to ninety minutes, to drink water or use the bathroom, but fall right back to sleep. Energy seems to concentrate in certain body areas. There's a knowing this feeling will soon pass as I recall the healing of my spine while lying for hours on top of a heating pad. The pain was nothing less than exquisite, the kind that makes you wish you were dead. I knew then God was healing me and did the best I could to get through it. Now it seems as if my sinuses are healing for tightness and pain in the temporal lobe persists.

Sun sits below the horizon when I slip into the bathroom to repeat prayers. Sleep engulfs me twenty minutes later but I soon rise to take a shower as Ruth begins to stir. She bathes while I consume a breakfast of cinnamon spice oatmeal and orange juice in the lobby.

The woman who checked into a room after us the night before sits at a nearby table with her daughter. Her little girl keeps looking at me and smiling. She reminds me of Abigail. I ask for her name while her mommy helps the hotel desk clerk put away the muffins. She responds shyly but her voice is so soft I have to guess at the name. Thinking her name is Sally, I tell her about the song "Sally Go Around The Roses."

"My name is Rochelle," she says in a louder voice.

I look down at my oatmeal embarrassed, but sense she sees something I don't. She continues to smile looking to my right.

"Is there someone with me?" I ask intuitively.

180

"There's a woman who is about your size."

"You don't see a boy or a man?"

Rochelle sweetly answers no. I smile and tell her it's my guardian angel for I'm never alone. Her mom returns to the table when she asks me if I know any songs about cars.

"There's a song by the Beach Boys called "Fun, Fun, Fun" from the sixties," I answer thinking Daniel's spirit, or another spirit friend, is letting me know I'm not alone.

Ruth is leaving the room to get coffee as I hand her a cup from the lobby. Since her new job deals with food delivery, she's eating meals and sampling food with other new recruits. We spend several minutes viewing my orb pictures as she savors the coffee. She's very doubtful and insists either my camera is broken or the orbs are reflections of something. I then show her my rainbow on the ceiling picture that could have been a reflection of the sun shining on a CD.

She stops denying the pictures might actually show something extraordinary after I tell her about the six favorite pictures displayed for my SOM 104 project. Ruth is suddenly silent upon learning that many classmates see spirit orbs as well. Dr. Bump even discussed her experience with orbs.

Ruth now announces I should submit the picture that looks like an angel welcoming three children to the shore in Fort Pierce, Florida. Perhaps the lady who does the angel series books might use it. As Ruth leaves for the day, I recognize a book or display of my photos will help to educate people.

It's wonderful to look out our window at the beauty of nature from a comfy, window seat. A park below our room offers hours of quiet introspection between bouts of work on my laptop. Unseen friends surround me as I rise to take a self-portrait. Many orbs are visible despite the huge, dirty, bedroom mirror.

We're in the heart of horse country and I relish the thought of strutting down rural, dirt roads. Rochelle and her mom Cherie are in the swimming pool as I head for the empty lot that's for sale a short block away. It's truly wonderful to walk slowly through what reminds me of Eliasa Hall, our old stomping grounds as pre-teens in Michigan. I'm still taking pictures of butterfly Heaven thirty minutes later.

Heading back to the hotel, I think about finding a treasure such as the rocks Samuel found. I look down, spot a golf ball, and pick it up for Ruth. It looks new and has the word women's on it as well as a picture of a ribbon. Daniel informs me it would be a good idea to walk more before my trip to Greece as I reach the pool. Rochelle is still there and smiles widely.

"Come on," she says from her perch on a float, "the water's really nice."

"Maybe later," ego lies as I head for the door now hot and tired.

It's been a long time since I've immersed my body in chlorine and I don't want to affect the healing process. I am acutely aware that everything absorbed through the skin affects physical well-being.

All beliefs are real to the believer. Soon I'll recall Masaru Emoto's scientific studies, changing the properties of water, with human thought. I'll also become educated about The Living Matrix, a documentary that shows even our bodies are the result of our thoughts.

It's a quick elevator ride to the room where I plop down on the window seat to look at my butterfly pictures. The sun peaks above the hotel and invites me to use my camera again. I'm ecstatic to see several magenta colored orbs in the picture before settling on the bed. What a blessing it is to do what I want, when I want. And that is to take a glorious nap here in Heaven.

Ruth scans TV channels for a good movie in the evening. It's been a while since I've watched TV so I set aside *Journeys Out of the Body*. After two hours of laughing, non-stop through several comedies, we fall soundly asleep.

I'm truly enjoying my freedom and sleep for another hour after Ruth leaves one morning. The lobby is nearly empty when I eat my oatmeal breakfast. This is a dream come true and I thank God for it. The fact that I've cooped myself up, mainly in one room, for more than a year, makes it all the more delightful.

This trip is surely a precursor to the great adventures I'll soon have in Greece and Turkey. The country area is abundant with forest-like areas and dirt roads. Sometimes I walk around the area taking pictures of butterflies, horses, and land. See-through white orbs, indicators of spirit friends, sporadically compliment pictures. They are particularly prominent in photos of nature.

Sometimes living in the Now has moments of forgetfulness. One morning, I leave the hotel to walk before it gets too hot. The

182

time is limited because I forget to wear walking shoes and sunglasses. I'm gone only fifteen minutes but during that time come across a store that sells lottery tickets. The thought of last night's movie about a big lottery win spurs me to buy a ticket.

Later while sitting in the cozy bay window reading *A Course In Miracles*, I see Rochelle and Cherie down at the pool. Cherie looks hot and bored as she watches Rochelle play so I decide to go down and keep her company. The visit serves to reinforce my belief in the Law of Attraction. After talking only a few minutes, Cherie reveals she has a gift of seeing and hearing spirits. I'm thrilled to let her know Rochelle does too. But, of course, she already knows about her daughter's gift.

We spend nearly an hour, thoroughly enjoying the time, discussing experiences. It's great to connect with a like-mind and I think the odds of such a thing are probably phenomenal. Yet, Spirit found a way. Rochelle informs me the spirit lady with me "looks yellow" after I ask if she's still there. I tell her it's probably a golden light. Cherie already mentioned that Rochelle asked why there are always lights around the spirits she sees.

When Ruth arrives back from her training session she insists on going out to dinner so I can have a hot meal even though she's already eaten with colleagues. We walk slowly to the barbeque place across the street. Ruth sips her beer and tells me about the food they ate during the day while I eat a chicken dinner. It sounds like the company she's with is a good one and I'm happy for her.

The old laptop automatically saves my work as I refine this book. And then the screen blanks out. This is different from the blacked out screen, experienced for years before I took it to the last computer wiz, who put in a new inverter last month. Although the screen is blank, it's not half as dark as before.

Last week for a few seconds, it changed to a light green color so I took a much-needed break. At this moment, I concentrate thinking that a message may be coming though. Daniel's essence fills my brain.

"Listen to me Mom. I want to talk to you. Do you recall the time we spent on the water in the dark? It was a time of great need, great emotion, and great feeling. A time of wonder and awe and yet a time of great desire to live, to be free of the powers that be. Do you recall the time?"

"No," I answer honestly.

183

"It's just as well for it was a time of great disaster where our lives were spared for short seconds before we were swept away into the abyss."

"What do you mean?" I ask with concern.

"They were times long ago in Atlantis when we were young, when our essence was young, and not as tainted as now. These times were times of purity and oneness with all. These times were times we now look forward to again for the time is nigh.

"We will experience these times again but first you must listen and learn. You must listen and learn to let go of the old beliefs you've harbored for so very long. These beliefs are the ones of restriction, of pain, of unnecessary suffering. You must relinquish these beliefs now before the end of days turns this world into a state of oneness again. This is a necessary process for all of humanity and not just yourself. It must be done within the next few years or time on earth will end. Do you understand?"

"I think I do," I answer back to the air, "but I thought we 'turned the tide' already. What are you trying to tell me?"

"That all are not yet onboard and you must step up your efforts to help assure that everyone is 'on the same page' so to speak."

"So other than writing these books and updating all my websites what's left to do?"

"You must step up your efforts in the online community and keep up the events you've been logging as of late. Continue your contributions daily as necessary for the next few months."

"Really?" I ask incredulously. "Daily contributions online? Won't that take away from the time I have to write the books?"

"You will find the time to do both. You always do. That is all I came to say today, that, and I love you, a part of myself I will never leave behind. I love you Mom."

An airplane passes nearby and I realize Daniel's essence is gone. The only thing left to do is stare at the old laptop blanked out screen, while I reach for the new computer to log onto the Internet.

It's another day of paradise as I head down to the lobby for breakfast after saying my prayers and taking a quick shower. As expected, Cherie and Rochelle have just begun to eat. I knew I'd see them for breakfast.

We share a table and have another pleasant talk while eating. Rochelle is wearing a new pair of sunglasses and she looks adorable, like a child superstar. She keeps looking at me; so finally, I ask if she has something to say.

"Around and around," she replies with a smile.

It reminds me of writing about how the car turned around and around on the Southfield freeway so long ago. I decide Daniel is using her to let me know he's around since I'd recently written about the incident. When I ask minutes later if she wants to tell me something else, she says she likes horses. I tell her my granddaughter has a little pony that she just loves.

Cherie notes Rochelle really wants a horse but they can't afford one. Tears fill my eyes with thoughts of Abigail. I push them aside making it a point to remind them that love and family are much more important than material things. Cherie leaves the table to get more juice. As I get up to go for my walk, I look deeply into Rochelle's eyes and ask, "Did you know me from before?

She smiles ever so sweetly and quickly answers, "Yes."

"Were you called Rebekah then?"

I watch amazed as she nods her little head yes.

"I'm glad," I remark softly as her mother nears the table, "to have helped you in the other life."

Walking away, I'm not sure why I asked the question. Yet, I've often thought this life ties up loose ends from the life when I was Samantha helping Rebekah to hide her Christian son James from the disbelieving king.

Ruth and I depart for home hours later.

A strong sense of karmic completion permeates days as I write. Although I know this is a dream of my own making, it seems necessary to finish the script my soul agreed to before coming to earth again. Currently, the only thing left to do is finish this book series and experiment with going into other realms to change the past and future.

I've broken my sleeping in sequence record again. I slept for six hours before waking upon returning from a long vacation last week. Now, I sometimes tell myself before bedtime the number of hours I'll sleep before waking. I've slept four to five hours without waking on several nights, but each time I wake there's a memory of dreams, or experiencing life somewhere else.

In this illusion, the deep state of sleep affords us the opportunity to communicate with our soul and connect more strongly with Spirit. It's now clear why, aside from the first two years after Daniel passed, when this body clung to dis-ease making it rise frequently to use the bathroom, I subconsciously programmed irregular sleeping periods.

Our dreams consist of times spent on other realms, messages from Source, and what our brain processes of daily activities. This is an important point to consider for everything we experience is subject to how the brain chooses to process it. Brain processing includes everything we see with our eyes, hear with our ears, read and react to, and sometimes try to ignore. These things often turn up during the delta state of sleep while dreaming. I'm grateful there's no TV or people where I live to distract me, and during dreams of Daniel, I rarely react with negative emotions.

The key to waking up from this illusion is mind training. It's vital to fill your brain with pleasant thoughts before bedtime. Many different tools help to retrain the mind. Audio programs designed for people to hear at bedtime are particularly useful to break old habits that no longer serve our new reality. I started the practice of falling asleep to positive affirmations or music sometime in 2005. Waking to recall empowering words, or beautiful music, is much more appealing than rehashing world news.

Perception rests on choosing while knowledge does not. Gary Renard's book, Your Immortal Reality, verifies what I've heard from my guides. Yes, awakening to the unalterable reality of One is a process. We learn the truth slowly, in a variety of ways, to help us adapt to a higher way of being. As our perception changes, so does our way of experiencing the world around us, and soon, we are at peace regardless of appearances.

All of this life is an illusion, and that includes the many layers we chose to put between God and ourselves. In Truth, there is no soul, no spirit, and no guides. In Truth, we are not separate at all. Renard accurately notes your immortal reality is the knowledge that real Spirit is whole and permanent. Anything else is illusion.

:-)

Chapter Twenty-Four

Gifts From Beyond

"It is one of the commonest of mistakes to consider that the limit of our power of perception is also the limit of all there is to perceive."
C.W. Leadbeater

A quick email check astonishes me. As I savored time in Ocala, others were busy helping me to explore new opportunities. The Center's "Leadership Council Contact List" now holds my name as Hospitality Coordinator, despite my reluctance.

Gifts from beyond are much more plentiful. During the first year after Daniel's transition, many gifts of beautiful golden orbs flowed from the back yard. I heard to take them into my heart and forehead and did so joyously, like a starving vagrant, not really knowing their value. At this point, almost twenty-nine months later, I see wonderful things unexplained by most people. They are precious gifts to treasure suggesting there's much more to life than what I have come to believe.

Memories of exquisite magenta colored orbs, gliding by my side while walking to see a Keys sunset in May 2004, fill me with ecstasy. The night of my birthday in 2005 stands out as well. I woke throughout the night to feel arms holding me lovingly, gently, as if cradling a precious baby. It was a glorious experience. The only thing that compares is the feeling during my near-death adventure. The thought of a beautiful large magenta colored orb, always there when I opened my eyes on New Year's Eve 2005, still fills my heart with joy.

My portable CD player soothes me. After Daniel transitioned, it sporadically changed songs and often repeated certain phrases. The player repeats words of comfort as well. For instance, when I returned crying to my car after giving the insurance agent Daniel's death certificate, it played, "It's okay had a bad day..." then abruptly changed to "Soak Up The Sun" by Sheryl Crow. It continues to change tracks, beep, or rapidly breeze through songs at certain times. The larger plug-in CD player in my room also changes tracks without me touching a thing.

Phenomenon lessened in 2005, after Daniel told me he was being reborn, so I treasure them even more. They remind me that we are spirit, pure energy. The essence of spirit remains after the physical host is gone.

Electronic equipment can "malfunction" cluing us into changing energy. My computer often seems to have a mind of its own. The TV is another example. As I taped political programs in 2005, it changed to a music video on the power of love. The TV switched channels many times to upbeat programs when I was feeling blue. It actually shut off as James and I participated in a serious "discussion" about divorce. "There are no laws except the laws of God," I'd said adamantly quoting *A Course In Miracles,* seconds before James raised his voice in anger.

Controlled by the rules of others and stuck in a marriage that stifles creativity, I'm fairly certain James feels the same. Yet, having gone through hoops to marry a Catholic in a Catholic church, divorce seems out of the question. Sensing soul disharmony once again, I know a choice has to be made eventually. The question seems to be timing. Guides still encourage me to stay.

We put ourselves under a false premise assuming there are laws other than Gods. As noted by Tara Singh in Commentaries on A Course In Miracles, man-made rules may be necessary for society to function but are based on insecurity and fear.

"Under the Laws of God, everything extends and creates because everything is one life extending itself in many different forms, shapes, and facets. But it remains the One Life. Nothing is outside of it, and in it everything is in harmony."

Projection seems to rule whenever James and I interact. Yet, alone in my room, each day brings more visions of orbs, flowing into me, tickling my skin with their increased vibration. I now actively seek to increase awareness of the unseen. Atoms float, along with other substance and matter, as I watch in open-eyed wonder. It's marvelous to see what's been there all along. There's no need for photos.

Ruth's celebrates her fifty-fourth birthday. But no one wants to hear of my spiritual journey so I leave my camera at home. Momma's nose is raw from scratching. I stay silent preferring not to enter the realm of drama. I'm back in my room after a few hours to pass the time copying more of the study bible before concentrating on *The Science of Mind*.

Life is beginning to get more mysterious and exciting. Messages continue to wake me but I'm so tired I don't usually write them down. This morning I recall hearing, *see exile and Kings*.

It's been several days since I've went online due to computer issues. Eager for adventure, sensing the necessity to experience new things, I now greedily scan the Internet for information on airline restrictions before my upcoming trip.

September brings new opportunities as I continue to volunteer at the Center. Samuel helps me set up snacks and beverages on Saturday night for *The Peaceful Warrior*. The movie contains many of the teachings I've learned and Samuel enjoys watching it.

Guided to join the church officially last month, I'm anxious to attend Sunday's member meeting. Today we vote for a new Co-Pastor. Wonder of all wonders, in order to vote, one must have been a member for exactly the amount of time that I've been one. There's no doubt that Dr. Charles Geddes will become our new Co-Pastor as I drive the two blocks to make coffee for the event.

I've wondered since May what it was that I had to sign but today the mystery is solved. This signature is the one Spirit requests. A sense of overwhelming joy fills me while signing to bring Charles into the fold. He's voted in as Co-Pastor, by a very small margin, as I breathe a loud sigh of relief and congratulate him. The Center will welcome him during Sunday morning service on the day many of us are off to visit the mystical land of Greece.

Monday brings the TDA loan check via mail. I quickly deposit it into the joint savings account held with Samuel at the credit union. It seems prudent to assure the money remains solely under my control.

It's becoming hard to concentrate on anything because I'm so excited about the trip. A recording project converting several old 45 records into mpg files keeps me busy. Songs remind me of happier times. Daniel's presence is strong and every day my mood and activity level improves.

A trip to Greece and Turkey is worth documenting in detail so I decide to shop for a new camcorder using my trusty Visa card. Since Aaron's morning call announced the court case as settled we should expect a check in the mail from the lawyer. I'll soon be able to pay the charges that James may not. Something tells me this video camera will be much better and less expensive than the last one. I'm back in my room minutes later with the perfect camera, and accessories, for much less than the old one cost.

Pictures of the scene outside my east windows, taken in the early morning with the new camcorder, amaze me once again. The first one shows a blue diamond shape in the top middle of the photo. Two rainbow-colored diamond orbs overlap one another to its left. There are other orbs in the photo but they're not as visible. A big X-shaped stream of white light extends from the middle of the sun. Four minutes later, a series of three photos reveal other spirit energies, some of which look like blue triangles and white seagulls flying through the air.

I'm beginning to find the separation fostered within Christian music unbearable and wish the radio stations offered spiritual music. My mind is no longer happy to imagine what it will do when Jesus comes and I don't expect God to reach down and wipe my tears away. I know without a doubt that God in within me and I am that perfect, limitless Being, the maker of my own destiny.

There's much less thought of separation from good now. Although a slight sense of restriction prevails, increasing unity with Good changes the currents of causation. The number of good things in my life has increased dramatically over the past month. Aside from the complete healing experienced physically, there is so much more to reveal.

Perhaps the change results from a daily ritual that includes treatments, study and visioning. It could be because of my positive attitude and willingness to let go of the past or the tithing in service and small donations to the Center. The change in inner thought, classes, books, and movies, makes a huge difference.

Many miracles have taken place since Daniel's transition. I've come to understand that he never was, nor will he ever be. I am not; you are not, for we are all illusions as in *The Matrix* movie series. This is crystal clear because of my experiences since Daniel's transition.

Life regressions have been instrumental in helping me to understand the nature of our true being. We are all spirits that have been on earth in physical form many times. We take on physical form to learn certain lessons, teach lessons, and remember our Divine nature.

Shortly after Daniel's transition, I vividly remembered a saying seen many, many years ago. I heard him tell me, "I never was and I will never be." His essence led me to a bookstore that was going out of business. The store manager told me they'd packed up all the spiritual books but said I might be able to find the book I sought on the shelves. I had no idea what the book was but knew it was spiritual in nature.

Many of the shelves were bare but I knew I'd find what I was looking for. I'd nearly given up hope when I found _The Prophet_ by Kahlil Gibran. The saying I'd remembered shortly after Daniel's transition was inside the book. I'll forever be grateful that Daniel's spirit continues to evolve into an even greater awareness of his true self, pure spirit.

After seeing _The Secret_, I recognize the miracles that happen to me every day and have learned to look beyond the physical. The broken windowpane that's graced my room for nearly twenty years, and holes in the ceilings, no longer disturbs me. I now thank God I'm spirit and wait for the next sign of where I am to be.

I depart for Greece in three days so perhaps when I come back God will have prepared the way further for my new life full of positively, good, love, joy, abundance and prosperity. In the meantime, I'm recapping examples of recent "miracles" for later review:

* The motion detector light, turning on for no reason in the empty den, is now totally ordinary. It turned on today as I sang along to a song about being happy in the living room. The light stayed on and turned off abruptly as soon as the song ended.

* I've sensed certain desired items would be at the thrift store. The first item was a spiritual CD by Karen Drucker, which was at the Center for more money than I had at the time. Inner guidance told me it was at the thrift store. The CD looked brand new and cost me only a dollar. I've purchased different things at other times and spent less than I thought the price was.

* I looked for a certain book for several weeks, and found it several times, but was not willing to spend the money the stores wanted. Knowing I could get a better deal, I envisioned someone donating it to the thrift store. The next day I found the book at the thrift store knowing it was there. I'd just bought several books

belonging to the same series the week before. The book had not been in the store at that time. My new book was sitting on top of a box, not yet put on the shelves. I bought it for a dollar.

* I went to purchase new prescription eyeglasses after telling Ruth that was my intention. She moaned over the fact that her glasses cost more than $400. Prepared to spend $200, with an eye exam if needed, I went to the usual place visited for years. A beautiful pair of glasses with a detachable sunshade was exactly as envisioned. I did not have to get an eye exam and the total cost was only $100. The price tags on the frames I looked at were $125 to $139. The lenses usually cost at least $59. I hugged the store's proprietor in my excitement when he told me the total cost.

* Samuel had to do volunteer service and Rebecca telephoned to ask if he could do it at the Center. This turned out to be a win-win situation for Samuel, the Center, and myself.

* Several times, I've looked at my hair when the sun shone into my room. It is most beautiful, with rainbow colored orbs, throughout many strands within a single hair. I have taken pictures of my hair and even tried to draw what I see. Nothing compares to the Beauty and Truth seen when looking at my hair under the sunlight. Everyone should see such beauty for it is astonishing!

* I can close my eyes now and see orbs in front of me that I cannot see with open eyes. It's very cool to see. As yet, they are evident only to my naked eye in sunlight.

* My command of butterflies is excellent. I envision seeing a butterfly flow past my east window and within a minute or two, it does. It's delightful to see.

* The thought of getting a loan from a forgotten TDA came shortly after I heard God tell me it was okay to go where I wished, for I am healed. The loan process could have been a lot more involved. But it went smoothly, exactly as envisioned, and I got the check before the Greece trip.

* I continue to see substance and matter that no one else who I know sees. It's in layers with the first layer being what I suspect to be neutrons, protons, and electrons. They flow very swiftly in all sorts of directions, circles, up, down, sideways, etc. Another layer appears as tiny amoebas floating around through the neutrons, protons, and electrons. There are also small things that appear somewhat clear that drift through the neutrons, protons, and electrons. I also see what I refer to as "the scanners" several times a

day. They are small gray orbs that are about 1/20 of an inch and look kind of like dust balls. There is usually a visible string coming out of them at one point in the circle. They jot back and forth in front of my eyes. Occasionally, I see larger grayish colored mists, or shapes, flowing into my vision.

* I bought a scratch off lottery ticket while in Ocala with Ruth. As I got into the truck for the ride home I said, "I would like to win three times." I scratched off the silver coatings to reveal that I'd indeed won. The amount was one dollar but it was tripled due to the card's guidelines. I left the ticket in the truck, for it was Naomi's truck we drove in.

* I shopped in at least six stores, over the course of several days, looking for a new pair of walking shoes for the Greece trip. Some did not seem to fit properly while others were too costly. It then occurred to me to start packing. I opened the closet to get the suitcase and noticed a shoebox on the shelf. The forgotten box held a pair of new walking shoes. They were perfect for my trip so the need for new shoes was already met.

* I decided to buy a new pair of sandals seen when looking for the walking shoes. They were the exact type of shoe I regularly wore and almost half off the regular price. The shoes in my size were still there when I got back to the store. When the cashier rang them up, the cost was less than fifty percent of the original cost.

* I lost my charge card one day while shopping for the walking shoes. I'd been home for about fifteen minutes when I got the idea to check my wallet to see if it was there. I remembered putting it in my "bra bank" in haste as I left the grocery store. I was in a panic and decided to return to the store. After I got into my car, it occurred to me to search the car trunk to see if the card fell into the trunk when unloading groceries. As I looked into the car trunk, something prompted me to look down at the ground. My charge card was laying a foot beyond the car trunk and only six feet from the street in front of the house.

* Upon playing the video I took in Ocala, it appeared that if I wanted sound from Greece, I needed to purchase a new video camera. The camera was only a few years old and I was hesitant to do so because of cost. The new camcorder cost less than $275. It's about one-fourth the size of the older one and weighs very little. What a delight to record with it because it's easier to use and fits

snugly in my right hand. It also takes pictures a bit better than the old one.

　　* I decided to see if I could make a payment on the Greece trip online but could not find the statement. After telephoning the charge card company, I learned they sent the bill several weeks ago. When I telephoned James about the statement, he said he made a payment on the card.

　　* I continue to get beautiful pictures of orbs when taking snapshots of the sun shining into my room. Pictures reveal orbs even when taken with my new Canon camcorder so no one can say it's a camera malfunction. I also continue to capture spirit orbs around family. And, I continue to capture substance and matter, orbs and such, in my videos, with the new camcorder. They are mainly magenta (the color of love associated with strength and spirit) and green (the color of healing/protection associated with growth and renewal). Lately, I have captured more blue orbs (the color of new life, associated with purpose and trust) and occasional golden orbs (the color associated with attaining or highest attainment).

　　* It was evident a new suitcase was needed while packing for the Greece trip. I spent several days shopping for an inexpensive, substantial one, to no avail. When I finally found something that suited me, I was not willing to pay the price tag cost. I've always had a knack of finding a marked down item that others overlook and knew I'd find something acceptable for $50. My new valise was behind another one. It was the only well made, brand name, travel case to be marked down to $49.95.

　　* After more than three years, the lawyer for Dad's wrongful death lawsuit finally made a deal with the defendant. I'd prayed on the settlement a number of times, concentrating on a more equitable and just resolution, to include the grandchildren. We recently learned the proposed settlement now includes Rebecca and Joel. The settlement hearing was today. It's still hard to believe the lawsuit is settled. Since I'm leaving for my first international flight in five days, it's nice to know there will soon be money to spare.

:-)

Chapter Twenty-Five

A Taste of Greece

"In the vault of the mind lie all the chains of bondage, as well as the key to freedom."
Paramahansa Yogananda

September 10, 2006 marks the day I leave, to bask in the energies of Greece and Turkey, for thirteen glorious days. What a wonderful opportunity to experience life in a greater way! Temperature promises to be between the mid-60 to high 70's leaving me grateful for cooler weather. Anticipation overwhelms me so Saturday night offers a mere three hours of sleep before waking.

Twenty-three people gather at the Fort Lauderdale airport for a flight to Atlanta, Georgia. The rest of the Religious Science Tour Group will meet us there. Weather delays our flight but it makes no difference for we're all extremely excited. Something tiny flies quickly, way above our heads, as we sit waiting for departure in the afternoon.

"What was that?" says the woman sitting next to me.

We both look up and behind us. The airspace is devoid of explanations to clarify what whizzed by.

"I'm glad you saw it too," I gladly reply while scanning the vast ceiling for dark shadows. "Do you see spirits?"

"Perhaps it was a bat," my new friend says with a shrug while looking anxiously though her purse.

"It was a spirit," I reply with conviction. "I think it's a blessing for the trip."

We board quickly minutes later after the late plane arrives to whisk us away. I'm greatly surprised to sit next to Roberta's 19-year-old son Matthew who reminds me strongly of Daniel.

"Wuzz's Up?" he asks with a broad smile showing beautiful teeth before falling asleep.

Tears gather upon remembering the term as part of Daniel's vocabulary.

Weather delays the transatlantic flight from Atlanta to Athens, Greece as well. It's my first eleven-hour flight so I'm a bit nervous. Tiny black Air France earplugs squeeze into ears as I settle back in the seat to watch *Mission Impossible 3* after dinner.

Switching the radio from channel to channel trying to hear the movie, I pass, and then return, to a tune Daniel's spirit directed me to tape days after his transition. It's the Red Hot Chili Peppers singing one of his favorite songs.

"I don't ever want to feel what I did that day. Take me to the place I love. Take me far away…"

Daniel's presence fills my brain.

"That's the song I was listening to on my iPod when the accident happened. I didn't plan the accident but the song made it easier for me to pass."

Rebecca, Terry, and Ruth spent quite a bit of time trying to determine what song he heard when the accident occurred.

I silently thank Daniel, while switching to the movie channel, as tears slowly drip down my face.

A computer issue interrupts the film so I take advantage of the break by switching to comfortable noise-reduction earphones. After plugging in the earphones, I realize the movie channel switched to a music channel. Daniel's spirit energy changes the channel again soothing me with words from an unfamiliar song, "I will always be with you."

Fresh tears fill my eyes. I know it's all God. Yet, as a human, I'm grateful for the luxury of hearing Him, through the essence of the spirit known as my last-born son.

It's soon my bedtime but the plane computer reminds us it's five o'clock in the morning in Greece. I fall quickly asleep realizing we'll be in one of most ancient capitals of the Western World, in less than six hours. We fly over London on Monday, September 11 at 7:30 AM. Our plane arrives three hours later in the city dedicated and named after Athena, Goddess of Wisdom.

=

The passport control line looks short but I'm feeling unbearably hot and faint. I move out of the procession to sit on the floor up against a wall. The line welcomes me after silently repeating a treatment for wholeness and health. Fresh excitement replaces the ill feeling of being on the verge of passing out from

196

heat and exhaustion. Twenty minutes later, we're through airport security and heading to the tour bus.

Closely-knit communities come into view as dry, dusty land surrounding the airport fades away. A tour guide suggests we take a power nap after arriving at the first hotel to deal with jet lag.

"I'm in Greece, I'm in Greece," my brain repeats, as I continually envision jumping up and down as if on a pogo stick.

Tiny 'smart cars' among a constant stream of motorcycles fly by. I wonder how larger families deal with the trend to use less gas. Our bus turns down a narrow city street. Is the driver taking a short cut to avoid traffic? No. The Divani Palace Hotel soon stands serenely on a narrow city street lined with cars on both sides.

We see its amazing architecture once inside. Many of us quickly walk down a short flight of stairs to see the archeological artifacts. The key lottery begins. Jessica and I score a room on the fifth floor. I began to video as soon as she opens the door.

"Hey," Jessica excitedly cries out in wide-eyed astonishment while waving her arms, "come here, look!"

Small twin beds, packed closely together, fill the camcorder screen before Jessica comes into view. She's jumping up and down on a tiny balcony hidden behind a floor length curtain.

The camcorder is in the lead as I step out to witness a stunning site. About two blocks and ten stories, to our left, the Athens Acropolis stands in all its limestone rock majesty. The zoom function of my new camcorder gives us a view of tourists milling about the base of what I think is the Parthenon (built of Pendelic marble in 447-432 B.C.). We giggle and jump with joy thinking we'll be there soon.

As tired as I am, it's difficult to nap before our first excursion to walk ancient paths. I stand outside trying to guess what countries the thirteen flags below us represent while Jessica settles down. Small balconies, with green plants and hanging laundry, line almost every building as far as the eye can see. Zooming in on flat rooftops, I marvel to think one could actually stand there and get closer to the sky. Jessica sleeps soundly by the time I plop on the bed, which seems like a small stone slab with lead covers and too-thin pillows.

It's time for our first excursion shortly after I fall asleep but I don't mind. My twenty-minute power nap seems enough as our group walks the few blocks to Athens Acropolis. Athens seems filled with large black and brown dogs that look like German Shepards. They walk about the city streets and lie on the ground at archeological sites as if to guard them.

We quickly move up streets made of large marble slabs, little pebble stones, or bricks. I bask in wonder of energy-filled air. It's awesome to see atoms fly haphazardly through the air. They appear much greater in number than at home and faster as well.

Now we're standing near the place where Socrates drank the hemlock that put his physical body to rest. The Theatre of Odem stands majestically below. I'm in a dream I dared to imagine many years ago while watching *The Tempest* on TV. Our tour guide announces that 26,000 years ago a man cut it out of marble to honor his beloved wife. My mind races while considering his gift.

The wind swirls and whips past as we continue our tour of the Parthenon to view the Ancient Agora marketplace below, where people shopped and ate so long ago. My camcorder records streams of bouncing energy but others have problems taking photos for their cameras refuse to work.

A stream of greenish-colored light flows for a fleeting second next to orbs near a scaffold. Multicolored orbs occasionally come in

line with the sun. They're diamond shaped in a variety of colors, royal purple (the color associated with healing, strength, and attunement), magenta, and rainbow.

Seventeen million people visit the site each season. We're told there's no touching, not even a stone, or a whistle will blow and we'll be arrested. Although tourists fill the land, not a single whistle blows. Everyone seems to have great respect for the holy shrine. The Erechtheum and famous Caryatids, young priestesses who support the temple's roof with their heads, affords a stunning site.

Many blue orbs fly by in energy filled air as I bask in the scene. Our limited time at the site does not seem enough. Yet, I know if I'm meant to stroll around the Theatre of Dionysos, Romain Agora, Kerameikos, and Temple of Olympian Zeus, it will happen at another time. We return quickly to the hotel to freshen up for dinner. It's impossible to rest before meeting others for the twenty-minute walk to the Plaka.

Several dogs grace us with their presence while we stroll down narrow city streets. I'm amazed to think the locals are used to living in such close proximity to their ancient beginnings. Many building walls along the way seem to be falling apart, have peeling paint, or graffiti on them. It makes for a more entertaining view as we dodge the occasional cars honking for us to get out of the way.

Arriving at our destination, we hurriedly climb a set of spiral, steel stairs to reach the restaurant's second floor. It's a small place with few tables outside. Jessica and I sit at a long table next to an open window as the sun begins to set.

Our meal consists of seven dishes that each table chooses as a group. The choices include meatballs, French fries, boiled potatoes, and sausages. I convince the others not to order them all. Wanting spinach pie, I savor the pita bread dipped in tzatziki, Greek salad, stuffed grape leaves, spiced fava beans, and pork. Oompa's fill the room as wine begins to flow but I stick with bottled water.

A visit to the bathroom (water closet – WC) amazes me. There's a toilet bowl brush next to the toilet. Is this a common thing in Greece? Do patrons clean toilets? I decide to video all the WC's we use to find out. Differences between Greek and American bathrooms will soon become clear.

The restaurant owner bids us farewell as we leave with satisfied stomachs to tour the area. Time passes quickly. We're soon searching for something to drink. Bars seem scarce. Another nearly empty restaurant welcomes us with open arms. We're quickly seated at a table on the back patio. I ponder what to have as everyone orders a drink. It's been a long time since I've drank alcohol so I order a Yellowbird; something my old bartender friend Jerry called a "girlie drink."

Catherine Ponder's insights on excessive drinking come to mind. I'm now experiencing more good in life. The thirst for alcohol is quenched for I'm following the right path for me. A sense that Spirit continues to guide toward ever-increasing wholeness, fully expressed through talents and abilities, overwhelms me.

It's clear why we're together when talk of departed family members becomes the topic of conversation. One member of the group still mourns over his mother's recent transition. Another is dealing with the suicide death of his daughter many years ago. I do my best to tell them we don't die, we just change forms. Those we love are always ready and willing to communicate. It's more difficult to explain that life is a lesson and everything happens to help us evolve. After last call, we walk briskly through the dark night on empty streets to the hotel.

I hop quickly into the shower to wash away two long days of sweat. Washcloths are missing so cotton underwear seems like a good substitute. Bone tired but clean, I relish the thought of a good nights sleep while settling onto the hard mattress. It feels like I'm lying on a slab of stone.

=

Our driver greets us with a hearty, "Yassou" for the longest bus-traveling day in the morning. The engine idles quietly while we wait for everyone to board. I'm totally amazed when a spirit orb enters through the narrow front door. Am I the only one who sees?

The trip to Mycenae begins at 8:30 AM when a Grecian tour guide announces her name. Valena is a tall, androgynous looking woman who talks very quickly. Many of us decide to call the likeable woman Val. She makes me feel at home, moving long slender arms and hands in rhythmic fashion with her words, just like my Italian ancestors.

The bus has no bathroom and for the first time in many years, breaks are out of my control. Limiting fluids during daytime travel, to lessen bladder pain and the urgency to void, seems wise. Munching on salted pretzels brought from home, I'm reminded of car trips, as we travel along highways passing through one-way tunnels dug into mountains.

Val entertains us with Greek myths and wild stories as we motor past dry land, scattered with clumps of bushes and low-lying trees. After a few hours, we arrive at the very narrow Corinth Canal where tourists mingle and bungee jumpers seek a thrill.

Greek music fills the air. Tourist shops line the road on both sides. We walk quickly past them for our time is limited. My video camera picks up a stream of greenish-colored light, between rays of golden sun, as several people stand in front of a roadside Palm Reader. We board the bus ready to move on to Epidaurus after a quick trip to the WC.

I'm in Heaven listening to Val talk of Greek food and more Greek myths. It's a wonderfully, luxurious world, away from the

200

seclusion of my sunlit room. The bus laboriously climbs long, winding roads. Each bend brings a fresh rush of excitement as we round the corner inches away from the edge of steep cliffs. Val keeps us laughing with her tales.

We arrive at Epidaurus, the 6th century B.C. Sanctuary of Asklepios, God of medicine, ready to stretch our legs. Epidaurus was a healing center for pilgrims from Greece. The ancient Epidaurus Theatre (end of 3rd century B.C.) holds about 14,000 spectators and is famous for its remarkable acoustics. Most of us climb the long, wide, marble stairs without pausing. I video my ascent amazed to make the climb so effortlessly. A path of small stones leads us to the theatre where we form a semi-circle around Val as she talks of history. I decide to climb to the theatre's top when she's done.

Joy fills me upon silently singing Karen Drucker's "One Small Step" while videoing the climb. I'm amazed to hear people speaking way below when I turn to document progress. Marble steps become narrower after passing new friends but I continue to video while carefully climbing to the summit.

Gratitude overwhelms as I sit on a stone seat watching others make the climb. This is a major achievement! It's like being on top of the world. The panoramic view is utterly glorious. I want to walk the perimeter, all around the top, but force myself to start the long walk back down to the meeting point.

Val shares more Greek myths as we leave the theater behind. We're soon motoring through a small town that reminds me of Key West. Cars and small trucks line narrow streets on either side but there are less people than the hippest part of the Keys. Much of the recently built town features new, red, shingled roofs.

The bus passes another grove of orange trees before our driver turns down a paved road that seems narrower than the last. If the mountains were not in view, I'd swear we're in Lower Florida cruising Big Pine Key now. Greenery increases when we turn at a sign directing us to the next site.

The majesty of Mycenae (Treasure of Atreus – 3,000 B.C.) comes into view as many of us ponder lunch. It was a fortified royal residence surrounded by Cyclopean walls in ancient times.

I stand before the Perseia Foundation House minutes later videoing the wonder of Greece as the group follows Val on a dirt road. Purple diamond-shaped orbs point the way to the Lions Gate.

201

Val speaks as I try to catch energy-filled air on video. She announces Greeks still to this day pour wine on the ground for their ancestors. I think about my family.

"Why, that's alcohol abuse," Terry and Rebecca would remark in unison.

Arrays of multi-colored diamonds grace my video display amid spots of sunlight. A stream of greenish-colored light flows for a fleeting second, before changing to rainbow-colored rays among white beams of light. Diamond shaped orbs morph into triangles when we near the site's entrance.

The Lions Gate, symbolizing the power of the kings of Mycenae – a city rich in gold according to Homer – is the entrance to Mycenae's Acropolis. A fleeting shadow zips by and disappears before we pass. I watch amazed as a member from our group climbs into a small cave just beyond the entrance for a photo. Am I the only one that detects the change in his body's energy?

Less than half our group has the same idea as I climb to the summit of the hill, to see Palace floors, before meeting Val back at the bus. I'm adamant about making it to the top even though I have to scurry back down to make our deadline at 2:30 PM.

A short while later we're having a wonderful lunch at an elegant restaurant in the countryside. My first taste of lamb in Greece is not as good as the lamb from a downtown Detroit Greek restaurant savored years ago.

The day continues as we board the bus. Winding roads remind me of bobby pins. Our driver slows down considerably when we approach Megalopolis. This land offers a stark contrast of dry earth, with scattered small trees and a bustling city below, near emerald blue seas lining a coast melding into the sky.

Val tells us how the Olympic Games began as we motor through the greener Peloponnese District. She talks of shepherds, Zeus, and Greek men participating sans clothes. "Remember three words about Olympic Games," she notes, "war without weapons."

We pass through a light rain as the Ionian Sea comes into view but it doesn't last long. As we motor slowly through a small town, the paved streets narrow again barely offering enough room for the bus. A lone woman dressed in black, as if in mourning, stands at the side of the road across from a small cemetery as the bus rounds a curve. She raises her long, skinny arm to wave as we pass and I wonder if she knows the bus driver. The road widens again as we leave the small town behind.

A car blocks our way when we drive through a larger town. It's a normal day in Greece. We sit quietly until a local comes out of a shop to move it from the middle of the street.

It's nearly eight o'clock as the Amalia Olympia Hotel comes into view. We're told it may not be too functional but it's very spacious. I immediately trod down a set of stairs to check out the WC while we wait for room keys. The stalls boast sturdy floor to ceiling doors. A toilet brush stands near each toilet.

The hotel is lovely but my video camera has difficulty taping for main areas feature masses of unseen energy. Dinner leaves much to be desired. The locally harvested meal is slow in coming and seems sparse. I leave the table tired and disappointed over courses of tomato soup, onion pie, coleslaw, carrots, broccoli and fish, bread and butter, and white mousse for dessert. I want dark chocolate!

It's important for me to assure my aura is as clean as possible before bedtime. But once again, a quick call to room service reveals there are no washcloths. I wonder how guests thoroughly clean their bodies without a small cloth or loofa and remain thankful for cotton underwear. Sleep soon claims me but I wake often to use the bathroom and sip water throughout the night trying to rehydrate.

=

Morning comes too soon. Jessica and I leave for a filling breakfast buffet after placing luggage outside the hotel room door at 7:30 AM. Val addresses us with the usual hearty Kalime'ra (Kah-lee Mehrah – good morning in Greek) as we board the bus. Our ride to the archeological site in Olympia is short. It's the flattest site we're privileged to visit and quite expansive, stretching as far as the eye can see.

A light breeze blows through my long hair while appraising the surrounding maple, olive, and cypress trees. I'm anxious to explore gravel pathways but stay close to the group as Val discusses history. Curious about an engraved stone, I ask her what it says.

"Flavius, a guardian, the son of Alexander from Fesaly, became a member of the Supreme Court of Athens," she replies with authority.

203

A narrow dirt path soon beckons me to stray from the group. Whirling noises lead me to an area with several small rooms. There are no roped-off areas here amidst huge slabs of gray stone. Stepping gingerly through a narrow entrance, and down to the dirt below, I find myself spellbound by the variety of ruins. Gray columns sit perched on ledges made of rectangular gray stone. The area leads to a smaller space marked with crosses, carved into a latticework of stone.

A man dressed in blue overalls, wearing a facemask, works at the far end of the area, oblivious to me. He's cutting weeds away from stones with a weed whacker. I'm in a world alone, videoing with his back towards me amid ancient artifacts. Sunlight streams between clouds minutes later as I head back toward the tour group. Orbs surround me so I try to discuss the phenomenon with Kim who uses a professional video camera.

"Do you ever pick up any orbs?" I enthusiastically inquire.

"What's that?" she replies with little interest focusing on a shot of the gray stone columns before us.

"Never mind," I tell her drifting away.

A man from our group, whom I feel oddly connected to, approaches.

"Sam," he says pointing to a number of relics lined up for display on one of the ledges.

"Hey, Ramon," I address him softly, turning away from my video subject. "I'm picking up so much energy here it's freaky. Do you know what an orb is?"

"Orb?" he says with a quick glance around us. "That's a glimpse into our future," he replies as we begin to walk. "Do you see auras?"

"No," I excitedly reply looking at the ground. "Do you?"

"Yes. Mine is red."

"What color is mine?"

"It looks grey today."

I finally feel in tune with someone as we continue discussing the meanings of different aura colors. He offers to help me up steps as we climb out of the enclosed walled area, and for the first time in a long time, I miss having the human comfort of a helpful male. The weed-whacking man looks up from his job and waves goodbye as we pass.

History holds no interest for me so I again stray from the group. A triangular shaped piece of what looks like striated marble draws my attention. It's smooth and about an inch long at its widest point. As I turn it over in my hand, it gives me the impression that yes; I've been in Olympia before. The feeling is undeniable.

Orbs, streaming from the middle of the sun, enthrall me after we leave Hera's Altar where the lighting of the flame takes place to signify the official beginning of Olympic Games. The mixture of multicolored triangles and diamonds are beautiful.

We soon enter a large rectangular area of dirt surrounded by grass. This is where the games began many centuries ago so we stage a competition of our own. I video the action as Matthew wins a dash from one end of the field to the other.

Val discusses Cleopatra and Anthony on our way to the Olympia museum. I begin to ask questions when she notes Cleopatra committed suicide. Val quickly reminds us, don't always trust the movies. Cleopatra and Anthony were most likely slain, I quietly note, to get them out of power. Val agrees it's possible because Cleopatra was powerful, and in her day, women were not part of the power structure. I smile and leave the group to walk through the Olympia museum alone.

We quickly board the bus minutes later, glad to finally sit, and ready to move on to the next stop. The land is a contrast of dry, brown dirt and weeds, among green crops and flowered trees, where sheep graze and chickens occasionally peck at the side of the road. Val talks of how the European Union limits farmers as to what they can grow each year so the soil stays fertile. Laughter fills the bus upon hearing many stories of how gypsies live and annually pass though the town of Olympia to help with crops.

Our energetic tour guide continues to entertain us with outrageous stories. Areas of widely spaced old homes, and towns, with newly constructed buildings three to five stories tall, flash by. Just when I think I may need to ask for a place with a WC, we arrive at a seaside restaurant in the middle of nowhere. The quaint eatery is ornately decorated with many antiques.

The view is fantastic. Butterflies and birds fly pass windows as we wait for our late afternoon lunch. I'm able to video mountains and water from my end seat at the table. Two satisfied diners skim stones over the smooth azure waters as we all happily take in the world-class view. I want to video every single second of the trip so I won't forget a thing. The view from the WC is almost as beautiful while videoing through an open window.

A delicious meal of cheese pie, Greek salad, fresh fish, potatoes, and grapes soon sits gracefully in my stomach. Blue and magenta colored orbs, amid changing energy fields, are recorded from the upstairs dining room window before heading to the bus.

I'm feeling so very grateful as we drive towards Delphi along the water. The beauty of the area astounds me. Val points out more churches, as I sit sideways, happy to have two seats to myself. My ears pop as the bus climbs laboriously up the mountain. Everyone jokes about the ride with its hairpin curves.

Shortly before six o'clock, Val notes points of interest while we drive through the quaint town of Delphi. Several people say they may venture out after dinner. I'll be taking it easy, eating with the group at the hotel, and resting as much as possible. The amount of exercise I accomplish each day still amazes me.

Finally, at the Delphi Amalia Hotel, it seems like Jessica and I again have the best room. Everyone tells us not to brag. Our corner view, outside sliding glass doors, reveals a wide expanse of mountains and water, amid lush green trees and blue skies, with scattered white and gray clouds. I'm ecstatic to sit on the small patio to smell pine trees and take it all in.

"Is this Greece or what?" I call back to Jessica as she rummages through her suitcase.

"It sure isn't America!" she giggles with delight while dressing for dinner.

Jessica leaves to exchange American money for Euros. A happy sigh fills the air after I settle into a white, plastic, patio chair to place my feet upon the railing. The camcorder sits on the windowsill, taping a glorious sunset, while I repeat the usual ritual. I'm still there thirty minutes later when Jessica returns.

The dinner buffet is satisfying but I'm too tired after eating to go anywhere. There's a line waiting for the elevator. I force myself to climb slowly up wide stairs to our third floor room ready for a hot shower. Tonight, I resign myself to using a pair of underwear for the rest of the trip.

What a joy to open the sliding glass doors leading to the balcony after a shower! The fresh smell of pine trees wafts through the room. I'm thankful my roommate remains unconcerned about leaving the door open throughout the night.

=

The CD player helps me to repeat treatments in my head before dawn. Birds chirp in surrounding trees as sunshine climbs mountains. A cloudless sky makes sunrise pale in comparison to my taped sunset. But it's so peaceful here in Delphi that I want to stay forever.

Jessica sleeps soundly while church bells join the chorus of chirping birds. It's our fourth day in Greece and we're beginning to feel an urge to slow down. I give her a soft poke on the shoulder while whispering, "Your bus awaits my lady."

"I don't want to get up," she quickly announces shoving her head back under the covers.

"We both need to eat and board the bus by nine o'clock."

After a few groans, Jessica rises to dress while I finish taping the sunrise. The camera fits nicely in a day bag when my mission is accomplished. I set luggage in the hallway and head to the oddest elevator I've ever seen.

It's unthinkable not to document this relic, for it's tiny, and lacks the security measures American lawsuits demand. There's only enough room for four tightly squeezed people and very little luggage. Someone from our group pulls open the wooden door so we can squeeze through the narrow opening.

The door swings shut as my companion fixes her hair using the square two-foot mirror hanging on the back wall. I reach out and easily push it back open amazed. With the push of a button, the elevator jerks, and begins to move down slowly. It stops after a few seconds. The light goes off leaving us in total darkness. We giggle knowing it's time to get out. The wooden elevator door opens easily when I push it with my right hand. We giggle again and walk through the narrow doorway for the last time.

The breakfast buffet is outstanding. I happily stuff myself with fresh figs and olives before rising to explore the hotel. Several tour members join me on the second floor balcony. Anna and Ramon are below us surrounded by a beautiful garden. The view beyond them is an exquisite mix of mountains, water, and green trees. "Smile, you're on candid camera," I sing loudly. They laugh and begin to tap dance near the huge swimming pool.

I want to stay but board the bus to visit the archeological site. Today's adventure begins. Val soon reminds us Delphi is geographically the center of Greece as she points out upper and lower ruins. We quickly depart from the bus to gather around her.

Ruins come into sight after climbing a set of wide, long, stone steps. I'm drawn to the relics outside like a moth to a flame, having little desire to visit the Delphi museum as Val buys tickets.

In spite of an urge to wander outside, I join others entering the museum. Video and photos are allowed as long as there's no flash of light. Val speaks as I wander nearby, videoing statues of mythological creatures called griffins. I'm engrossed with the thought of living during those times.

Our vivacious guide discusses the "Sphinx of the Naxians"

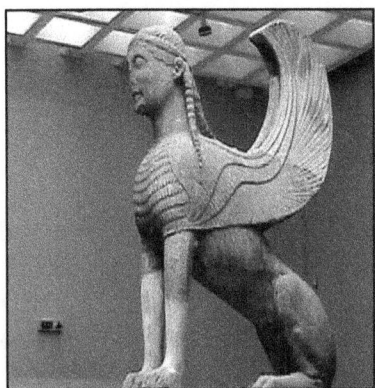

as the head of a caryatid (550-540 B.C.) and scenes of battle draw my interest. Battle scenes, depicted on slabs of stone, fill me with sadness. I'm abhorred to see a man's leering face, with his tongue sticking out, etched into a soldier's shield. Marble and stone relics, depicting lion's heads, fill me with an unexplainable sense of gloom.

Macedonian artifacts entice me so I film them before passing a small group of students sitting on the floor carefully sketching the "Charioteer." The camcorder captures their artwork before moving on.

Much too soon, we have less than an hour to explore the archeological site. Val warns us of a steep incline as I trudge up the stone path to see the ruins above.

"Bathrooms," Val says hurriedly, "we must use the bathrooms before we leave here." "The bathrooms are right here," she says motioning with her hands. "First door is for girls and for the boys it's outside behind the bush," she jokes.

The group roars with laughter.

"They don't need any encouragement." I tell her.

"It's not a hard thing for us to do," one of the men pipes in with a wink.

There are no roped-off areas here but we stay on the gravel path following Val. A scorpion passes to my right as we rapidly climb the archeological site. Val speaks quickly when I point it out.

"We call it the forty legs."

I video the air that seems more densely packed with Stuff of Matter than it was inside the museum. Val verifies what I see and feel by noting that the site has a special energy.

"And of course you must remember that this whole thing was a performance, a reenactment," she says as I wonder what she means. "Keep in mind that this was the network of information, the Internet for these people."

It was also the meeting place for duelers from ten neighboring tribes to try and find bloodless solutions to issues. I stop paying attention to focus on the sun amazed at the orbs my camcorder detects. It looks like a stream of purple, turquoise, white, magenta, and multicolored circles and diamonds, amidst a cascade of green flowing energy. Val announces there's no time for anything now for we are to be back in Athens at a certain time.

"I'll take a taxi," I joke while videoing the 4th Century B.C. Temple of Apollo below us. "I'll meet you there."

A whistle sounds repeatedly in the distance as I stand at the edge of the cliff taking in the spectacular view. Dense Stuff of Matter flows erratically all around.

"Isn't it beautiful?" I ask hearing someone approach.

"I can't get my camera to focus on anything to take a picture," a dismayed man remarks.

I know he doesn't see the energy fields.

Val is hurriedly walking back down to the bus. I ignore his remark, continuing to video, while following in hot pursuit. Unwilling to depart, yet knowing I must, I stop abruptly on the gravel path near the entrance. If it's meant to be, I'll return, I promise myself before moving on.

The boring bus ride gets very exciting when we attempt to travel down a narrow city street. A huge Mercedes Benz tanker truck sits to our left making it impossible to pass without riding up on the sidewalk. Our bus driver stops, puts his right hand up as if to assure the other driver, backs the bus up, and then waits patiently for the truck driver to make his move.

We sit in anticipation wondering how the truck and our bus will be able to pass. The trucker pulls his mirror out and continues to sit staring at us. Dumbfounded, most of us begin to laugh nervously at what appears to be a standoff. It soon looks like our bus driver wants to pass while driving on the narrow sidewalk. He begins to curse in Greek upon seeing the trucker blocked our route with his mirror. Now it sounds like he's asking the trucker what he's doing.

Our bus begins to move forward but stops abruptly when the trucker raises a finger. His mirror is still out as he inches toward us. We hold our breaths while I video the mere two inch space between vehicles. Just before the mirror hits us, he pulls it back. As the drivers begin to pass, they yell at one another while we sit mesmerized by the close proximity of the vehicles.

"If the windows were rolled down we could write our names on the tanker," someone remarks from the back of the bus.

"Let's bless it," I enthusiastically reply.

We all laugh nervously but breathe sighs of relief when the tanker finally passes. Everyone begins to happily clap, hoot, and whistle, congratulating the bus driver for his expert driving, as we slowly pass a steady stream of small cars. It's taken us more than fifteen minutes to move two blocks through the town of Araqueba. While we sit stopped, again in traffic, trying to pass small cars to our left, I'm struck by the town's layout. A bevy of stairs, between buildings, looks very old.

As usual, Val reminds us to wash our hands before eating when we stop at an elegant restaurant for lunch at two o'clock. Water tanks high above toilets soon amaze me before settling into my seat with a view. I'm again impressed with Greek food but disappointed over the dessert of fruit.

We continue on hoping to reach Athens quickly. An emergency bathroom break halts the journey less than forty minutes from the inner city.

"There's a McDrive guys," I announce with a hearty laugh as we pass McDonald's.

The sound of laughter fills the bus as we pull into what Val refers to as a filthy McNasty gas station.

"Remember girls," she says adamantly, "don't touch anything!"

Ken is making an announcement as I board the bus ten minutes later. "Also," he says with a straight face, "when we get to the resort I'll give you my room number and cell phone number, to call if you have any concerns, or want to tell me what hospital you're at or…"

Someone behind me promptly adds, "Police station."

We all giggle as Ken repeats the words. His voice trails off at, "and churches for others," as we enter the inner city traffic, which looks backed up for miles.

Ken considers the traffic and then notes the cost of optional excursions on our upcoming cruise. Although it's an extra cost, money is no longer a concern for I have my trusty Visa charge card. This is my chance to break the thought of limitation held so strongly for decades. I ponder which excursions to take while Val remarks on traffic control by noting that people with cars can only drive on certain days.

The scenery continues to change. One or two-story buildings are now a rare sight. Taller buildings, closely packed together leaving no room for yards, are more prominent. It's much different from my current home of Fort Lauderdale where adequately spaced one-story houses are the rule. Val tells us it was not always that way, but over time, laws allowed builders to block the view of the Acropolis with monstrous concrete buildings.

I watch traffic amazed as motorcyclists make their own lane by riding between cars before stopping at traffic lights. It's something I've never seen so prominently before. But drivers don't seem to mind, as four-lane highways turn into six, and then seven lanes, while we wait for lights to change.

As we drive through the "red light" district a man in the rear of the bus calls out, "Stop the bus," and we all roar with laughter.

We're on a roll as another asks in a serious voice, "Val those stainless steel tanks on top of buildings, they're ouzo?"

"Ouzo would explode," she tells him with a laugh. "Remember, I told you it looks like water and tastes like hell."

The bus breaks out into another fit of laughter as we round a curve. After 850 kilometers, we're back where we started for another night at the Divani Palace Hotel. Jessica and I settle down for a two-hour nap before dinner.

Like our first night, we again walk to the Plaka but this time visit a more elegant restaurant. I'm impressed when waiters put oil-soaked, black, Greek olives on the table instead of the usual rolls or bread we get at home. The excellent meal of fried cheese (saganaki) and seafood crepes satisfies. Jessica and I rise to leave after paying our share of the bill.

"We'll be okay walking back alone," I assure friends.

Waiters approach with trays of free after dinner drinks.

"Come back Sam and have a drink," several members of the group chorus as we slowly make our way through the maze of outside tables.

"You can have mine," I announce continuing to walk away.

"Sam, come on and join us," they insist motioning with their hands.

A waiter turns toward me and motions as well. "Sam, come, come Sam," he says as another waiter places his hand on my arm and leads me to the tray of drinks.

"Where are you going without this?" another waiter asks holding the tray out in front of me.

"The owner addresses me as well. "Where are you going without this? It's good for the digestion."

"Is it ouzo?" I ask silently reminding myself alcohol decreases the body's vibration.

"Sweet liquor," he replies enthusiastically.

"Oh," Jessica says coming up behind me as he holds out a small shot glass, "sweet liquor."

I see no way to back out politely and decide to join the group in a toast after Jessica takes one.

"Oh, alright," says I taking the shot glass from a waiter's outstretched hand. "Okay, so it's not ouzo."

"Yamas," the owner shouts.

We all raise our glasses and repeat the word ready to drink.

"The best city in the world, now, just one sip," he instructs as we all slug down the shot.

"Thank you," I tell him after downing sweet-tasting, syrupy liquid. Turning to our friends I calmly announce, "It was good. If you find us in the street on the way home you can just kick us down the hill."

Jessica and I make our way back down the stairs to Plaka streets. After we stop at a vendor stall so Jessica can buy a souvenir, we head quickly back to the hotel. The brightly lit Parthenon in the distant hill guides us back safely.

=

My brain records a message the next morning upon waking. *There's much more to life than we will ever know at any level.* I write the words on paper before quickly dressing for breakfast.

Our group happily boards a bus to the cruise port after checking out of the hotel. Excitement fills the air as the new tour guide begins our ride with a warning of long lines, due to 2,000 people boarding the Sea Diamond, for passage to the island of Mykonos.

Dr. Bump takes the microphone to give thanks to Homeric Tours and our personal tour guides who are church members. We close our eyes as she begins to say a treatment of thanks to everyone involved with the trip. I don't pay much attention but am encouraged knowing all is well as she continues.

"...we allow and accept, and know, that our voyage to Mykonos is perfect in every way, that everyone, and everything, is functioning perfectly, on time, and in Divine Law and Order," she notes with authority. "Spirit is with us, guides us, goes before us and makes our way safe, smooth, comfortable, and oh, so joyous."

I mentally agree, smile and nod, as she continues.

"We are the right people, in the right place, at the right time for the Holy Spirit to be made manifest as this most glorious trip, as we extend this second leg of our voyage, and for this we give thanks and we affirm it by saying and so it is!"

It's shortly before ten o'clock when we pull into the port where the Sea Diamond sits.

Our bus guide excitedly notes, "There is no line-up and we are really lucky."

Several of us cheer knowing all is well just as Dr. Bump said in her treatment. She jokingly asks if I've found a WC to video as we breeze through the line. Laughing loudly, I tell her the K.E.A. Special Missions sign on a door is much more interesting. We pass quickly through the port and are soon on the ship for a five-hour cruise.

Past Sea Escape gambling day cruises pale in comparison to being on a ship in Greece. Filled with excitement, I scan the booths lining inside walls as they fill with people. My mission is to video as much as possible. As the rest of our group relaxes, I boldly video the WC after helping someone turn on the water faucet. The Orient Queen sits at dockside. We'll be on it in four days for a longer cruise of the Greek Islands. I move back outside to video it as we pull out to sea.

We're sailing into darker blue waters as a strong wind whips about the ship. I'm amazed to hear announcements in several languages. A small submarine catches my attention for several minutes before slowly sinking back down under the sea.

The excitement builds as we near the island. Mykonos is named after the son of the legendary king of Delos, Anios, descendent of god Apollo.

It's extremely windy and about 60 degrees as we disembark. I'm one of the first to lead the way off the ship. Anna and I soon crouch behind a short wall to avoid the wind as we wait for luggage.

With possessions in hand, we board the San Marco Hotel bus ready to begin our island adventure. A hotel representative takes roll call, making me feel like a kid again, as we drive down a narrow seaside road. His accent is thick and it's hard to understand him. We giggle while taking in the expanse of whitewashed buildings as the sun sets to our left. It seems like we're almost at the end of the road, when the bus makes a right turn, to chug slowly up a long hill.

The San Marco Hotel stands mid-way up the hill. We disembark near lavender colored bougainvillea bushes listening to small birds flying nearby. The hotel looks amazing but seems short-staffed. I walk over to video the awesome view of sky, mountains, and sea, beyond the hotel's swimming pool as we wait for room assignments.

It's seven o'clock on a Friday night in Greece, and I'm happier than I've been in ages gazing at a panoramic view, before heading to the WC with a gal from our group. We enter a large elegant room with marble floors, private stalls with massive floor to ceiling doors, artwork, and decorative baskets. Each stall has its own piece of artwork hanging on the wall. One stall is extremely large and has a shower as well. Toilet brushes sit stationed like soldiers next to each toilet.

After taking care of the task at hand, we exit to find we were in the men's WC. We're too tired to care. My camcorder documents that the ladies room is exactly the same. I slowly move on to video the rest of the basement that includes a gymnasium, dress shop, and bar.

It's almost eight o'clock by the time Jessica and I trudge up the hill to Room 404 in the fourth building. I'm grateful a bellhop is bringing our luggage with a jeep as I hear Jessica lagging behind me in the dark.

"I have the key," she calls out laboriously, as if I didn't know.

214

"You check the buildings to see where we are."

I'm getting out of breath myself but am happy to note our view will be better the higher we go. I just know we will face the sea.

"Oh, whee," Jessica says as she continues to climb through the silent night breathing heavily.

We're faced with a set of stairs after reaching the last building. I climb alone to find Room 430 facing north towards the heart of the city. "It's not up here," I call down to Jessica. She is leaning over now trying to catch her breath.

Suddenly feeling tired, I slowly climb down the stairs. Jessica trails behind as we walk around the building to a smaller set of stairs. I push ahead to quickly pull open the massive wooden door at the top. A large dimly lit room looms before us as we slowly move forward together. We breathe a sigh of relief at the first doorway.

Jessica plops on the first bed as I head toward a set of small, wooden, balcony doors. I'm ecstatic to see our room faces west, towards the sea. There's a bird's eye view, and a furry of activity below, as members of our tour group happily enter rooms.

Stomachs soon cry out for food. Jessica decides to rest before eating in the hotel restaurant. I get a sudden spurt of energy and quickly dress to meet thirteen others catching the bus into Chora for dinner. It's a full bus. We weave through the night towards sparkling red, white, and blue lights while listening to Greek music.

The bus comes to a slow halt. One by one, we disembark to follow Ken on the dimly lit road. A series of narrow stone steps soon takes us through a small restaurant, disappointing the owner. Kittens in a box call out for attention but we pass them to climb briskly up a few more steps, anxious to reach our destination. We're going to have a drink at Kastro's Bar and then move on to dinner at the restaurant of a friend Ken knows.

"This is the taxi stand in case you miss the bus," Ken tells us as we continue walking.

He leads us down streets with whitewashed, cobbled pavements before passing through an intersection crowded with people. A huge white pelican walks among the crowd. Ken acts like a father as he guides us through the countless labyrinthine alleys. When we stop to wait for group members to catch up it's nearly ten o'clock.

There seems to be a never-ending stream of steps to climb. Ken stops again at a busy restaurant and tells a lanky man named George to prepare a table for us. Walking through a wide-open space, we reach another alcove that leads though a maze of tourist shops. White and aqua blue buildings, some with blue shutters, flow past as we step swiftly on the uneven stone and white, painted, cement path.

Music fills the air when we round a corner and pile into Kastro's bar. Ken lags behind to wait for the others after instructing some of us to get tables near the water. He suddenly appears in a doorway to our left and motions, "this way," as I protest when the waiter seats us near the front door. The waiter apologizes as I rise to follow Ken videotaping our approach to a bevy of tables near the water. When it's apparent several people moved to allow us the view, we thank them for moving.

Although I'm gifted with one of the few seats closest to the water, it's too dark to video beyond the restaurant floodlights below. Looking out the open window, I notice a number of large gray rocks. A man in blue jeans, wearing a black jacket, sits upon one facing the sea. There's a woman crouched holding him from behind, as if she wants to be sure he doesn't jump into the water below. I watch for several minutes while waiting for my white wine.

Soon we are back at the Taverna restaurant. The white pelican approaches and stands in our way as we clamor to take its picture. We pet him before sitting at a long table in the large courtyard.

It does not take long for George to pull several women up from our table, one by one, to dance. Our table is outrageously loud by the time we finish eating and Yia'sou (meaning health, cheers) fills the air.

George brings us a free round of Tentura, cinnamon-tasting liquor. I think twice before accepting it for now two glasses of wine swim in my belly. The waiter soon delivers our checks. He pours everyone another shot of Tentura and leaves the bottle on the table.

"That concludes our drinking for the evening," I say after downing the second shot.

"You're not running with us?" one of the guys asks as we all stand to go.

"Not tonight baby," I reply with my video trained on him. "You find the hot spots and let me know where they are tomorrow."

The open-air restaurant is empty as I video George dancing Greek style by himself to the music in his head. I make my way through the food market, videoing fresh fish laid out in bins, while a few of us head back through the city maze to the bus. It's past midnight as we listen to what sounds like Greek disco music while driving through the black night to the San Marco Hotel.

It feels close to Heaven on earth as I settle down on the hard mattress for what I hope will be a good night's rest. I'm overjoyed to take a break, finally, from the hectic schedule that ended up at a different hotel every night.

Jessica rolls over to tell me not to close the balcony doors. The room is hot but the air conditioner doesn't seem to work. I'm too tired to complain about it now. We leave the balcony doors open all night to bathe our bodies with fresh air. Each time I wake to use the bathroom, I peek out beyond the balcony and hotel lights, to squint at the black hole directly in front of us.

=

Chirps from small birds fill the air in the morning. I move slowly, beyond slotted, wooden, balcony doors, for the first daylight glimpse of our view. This is Heaven on earth! The Aegean Sea sits smack in the middle of my sight, beyond white adobe buildings with blue doors. Whitecaps flow quickly away from the mountain beyond as I settle into a chair with my CD player. Jessica sleeps while I silently repeat treatments before waking her for breakfast.

Our building looks much different in daylight. The large, empty, common room holds a pool table and bar that looks neglected. The other end of the hall contains another spacious sitting room. No one is there when we head out the back door to find two sets of gray stone stairs, one leading up, and the other down. A blue table, with white chairs, sits before us. There's no exit so we turn back relieved to see a side door that leads to the street.

A calico cat with brown eyes greets us immediately. She purrs as we pet her before heading down the hill. Jessica decides to take the stairs as I video, slowly trudging down the moderate incline. I'm highly impressed with what I see. It's my first experience staying at a pricey resort in a foreign country and I want to document every second.

Purple and magenta colored orbs grace me with their presence. I quickly walk up red and gray tile stairs to stroll through another area. It's decorated with a canopy, protecting two brown wicker couches, to my left and right. A small table sits in the middle. Another set of red and gray tile stairs leads to the main hotel building. Jessica and I meet there before moving down a set of stairs to the restaurant.

Our exercise levels are much higher than at home. We both eat more than usual no longer concerned about body weight.

The maid sparks a fit of quiet giggles as we slowly climb the hill back to our room. She's wearing a pair of tan capri's and a sleeveless, black, string top. It's unusual attire for American housekeepers.

"Taking the stairs is less strenuous," Jessica notes with a sigh.

I tell her we'll do that for the rest of our stay.

The calico cat follows us into the building. It walks back out when I open the blue, wooden doors in the common room. I move out to the terrace and easily step over the wall onto our balcony. It's easy to enter the room. We still don't know how to work the air conditioner so we've left the balcony doors open to fill the area with fresh air.

Jessica reads the hotel information.

"We have to leave the key on the wall over there," she says pointing near the door. And all the doors have to be closed in order for the air conditioning to work."

It seems like an impossible task if we only have one key.

The cat strolls into the room. It quickly settles on my bed as I video a catamaran sailing on rough seas.

"Remember what I told you kitty," I say with conviction turning around to address the cat. "If you have fleas, and I know you do, you must keep them on your person."

The cat stares up at me before closing its eyes to nap.

Jessica soon joins a group to tour. I stay at the hotel anxious to let my family know all is well. There's a bevy of computers, hooked up to the Internet, tucked away in the main building. Dr. Bump offers me her unused time to check and send email.

Splendor surrounds me. It's a perfect day for adventure and exercise as I later begin my search for the highest accessible spot behind the hotel. After investigating our building's roof, I walk down several sets of concrete stairs to climb the hill behind it.

It's been a long time since I ventured out in an unfamiliar place alone but I'm raring to go. The road turns to gravel as I walk behind what looks like a caretaker's small home. A ladder rests on the side of the white, adobe building. I consider climbing it for just a moment but decide to video the sparse vegetable garden instead.

Large stones lie in the dirt hill beyond the garden. The caretaker's roof appears below me after paving a path around them. The view is not as pretty as the one from our balcony. As I look towards the sun, a beautiful stream of green and violet blue seems to flow forth to embrace me.

"And so, that concludes the back alley hotel portion of our program," I announce out loud. "Thank you for watching."

Foliage is an amazing mix of what looks like cactus, brown mounds of weeds, dirt, and rock. I'm happily rewarded with a breathtaking view after climbing further up the hill. The camcorder picks up orbs of royal purple, and streams of green-blue light, before I head back to the room for a short nap.

Jessica makes it back in time to take the bus to town for our Saturday night in Mykonos. Narrow cobbled streets lead us past whitewashed houses, elegant nightclubs, restaurants, and chic boutiques with clothes, jewelry, and works of art. Many houses feature balconies. It's easy to recall countless Keys trips enjoyed with James while sipping Spanish coffee at Kastro's bar.

Taverna soon welcomes us for dinner. After we eat, the waiter again leaves a bottle of Tentura liquor on the table. I notice there's no label on the bottle as everyone toasts. Tonight I'm inclined to join the late night crowd to cruise the scene.

Several minutes later, we arrive at Piero's, a dark, outrageously loud, disco bar. I order a glass of wine but feeling tired, head back to the hotel with Jessica before finishing it.

=

Jessica joins members of our group in the morning for a trip to the sacred island of Delos, the ancient capital of Greece, while I enjoy the luxury of sleeping in. According to mythology, Delos stood still on the waves of the Aegean so Leto could give birth to Apollo and Artemis (Diana) on the island.

The sound of children wafts into the room through balcony doors shortly after Jessica departs. I rise to see two, unsupervised, young boys streaming pieces of what looks like toilet paper in the wind, from the balcony to our left. White streamers float softly up into air with the breeze. One falls to the ground when the youngest boy, who looks about four-years-old, lets it go.

The older boy jolts downstairs, retrieves the streamer, returns it to his brother, and stands beside him waving his own long flag in the wind.

Small birds dart across the courtyard as the boys mix their streamers together. A disinterested maid drags laundry out of a room from the building across the courtyard.

After another restful day at the hotel, I board the bus with Jessica before sunset. This time we stop to hold the six kittens while passing through the thoroughfare. Water laps softly on the shore as we make our way to the free jewelry reception held in our honor. After sampling a glass of wine and some food, I sit patiently waiting for the reception to end. I'm only interested in a butterfly pin with yellow diamonds, which I cannot afford even if they had it.

One of the owners starts a discussion with me. He seems familiar and notes how difficult it's been for the family since their father's death. We talk of the Otherside for the next thirty minutes, until the group leaves to watch the sun sink into the sea, while having cocktails at Kastro's bar.

Maria, the owner of Chez Maria's Garden Restaurant Bar, greets us a short time later as we enter her foliage-filled area. Polished wooden beams grace the ceiling. They hold a bevy of lush green vines cascading all around the room. I adore the ambience and video the décor of many small rooms to my left.

We eat happily by candlelight while listening to beautiful French music. Costs no longer concern me. It's easy to charge the meal to my trusty Visa card. There's a knowing that all is well and Dad's lawsuit will be more than enough to pay the bills.

Tourist shops line cobbled paths as we stroll after dinner. Sets of stairs, between shops, lead to apartments. It's our last night in Mykonos and the thought of our destination fills me with delight.

The Montparnasse Piano Bar is packed. We enter just as the singer belts out Barbra Streisand's "Memories." Smiling broadly, I fondly recall years as a waitress in Detroit at the popular Sing Along. Some people depart gifting me with a seat directly in front of the singer. It's the laughter I'll remember as she entertains us.

The waiter asks for our order. I'm feeling good remembering my drinking days.

"I'll take a Zombie," I innocently announce.

"I don't even know what that is," he says while reaching for a drink menu behind me on the round table. "Oh, yes, I see," he remarks with a chuckle. "It looks like a good drink."

"Enjoy your drink Sam," he says minutes later while placing it on the table.

I wonder who told him my name and then entertain the idea of seeing the singer in the States. As I slowly sip the Zombie, Pamela Stanley tells us she'll be at Chardees less than a mile from my house right before Thanksgiving.

"Is there a straight man in the house?" she sings, as we all burst out in raucous laughter.

Her song fits perfectly for we're in one, of many, area gay bars. The Zombie drink soon affects me. As Pamela's voice fills the area, I'm grateful there will be no putting aside my self respect, to search for slime after a few glasses of wine, ever again. When it's time to go I'm glad Jessica is with me for it's been more than nine months since I've drunk so much.

Everything seems surreal as we make our way back down to the water's edge before boarding the bus. It soon occurs to me my roommate's mannerisms are much like my own. I quickly decide to pay more attention to thoughts before blurting them out.

=

It's our last day at the San Marco. After a hearty breakfast with Jessica, I board the bus for a quick trip to Delos. Excitement quells when the Blue Ferry spokesperson informs me there are no ferries to Delos on Monday. The island is under the protection of the Greek Ministry of Culture. It's closed every Monday to care for the environment and allow everyone a day off.

Walking along the water's edge, I push disappointment aside and decide to explore. Small chapels and whitewashed windmills line the picturesque harbor. Buildings block my path forcing me to find another way to walk near the sea. Large stones now line the shore. A lone fisherman, wearing a white beret, casts his rod into the wind as I try to get back to the water.

The old-fashioned landscape makes my heart ache for a simpler way of life. Surprisingly few people stroll nearby as I make my way up small dirt hills to find two whitewashed chapels. Stepped arches feature stone crosses at the top. They're painted burgundy just like the window shutters. I stop videoing to take a picture of an arch on the roof of another chapel. It looks like a doorway to Heaven.

A Greek man, wearing one plastic glove, talks to an older woman down the street. She's wearing a bright red sweater. Three pelicans stand beyond the low, white wall to their left. It looks like they're eating fish. The man stops speaking, looks over at the birds, and says something in Greek. The woman immediately leans over the wall and begins to chastise one of the pelicans.

She seems quite upset when the pelican keeps trying to pick up something from the ground. It looks like a gray, slimy object. The object falls from the bird's mouth but it bends its neck and scrapes its beak across the ground to pick it up again. The woman continues to scold as she moves briskly around the wall. After the bird drops the object for the third time, she plunges her hand down, grabs it, and seems to say, "Now, you can't get it again."

Since the show is over, I move on to use a public toilette near the bus pick-up point. Two, clean, private stalls with one sink stationed outside the buildings soon sits before me. Chora's flat-roofed buildings hold a certain appeal. The camcorder records one last panoramic view when I step beyond the stone wall enclosing the area. An urge to stay where people are friendly, and seemingly free of greed, overwhelms me.

The bus moves on while I video minnows at the water's edge.

I'm not ready to leave but know I must for we'll soon be on our way to board the Orient Queen for a four-day cruise of the Greek Islands. As I ponder whether to take a cab back to the hotel, I spot another empty bus with its door open and board it. The bus driver enters several minutes later. He sits in the driver's seat without looking inside the bus. I've traveled with the burly man several times but don't remember his name.

"Hello," I say as he begins to shut the doors.

He turns abruptly to stare at me sitting in a middle seat, smiles broadly, and replies with a thick accent.

"Hello, I'm off duty now but another bus will be by in an hour."

I frown as he reopens the doors and tell him I don't want to wait.

"I'm eating lunch now," he says, grinning while waving a brown paper sack, "but you can join me if you like. I usually eat by the new port and then go back to the hotel."

"How long will it take?" I ask not wanting to engage a taxi or stand around for an hour.

His round face morphs into a wide, endearing smile.

"Well, my break is thirty minutes."

"Sure, I'll go with you."

"Okay, I am Kosmas. What is your name?" he asks stretching out his huge hand.

I move slowly from my seat to walk towards him. We shake hands, and after I tell him my name, we're on our way. The new port is minutes away. He turns the engine off and opens the bus doors before quickly climbing down the steps to hold out his hand helping me down as if we're on a date.

"I like big ships," he says walking briskly toward the long dock.

I'm a bit nervous following him but soon he slows down allowing me to catch up.

It's clear he's a sincere man when he starts talking about his departed mother. Sensing she has a message for him, I softly relate the words that pop into my head, without paying attention to what they are.

"My mother would really like you," he says opening the brown, paper sack and pulling out a huge submarine sandwich.

He breaks it in half and offers me the largest half.

"No thanks, I'm not hungry."

We're at the end of a pier when he's done eating. He stuffs the empty, brown sack in his pocket and asks if I'd like to try something fun. I look at him not knowing what to say as he quickly grabs a taut, sturdy rope that holds a huge ship to shore.

"Hop on," he tells me with a broad grin. "Don't worry. I will make sure you are safe."

I feel like a little kid stepping up on the rope. He carefully swings it back and forth while making sure I don't fall. My face flushes. I'm suddenly aware that what we're doing could be dangerous. He stops the rope and easily lifts me down to the ground.

"Fun, eh?" he says with a grin. "Well, it's time to get back to the hotel."

I follow him quickly back to the bus. We make small talk during the short drive back. Kosmas turns the bus engine off when we arrive at the hotel. He turns, looks deep into my eyes, and lowers his voice.

"When are you leaving?"

His face mirrors disappointment when I tell him in two hours.

"I wish we'd met when you first came. There's so much I'd like to show you. When will you be back?"

"I don't plan on coming back."

"Perhaps you will," he announces as he helps me down the bus steps, "or perhaps I will come to America."

It still feels like I've been on a date as I quickly log onto the Internet. Ruth answered my email. She bought another ticket to see Barbra Streisand in October at the Bank Atlantic Center in Fort Lauderdale. Even though she couldn't get a seat next to her and Naomi, I'm thrilled to know I'll see the great Streisand in person after years of buying and singing along to her records. The $203 is small change compared to seeing a living legend and I plan to reimburse Ruth with money from the TDA loan.

Jessica gifts me with a small, silver, butterfly pin encased with rhinestones when I return to the room.

"You're a really good roommate," she announces, "and you deserve nice things. Although they're not yellow diamonds, it's a start."

We soon board the big bus with others after one last look at bougainvilleas and pineapple palm trees reminding me of Fort Lauderdale. Our ride to the small old port is almost too quiet.

"Since we're going to the old port we will not have to walk a long distance with our luggage," Ken assures us. "But this is where it could all go wrong. We must all stay together and help one another. Once we're on the ship everything is terrific."

Jessica and I giggle with anticipation as Ken talks about what to expect onboard. It's late afternoon upon arriving at the small port. We help one another cart luggage to the middle of the small, concrete dock, like a cohesive group of ants. Strong wind whips around us as Ken speaks again.

"This was very easy. Now, with a little bit of luck we'll be onboard watching the sunset before dinner and a show. There are other ships here so as tenders pull up ask them, is this going to the Orient Queen?"

Hours seem to pass but it's less than forty minutes when the first harbor tender approaches. It looks like a small fishing boat and glides past us to stop near the beginning of the dock. Passengers disembark before the tender quickly pulls away and heads back to one of several, large cruise ships about a mile away.

Other tour groups now wait impatiently upon the wide dock as the sun begins to set. We stare at one another in disbelief wondering how long the process will take. Too few tenders continue to drop people off. After a time, they begin to take new passengers out to cruise ships. No one approaches our group. It's clear the tender boat operators speak only Greek. They transport many passengers as the sun sets before us.

It's cooler now and many of us put on hats and scarves. After two hours of waiting, Ken approaches a Greek-speaking tour guide who seems to know the system.

A larger, ferry-type, tender pulls up to the dock in front of us just when we're beginning to become disillusioned. The Greek tour guide motions us forward. Glad to be out of cold wind, we leave luggage behind, with Ken to take on another tender as two Greeks help us aboard.

It's my first trip on a tender boat. I'm thrilled but a bit apprehensive as the tender pulls up to an open doorway near the bottom of the Orient Queen. "We're home, for the next four days," I remark happily. "And there's the door we're going through in the middle of the ocean, okay."

Burly Greeks help us off the tender to the gangplank. After getting the key, Jessica and I practically run to our room anxious to change for dinner. Disappointment is hard to disguise when we enter the tiny, dark, space. A full-size bed, that looks way too small, sits a mere yard away, shoved up against the back wall. A mirror covers most of the room's length on the back wall and another floor length mirror sits on the wall besides the bed.

"This isn't going to work," I adamantly announce looking at Jessica.

"No, I don't think so," she replies shaking her small head back and forth. "We need to get a room with two beds."

The line to change rooms is long but we're quickly rewarded. Within the hour, many people in our group have their own DA cabin on the seventh deck. I'm in Heaven once again retiring for the night directly after dinner as we sail on the Aegean Sea. It's been a long but satisfying day and I want to repeat my treatments before drifting off to sleep.

=

We assemble in the Star's Show Lounge after a filling buffet breakfast the next morning. Our group disembarks shortly after seven o'clock. As fate would have it, I'm in a tour group identified by my maiden name. Surely, this is a sign that I'm in the right place at the right time!

It's windy and the sky is filled with gray clouds at the port of Kusadasi, Turkey. A small modern looking structure, with glass panels reflecting beautiful mountains, stands before us. We walk briskly down the long dock to customs while I video lettering on the building. "When in Turkey...Do what most Turkish people do."

Several men stand at the entrance holding signs with names. We glide past them to a multitude of buses on the other side of the building. A Turkish flag waves in strong wind. Our bus, number twenty-eight, is the last one. My knees ache while climbing steps. I quickly plop into an empty seat, behind the bus driver, to easily video scenery.

A large map hanging at the front of the bus occupies time as we wait for more passengers. The word Mesopotamia, in bold black marker, fills me with excitement. I envision myself washing laundry in the Tigris River. An infant, wrapped in a coarse dark blanket, lies next to me on the ground.

Today's adventure will be on the other side of Turkey, at Ancient Ephesus, near the historic town of Selcuk. Our short, energetic tour guide describes the area in broken English as she smiles brightly. Just as our tour routes in Greece, many of the buildings we pass have several floors and appear fairly new. I'm astounded to hear, the population includes 50,000 people in winter and 300,000, with nearly 700 hotels, during the tourist season.

The perky tour guide proudly points out Adaland, one of two Turkish water parks. As we quickly pass, she notes it's the biggest water park in Europe. The sun rises above a mountain to reveal its Russian design.

"We have no idea why it has Russian architecture," she tells us nervously amid everyone's laughter.

Changing the subject, she informs us, "Ancient Ephesus is one of the most important ancient cities in the world. It has four settlements. Today we will visit the third settlement. Current thought notes the foundation of Efes, the city of the Mother Goddess, was built by Amazons who were human warriors in 14th century B.C."

The bus driver weaves down a two-lane road of tar, often straying into the other lane as we round curves, while following two other buses. After what seems an eternity, but turns out to be only twenty minutes, we arrive and disembark to file through turnstiles. A short stout man, dressed in casual clothes, stands at the rows end inside the area. He looks like a character in "The Soprano's" watching us as we slip tickets into the slot, which causes a turnstile to move.

Another younger man dressed in jeans and a white tee shirt approaches our guide and smiles. He begins to talk with her as she walks to a large map of the area on stilts.

"First of all, let me introduce you to our photographer in Ephesus," she tells us motioning to him proudly. "He will be taking your several photographs, of course, if you let him. It is his job here. He is working as a photographer in Ephesus and in the end when our tour is ending, he will be waiting for us with your photographs in front of our bus. If you want to buy, if you like them, you can buy but it is not an obligation."

The tour group quickly continues past Roman baths and Basilica as our guide begins to explain the early days of Christianity.

"In the first years of Christianity, Christians were thrown to the lions," she explains with a hint of sadness in her usually perky voice, "so people had to design a way to know if they could talk about God with someone."

A sense of doom overwhelms me thinking I was one of those unfortunate souls thrown to the lions. Our guide picks up a small piece of clay, which looks like an old piece of pottery, as she notes the people's use of symbols. She quickly draws a fish on the cement wall before heading down the gravel path.

As we move on to walk through the Odeon, a sense of familiarity overwhelms me. Built to seat 1,400 people, the first few rows are made of marble, while the rest are stones melded into what appears to be some kind of mortar. The upper part of the theatre is decorated with red granite pillars in the Corinthian style.

Our group gathers below but I climb to the top for a birds-eye view. I spot a piece of clay next to my foot and use it to draw a smiley face on the step above me before joining the others. A skinny black and white spotted cat appears as we move towards the Arcadian Way where Mark Anthony and Cleopatra rode in procession. It reminds me of the photo I saw in the study bible, months before I knew I'd be in Turkey.

The cat, I sense, is a guardian. It looks at me, meows politely when I thank it for guarding the area, and jumps up to lie on a large flat slab. As I turn to catch up to the group, it occurs to me I've walked miles every day without feeling any detrimental effects. It seems like a miracle, for although I walked back home, distances were much less. I'm pleased as the photographer turns around to take a quick picture of me to document my accomplishment.

The path is paved with a variety of large, flat, misshaped colored stones so it's easy to catch up with the group quickly. I video a multitude of caves in the distance as our guide discusses ancient times. The surrounding energy is unbelievable. A number of people note goose bumps.

Starcke explains, all we see is Spirit appearing at the material level. It's all Divine energy. Everything represents the Presence and ninety-nine percent of what we see is empty space, consciousness. Unformed Stuff of Matter fills this space.

My eye catches a large piece of stone, with what looks like a delicately carved angel, resting upon another stone slab. It is Nike, the Goddess of Victory. The photographer asks me to pose and quickly snaps the shot.

Our allotted time to tour this magical site seems way too limited. Archeological masterpieces are everywhere. The line moves slowly as I wait to get the power of Hercules by simultaneously touching both sides of Hercules Gate. When it's my turn, I stretch my short arms out. They barely touch two massive carved columns. The photographer takes another picture.

The energy surrounding us invigorates me. Numerous recessed archways catch my attention as the guide talks about houses. It looks like houses were made of red and gray stone. Increased spirit activity lurks beyond doorways. But nothing out of the ordinary shows up in video. I silently thank spirits for letting me sense them in the dark behind iron bars. It seems appropriate to bless and release the energies to other areas. Yes, my work as a Lightworker accelerates here!

Our group passes Hadrian Temple, walks down narrow steps, quickly skirts by the souvenir shop, and continues on to the Library of Celsus. C. Julius built it in honor of his father in 135 A.D. I videotape the Agora after walking down another set of steps on the other side. Everyone else climbs nine stairs to the salon to get a better view of statues in the library. Air is alive with densely packed Stuff of Matter. Everything feels familiar and I sigh trying to remember ancient times. Someone calls me from a distance.

My friends stand near a footprint, carved into marble, when I finally join them. The footprint leads the way to the Brothel. Ramon and I walk slowly from the House of Love while multicolored orbs stream from the sun. When he moves further up the marble road to catch up with Anna, I thank unseen spirits for appearing to me in such beautiful forms.

Our group continues to follow the perky guide as she moves quickly down the marble road. She turns to climb two sets of stone steps into the Great Theatre. The Great Amphitheater where officials arrested St. Paul and cast him out of the city holds much significance to me. It has a capacity of 25,000 spectators with twenty-two flights of stairs, each set by three circular rows. I'm full of energy while climbing higher for a better view. Multicolored orbs, amid green and yellow-gold energy fields, appear as if coming from the sun.

"This is where the lions were," one of my companions says.

Chills fill my body. I again sense life as a persecuted Christian, thrown to the lions, in ancient times. Colorful spirit friends surround me. It takes too much effort to listen, for now I know without a doubt, I died there many years ago. Birds' singing in the distance draw me away as the guide discusses how victims were led to their deaths.

Moving quickly down the steps, I begin to walk the gravel path of Harbour Street. Two dueling cats linger in front of me. My video takes in the action as I silently emit love. I'm still thinking about being fed to the lions and do not wish to investigate the past life. As cats continue to growl, I leave the area.

Currently in November 2009, a sense of wonder and completion fills me having just returned from the Tampa Hay House conference. It was not my first intention to go, but when Mary contacted me asking for company at what she referred to as the "woo, woo conference," I immediately envisioned giving my second book to Louise Hay.

The thought of attending stuck with me for several months until a week before the conference when I finally decided to visit Mary in her new lakeside home. We arrived at the conference site the following evening. The next morning, I registered for the day's pre-conference session along with the general Saturday and Sunday conference.

Pre-conference choices were limited for most sessions filled quickly. But I wasn't disappointed because I didn't feel drawn to them. Denise Linn, a soul coach I'd never heard of who specializes in past-life regression, seemed the perfect choice. I've learned that recalling past lives is useful in releasing stored negative energy and am ready to expand my knowledge.

"I don't believe in coincidence," Ms. Linn announces calmly as I enter the room. "You will be amazed to find that where you sit is exactly where you need to be."

As her words echo throughout the large room, I walk slowly to the front knowing an empty, unsaved seat will be there. A seat in the second row beckons as I ask the lady on the aisle if it's taken.

"No," she says quickly taking her bag off the seat.

Another woman rapidly places a chair next to her as Ms. Linn begins to speak again. Minutes later, Denise asks us to participate in several mind exercises in groups of six. As the front row turns to join us, I wonder why I'm in a group of women, one of whom has a small service dog. It's soon clear that we have two things in common. All of us feel we were unwanted or "accidental pregnancies" and most of us felt unloved while growing up. We each appear to have, or have had, a variety of medical conditions. Three of us report spinal issues.

I seem to be the only one who previously investigated past-life regression. The excitement builds as I ponder the possibility of finally ridding myself of the last medical condition that still seems to occasionally surface. Learning the source of this spinal malady seems like a good way to rid myself of emotional manifestations that hold it in place.

The exercises are exciting as we imagine everyone in a past-life, focus on a past-life of our own, clear negative energies, and determine our totem animals. I'm amazed to vision lives for each of the woman and deliver a meaningful message to one of them during our first assignment.

Two women in the group describe me as a healer who grows herbs to help the community. Others render memories of me as a teacher, a nurturing muse, and a loving, giving soul. When the gal with the service dog speaks about my past life, her eyes fill with excitement.

Their memories appear to match the past-life just imaged as a Shaman in olden days. People eventually turn against him. Someone pierces his back with a spear before he passes to the Otherside.

I'm vaguely familiar with the concept of changing the past and future through decisions made in the present. The possibility first presented itself as I laughed through the trials of McFly in the <u>Back to the Future</u> movie series. Since then, I've discovered that *choices in the present manifest exciting and new things in the future. Denise now informs us we can use our thought to go back into the past to change the present. It's an exciting possibility.*

In Time is an Illusion, *author Chris Griscom notes any thought eventually connects to its counterpart, which images back via manifestation. For instance, posing a question before bedtime can often result in an answer before dawn. We become much more careful with our questions, projections, and desires when we become aware of the "circular arcing" relationship of cause and effect. Manifestation that stems from the level of cosmic synergy pulls in the natural flow of creative synchronicity. This type is preferable to manifestation by the force of personal will, which involves ego.*

Using Denise's idea of changing the past, I envision showing the small village my light body, while reminding everyone we are Light. Slowly, one by one, the villagers remember. They begin to display their real nature, a pure, beautiful, energy of radiating white light. We joyously build a city of glistening Light beings whose nurturing actions mold a new world. News of our city spreads across the land. I'm ecstatic to transmute this negative energy and bring it to the Light of God. When the assignment ends, I gulp water feeling the familiar heat of increased vibration.

The now familiar counterclockwise swirl of energy circulates above my head as I envision the first life lived with Daniel and Rebecca. I regress back to the first time the master of the house calls me forward. Before he has time to abuse me, I stun him by revealing my radiant Light body. I speak softly of our true nature while radiating pure, beautiful, white light.

The master is quickly disarmed. He no longer wishes to feed his ego with worldly pleasures but begins to recognize there's more to life. He cannot deny the pleasure of feeling the One within as his own Light body begins to shine. History changes as we remain in the lush Nubia garden with his wife and son.

Two days later, I enter Denise's shorter session early, wondering why once again. An aisle seat near the front beckons. The couple before me seems vaguely familiar. I've seen them several times over the past three days. My auric energy field expands to insure that only those people at, or above, my level of vibration will sit nearby. Several dozen people parade up and down the aisles looking for seats. The three seats next to me remain empty. It's as if the empty seats are invisible. No one even points to the row where I sit.

Right before the session begins an older woman asks if the seats are taken. I answer no and remove my tote bag from the chair beside me. The older woman, who appears around my age, takes the seat furthest away and seats the man and woman with her closer to me.

Denise guides us through an exercise and I note with great clarity that the man in front of me was very eager to come to earth at this time. When the chairs are turned around, the man, his wife, and the lady beside them are in my group along with the newly seated woman and man.

Once again, as assignments unfold, I consciously find myself in a past life with three people from the group. It's the life where I was persecuted as a Christian and thrown to the lions. This time I not only forgive the rulers (the man and wife who sit in front of me in this life) and the guard who opened the barred prison to lead the Christians to death (the young man who came with his mother and sister) but change the outcome as well.

I envision showing my radiant Light body to the young guard as he opens the prison doors. He quickly remembers our Divine nature, and instead of following orders, leads all the Christians through darkened catacombs to freedom. We live together in peace, and joy, fostering a city of radiant Light bodies. The knowledge of our feat spreads across land to change the world.

As I listen to the groups depictions of my past lives, it seems they have not envisioned this life. The man, who was ruler in the past, saw me as an inspired chemist, with wild hair. His wife caught a glimpse of me as a loving, giving being. The lady sitting in their row saw me as a talented lion and tiger tamer, who loved and was loved by the animals, while the brother and sister appeared unconscious of previous lives.

I leave the room astonished to have now transmuted negative energy from three, possibly more, past lives. It feels great to clear the path of energy from dysfunctional emotions and beliefs and become a co-creator of reality. Since I've changed those past lives in my mind, it's clear that subsequent lives will change as well. But unlike the movie The Butterfly Effect, I do not expect undesired results in subsequent lives. Only time will tell if the few remaining symptoms I occasionally feel will dissipate.

Chris Griscom notes by using past-life regression, we are able to reshape the magnetic astral connections that allow them to continue to play themselves out in this lifetime. This frees the essence of the soul's energy to move through us again, more perfected. And as we release these memories within ourselves, we trigger their release in others.

We must imagine ourselves always in the Now to transcend this illusion. Dr. Page notes, there's no past or future, only different opportunities to show who we are. The past and future exist only in our small minds. We can change them while living in the Now.

Two men stand outside the public WC taking money from all who enter. They frown and adamantly wag index fingers back and forth to stop me from taking pictures. A brown sign with a picture of a small child sitting on the toilet notes, "Fifty cents is enough to feel the magic atmosphere." I'm pleased to get change back in Euros.

A bevy of souvenir shops line the gravel road leading to the bus making it impossible to avoid persistent vendors. Canopies of white gauze-like material shield multiple stalls from the sun. Although I want to see everything, our time is limited for soon we'll be dropped off to shop in town.

"No thank you," I say kindly to each vendor standing between the bus and me.

"Just looking, just looking," a vendor wearing a white tee shirt says loudly while vigorously pointing to his stall. "Just take a look."

My pace quickens as each merchant tries to lure me into his stall to view merchandise. One magnificent camel, its mid-section draped with a colorful blanket, sits on its haunches ahead of me. A sign next to it notes, "If you want to take a picture you MUST pay money, one dollar, one euro." I smile at the ingenuity of the camel's owner and move past him quickly.

A short, dark haired, middle-aged man in jeans stands before the display of pictures next to our bus. He reaches out to hand me several photos when I begin to pass. I can't deny they look great, and since I have very few pictures of myself, buy them all before boarding. We're soon on our way back to the town of Kusadasi. Many of us get off at a recommended store blocks from the ship to shop for twenty minutes.

"You walk toward the ship, no problem," Ken assures us. "Shop and bargain, and walk back to the ship by no later than when we set sail at 11:15 AM."

A younger woman weaving a rug outside a shop immediately mesmerizes me. Her manicured hands work skillfully, pulling out sections of string, as she weaves colored wool between them. The repetition reminds me of two boring jobs in the auto industry, working at age seventeen with Momma, and then twenty in my uncle's shop making car parts early in the morning with Ruth. I'm grateful to be rid of the lifestyle of a young single mom often working two or three jobs at a time to make ends meet.

I enter the Caravanseral to walk quickly through the rug shop and open courtyard before climbing the stairs back to the street. My eyes rest on a small blue hotel sign, "Liman Hotel (Mr. Happys)." Daniel's essence surrounds me. I smile broadly upon recalling the name that was dear to my beloved son. As a young boy, "Mr. Happy" required many hours of dedication behind closed doors. My heart sings while moving toward the long line of people leading back to the port.

A short nap refreshes before rejoining the group in a lounge. Ken discusses our next stop.

"You don't need to pay for a tour," he tells us with authority. "Taxis will take you to where St. John the Divine stayed, in exile from the Roman Empire, while dictating the apocalyptic Book of Revelations to his pupil Prochoros in 95 A.D. Just be certain you get a tender number from the reception desk."

I'm blessed with endless energy after a buffet lunch. It's the perfect time to tour the area. The ship's highest accessible spot offers a place to video eight minutes of aquamarine sea. White table canopies wave in the wind below. The camcorder focuses on a hot tub and swimming pool, before zooming in on widely spaced cruise ships, in front of majestic mountains.

A fellow traveler, exercising in the gym, offers a short respite from the wind. After our chat, I spot Ramon sitting in the Venus Disco Bar up on Compass Deck 11. Polished wooden stairs lead me to a field of fake green grass amid numerous lounge chairs. Loud Greek music echoes throughout the empty area as I push the heavy bar door. A quick look reveals the spiral shaped staircase of polished wood that I must climb to reach him.

He sits alone staring at me as I approach.

"Are you hiding on us or what?" I ask loudly to be heard over the music.

"How you doing?" Ramon asks with a sly grin before taking a long gulp of beer.

Barely able to hear his words amid blasting music, I quickly move on to video the deck at the front of the ship with its helicopter pad. Sparkles of bright green and magenta accompany me while videotaping shimmering sea. Birds glide by as I take in the breathtaking view of water, sky, and majestic mountains while we sail for Patmos forty-seven miles away.

We're closer when we pass through the Strait of Samos also known as the Strait of Mikali. It's the narrowest point between Greece and Turkey passing the island of Samos, famous as the birthplace of Pythagoras.

Arriving near the small (thirteen square miles), serene, island of Patmos, we wait for our turn, while people with booked optional excursions board the tender. It's a small white ferry-type boat featuring polished wood seats decorated with thin cushions.

The usual spirit orbs grace me with their presence as we disembark in front of the Blue Star Ferries building. I purposely lag behind Jessica to talk with other members of our group.

"Let's see how many we can fit into a taxi," I tell them excitedly while videoing the mass of tourists arriving on buses and boats. "We'll pretend we are in college."

"Sam, Sam," Jessica shouts from ahead pointing with vigor at something beyond a tour bus.

It's hot and sunny as we quicken our pace to catch up with her at the outside taxi station, which is thankfully in the shade yards away. Four of us soon pile into a cab with shoulders and knees covered hoping to tour the Monastery of St. John. It's on one of the island's highest points and houses priceless icons and manuscripts.

The young taxi driver wears a white tee shirt and black sunglasses. He follows a tour bus up the winding tarred road while local music blares relentlessly from his car radio. We each try to get him to turn down the radio but he speaks very little English. The bus quickly moves out of sight. We look at one another wondering if the choice to tour alone was wise. Soon our handsome driver pulls ahead of several parked buses, stops the taxi, and opens the doors. He refuses money when we hold it out asking what the ride cost.

"Here, one hour," he tells us in broken English before swiftly driving away.

"Are we going in here?" Kim asks pointing ahead to a brick enclosed area up the hill.

"Yes," Jessica answers while shifting through her purse.

"How do you know?" Kim asks with a note of concern.

"Well, he said cave of Apocalypse."

I look at the open iron gate that's now in front of us and notice a sign embedded in the faded, brown, brick wall to my right.

"Holy cave of the Apocalypse, I was on the island of Patmos."

We enter slowly walking on a cobbled street. Stone benches sit underneath shade trees. The faded, brown, brick wall to our left extends progressively, from about seven to fifteen feet high, as we move further into the complex amid departing tourists.

A large sign on stilts reads, "We welcome you to our Monastery. Please be aware that you are in a holy place of worship. Proper attitude and dress are therefore requested. Tank You."

The misspelled word causes giggles as we pass the sign.

A throng of tourists now walks before us. We follow them to a small, white building with a narrow doorway. Many people stop, before entering, to take a picture of a mosaic tile image above the door depicting St. John dictating to Prochoros.

"Careful Sam," Jessica says as I video the city below from the cliff on the left.

The wind whips around us while I record a panoramic segment of the area sensing spirit friends.

"Come on Sam," Jessica calls out as the women move through the narrow door.

I continue to video after we enter a small alcove. There's a brown, polished, wood door to our right and a small, brick, arch-shaped opening above. It leads to a set of narrow cement stairs to our left. The cost to continue is a mere five dollars.

Wooden ceiling beams and beautiful green foliage complement the room beyond us. Open, white, arched windows, and a white door, highlight the area. Two women, speaking a foreign language, trudge up very steep stairs to our right in the courtyard beyond. Watching as they grab handrails on each side to pull themselves up, we don't need to know their language. We smile and nod our heads as they slowly move forward.

Our trek continues down a different set of steep stairs. Other tourists pass us on their way out. A new set of narrow stairs looms before us but now a line of tourists, on either side, impedes progress.

"We're just going to have to push our way through," I remark thoughtfully to the others, "or we will be here all day."

I take the lead after videoing the landscape of mountain and sea beyond white walls. We move to the bottom of the stairs when there's a break in the slow traffic. The line comes to an abrupt halt at the entrance to a small room. Now we wait wondering what the room holds.

"Probably no photos allowed in here," Kim notes as we start to enter, "no flash allowed."

The darkened room beyond is small and nearly full of tourists.

"Please, please," says a stout, middle-aged, bald man, holding up his hand to stop us.

I sense this is the closest thing to the cave where St. John is said to have lived, and intuitively know, he thinks we are with the larger tour group around us.

"There are only four of us," I tell him holding up four fingers.

Another Turkish-looking man inside the small room speaks.

"Four would be perfect," he says with a flourish of his hand to wave us into the room.

"Come on, let's go," I command thanking him while nudging my companions forward.

Lavish wood antiques adorn the arch-shaped room with its high cement ceiling. Tourists stand before an altar with two red, burning candles. I move to the left covertly videoing a disinterested bearded monk. He's wearing a tall, black hat and scanning the crowd.

Air seems dense with activity but my eyes see nothing out of the ordinary. Someone mentions 95 B.C. as I sense the unseen.

Weaving deftly through the crowd to the far end, I'm able to spot what looks like a cave inside the room. It's crowded with people. I covertly video art on the walls and massive ornate moldings of the room I'm in.

A brilliant odd-shaped orb, of royal purple, appears amid a field of purple and light blue mist when I approach a small, open window. I cannot see it physically, but feel it (and later verify the phenomena when I play back the video). The Stuff of Matter changes constantly as I stand in front of the ornately framed picture of someone holding a halo-bathed child on the back wall. It is, I suspect, St. John.

I trust the unseen, and know I've experienced something few people do, while quietly whispering to Jessica, "I'm going out."

"This is amazing," she replies. "Did you go into the cave?"

"Don't need to," I reply heading back through the throng of people to the door.

A rooster crows in the distance as I spot an orb with my eyes. (When I view the video later, the green and magenta colored Stuff of Matter reminds me of videos completed earlier in the year.)

I'm still shaking with excitement when Jessica joins me outside the room. We remain unaware that walking down the steps to the Grotto leads to niches in the wall that mark the pillow and ledge, used as a desk by the author of the Book of Revelation, and the crack in the rock, made by the voice of God honoring the Holy Trinity.

There's so much more to see but it's time to meet our taxi driver. We stop to use public toilets on our way out. They're clean but lack paper so I'm grateful for the extra tissue in my pocket.

Orbs are everywhere minutes later as I video a lovely looking tree-lined, dirt path. I sign deeply knowing it will remain unexplored.

"Sam," Jessica calls, "come on."

"I'm coming," I tell her distracted by orbs. "I'm just catching some special light. You see that? As they say on the ship, they won't go without me."

I'm in no hurry to leave, while videoing white-gold streams of brilliant light from the sun, along with a display of purple, orange, and magenta orbs, amid green mist.

We walk briskly back towards the entrance a minute later. Our taxi driver arrives immediately. The four of us quickly pile into the car ready to go back to the ship. His radio is still too loud for us to communicate. We tap him on the shoulder, point to the radio and motion with our hands, pretending to turn a dial.

He drives quickly after turning the radio down. Our taxi soon passes the road leading back to the ship. We have no idea where we're going and joke about being kidnapped in Turkey. It's time to put our faith in the Universe and trust we'll end up where we're meant to be. After a few minutes, our driver stops in the middle of the street where tourists mill about as if anxious to get somewhere.

"Be here 5:30," he turns back to tell us before we open the door.

"What time is it?" I ask.

"It's a quarter to five," Jessica answers as the taxi driver moves quickly away.

The four of us stare at tourists walking up a long hill behind a short, white, stone wall. Jessica gets advice from a group of tourists as I video the Orient Queen below. I hear her tell the others we need to climb the hill.

"We got to hike all the way up there?" I ask incredulously. "Are you kidding me?"

"See that castle-like building behind the other one?" Jessica asks. "That's where we need to go."

Looming before us stands a broad staircase leading to the monastery's entrance, built more than 900 years ago. Green moss grows out of gray stone walls to our right as we climb. I lag behind minutes later as we walk through an enclosed area of tall, decorative, white buildings with brown shutters. The other women are looking at sale merchandise when I catch up. Not interested in shopping, I move ahead.

After following a couple down what looks like a narrow alley, I come across a sign that points back to the monastery. A line of tourists, weaving further up the stairs, soon looms before me. It seems almost fruitless to join them for there's not much time left. Two older men walk slowly ahead with canes as I video their climb.

Suddenly, I spot two women from our tour group heading down the stairs.

"I'm so glad to see you," I tell them with relief. "If you see my people please tell them I'm here."

240

The women point to the top of the stairs. "They're up there," they say in unison, "Audrey and…"

I quickly interrupt them pointing down the hill. "Thanks. No, I'm with Jessica, Kim and her mom. They were shopping so I left them down there."

They smile and nod while continuing down the stairs to avoid stopping the line.

The throng of tourists slowly passes through a courtyard of sale merchandise but I keep moving ahead towards the Monastery of the Apocalypse. I want to, at least, get a glimpse of the library and treasury of relics, icons, silver, and vestments of luxurious fabrics.

Another set of steep stairs stands in my way as I follow the large man with a cane. We soon pass quickly through an area, with three colorful mosaics recessed in the wall, which opens to a large square. The monastery's bell sits beyond a white stone arch amid a clear blue sky. Its sturdy rope hangs down into the courtyard.

Suddenly, a tour guide speaks from a room filled with people ahead of me. Her accent is so thick I cannot understand a word she says. Daniel would love the room my eyes now rest upon. Beautifully painted walls and ceiling complement the ornately carved wooden door and moldings. I record it all before moving slowly to another majestic room.

A man approaches just as a line of green and magenta colored orbs fill the field. I only understand the word "Madame," but know he's telling me I can't video as he wags his finger back and forth while speaking. I keep my camera on but aim it at the floor and catch a few more orbs while slowly walking away.

The room I'm in now is too beautiful to describe appropriately. It has majestically painted walls and things hanging from the ceiling, which look like large, silver, Christmas tree ornaments amid temperature gauges. I sense spirit activity and think I'm seeing large silver chandeliers in a room with walls of glided gold.

Four black kittens sit clumped together outside. They rest quietly around a small pineapple palm tree in a large, orange, clay pot near the WC. One looks up at me as I reach my free hand out to touch it. The others don't budge at all. Nothing can capture the smell in the WC so I decide to wait until we get back to the ship.

The stairs to the small museum of priceless treasures loom before me but I decide to skip them after passing a burly man with a flowing beard dressed in black. I've missed the monk's dining room and the old bakery as well but am happy to see Jessica in the courtyard.

"Honey, I'm home," I say with delight.

"I lost Kim and her mom," she answers with a note of concern pointing down the hill. "They stopped to shop."

"Yeah, I know. We have fifteen minutes so I was thinking of starting down."

"I haven't gone up yet," she tells me heading for the museum stairs.

"I haven't gone up either but we only have fifteen minutes."

"Well, let's rush up and rush down," she says walking briskly ahead.

"Okay, we don't want to miss our number four taxi," I note, trudging behind her as she ascends a set of narrow gray stairs.

Two signs lead to the museum. One sign points to a set of stairs that I choose to avoid.

"Oh, this is the place I'd like to spend some time in," Jessica says looking beyond the museum entrance. "If I could find stairs to go there…" A large room with an open window looms at the end. "If I can just find a way to get up there…"

I look into the museum and notice a sign that notes the entry fee is six Euros. "Oh, we don't have time and it costs six Euros," I call out to Jessica as she delves further into the room beyond.

"We don't have time anymore," she replies turning around to enter another room that she thinks might be a little cell. "Watch your step," she warns while looking back and moving down a step.

I follow her into a spooky, dimly lit room thinking of the long trip back downhill. "This is where they kept the bad priests," I announce passing a barred window covered with plywood.

Jessica moves way ahead of me toward the daylight steaming though an open window as I look up to see a log ceiling.

"Let's go back down," she says. "All roads lead to the exit, hopefully."

I follow behind her at a fast pace. We have thirteen minutes to get back to the point where the taxi dropped us off. The walls edge offers a panoramic view of the scene below us.

"I'm starting back down," Jessica says continuing behind members of our tour group.

"Okay, I'll meet you," I reply, sighing over the magnificent blend of land, sea, and sky.

Time slips away while I allow myself the freedom of being in the Now. The peace and stillness of heart and mind overwhelms me. A car backfires as I make my way back along the white wall.

Jessica calls out, "The taxi is here Sam."

The four of us pile into the number four taxi not really knowing if we're on our way to the ship. We have two more hours before the ship leaves.

"So how many kids do you have?" Kim asks politely making small talk.

"I have a daughter that's thirty-three," I reply.

"Just one?" she asks. "Don't you have a son?"

"Well, yes, I have a son but he's a spirit now."

The taxi radio blares as the dispatchers' voice fills the air. We watch with apprehension when our driver comes within inches of hitting another car as we barrel down the road.

"That was fun," Kim replies clutching her camera to her chest.

"Oompa," I say cheerfully noticing other drivers moving way too fast along the road.

A purple and blue triangular set of orbs enter the car on my side as Kim changes the subject to our uphill adventure. Minutes later, the driver delivers us safely to the pier. We're soon on the Orient Queen heading for the island of Rhodes.

Moving to the dining room after a nap, once again I'm glad Daniel guided eating habits months before the trip. Now I eat more slowly, keeping my mouth shut, while paying attention to the people around me. I'm grateful to have changed my bedtime as well for our early morning jaunts would be hard to do if I still went to sleep at 3:00 AM.

After dinner and the Greek dancing show, a number of us meet in the Venus Disco on Compass Deck 11 to dance. The Myers rum and Coke mix in my brain as I watch the others until a man

243

from our group persuades me to my feet. It's been many years since I've danced. Expressing myself through music feels great.

Exhausted and out of breath after a short time, I stop and head back to my quiet room. Disappointment sets in when the treatment CD plays without fanfare. Sleep comes easily.

=

My CD player again operates normally in the morning. A small elevator leads me to the breakfast buffet after the daily ritual. Streams of blue flow from the crescent moon as sun begins to rise. Atmosphere changes entertain while sipping cappuccino.

A young Indian man clearing tables soon asks if I need anything.

"No, thank you," I reply, with a smile staring at his pock marked face. "I have everything I need."

"Have you ever been to India?" he politely inquires.

"No, no, but I'd like to go there."

"You should come. You can stay at my house in NGO and it won't cost you a thing. I'll take care of everything."

I'm stunned and stare with disbelief before replying. "Thank you. I'll consider it."

He nods his head and moves on to the buffet as Kim and her mom sit down.

"What was that all about?" they ask in unison.

They're concerned when I tell them. Kim quickly asks if I gave him my room number. I assure them I have not.

Conversation moves on to the day's excursion at Rhodes. It's known as "The Island of Roses," where hillsides greet visitors with displays of rock roses.

The old fortified city, built by the Knights of St. John of Jerusalem, looms before us later as Jessica and I disembark. It's a short distance away and looks like an old castle. I'm truly living in the Now videoing our approach from across the street a block away. Tourists from various countries head toward arched entrances, amid the sound of police whistles. I stop to video a souvenir stall with seashell wind chimes like the ones sold at home.

"Today we are in…," my voice trails off. "Where are we?"

Jessica, unconcerned by my memory loss, quickly answers. "Rhodes."

"Yesterday we were in Turkey," I note. "I'm not sure if this is a Greek island or if we're in Turkey."

Medieval walls, enclosing the old inner city, extend more than two miles before us. They vary in thickness from six to forty feet. Spirit friends are near as a traffic cop, wearing a bright green vest, blows a whistle to help us quickly cross the busy street. A cobbled path on the other side makes me feel sorry for people with thin soles on their shoes. It feels like we are walking on little solid eggs.

Excitement fills the air as we pass through St. Catherine's Gate. Shops on either side of the paved path compete for attention. Overpriced ship beverages spur me to seek out a grocery store. I still limit fluids when on excursions, to reduce bathroom trips, but now feel very thirsty. My small water bottle is almost empty and I need more water, and Diet Coke, for the ship. It seems odd, but the soda no longer causes my bladder to burn.

Everything interests us as the path changes to large, flat stones. We giggle with delight when Jessica fondles small purses that look like kitties. My video quickly documents artwork hanging outside a shop. Orbs from the sun catch my eye before spotting what looks like a knight in shining armor. It's on top of a gray and red stone building to our left.

"Look, look," I call out marching toward the Clocktower entrance before quickly ascending a set of narrow stairs. "Will I be meeting you at the top?"

"I don't know," Jessica replies as she continues to take pictures with a disposable camera.

"Well, I can meet you on the way down," I announce, continuing to climb to an egg-shaped cobblestone path.

No one is around as I reach for the brass handle on an ancient wooden door. It fails to open the door. Jessica sighs behind me. We shrug shoulders before moving down the cobbled path to another entrance. There's so much to document that we constantly look in all directions to avoid missing a thing.

It costs five Euros, including the drink of your choice, to visit the Clocktower. Our time in Rhodes is limited so we slowly make our way to the castle in the hot sun. Jessica's shoes have thin soles making it tough to walk on the cobblestones.

"There's shade up here Jessica," I announce. "Can I entice you to move faster toward the shade?"

She groans as I quicken my pace to reach the shaded archway where our path flattens out once again.

We bolt through the iron gates of the Palace of the Grand Master of the Knights of Rhodes feeling victorious. The magnificent, gray stone building looms before us looking like a medieval castle in a fairy tale. Jessica and I pass through the huge arched entrance, pay our admission, and trudge slowly up two, long, flights of wide stairs.

"Do we have to walk down too?" Jessica asks.

"Well, we can always jump out a window," I reply with a chuckle.

The Archaeological Museum within the Grand Master's Palace is nearly empty. I'm in awe looking at what appears to be delicate golden statues while wondering why there are so few tourists. Multicolored stone walls remind me of two basements of multicolored cement left behind in Michigan many years ago. The days of painstakingly painting my home are well behind me.

It's difficult to believe the building was Hospital of the Knights as I wander the area spellbound. Superb mosaics are just as impressive as the polished wood ceiling several stories above. A delightful breeze summons me to an open, wooden window for a few fleeting seconds. There are no screens to block out incoming birds or bugs.

Two large birds rest on top of another window inside the gargantuan room. I point them out to Jessica. One leaves its post in the sun to glide swiftly past as we giggle in delight. I consider it a blessing, sensing spirits, as we move on to other rooms.

Jessica gradually shuffles on. I stop frequently to video antique wood and golden angels, while skirting around roped off mosaic floors. Delicately hand carved antiques stir memories of past lives. The intricate craftsmanship is amazing. It no longer matters that Jessica is out of sight as I navigate a maze of narrow stairwells, small rooms, and long hallways.

"Hi honey," she says later after I climb a set of stairs to reach the open courtyard.

We leave together discussing how our lives changed while strolling past medieval buildings, towers, turrets, and emblazoned facades. It's such a pleasure to wander through the winding alleys. Many cats grace us with their presence. Vines, overflowing with grapes, hang above doorways in an empty back alley before we enter the throng of people once again. We happily head into the bowels of the city knowing souvenir prices will be cheaper the further we are from the port.

I'm thankful to document the picturesque city with video. Jessica heads towards the Old Town Theatre and Greek Folk Dances while I investigate the architecture of brown, stone buildings. A rooster's crow summons me forward, past narrow alleyways lined with motorbikes, to a large pen where it sits among a bevy of chickens.

Passing the fenced-in ruins of the Roman Public Building of the Agora, I nearly trip over a snail shell, and stop to put it in my bag. Motorbikes fly past when I turn left to move down a narrow cobbled path. Two small boys speak to each other in Turkish as they look excitedly at several magazines hanging from the wall of a small stall. They appear five to seven-years-old and walk slowly away as I approach. I chuckle softly while passing girlie magazines.

Inner city, narrow, cobbled paths are devoid of tourists. A neighborhood convenience store sits hidden among private apartments. I head back to the ship after purchasing liters of Coke and spring water, both for less than a dollar. A tourist-filled courtyard leads me to the street beyond medieval walls.

It's soon a pleasure to sit outside in the sun sipping tea with members of our tour group. Feeling homesick when the cup is empty, I rise to use the ship's Internet. Forty dollars for thirty minutes seems reasonable since I'm on a cruise ship in a foreign country.

Ruth's email notes her second attempt to get us seats together for the Streisand concert was unsuccessful. "Anything better would have cost us a thousand dollars," she writes. "I checked two other websites and the best tickets left were going for $20,600. Don't want to see her that bad so we'll have to take binoculars."

I'm just happy to be included for I thought Barbra stopped touring.

"There's going to be a Captain's Cocktail Party before dinner tonight," I type filled with excitement. "This is way cool. I will not be back on the Internet for there is just way too much FUN to have :-) See you soon for we board our plane Friday at noon :-("

A short nap rejuvenates me before the evening's festivities.

Enjoying the night's entertainment in the Star's Show Lounge after dinner makes me feel like part of the "Jet Set." My

247

friend Luke was a great fan of the Broadway performance Cats and often spoke of it. Having missed the show, I'm now pleased as actors grace the stage in a variety of cat costumes.

=

Red lights line the shore before dawn as we dock on the eleventh day of our trip in Heraklion, the capitol of Crete. It's a mountainous elongated island, the biggest of the islands, and the mythological home of Zeus.

We board an excursion bus to visit the reconstructed Palace of Knossos and Archaeological Museum before eight o'clock. Sir Arthur Evans discovered the elaborate palace in 1899 and it dates back to 4,000 B.C. It's the mythical Labyrinth of King Minos and the seat of ancient Minoan culture. Our group will view fantastic palace ruins for ninety minutes before moving on to the archeological Museum in Heraklion.

A petite tour guide continuously scans the area for the rest of the group after we leave the bus. She looks like a little bird, perched precariously on a branch, as she stands tottering on a low wall holding a sign with the number two.

Orbs reflect in the sun as she discusses the palace layout. Triangular shaped orbs of orange, purple, magenta, and green are much more interesting as I wander alone on a red path. The orange orb looks like two triangles with one facing up and the other down.

Watchful guards are not as evident as we tour the fantastic ruins. Sensing unseen company, I follow a brilliant stream of green mist further down the path. The mist changes to reveal a variety of rainbow colors. Wonders totally mesmerize upon entering a palace room near the north entrance. Many multicolored orbs flow in through the window to greet me. After thanking the Universe for my gifts, I continue down the path to join others.

We stand in a slow moving line to view a mural of some mythological creature on the back wall of the Throne room. A dove coos in the distance. I long to sit in the shade on one of the benches beyond the short,

stone wall but console myself by videoing one of many cats on the immense property.

Later in the restroom, we pay a dollar to get toilet paper from a friendly attendant. She speaks Turkish and holds up her hand to stop me from taking her picture. I use the tissue in my pocket instead of the thin sheets of paper handled by the stranger. I'm soon happy to sit on the bus as we make our way to the archeological Museum in Heraklion.

Unlike the nearly empty museum in Rhodes, a multitude of guides, all talking at once, pack this simply styled building. I move at my own pace ignoring them all. The museum displays many treasures found during excavations, mainly contained in glass display cases. Long windows line the top of the walls offering natural light.

Women guards, dressed in skirts and summer tops, ignore me as I wander through the museum away from tour guide clusters. Video records marble and alabaster figures before filming multicolored pottery. It's soon my pleasure to move outside, away from the crowd.

Numerous small gray taxis round the bend in the road as I watch while waiting for the rest of the group. When the rain comes, I escape to a covered ledge and watch it flow. The air now seems more densely packed with swiftly moving Stuff of Matter as I stand happily with a member of our tour group. A large trailer that functions as the museum restroom stands before us. It reminds me of the Indian reservation off Alligator Alley in the Florida Everglades. The door is wide-open, exposing small, open windows above each stall.

Later, our tour guide discusses fountains and drinking water as we make our way to the shopping area in Heraklion. The Morosini fountain at the center of town is alive with pigeons. I pass quickly to find a stall with soaps made of olive oil and sandalwood. They are unique and lightweight gifts. Back on the bus, several of us point to a McDonalds on the way to the modern harbor. We board the ship before eleven o'clock in the morning.

Gray-white, puffy clouds highlight a baby blue sky as the ship cuts through tranquil waters. Hours later, as we sail through waters of dark blue to sulphur green, the view approaching Santorini is spectacular. Many of us enjoy it from the ship's windy open decks. Santorini is a breathtaking island accessible only by cable car or donkey.

It's soon time to tour the town of Thira on the northern edge of the Sea of Crete. Thira is set on top of sheer cliffs that lead to a precipitous summit 1,916 feet above sea level. Severely damaged by an earthquake in 1956, it has largely been rebuilt. A crescent shaped rim of cliffs around the harbor, formed by a volcanic eruption occurring in about 1,500 B.C., encases the town. The massive eruption caused half the island to sink below sea level forming the bay now called 'Caldera.'

A reminder of tender guidelines, spoken in three languages, breaks through silence. Our group must get a tender boat disembarkation number from the Information Desk and wait in the lounge until called. We'll explore on our own what some people say might be the fabled lost continent of Atlantis. Conversation focuses on two routes up the mountain. The donkey ride seems much more appealing since I've already experienced being on a crowded cable car, in Vancouver, years ago.

"I'm going to take a donkey up," I finally announce to those around me on the small tender.

"Are you?" Someone asks. "Won't that take longer to get to the top?"

"It's probably slower but it doesn't matter," I calmly reply. "It's the ride that's important not the destination, it's the journey."

Several foreigners began to clap and sing as we slice through deep blue sea. Everyone smiles and claps along.

We soon begin the long climb to the donkey line. It's filled with people and coils up cement steps shielded by stone walls on either side.

"I wish I could capture the smell to put a little more realism into this video," I remark to companions with a grin.

Minutes later, I'm perched securely on a brown donkey. The polite donkey climbs slowly up 566 long, wide, steps on the zigzag path. It periodically stops to allow other donkeys to pass on their way back down the trail. I thank him and let him know how much I appreciate his gentleness as we mosey past donkeys and people walking in the opposite direction on the stone path.

"You're just too good to me," I remark nervously, patting the donkey's neck affectionately with one hand, while holding the operating video camera in the other.

My words make a difference as the donkey continues to move steadily up the path. We quickly leave others behind as their donkeys stop to rest.

"Did I tell you I love you donkey?" I ask as the donkey moves forward with its clanging bell necklace. "Yes, I do. You're a wonderful donkey. You may go at your leisure."

I need no assistance to control my donkey for we are one. Although it's difficult to hang on and video as the donkey climbs, I'm having the time of my life. I giggle as the others catch up and pass for now there's a Greek man prodding their donkeys to move faster. Love and gratitude overwhelm me when we reach the top. I'm immensely happy to have chosen such a grand experience.

A spectacular, panoramic view sits below. Ships look like toys in a bathtub. Rays of light from the sun touch the Aegean Sea, amid small islands beyond the cliff. My SOM friends and I stroll past blue-domed churches, and white washed houses with blue shutters, before stopping to enjoy the sunset. It's a pleasure to stand near Franco's bar overlooking the harbor. Piano music wafts through the air as orbs stream from the sun.

I move on to step 573. A familiar song fills the air. I've passionately sung Bonnie Raitt's "I Can't Make You Love Me" during many times of turmoil. "I feel the power" fills the air as my camcorder zooms past an empty bar, to video the sea, beyond an open door. I'm happy just to be where I am. The throng of tourists embraces me beyond step 588 as I video the sea near the Hotel Atlantis.

An entirely different experience waits on the other side of the island. Small cars, motorbikes, and buses travel amid residents moving to and fro. Tree trunks painted white look too sterile. I quickly make my way, along the wide street, back to small, cobbled roads.

A skinny pre-teen boy wearing a white tank top, shorts, and cap sits up against the wall overlooking the sea. He plays a harmonica and beats on a tambourine. As many others, I drop coins into the plastic container at his feet before moving on to look for friends.

Kim and her mom are a short distance away at the café Del Mar overlooking the harbor. The houses below look small as I video while discussing my donkey ride. Beautiful classical music wafts through the air.

"I can see our long walk down," one of the women notes looking over the edge of the white wall.

"Oh, I'm not walking down," I quickly announce. "I'm taking the cable car honey. There's no way I would walk that."

The sun continues to set while we enjoy cocktails and snack on chips.

"I just remembered," I note with surprise. "I blessed my donkey and patted him and now I'm eating chips with that hand!"

"Oh, oh," Kim says. "Would you say that again for my video?"

I oblige her with a smile while eating another chip.

"What's that?" she remarks hearing bells in the distance.

"Seven o'clock. It's the church bells."

"What time do we have to start back?"

My eyes remain on the gorgeous sunset above our ship, sitting amid small mountainous islands and sea.

"We have to be back by 8:15 at the latest."

"It's going to take us a good twenty-five minutes to walk down."

"Did you ever see that movie staring Nicholas Cage and Meg Ryan where he's an angel and she's a doctor? I'm reminded of it now, for in the movie, all the angels stand to watch the sun and I'm seeing a lot of magenta colored orbs."

"What do you mean?"

"Remember when you got all that static in your video?"

"Yeah, that was weird," Kim replies, looking perplexed as she scans the sky.

"That's when I saw a lot of magenta colored orbs too," I tell her filled with wonder, as a strong wind whips around us. "It's a sign of loving spirit energy."

"There go the donkeys," her mother calls out from the table behind us. "They're taking them to bed."

We continue appreciating the moment while videoing the scene below until it's time to return to the ship. All too soon, the serene restaurant view is behind us. Our pace quickens after sprinting down narrow, gray stairs. My breath stops briefly, upon seeing the most spectacular sunset that I've ever been privileged to view. After a quick glance, I push past the tourists standing against white walls posing for pictures.

252

It's a struggle to return to the ship because I want to stay in this land of luxury and freedom. Music from a local bar fills the air as I ponder how to make a living that enables me to prolong my stay. "You don't have to worry if you have no money. People on the river are happy to give." It's Credence Clearwater Revival singing "Proud Mary," the song Tina Turner sang so well.

A long sigh fills the air as I continue down wide, gray steps, yards ahead of Kim and her mom. The cobbled path takes me to another set of steps leading up to a magnificent display of fresh vegetables and fruit.

"Where are you going Sam?" a friendly male voice asks.

"Cable car," I reply out of breath looking up to see several SOM friends coming from the opposite direction.

"We're walking down the donkey path," he replies as the group quickly passes me. "Join us. The cable car line is about a forty-five minute wait, too long to make it back on time."

"Thank you for being here," I reply with joy making an abrupt turn to follow them.

Before long, we begin to sprint down the steep zigzag of 587 stone steps. The islands beauty again summons me to stay even as I note the ship's lights cutting through twilight. It's difficult to concentrate as I take in the landscape while avoiding piles of donkey dung. "Goodnight, sleep well," I tell the donkeys passing to the left.

My friends are now out of sight as I pause to rest amid the

tingling of donkey bells. A long donkey parade moves up the steep cliff to sleep.

"Okay, let's not trample the lady," I remark loudly weaving through the steady mass. "Goodnight guys, sleep tight."

"Sam, I can't believe you're walking down," one of my SOM friends says from behind me.

I turn as a hand brushes against my shoulder to see two men on donkeys.

"Don't touch me when I'm videoing and avoiding donkey dung," I reply with glee.

They pass and continue down the wide steps. Locals asking for payment to walk on the path accost friends ahead of me. I've already paid one a dollar and been approached by another for payment.

"Just walk away with a big smile on your face," I tell Roberta.

"Good advice," a stranger declares as he quickly passes by, "for that's just what you have to do. Just walk away, you're absolutely right."

We all meet again at the tender barely making it back in time before the Orient Queen sails for Piraeus.

Actors sing, "Tears on my pillow" as I enter the showroom after a short rest. I'm a master of emotions glad to be in charge of my own feelings. No one causes tears unless I allow them to and I choose not to give away my power. I'm so grateful to be on my own enjoying a live show on a ship in the middle of the Aegean Sea.

Later after paying my bill for costly bottled water onboard, I set my large green suitcase outside the cabin door. At this point, I'm delighted when the CD player skips over several tracks of the treatment CD to play "The Best is Yet to Come" by Carole King. It's great to sense Daniel's presence and know there will soon be more manifestations in my life. Sleep comes after realizing I'll get my passport back in the morning.

=

We sail through the night.

In the morning, the CD switches between "In the Name of Love" and "The Best is Yet to Come" when I repeat prayers.

After a hearty breakfast, I walk with my SOM friends past the ship's duty free shop for the last time on our way out to the sunlight of Piraeus. It's September 22 as the Homeric Tours representative leads us to the bus for one last ride to the airport. A small white orb follows alongside us as I video the ride not wanting to miss a single thing before our long flight home.

The airport looms before us much too soon for me. We're quickly herded into a small glass enclosed area. Waiting for our flight to depart is pure agony. Many of us feel as if in quarantine. When we venture out to use the WC, beyond our cage, it's clear we must go back through security to return to the group.

The outside air temperature is fifty degrees below Fahrenheit as the plane nears London. I'm astonished to note we're moving at 632 miles an hour. We've traveled 1,471 miles in 169 minutes. There are eight hours and forty-nine minutes to go when my fifteenth videotape ends. Grateful to have made the trip that widened my horizons in a whole new way, I store the camera away.

:-)

Chapter Twenty-Six

Contrasting Times

"A mind is like a parachute, it has to open to work."
Frank Zappa

The Center is now a major part of life. Spiritual studies and computer work keep me busy between events. My new project involves transferring camcorder videos to the laptop. It's easy to do because the new camcorder came with computer software.

Ego informs me everyone wants to see videos of Greece and Turkey. I promptly contact family members after completing the first DVD to schedule a viewing. Nobody seems interested. Ruth wants to plan a Tampa trip to see our sister Sarah. Rebecca asks me to stay with Samuel, for five days, when she goes on her first cruise. I happily agree to both opportunities.

Samuel, Princess, and Kitty become the focus of my attention four days later.

I'm still looking outside myself. The horoscopes in Horizons Magazine garner interest upon returning to the house on 47th Drive. Ms. Lee's predictions are particularly encouraging. It's oddly reassuring to know that beliefs, dreams, and goals will evolve and change. I'll continue to purge things not for my highest and greatest good for a few years, but after Pluto's transit, will be better than ever, with no worries.

Now it's easier to create a new life consciously making changes as needed. Emotional reaction fades quickly. When James angrily reacts because my Visa bill is over the usual amount, I calmly take full responsibility for travel expenses. I'm grateful the TDA loan money will cover monthly payments until Dad's lawsuit check arrives.

A bit of the daily visioning process flows from brain to lips as soon as he leaves the room. "I am grateful for my generous and considerate husband who sees the Truth and values experience enough to do what is right."

The telephone rings. It's back in my room for James' friends now contact him through his cell phone. Someone at the Center wants to know if I'll be in charge of a snack table on Saturday. The Center rented out space for a health fair and agreed to have snacks available for the public.

"I know you're Hospitality Coordinator," Mark notes cheerfully. "We just need someone for eight hours to sell healthy snacks to people who attend. We'll reimburse you for the cost of the snacks and you can keep the profits."

I quickly agree to help. My world is still a mix between SOM, and ego-based desires, as I hang up the receiver to quickly log onto the Internet. It's easy to change the signature line in my email from the old business motto to "Promoting Spiritual Growth through Peace, Love, and Harmony for all living things."

Questions on topics researched for the business are referred to colleagues before signing petitions to end battles in Iraq and Darfur. Rev. Bump's email, thanking tour members for experiencing Greece, prompts me to offer copies of my DVDs. There's still a strong feeling of lack and limitation as I ponder the costs. Yet, I'm sure my SOM friends will treasure the gift.

Anna's email arrives asking if we can get together after church on Sunday morning. I thank Spirit for another friend of like-mind but decline thinking it would mean another service to attend. The Internet connection breaks off after emailing her my telephone number so we can choose another time.

Leah and I share lunch and a movie later in the week. The thought of sharing experiences with her fills me with joy. It seems like divine intervention that we're so much alike despite our difference in chronological age. I immediately love her condo for it sits on a canal yards away from a man-made lake. During lunch, we talk like two castaways glad to be home and lose track of time. There's barely enough time to get to the movie.

Today's date is 10-5-2006 and now it's 9:37 PM. The printer continues its odd behavior noting it is 1-5-1970 at 2:14 PM. The difference in dates and times is now standard. I ignore the phenomenon to finish studies before quickly falling asleep.

The next morning a sunrise message prompts me to wake.

God is the Creator of all living things.

It's shortly after daybreak when the morning ritual completes. My printer's display claims it is 1-1-1970 and 11:55 AM.

Buying food for the health fair offers a refreshing break. Choosing portable healthy foods is easy. I purchase individual cheeses, apples, juice, low-fat treats, and other things before dropping them off at the Center on Friday.

Saturday is the nineteenth anniversary of my marriage to James. Scattered clouds fill the sky. I rise early to dress and drive to the Center. The parking lot is empty and there's no sign announcing the event. For the next hour, I make coffee and set up the food table.

The day is excruciatingly long as ten people trickle in. Vendors leave by two o'clock. Most of the food is left for the Center but I depart happy to be of service and surprised to be reimbursed.

More people attend Sunday night's service the next evening so I'm ecstatic for Rev. Van Damme Rance and Rev. Rance. They focus on love and clearly adore their occupation. It's truly a joy to see more people appreciate their message of Truth. When the service ends, I thank them both before quickly cleaning up the coffee station.

Twenty-four hours later, Rev. Peck welcomes guest speaker Paul Bunting at the "Sisters in Spirit" Covered-Dish Dinner. Paul is a Fitness and Alignment Yoga Instructor, who speaks on "Total Alignment Science." I'm not a fan of Yoga but enjoy all of Heidi's events for she's always upbeat and friendly. She intuitively knows what I need.

Paul's talk is interesting and soon I'm up along with everyone else doing an easy exercise for the spine. It's wonderful to be around other women of like-mind.

The following morning, I'm drawn to check email after repeating the usual treatments. A message from Mary surprises me. It begins by noting there was no answering machine to take a message when she telephoned. As I continue to read, it's obvious she has better things to do than respond to three weeks of forwarded political petitions.

Her husband Seth is on Hospice at home. The incurable disease that left him deaf, wheelchair bound, and unable to care for his basic needs for many years, is running its course. Mary asks for prayers to help him peacefully pass to the Otherside. I telephone her immediately, agree to contact ministers, and arrange to visit.

Driving westward during the forty-minute drive to Seth and Mary's suburban home affords me the pleasure of seeing a beautiful sunset. A huge, red sun peeks out occasionally, amid clouds of pink, orange, and gray, making the ride an unexpected pleasure. It slips below the horizon when I reach their manicured lawn and pull into the wide drive. A friendly nurse opens the front door. She slips quietly into the dusk after letting me in.

Mary's voice leads me to the master bedroom. Tension and anxiety fill the air as I make my way across the polished, hardwood floors. Seth, who now looks like a skeleton, lies in the middle of a hospital bed with closed eyes. Mary talks to his mother who sits quietly in one of several chairs around the bed. Both women appear exhausted.

"Time to take a break Mom," Mary announces.

The older woman rises and slowly makes her way to the outside patio to smoke. Mary and I take over the watch. My friend describes the last few weeks noting Seth's mother has already lost a daughter to cancer. We sit and chat for several hours.

I'm shocked when the two women agree to let Seth watch his favorite "CSI" TV show. They position his lanky body into a wheelchair for the trip to the living room. I quickly excuse myself preferring to sit on the back patio. The beautifully landscaped yard is a pleasure to see. It's soothing to gaze at the swimming pool, and multiple statues of creatures, as I decide the best way to help Seth.

When Mary joins me, we talk of the good times Seth enjoyed despite ever-increasing limitations. Those times are over now. It's clear Seth wants to go Home but he's afraid of dying. Mary sounds afraid of the unknown as well.

"No one really dies Mary," I say filled with emotion. "Daniel taught me that."

"Well," says Mary with a sly grin while kicking off her shoes, "we'll see because Seth and I made a deal."

"A deal?" says I filled with curiosity.

"Yes. A deal that he will contact me from the Otherside, showing up here in a different form. We're still working out details, but he's agreed to let me know he's okay, once he gets over there."

"That's a great idea Mary," I say reaching over to pat her hands as they rest on the patio table. "So has Seth said why he's afraid to go?"

I listen as she describes the dark figures Seth complains about upon closing his eyes. Clearly, his state of mind must change and watching "CSI" doesn't help. Should I mention it now?

Thoughts focus on many ancestors who helped me from the Otherside.

"Was Seth ever especially close to a departed loved one?"

"His dad," she replies softly. "Why do you ask?"

It takes several minutes to relate a few instances where Daniel and others reached through the veil to convince me there's more to life than we can possibly imagine.

"His dad," I say reaching for her hands again, "can help him pass peacefully but you're going to have to help him change his state of mind."

She looks at me wide-eyed, pulls her hands away, and indignantly remarks, "I'm doing all I can."

Obviously, it's not time to elaborate so I reassure her.

Seth's mother opens the new French doors from the kitchen to let us know "CSI" is over. She needs help getting Seth back to bed. It's clear the two women have lots of practice as I watch them lovingly transport him, from leather couch to wheelchair, and back to the comfort of his hospital bed.

"Nothing is going to happen tonight," Mary notes after he settles in bed. "You might as well go home."

Promising to return the next night, after the hospice nurse and other relatives go, I quickly leave. A plan to help Seth forms on the drive home. It's no surprise that the daily random reading notes we are never born, and cannot die. It's time to help Seth accept the fullness of his own Divine Well-Being.

A bird's chirping fills the air as *Love is all there is* rings throughout my brain the next morning. I'm not sure where the words came from. It really doesn't matter, for it's something I've believed in all my life.

After repeating the usual ritual, I make a copy of the Delphi, Greece sunset adding beautiful piano music. I then copy another video for Seth of a sunset in Green Turtle Key. It's the sunset originally taped for James' father Zephaniah, thinking he could watch it as he slipped to the Otherside. I place the disks in a bag, along with a fragrant candle and some sage, believing Seth will appreciate my efforts.

Something prompts me to open the closet door. I know why when eyes rest on a container filled with needles from our 2003 Christmas tree. Their scent always lifts my mood and I'm certain these Michigan pine tree needles will energize the atmosphere at

Mary and Seth's. After grabbing an empty small plastic container from the kitchen, I fill it with pine needles without another thought before tossing it into the bag.

Day passes quickly and soon I'm at Mary and Seth's doorstep once again. Seth experienced nightmares throughout the night so it's easy to convince Mary that "CSI" is not appropriate to watch. We light the candle and fill the air with lavender. Mary watches as I sprinkle sage in the corners of the room while saying a silent clearing prayer.

Seth is not interested in watching the sunset videos on his laptop computer but breaks out into a wide grin when Mary shoves the open container of pine needles under his nose.

"Ah, I miss the smells of home," she notes with glee.

Seth is never left alone. Each evening I return to fill out the bedside "watch schedule" with Mary and Seth's mom. We talk of Seth's dad and happy times, long past, and soon, Seth sees his dad instead of dark figures. The time for him to pass is closer than ever before. He refuses food and limits liquids to only what's necessary for drugs to settle down his throat.

The ever-burning candle flickers as Mary rises to answer the phone. She returns happier for more relatives will visit the next day.

"There will be five people here tomorrow so you can take a break," she tells me with a smile. "I know you're leaving for Tampa in three days. This will give you a chance to get a tune-up on the car. Next weekend we'll probably have a party for Seth."

Seth mouth tries to break into a smile as Mary reports it's what he wants, a party to celebrate his release to the Otherside. I leave for home hours later to repeat prayers before sleep.

An email from Leah, saying she misses me, arrives the next day. I miss my like-minded friend as well. Our subsequent telephone conversation reveals several similarities between her and Mary. Leah understands my commitment to Mary and notes she would have appreciated emotional support when her husband was slowly dying.

I leave for the car repair shop after our lengthy conversation.

Since I'm driving to Tampa, it's important to make sure my nine year-old car is in good running condition. The tune-up costs more than $250 but I know James will cover it. It's cheaper than buying a new car.

Mary telephones the next day to let me know there's no need to visit. Seth passed over to the Otherside. She's busy planning his celebration party amid a house full of relatives. We schedule time for memorial posters before the conversation ends.

The costs of my adventures have now exceeded the amount received from the TDA loan. Dad's lawsuit is still a pipe dream so it seems reasonable to make money by selling the prescriptions I no longer take. Four bottles of Elmiron sit unopened and at $400 per bottle, it seems wasteful. I'm dismayed to hear it's illegal to transfer or sell prescription drugs.

Later in the day, Wednesday evening's service delights me. Rev. Peck always has something valuable to say. As her voice fills the room, the One Spirit Chorale sings beautifully in the sanctuary, making me second-guess my decision not to join them on Monday and Wednesday nights.

A phrase fills my head upon waking Friday morning. *There's going to be a heartache tonight.* It's a line from a song by Rick Nelson. Since the family weekend trip to see Sarah is today, I'm glad to sleep longer, often fifty minutes before waking, and sometimes up to three hours. I've also begun to dream again.

Family meets at Momma and Terry's house. Terry, Rebecca, and Naomi's nephew pile into Ruth's black Chevy van for the drive. Momma and Samuel decide to drive with me. When Ruth veers off the turnpike to pick up Sarah from a nearby town, I check us into the usual three-bedroom villa in Orlando. Momma immediately settles in bed to nap before Dolly Parton's 20th Dixie Stampede.

Later, the show is delightful and everyone has a good time. I do my best to stay positive and focused on Spirit but get drunk on two glasses of wine. Everyone roars with laughter when I stumble out of the van and try to open the villa door without success.

At Busch Gardens the next day, we get a wheelchair for Momma so she won't have to walk. It's great fun to move to the head of the lines with her. She seems to enjoy herself even though the Band-Aids on her nose and chin fall off when doused with water. Momma scolds us like small children for taking her on the water ride.

A nervous Rebecca holds a small orange tablet near my lips as we stand in line to ride the Kumba rollercoaster later in the day.

"What's this for?" I ask innocently.

Rebecca stares at me pleading with her eyes. "Mom," she says lifting the pill closer to my mouth, "take the pill. It's a baby aspirin. I've heard it will stop a heart attack. I know you say you've been healed but I don't want to take the chance."

My wide-faced smile covers the fleeting thought of an attack as I cater to her by swallowing the sweet tasting pill. After all, it's the first time I've been on a rollercoaster in more than thirty years since the diagnoses' of heart murmur, mitral valve prolapse and heart arrhythmia. The jerky ride is over quickly. Upon remembering I've never liked rollercoaster rides, I decide not to ride again. We head back to the comfy villa after dark.

Everyone wants to return to the park the next day but I opt out agreeing to take Momma back home while the rest of the family enjoys themselves. Our drive down the turnpike is easy. Momma is ready for a nap in her own bed after a leisurely lunch. I'm free to finish the day with uplifting music and a quick jaunt to the Center where I make coffee for the evening service.

Words and moving pictures often come right before opening eyes in the morning, especially when I ask a question. Before falling asleep I ask, "Why am I here now?" In the wee hours of the morning, I hear it's my life to do what is right.

After using the bathroom near dawn, I fall quickly back to sleep but wake minutes later upon hearing "Mother," as if Rebecca calls me insistently. My heart still pounds erratically for the dream seemed so real. Still not sure if dreams are subconscious thoughts, or experiences on another dimension, I vow to keep documenting them. The day passes quickly.

Dr. Bump's new SOM 200 series class begins in the evening. It's wonderful to be with friends of like-mind once again. The class promises to enlighten for it's based on *It's All God* by Walter Starcke.

I'm happy to verify what I intuitively know; God and I are one, the "Double Thread" as Walter puts it. Once you understand that and treat everyone as yourself, or how you prefer to be treated, everything becomes clearer. Knowing you are an extension of one Being helps to avoid judgment of other extensions who may not know of our oneness yet.

We are spirits in human form. As Joel Goldsmith notes, in *Infinite Way*, "...Spirit made visible, or Consciousness expressed as idea." It's impossible to honor God without knowing other parts of

263

God. Loving God and loving others are the same for we are one, just bits of the whole. There is no not loving for it's all love to all, the whole.

During class, it's surprising to note the myths I've learned. For many years, I really believed God wrote the *Bible* because it was "the word of God." I also believed we should be fearful of God, because we were separate, and suffering was God's way of punishment.

The greatest lie I believed was that hell is a place you go to when you are a bad person. I made my own version of hell for most of my adult life by believing there was nothing more. Nowadays, I know life is what I make it to be with thoughts and actions. We are unlimited in what we think and can manifest.

I'm going to like the daily journaling required for this class. Listening for Spirit and recognizing the spaces between ideas is the only thing that's real. Dr. Bump notes, "We are a spiritual cause and treatment changes consciousness, Mind changes the effect." Therefore, it's vital to believe firmly in what you treat for, both consciously, and unconsciously. Dr. Bump claims repetition is the key to successful treatment. After cleaning up the coffee station, I leave smiling, happy to be involved.

Sleep comes easily but I wake throughout the night as usual. At one point, I see a small girl and know it's Abigail. She's holding her daddy's ashes and letting them go by the ocean. *Abigail needs to let go of her daddy* fills my brain. Small bubble-like forms drift past vision upon opening my eyes.

I'm happy to report Rachel and Abigail joined the family for a few days of our 2009 Florida Keys vacation. We stood on the old Bahia Honda Bridge at sunset on Saturday and released Daniel's ashes to the air and sea. The wonderful time filled with love and appreciation, for the oneness of us all, as we later sat on the pavement sharing favorite memories.

Victory is the mainstay of fear fills my head sometime later. I fall back asleep thinking it's an odd thought.

A moving picture unfolds behind closed eyes when waking to greet the day. The movie shows an ocean with mountains in the background. I'm spirit ascending into a somewhat pink sky. I open my eyes and hear, *That's all Mom*, just as Daniel would say it. The usual "stuff" is flowing around the room but not the bubbles. It looks like atoms flowing haphazardly among microscopic forms. Forms include transparent circles and something I refer to as "scanners" with strings.

I stop writing later to accept the orbs facing me. "Thank You," I tell the air before starting the night's homework. It's interesting to see a mention of Paul while reading. I bought two copies of the book Paul while in Greece, one in French, and then one in English, without really knowing why.

Walter Starke claims without Paul of Tarsus it's doubtful that Christianity would have spread throughout the world. After overcoming many shortcomings such as his sense of self-importance and contradictory judgments, Paul experienced the mystical level, direct contact with "Christ Consciousness" (awareness of the soul's oneness with God). Knowing it's possible to experience such a thing spurs me forward.

:-)

Chapter Twenty-Seven

Changing Scenery

"The true self is continuous and unchangeable. The reincarnating ego belongs to a lower level, mainly the world of thought. It will be transcended through self-realization."
Ramana Maharshi – Time is an Illusion by Chris Griscom

Mary is ready to start a new life after years of working full time while caring for an ailing husband. Her courage to face the unknown as a widow amazes me. A strong sense of Mary's new freedom permeates the house as we plan the celebration party. She sorts through Seth's things as I help her friend from Michigan with memorial posters.

We deliver cookies to Seth's hospice team later in the week. Mary drives while reciting her to do list out loud. As I focus on billowing clouds, all at once, clouds and sky change colors from white, shades of gray, and sky blue, to brilliant pigments, like those in the *What the Bleep* movie.

A stream of sea foam green, ascending in an upward funnel towards the heavens, appears directly in front of me. Lilac-colored clouds drift on both sides of sea foam green, while a beautiful turquoise color appears on each side of the lilac. Sky blue emerges, amid clouds of a different blue shade, directly above the sea foam green funnel.

The scene is strikingly beautiful and I have to tell Mary about it when she asks what I'm staring at. Brilliant colors only appear while wearing Polaroid sunglasses. Yet, I have never seen such a display before. It's what I think Heaven may look like, strikingly beautiful, really beyond the description of words. I truly hope it's a sign of things to come.

Today's email reports NASA's Solar Dynamic Observatory flew past a sundog and destroyed it. Plate-shaped ice crystals in high, cold, cirrus clouds form sundogs in the sky. As ice crystals drift down, aerodynamic forces tend to align their broad faces parallel to the ground. A sundog appears when sunlight hits a patch of well-aligned crystals at just the right distance from the sun.

While looking at the video offered by NASA, the sundog's tints remind me of unusual colors seen in the sky. The video also explains how waves reverberate in the atmosphere whenever geomagnetic activity occurs.

Frankly, there's much more beauty here than we allow ourselves to see. If we truly tuned in to the splendor around us, we would never get anything done, for we'd just want to spend our time gaping in awe.

Sleep claims me after a busy day but I soon wake to remember Kenny, someone I barely knew. He was a lone guy who periodically danced with me at Pompeii, a nightclub near Detroit, in the wee hours of the morning after work. He always seemed serene, peaceful, and friendly.

Hours later, I wake again remembering Diane, always smiling with her one crooked eye. I went to college with her in the early 1980's. It's strange to think of two unrelated people whom I have not seen for decades. Do I see them because they passed on?

A book from Mary helps to lull me back to sleep. It's clear nothing happens by chance. Reading about mental mediumship types in James Van Praagh's *Talking to Heaven* empowers me. Van Praagh notes we are never alone for guides are always with us. I'm excited to know the pictures that flash through my mind are a sign of clairvoyance. It's reassuring to learn that clairsentience (sensing the unseen) and clairaudience (hearing the unseen) are part of my recognized psychic abilities.

Another message wakes me after drifting off to sleep. *As ... we are in a constant state of influx.*

Later, I dress to see Barbra Streisand at the BankAtlantic Center. Light traffic accompanies me while driving down the highway to meet Ruth and Naomi. Ruth is happy when I reimburse her for the ticket. We speculate on when the settlement check from Dad's lawsuit will arrive while eating at a Steak and Shake restaurant.

Our mezzanine seats sit several rows apart. It no longer matters when Barbra's magical voice fills the air. When she talks of the political atmosphere, a man boldly sprints forward and douses her with liquid from a cup. Barbra barely recognizes his gesture. She continues to speak, and breaks out into song, while security guards haul him away. The upheaval becomes a non-event as she continues like nothing out of the ordinary happened. After several encores, and a short period in the souvenir line, we leave happier than before.

Loving energy overflows as the little car weaves through heavy traffic. The house on 47th Drive seems empty and cold while quickly moving to the sanctuary of my room. There's no doubt that the best is yet to come as I drift off to sleep.

A vision of Daddy's father wakes me near dawn. Grandpa comes into the room and asks if I want to play baseball. He says he was very good at it. His 100-year-old body changes to one of a young boy as he speaks. At this moment, Grandpa looks like a twelve-year-old boy from India with black hair.

It's clear I can change my form into that of a young girl and be just as good at baseball as he is. I've always relished my baseball-playing days in middle school and readily agree to play ball. A gentle rain taps on bedroom windows when my eyes open. There is no pain, anymore, of letting old beliefs go.

New possibilities fill my brain at sunrise upon hearing another message. *There is only one universe. I am in the midst of making copies.* I quickly rise to pray and study.

The book about Paul calls out to me from its perch on the bookshelf after completing the week's SOM assignment. I reach up, pull it down, and glance at the pictures. Words come into my head while viewing page 56, "Philippi, view of the Via Egnatia." *I have traveled that road many times.* Reading on, I'm surprised to learn Philippi was in the "district of Macedonia." Something tells me I lived there as a Roman. I recall wanting to go there while in Greece.

The day passes quickly filled with study, family duties, and the Center's evening service.

Another message comes minutes after falling asleep. *There is nothing between the illusion and the soul.* The shape of a large bird or butterfly, along with three blue orbs, appears behind closed eyes. Magenta, the color of love, surrounds orbs before they merge.

A brilliant sun shines on my face in the morning. The day's ritual begins. This week's "ah-ha" is that, the results are insignificant. Only the spirit in which you do something matters. A spirit of Love is vital to action in Truth. I currently wonder if the consciousness of Love fills mountains. If not, why do most people feel attracted to them?

Conversations of Seth Volume One soon fills me with glee. It's quite informative so I silently bless Leah for cleaning out her bookshelf. I am, and always have been guided. The book confirms my beliefs. Yes, I am here to be a co-creator with life energy!

Weary eyes close as sleep beckons. Book topics often come during the dream state. This is the case with my next waking thought. *It's like what you would expect Heaven to be.* "This relates to Seth's material," I think, before drifting back to sleep.

More words fill my brain eighty minutes later. *I worked for three years in a village called the Tender of Awareness. It was a beautiful city and the people were filled with joy.*

Based on the instructions in *Conversations of Seth Volume One*, I've been building an ideal world in my mind. Money has no value in this place and all needs are met. Everyone treats each other with love and respect. This ideal world is Heaven on earth, where everyone recognizes we are unique parts of God, here to expand All the Good There Is.

Life becomes more like the world I dream of as conflicts between James and me lessen. The only time there seems to be an issue is when my charge card bill is due. It seems prudent to keep some of the TDA loan proceeds in the credit union. James appears resigned to paying the bills but scrutinizes every charge. Glad to have money again, I go online and transfer $900 from the joint account held with Samuel to pay on the Visa credit card.

Prayer treatments are working. Yet, James and I continue to separate. It's necessary for our souls' growth because our paths are vastly different. Only time will reveal when the final break will occur but I sense it will be through Divine Timing. The Center, and friends of like-mind, keeps me focused and moving toward the goal of helping humanity to recognize its spiritual magnificence.

Reminders sit in several places for lately I've been very forgetful. It's a side effect of living in the Now. Sometimes it's embarrassing, like when I insisted that Daniel's Web hosting renewal was paid for, only to learn it was not.

The chore list reminds me it's time to set up the Center's snack table. We're showing the monthly movie in a small classroom today so there's only one table to prepare. I take an empty seat as the movie starts. It soon feels as if a cat is brushing by my leg. There are no animals in the Center. An image of Seth's smiling face flashes through my brain. Mary still waits for a sign from him and now I think it may be in the form of a cat.

I email Mary later to relate the "cat experience" before settling down on the futon to read *Far Journeys*. Reading the book creates odd dreams of traveling between planes.

Perhaps, if we are worthy enough, learn, and have enough power, we may be able to travel between planes, but I wonder for how long. Based on research studies described in the book, many people experience higher realms of consciousness. They often connect with entities that guide and teach.

Monroe's website notes off-campus programs are learning exercises with the Hemi-Sync® process, helping participants move comfortably along a continuum of consciousness, shifting between one phase (or focus of consciousness) and another. I want to learn how to control these phase-shifts to visit and integrate non-physical energy systems. Hemi-Sync®, using audio sound patterns to achieve expanded awareness, looks mighty interesting.

Today, I'm grateful the excruciating pain from an abscessed tooth is less than it was yesterday. It has taken a bit of thought to figure out how I attracted this experience. Although most medical issues are a thing of the past, dental issues still seem to pop up occasionally. This issue is odd because the tooth in question already had a root canal, and has a crown and a post.

I've heard that issues with teeth signify the letting go of family. Nevertheless, I have chosen this experience for two reasons. I needed a reminder that pain experienced here does seem very real and it's important to recognize that fact. Even though this is an illusion of my own making, this kind of pain makes it seem all too real. That is something I need to recall when hearing of the pain others experience.

Consulting my Inner Self, I've learned that this pain is part of the purging process. My soul chose to experience it so humanity can break through the negativity that seems to surround us. There is no need to help humanity further, for all my soul's karmic debts are paid. There is no need to reincarnate in the illusion.

Specific words came to me a short while ago. "The past is gone. It's time to move on." These words spur me forward. I know now it's not necessary to help humanity from the Otherside. Will helping keep me in the illusion? Clearly, I must allow the soul to decide what to do after my physical body transitions.

270

"Twelve Signs of Spiritual Awakening" by Geoffrey Hoppe and Tobias, found on the Internet, helps to verify what I intuitively know. All the sudden changes in my life reflect a changing consciousness. I'm grateful to know body aches and pains are the result of intense DNA changes. Withdrawing from family seems easy, as I trust most karmic debts are paid. There's only a pull to continue helping Rebecca and Samuel but I'm not sure how it will be done. I look forward to developing new relationships with family and friends based on new energy, without karmic attachments.

Knowing unusual sleep patterns are part of the process eases my mind. I so look forward to sleeping normally in the future. Physical disorientation and increased "self talk" are part of the process as well. Reading that the conversations in my brain will increase and become more insightful fills me with an increased sense of well-being.

I can relate to almost every sign. A feeling of loneliness, even when in the company of others, seems ever-present, along with a loss of passion. It's calming to know that shutting down for a brief period, in order to assimilate "the new Christ-seed energy," is normal. It makes me feel better to know that difficultly in relating to others, and a desire to flee certain people and crowds, is part of spiritual awakening too.

A deep longing for Home challenges me for it's often hard to get anything done. Although I sense completion of karmic cycles, at this point I'm not certain my contract is fulfilled. I do not wish to enlist for another tour of duty here but am ready for the challenges of moving into New Energy. Spirit needs me here now to help others make the transition.

I have spent a lot of time thinking about how my particular spiritual awakening occurred over the past five years. Prompts and life changes are recorded in this book series and there's a synopsis of these steps in notes at the end of this book. [57]

A yellow legal pad, under the futon near an ink pen, makes it easy to document early morning messages. I wake hours later and wonder if the words in my brain relate to Robert Monroe's books. *You too can go to dream world.*

The next morning I ponder the identity of Alex as new words fill my head. *Alex is faithed. The faith in this entity comes from many sources.*

Minutes later, more words come to fill me with joy.

Then within a day, within the last few minutes, we shall be called Home.

I so long for Home.

:-)

Chapter Twenty-Eight

Part of the Divine Plan

"There is a soul force in the universe which, if we permit it, will flow though us and produce miraculous results."
Gandhi

Activities beyond the confines of my room increase in November. I'm back to picking Samuel up from school biweekly besides attending the Center three or four nights a week. Some people say I'm lazy living off of James but it's part of the Divine Plan. I'm doing exactly what I'm supposed to do, increasing spiritual growth of others and myself by learning, teaching, and helping those who seek assistance.

There's no doubt "they" come from the sun when photographing the unseen. Countless multicolored orbs, nurturing friends sent from above to let me know I'm not alone on this path to help humanity, fill me with ecstasy. The stained glass trinket lies packed away for hurricane season, so no one can say it affects photos. Orbs of various colors, green encircled in red, blue, red, and rainbow, amid streams of rainbow colored rays of communication fill me with joy. I know it's Truth when new words fill my brain. *The Stuff of the Universe of which all things are made.*

Far Journey's by Robert Monroe is amazing! For two days now, I have agreed to allow higher entities to lead, guide, and protect as spiritual consciousness grows while I rest. A flash of Daniel's face, very small as if far away, comes before rising. He repeats four important words before disappearing.

"We are all God."

The TV turns itself on later in the afternoon as I ponder a talk with Aaron about Dad's lawsuit. I push several buttons on the remote control but still no sound. When I push the power switch off, the TV turns back on with sound. The show is about Detroit cops. I sense Daddy's energy. He's happy about the settlement. After thanking him for coming, I switch it off and walk away. It stays off.

Sleep comes easily but I wake throughout the night. At seven o'clock, I finally rise to document words ringing through my brain. *Our relocation is a process.*

It's time to repeat the "World Healing Meditation" and my usual treatments before studying for class. Today is a post-Greece party and I want to study before attending. When the party ends, I'll go to Rebecca's house to stay with Samuel while she's out of town.

Twenty-two minutes after falling asleep later, still in a dream-like state, I recall telling four women of my intention to be with them soon but sadly, not soon enough for me. Two favorite aunts, Momma's mother, another aunt and cousin, come to mind before rising to pack a small suitcase.

Driving down the expressway is a pleasure for it's such a beautiful day. The party is at a splendid house on a man-made lake, where the Everglades flowed freely a few short years ago. Although it's very beautiful, I cannot help but recall the natural beauty the exclusive housing development marred to build upon the land.

Rebecca is glad to see me after dusk. It soon feels wonderful to sleep once again in a real bed. I wake abruptly after hearing words related to *Far Journeys. "You'll transfer on day eight."*

My lovely daughter sits drinking her morning coffee on the back porch as I venture outside. A vast pile of laundry covers the laundry room floor.

"Thanks," I say reaching down to hug her as she sits in a white, plastic, porch chair, "for letting me come over a day early. It's wonderful to sleep in a bed."

"I don't understand why you're not sleeping in your own bed," she calmly replies.

"The marriage is over," I announce while settling down in a chair away from billowing cigarette smoke. "It's just a matter of time now. So, is there anything special you want me to do while here?"

"Just take Samuel to school and drive him home," she says springing quickly from her chair, "and love the animals."

She moves into the house to get ready for work while I start the laundry.

The day passes quickly. Samuel seems glad to see me when I pick him up from school. We watch his favorite TV shows while waiting for Rebecca to return from work before eating dinner. I'm in bed before either of them savoring the good energy of their home.

Rebecca leaves for her trip the next morning as I drive Samuel to school. Washing more laundry between studying for class keeps me busy until it's time to pick him up again. Samuel keeps me occupied until it's time for class.

All the lights are green so I don't mind the extra twenty minutes that it takes to get to the Center. Leah approaches me during the break to schedule time together. She quickly agrees to dinner at Rebecca's house on Thursday. It's been a long time since I've prepared a meal and sat at a table with others to enjoy it.

...but my friend, no more pain, only joy, fills my brain at dawn. Familiar warmth radiates out from my chest. Sleep prevails after using the bathroom. Daniel wakes me later to get Samuel to school on time.

"Hi Mom," he says cheerfully.

It's a joy to be with Samuel but I can't seem to get much done. I fall asleep while reading. Kitty startles me awake. She leaps onto the bed, walks across my legs, and leaps back down to the floor.

Samuel is late for school the next morning after we sit in a turnpike traffic jam. Several other students are late as well, so this time, there's no penalty for tardiness. I decide to shop for dinner on the way back to Rebecca's house and soon find myself searching for another foam pad at the discount store. The futon back in my sunlit room has become increasingly uncomfortable.

A case of spring water and blank DVD's go into the cart. It seems like a costly venture to offer multiple DVDs to tour group members but I'm not concerned. It feels great to remember the trip of a lifetime and our time together. Costs go onto the trusty Visa card knowing my prosperity treatment works, even if results are still invisible.

After storing the food at Rebecca's, I'm grateful to use her desktop computer. Mine is acting up again. Editing the ninth video, adding music and picture slide shows, is easy. I get the external hard drives from Rebecca's hall closet to back up my work. It seems prudent to keep the drives and other collectibles, stored for safekeeping before hurricane Wilma, at Rebecca's house.

The day again passes quickly. Leah arrives in the late afternoon for a dinner of porcupines (lean ground round mixed with Rice A Roni), rice, and broccoli. Samuel and Leah talk as if old friends while I put the meal on dinner plates. It's clear Leah and I need more time to share notes and experiences. I agree to call her after Thanksgiving before she leaves for Rev. Charles' Thursday night class. She speaks so highly of the course that I'm ready to take SOM 101 again.

More words related to *Far Journeys* come the following morning. I quickly remember that Rebecca will be home tomorrow. Daniel's spirit then relays a message.

"She will live a good life Mom."

It is an old message heard before.

Rebecca has been in Washington for five days now. Samuel and I have gotten along very well. Princess is eating and not sulking as usual when Mommy is gone. Ruth got Samuel from school today to spend the night with her and Naomi. I was supposed to go to a party but didn't and now am nagged with the thought of being alone.

My CD player is on when I reach down to gather nightclothes from a travel bag. I lift it from the floor to place on Rebecca's bed while thinking about the SOM class book *It's All God*. In the book, it says aloneness is really all-one-ness, the recognition that we are never alone, for all is God, and we are a part of the Universe that is God. Extraordinary things like this serve to confirm my beliefs.

The CD quickly changes tracks a few times to get my attention. Isaiah's meditation CD, which I keep telling myself to listen to every day, but don't, is playing. Now I lie down to listen. Isaiah's soothing voice guides me as I send purifying, cleansing, white light from within my heart's core throughout the universe. My physical body seems nailed to the bed. Yet, there's a strange sense of being lifted heavenward by unseen energy.

What a great feeling to know I'm not alone and furthermore am not really human at all! I, like everything else, am an illusion made for an, as yet, unknown purpose.

Humanity is one of an infinite number of entities and things that makes the whole of God. We are beautiful Light Beings, pure energy in material form, having a physical experience. As I write this third book, I'm now perfectly clear of my role. It's my charge to awaken parts of me still sleeping in the dream for it's time to awaken the God within.

We somehow lost sight of God-given abilities after agreeing to experience this realm of consciousness. In the course of experiencing the dream, we continued to spiral into denser and denser realms leaving our true Self behind. It's time to remember who we are and return to the Godhead, to Spirit. My soul agreed to spread the word by discussing the many experiences that affected this physical body.

In doing so, if one is open-minded to believe beyond a rigid set of beliefs, one will clearly see there is so much more to life than anyone could ever comprehend. Thoughts and words make our physical reality and now that physical reality is manifesting quicker than ever before. It's vitally important that humans remain positive in thought for what we concentrate on manifests to become our reality.

It is my understanding that some souls chose to stay a bit longer in the dream of forgetfulness. But it's important to note that the Godhead has never, and will never, be disrupted.

One can see Omnipresent Consciousness as a vast collage of everything that exists. One may take a photo of the collage and make a puzzle but it does not change the collage. One may separate the photo into unique puzzle parts but that has no affect on the collage. One may even disconnect the parts of the puzzle and separate them to the four corners of the earth, and beyond, but it still has no affect on the original collage. Eventually, the puzzle parts will come together and disintegrate having never been "real" at all. The photo will be no more, but the collage remains perfect, whole, and unaffected.

This physical body is a part of the dream puzzle associated with the photo of the collage. Yet, I am in Truth a part of that perfect, whole, and unaffected collage of Spirit. There is nothing to separate me from Spirit but my human thoughts. The more I focus on Spirit, or whatever one refers to as God, the more my life here unfolds in perfect and Divine Order.

Time here is most gratefully shortening for my work on earth will soon be done. And I say that with tongue-in-cheek even knowing there is no work to do.

I now believe a spirit can stay 'in the middle' to help humans still in the dream and that is my human plan. Spalding reports there is no definite time between passing and rebirth. It seems likely that the soul chooses the time of rebirth but I sense there will be no need for rebirth into human form for me.

Yet, as long as I still seem to be here in this realm, it seems that something should occupy my time. Since there is no what some would call a significant other or partner to consume the time away with, it must be filled with something. And writing these books seems to occupy my mind between trips to see friends and leisurely excursions, which are so much better shared.

So, really, it makes little difference to this soul whether one believes in the Vital Life Force or not. Yet, doesn't it make sense that if you're here, and your thoughts make your world, you would transmit positive thoughts and have a good time? Wouldn't you want to know it's possible to accomplish your dreams and live a life worth living? Wouldn't you want to be the very best you can be?

I admit I've been struggling with what to do about this dream. Specifically, what to do about the information I learn concerning things like global economic collapse, one-world government, aliens, genetic evolution and the like. Once you know it's all an illusion, you can disregard it knowing your thoughts can create a different reality.

Although I still wonder what it all means, spiritual leaders note we are a holographic universe, a microcosm of the macrocosm containing all possibilities. Dr. Page notes the hologram is a product of light beams that creates the illusion called matter. Everything is here but we need to raise our consciousness to find it.

To humans, it's kind of a smoke and mirrors effect with thoughts directing possibilities. Although one part of us is fully aware of what we're doing, we rarely have a conscious clue. We begin to notice this hologram when we change the way we think. Dr. Page notes, "...our own holographic image is still developing as we continue to align our soul's intentions with our manifested self."

Nothing is solid. New holographic images are continually produced in response to collective awareness. Please remember, we are living in a virtual reality field. It's important to test it through intuition, feeling into the vibration of our heart to see if it resonates with our truth.

Are there enough of us here to change the reality we see? How many does it take? Can I change the entire reality of the world by myself? I doubt it, for every time I leave my sanctuary of a home the ball game seems to change, as more people become involved throwing their beliefs and thoughts into the mix.

In his book, The God Code, Gregg Braden notes it takes only the square root of one-percent to make a difference. That means in a world of six billion people, it only takes a minimum of 8,000 people to begin to change the world. We have many more than that working all around the globe.

So what am I to do in the meantime? That my friend is the question I seem to be faced with. I have tried a number of methods to deal with this illusion, yet, everything seems lacking, if only in one aspect. Attending events, where people of like-mind may gather, has of late proved fruitless. Mingling with the speakers seems more promising for I seem to have more in common with them than the audience in which I sit. Yet, I really do not see myself up on a stage giving sage advice. My role is to write and lead though example.

For many months, I remained in seclusion, and some would argue I still do, but that does not seem to be the right way to live either. Even though I'm well ware of the God Network it seems that some physical relocation on my part is needed to fully connect on a physical level.

If I stay in my own dream world of a sanctuary, going out only for necessities, how will I connect with others like me? I now conclude that venturing out to events where there will be more of "my kind" is vital, despite the fact that when I do, I feel more like a contributor than a student. But isn't that what people do at the stage I seem to be at, contribute their consciousness to events?

I must also continue to quiet the ego within, which often successfully controls my brain by filling it with constant 'self talk'. Although talk is now to a large part limited to repeating, "Grateful I AM, I AM grateful," it still does not allow my small mind to silence itself.

Sometimes I feel the need to meditate once again thinking I need information to progress further. However, at sporadic times such as the day after November 11, 2009, when another Gateway opened, I more strongly felt the familiar connection to Source.

It has been quite a long while since I've felt any physical discomfort that could not be thought away but this week was

279

different. The excruciating pain in an abscessed tooth drove me to the dentist. She sent me to an endodontist who prescribed antibiotics and painkillers.

For three days, I took pain pills delving back into the world of limitation left so long ago. I'm not proud to report most of my time was spent sleeping but it seemed all I could do, even as I constantly treated the issue as cured. Now I've come to the realization the experience was, and sadly seems to continue to be, a purging of what is left of the denser, darker energies within.

By the fourth day, the pain subsided enough so I could stop the pills. I still was not feeling up to par two nights later but felt guided to answer a request to attend Charles' meditation on November 11. Since I live mainly in the Now moment, it did not occur to me what an auspicious day it was. I didn't consciously remember several Lightworker emails received on its importance.

Three men and I joined Charles in a short reading of Rumi's work before engaging in a fifteen-minute meditation. As Charles led us, we gathered everyone seen and unseen, into the room to share and spread Light throughout the world. I called forth everyone I knew, including members of the Global Prayer Project, who I meditated with the previous night via Webcast.

The power that filled me was undeniable, as I remained grateful for air-conditioning, which offered a steady stream of cold air despite the cooler Florida night. This time when my body filled with heat, it was much more bearable as I held the Light, spreading it, as done the night before.

When we were done, I was grateful to hear the young man next to me report that he too felt the heat. Charles shared the need for someone to design a flyer for the upcoming holiday concert. Since I've designed flyers using a software program, it was easy to oblige. Yes, it was one of the reasons intuition prompted me to be there. The God Network is always working and we need only to tune in.

I was home an hour later and soon in bed, sporadically rising every fifty or ninety minutes, each time recalling a glimmer of something, but unable to recall what it was. Exhausted at dawn, I rose again, and this time, remembered.

A voice told me I was getting more power. As I lie still to receive it, I felt the familiar heat spreading from my heart's center throughout the body. The heat became almost unbearable. This time

I did not throw off the bedcovers, but remained still, reminding myself that's what I'd done so many times in 2006 and 2007. I laid there feeling my entire body vibrating as if plugged into a light socket. I have felt this energy before but not, to my recollection, to this extent. And when I thought I could not stand it any longer, it seemed to be over.

I opened my eyes and raised my head slowly still feeling a counterclockwise rotation of energy circulating directly above my head. Again, it's now a familiar feeling, but not to this extent. This strong beam of energy came undoubtedly from Source, the Universal Cosmic Energy that will help to bring me Home again.

Gratefulness overwhelmed me as I thanked God for the experience and for carrying me through it. My brain began to kick into gear but could not deny what occurred. Failing miserably, it tried to convince me the communication was not from Source. But I now know how Source works. It never demands but guides by communicating certain things. It is always my choice to follow up on the communication or not.

For instance, before going to bed I asked if I should attend the "I Can Do It" conference. The 74-degree room felt uncomfortably cold even after putting on pajamas and a pair of socks before crawling under bedcovers. When I woke the next morning, I heard I would meet a man at the conference who would help me greatly in the days to come. The all too familiar heat consumed me when the message came through.

A few days ago, I heard there was an energy field above my head that I could tap into at any time. I need only to remember it. An unconscious deep intake of breath brought me back to full consciousness as my body shook with vibration. It vibrated vigorously for several minutes afterward.

:-)

Chapter Twenty-Nine

Manifesting Money

"If you change the way you look at things, the things you look at change."
Wayne Dyer

H*e has met the needs for whom they share.*

The confusing expression wakes me before dawn. Sleep reigns after logging it on paper, until *Theolapodolipis* enters my brain. I'm unsure of the spelling but log the word anyway. My throat is dry as usual so I sip water from the bottle nearby before rising to use the bathroom.

Copious amounts of fluid again seem to flow from within, while sitting, for what seems like the tenth time since going to bed. I wonder where it all comes from but sense the process of cleansing, and purifying, continues.

Windows remain open as a cold front passes through. The temperature is in the 60's and it feels quite comfortable while repeating prayers amid twinkling wind chimes.

Aaron telephones hours later. He has his check and we should expect ours soon. Dad's lawsuit, I'm very grateful to hear, is settled. We discuss finally laying Dad's ashes to rest before ending the call. There's a strong sense that I'll be in Michigan, to support Aaron, when he moves the ashes from his closet.

This money will pave the way to travel between classes because life is too short to be limited. For now, loan proceeds will help to make payments on the charge card and the loan. It doesn't cost anymore to pay in installments, and it makes sense to leave money in the bank to travel. I quickly log onto the Internet to transfer another $900 from the TDA loan proceeds to pay Visa.

Daniel's essence warned me in 2004 not to keep funds in government bonds or banks. Repeated warnings of global economic collapse prompt me to follow inner guidance. My future as a Lightworker is now secure knowing God as my true Source.

282

This new influx of money also makes it possible to donate more. The Center makes my life better by helping me to think for myself instead of clinging to old beliefs. Supporting the services I regularly attend makes sense. It will be wonderful to slip fifty and one-hundred dollar bills into the basket, knowing non-salaried evening ministers will benefit, as well as the Center itself.

A stray thought of illness surrounding Ruth's childhood friend Beth comes to mind later in the evening. I recall dreaming of her and sense things are not well. Fond memories of loving help on Christmas Eve before she slept on my old, brown, velour couch surface. These memories are very special since I don't host Christmas anymore. I'm interested in reestablishing our friendship because good friends are hard to come by, especially as we age.

It seems prudent to get Beth's email from Ruth so we can reconnect. Ruth answers the telephone and quickly notes she hasn't heard from Beth in a long time. When I suggest we visit her in Texas, she considers the possibility.

"You know," Ruth says, hesitating as if in deep thought about what to say. "Beth never really liked you because you used to be skinny. Didn't you tell her she weighed too much?"

"I'm a new person Ruth. Now I understand we take on a specific physical body to learn and teach lessons. I believe Beth weighs more than four-hundred pounds to teach us unconditional love. And I would love to see her in person to let her know she's okay, just the way she is. She was always so helpful spending the night on Christmas Eve as we labored making Christmas dinner."

"Well, I'll give her a call and see if we can go out there sometime but getting off work may be tough for me."

When our conversation ends, I quickly email Beth. It's vital to relay how much her help during the "good old days" meant to me. They were times when we had no idea how great we had it with friends and family. The email flows into cyberspace after I sign it with blessings of Love and Light.

Emails from Anna and Mary warrant attention. Anna asks if I'll be at the next Course in Miracles study group, on the first and third Thursday of each month. This presents a dilemma, because I plan to join the Thursday class taught by Charles. Mary notes a friend from Michigan is coming to visit. She asks if I know about a psychic they will see. After answering emails, I spend hours updating Web pages on the business website. I envision the business sold but since it's now Internet based must keep it up-to-date.

Days fill with a mix of prayer, study, and computer work while transferring videotape from Greece onto DVD's. The tenth DVD takes much longer to complete. There's just too much fun to have. I'm spending more time at the Center now, sometimes five nights a week, enjoying movies and sporadic classes.

Multicolored orbs are common in pictures taken while standing in front of two bedroom windows facing the rising sun. Dots of pure white among orbs of blue, green, red, and rainbow, all within rainbow colored streams of light rays, speak a language I have yet to learn. But I know, they are communicating.

Changing reality with my mind seems much more possible. Although I still feel a need to sequester myself, James and I are now more cordial to one another. It's clear we live in two different worlds, but then again we always have. The time for me to leave my world to play in his is over. It appears he will never play with me in mine so it's only a matter of time before we part.

It's time to stop using others as an excuse for not evolving. I must reclaim my power. Yet, there are fleeting times when I wonder about moving on. How will I support myself? Each day seems to bring more awareness that God is my source. I am where I'm supposed to be for now, doing exactly what I'm supposed to be doing. It's wonderful to take care of only myself, healing dis-ease that plagued me for decades, as I evolve into a more spiritual human. What a blessing to know that the more conscious I am, the more I automatically produce harmony in place of dis-ease!

I've controlled surroundings by purely physical means for most of my life. It's time to let go and let God, to get out of my own way and use mental methods to shape a new life. Daily confirmation assures; what I do is right for me. Chosen books, Internet websites, and classes, all verify the power of mind working through Universal Laws. I'm grateful to know the All Originating Spirit, Omnipresent Consciousness, God, whatever you care to name it, is a Spirit-Intelligence of limitless capacity from which we are all formed.

Dis-ease lies in the mind, the only conceivable channel between psychic and physical planes. Everything on the physical plane is first conceived on the psychic plane, and everything created, is a manifestation of Originating Thought. Our mind is a distribution center for the entire Power-in-Action of the originating Thought, giving us the ability to manifest at will. Since the characteristic of Spirit-Intelligence is Thought, changing perception to more closely align with *It*, will change the world I eventually experience.

It's time to revert to my original state of BEing. I have seen, and unseen, assistance to do so. The Center helps me to omit past beliefs. I'm grateful for the vision board process learned in class. It's empowering to picture myself in different nurturing places, vacationing with family and friends, enjoying a life of service and joy.

Positive affirmations help to retrain my mind and replace lies of limitation. Visioning complete and unending happiness for all of humanity will soon be my goal, but first, I must achieve it for myself. Constructive thoughts rule when alone in my room but I need to expand that practice to other areas.

Entertaining consistent constructive thoughts, in the midst of those who think otherwise, is essential. It must be second nature to think constructively and vision a New World. Knowing Infinite Power is at my disposal makes the job easy. It's both amazing and delightful when outside events and circumstances aid me.

The kingdom of God is within. It is time to bring the knowledge of this awareness back into the hearts and minds of humanity. We all play a part in acknowledging the Spiritual Truth that Jesus and other great masters taught and demonstrated.

After a while, I will have no doubt that a means to achieve what I desire will manifest as God works through me. By passing on what I have, I'll make room for more good in my life. I will learn the joy of infinite supply by freely giving happiness, service, peace, money, and love. Space, time, and limitation will fade away as I use spiritual gifts for the highest good of humanity. The recognition of being a channel for Power to work through me will be overwhelming, especially when working with others to spread Light and Love throughout the world.

Sensing my new role has begun, I leave my sanctuary for the Center's Wednesday night service. The event ends soon after placing my first fifty-dollar bill in the donation basket. Still in a contrasting environment, I shut down the audio system and rush home to eat before meeting the family.

People fill the bar, Terry's workplace, on this night before Thanksgiving. Since they offer Karaoke, Rebecca goes up once a week to sing and drink free beer. It's easier to be with her, Ruth, and Terry in a fun atmosphere filled with the energy of music. I settle happily onto a stool to pore over the songbook. Later, Ruth belts out "Bobby McGee" by Janis Joplin to the happy throng of barflies before calling it a night. I'm proud of myself for nursing one glass of wine over the course of two hours as I head to the car.

Reaching home minutes later, I see James returned from fishing in the Everglades. He sighs loudly while closing his bedroom door as I softly repeat prayers of gratefulness. The prayers have been a part of my daily treatment work for many months now.

I'm thankful for a multitude of invisible things including perfect health, a generous, considerate husband who cares enough about the Truth to do what is just by God's Law and a loving, joyous, giving of all things good family. Visioning includes affirmations on the abundance and prosperity that continues to come (allowing me to give to humanity in ever-increasing ways); friends of like mind; the wholeness, joy, beauty, good, and truth within that spreads out onto all whom I come in contact with and my ability to teach humanity in ever-increasing ways.

The next morning, I recognize there's much more to be thankful about. The support that I get from Mind, Omnipresent Consciousness, Cosmic, God, for lack of a more fitting word, is awesome. It is much more than a CD player alerting me of unseen guides by haphazardly changing songs. It's more than seeing brilliantly colored orbs that rarely grace my physical sight, or occasionally appear in pictures Mind tells me to take. It is more than brilliantly colored iridescent clouds I have begun to see in the sky. It's also more than getting all green lights or parking spaces when I want them.

This Omnipresent Consciousness is even more than the normally unseen universe of matter spinning and bobbing wherever I look. It's more than the occasional computer glitches alerting me to focus on the message of Spirit coming through. And, it's more than the wonderfully good things that continue to come my way. It is even more, dare I say, than the presence of the spirit known as my last-born son.

After falling asleep at midnight, I wake hours later to say treatments and listen to Isaiah's meditation CD. Daniel and the others are with me. With eyes shut, I again see more of Reality than with eyes open. The orbs, or spirits as I think of them, are always there and their number is great. The number differs at various times but I am never alone.

Treatments focus more on prosperity including the sale of the business. I manipulate an image of a check shown in *The Secret* and write it out to myself for the sum of 1.2 million dollars, the amount I expect to get. The image and pictures of beautiful areas to visit in the future now sit on a new vision board.

From January 2007 to April 2013, I've visited thirteen U.S. states, several islands, and six countries.

Quickly changing my focus of attention before 10:00 AM, I decide to take quiche baked the day before to Terry and Momma. It will give Amos something to eat upon arriving early for Thanksgiving dinner with his ever-present hunger.

Terry sits outside at the patio table with two buddies as I pull into the drive. They greet me warmly before I quickly move into the house to place the quiche in the refrigerator. A 22-pound turkey sits on the top shelf as I wrestle negative emotion. I usually put the turkey in the oven the night before dinner.

Terry thinks it will cook in four hours and seems surprised when I announce the meat is much more tender if cooked slowly overnight on a lower temperature. He seems to take the news well and only comments on how he's looking forward to eating quiche.

Later, my aura stands out in the mirror after a shower. It's beautifully white and more than a half-inch thick. Does the combination of bathroom lights and steam make it easier to see? I stand in the steam-filled room joyously moving arms while watching the aura flutter.

James soon tells me Prudence birthed four kittens but none survived so he "took care of them." Poor Prudence is now on the back porch trying to carry one of Wylie's three kittens out into the yard. She finally kidnaps one and James comes to my bedroom door to spread the news. I listen without comment knowing, cats like humans learn from their own kind. Maybe this is her first time being a female cat. I've done my best, without physically interfering, to help her learn how to nurture herself and offspring.

The now familiar flash of heat and tiredness comes quickly as I update a page on the corporation website that has not changed in three years. I stop, lie down, and close my eyes to get the message. Abigail and Rachel will not be visiting us at Terry's and Momma's today. I'm not surprised, or very disappointed, for they are, for the most part, out of my life now.

I hear things will happen quickly. I am to release business newsletters, via the Internet, free of charge. Announcements through the email update (that I've let stagnate for most of the year) will increase visibility.

A short nap refreshes before rising in the early afternoon to dress for dinner. James and I drive in separate vehicles to Terry's house. This year there's more people so Terry sets up three tables, end-to-end, stretching from the living room to the hall. His friend, a minor league baseball player, helps as the rest of us chat with three members from Naomi's family.

Momma wears my favorite blue denim outfit, which no longer fits me, for I've lost more weight. It's nice to see her wearing good clothes. Amos is not as tan, but looks clean, and wears clean clothes as well. Rebecca is the last to arrive with Samuel and Princess to keep Terry's chihuahua Baby company.

Dinner has its high and higher points. The turkey is cooked and James sits next to me. He seems happy that the family still includes him even though everyone knows our marriage is vastly different from before. I have no regrets or ill feelings. Our time is over and he's making it easy on himself and me. Spirit will direct the time for us to move on to completely new lives. I expect to include him in my life even when our living arrangement ends.

Amos doesn't speak very much and quickly falls asleep on the couch after eating. We know he's homeless again but refuse to see he is holding the darkness so that we may know the light. He wakes to participate in the usual family telephone calls. Terry's son Joel is doing great in Kentucky with his mom. He's wrestling again and I know that is where Spirit has set him to be. It's a pleasure to learn that Daniel's essence continues to support Joel's efforts. Yes, he visits Joel too!

After saying goodbye to Joel, Terry telephones Aaron to discuss arrangements for Daddy's ashes. We all listen before talking with him ourselves. Aaron now doesn't think it necessary that we lay Dad to rest by having a service or party. He does not seem to understand that Dad had other relatives besides us who might want to say goodbye. I take the phone next but just cannot get through to him before passing the receiver to Ruth.

288

Aaron reports he's thinking about putting Dad's ashes in the cemetery near his house, where one of the Temptations is buried. Ruth reminds him of Dad's wishes to be at the cemetery with the rest of his family. She stresses it was what he, Aaron, said he would do when lawyers settled the lawsuit. It's downhill from there and she ends her part of the conversation by asking him to sleep on it.

Ego rises, reminding me of the past, fearful of the future. As a reformed smoker, I find it difficult to see Ruth and Rebecca back to smoking cigarettes along with Terry. The planning of Samuel's birthday celebration, without his participation disappoints me as well. I leave for home allowing egos to upset, including my own, which seems to pop up out of nowhere.

Later, I decide the day was enlightening. There were moments when the family noted how weird I was because I'm no longer like them. The support I get from Spirit is more than enough to make up for the lack of support from my human family.

I look ever so fondly to being back in the merging orbs with others. 'Home' seems so far away now, but thankfully there are only about eight years left here until I return. Spirit will insure my abundance and prosperity along with the ever present wholeness, good, and love filling me now.

Checking email, I'm grateful to see Rev. Peck sent something about people coming into our life for a reason, a season, or a lifetime. I'm happy she's thankful that I'm in her life for she makes such a wonderful difference in mine. Sleep comes quickly after shutting down my laptop.

James knocks on my bedroom door before entering in the late morning.

"My mom died yesterday morning," he says without emotion. "I'm on my way to help my sister move her stuff from the nursing home."

I stare at him in disbelief as a feeling of compassion overwhelms.

"Is there anything I can do to help?" I ask, rising from the computer task chair to hug him.

"No," he says, holding out his arm to stop me while turning towards the door.

I stand still unsure of how to react.

"Can I help somehow with the services?"

"Mom didn't want any fuss so we're not doing anything now," he replies with authority. "There's nothing to do."

He begins to leave the room as my mouth opens in astonishment. It's a mystery why he didn't share the news earlier. Did he know yesterday?

"Let me know if there's anything I can do," I announce as he slowly passes through the living room and out the den door to his van.

Family differences are clearly apparent when I call relatives to report the news. Upon ending the conversation with Rebecca, I give up trying to make sense of everything. I decide to mine the Black Friday sales instead. It's time for a new approach to life's dramas. I have never shopped for "unnecessary items" but there's now money to spend since Dad's lawsuit is settled.

"Time to treat yourself," I hear while making my way to Circuit City.

A CD by Third Day catches my eye while scanning the Christian music. I grab it and head back to the entrance for a shopping cart before scanning the store for Christmas gifts. There's a nifty am/fm cube radio alarm clock with eight soothing sounds for less than six bucks on a display near the door. I choose several for friends and one for myself before moving on.

The check out line is a long worm of customers weaving between bins of impulse purchases. I join the throng of customers looking straight ahead until Daniel's voice enters my brain.

"Look in the bin Mom," he says. "There's something there for Samuel."

The bin to my right overflows with small packages holding something to do with game systems. I'm not sure what I'm looking at, but the words Nintendo catch my eye. I assume it's some kind of game and silently answer the voice in my head.

"I don't know if he has this one."

"Just buy it Mom, from me," Daniels' voice echoes in my brain.

I place the plastic package in my cart before charging everything and heading home. James returns home to announce there will be a mass for Martha next weekend, with burial afterward.

"Don't you want some help contacting the out-of-town relatives?" I ask, remembering that when Daniel passed, Rebecca and Ruth contacted everyone while I remained in a fog.

James looks down at the floor.

"We're not contacting them just yet. It's limited only to close family," he replies, before walking briskly away.

Although I'm not yet aware of it, James is further ahead, in the game of life, for the trick is to limit negative emotion. James was the perfect husband to help me move out of the illusion. His usually slow and carefully thought out words and actions gracefully displayed the art of non-reaction.

I'm guided later, while on the Internet, to download a free music track "Poonthen Raga-Anandabhairavi," a healing song by Chitra on their "Enchanting Memories Album." It's a song played in India's hospitals during surgery, proven to assist in healing.

You give what you got and you get more, rings through my brain upon rising the next morning.

A letter addressed to me, from a lawyer in Detroit, sits in the mailbox when prayers and study are complete. The envelope holds a check for ten-thousand dollars, the amount allocated by the courts to settle our lawsuit for Dad's wrongful death. After a few minutes of crying, I make a copy of the check before logging online.

Mary notes in a group email that she finally received the awaited sign from Seth. He sent a cat with a raccoon tail for her birthday. It showed up at his cousins' house in Miami a few days before Thanksgiving with the knowledge that she would be going there for dinner. After remembering Seth said he would come back as a cat, they took very good care of it until Mary arrived. As soon as she saw the cat, now known as Sethala, she knew the gift was for both her and her younger cat Michgi.

"The older ones don't care about anything but sleeping," she informs us. "Michgi needs a day buddy now that Daddy is gone. Introducing Sethala, four-months-old, 4.4 pounds, sweet and cuddly as can be, with fur that is as soft as a rabbits and a purr that sounds like the Mazda motor in my car. Her tail looks like a raccoons. Now that's interesting for raccoons were invading the back yard while Seth was on Hospice, until I exterminated their grub food source. I am blessed with my fourth feline. You just get used to doing tail counts before you close up the house and leave. Cats are like potato chips, you can't have just one!"

Happy Seth's spirit came through as planned, and that Mary recognized the occurrence, I share the news about James' mother and the four stillborns Prudence had on the day she passed. Poor Prudence had five stillborns. Four were born on Thanksgiving and the fifth the day after. Right now, we have six cats. Wylie's three kittens are about six-weeks-old. Her son Bart, from the litter before, plays with them all day.

Another email, from Leah who is nursing a cold, garners attention. She wants to get together for lunch and a movie. I'm glad to reply letting her know Dr. Charles stepped in to do class for Dr. Bump. Leah and I plan to share a dinner before Rev. Lockard's night class on December 1.

How wonderful to reach another milestone in this time-space continuum! I no longer seek advice from outside my limited physical self. Really knowing this is an illusion, I've basically just given up. If everything I think and see and hear, even when sleeping, is an illusion, why should I believe any of it. Why indeed should I trust it to lead me back to Source without knowing if it ultimately keeps me locked in the dream just due to my belief in its value?

And yet, while I still seem to be in this body the game must continue. Although I know this is an illusion of my soul's making (perhaps my spirit's making), it's coming to an end, for now I know this is not all there is. I lost my way in the process of seeking new ways of being and experiencing life. But now, I am returning to Source.

I've done my homework and covered all the bases I know to ensure that the karma of this, and every life, is complete. A sense of balance fills days. I now choose to get help from that part that leads me to the end of birth and rebirth, without making more karma.

The basic teachings of Michael tell us karma is a law of balance, either experiencing both sides of intense experiences throughout many lifetimes, or meeting other challenges that help us grow. Yet, Emmanuel notes karma is really a mode of learning not "a balancing of books." Karma is a set of circumstances humans choose in each life they live to find areas not yet in Truth.

We seek Truth to finally return to the One in which we live, and move, and have all BEing. As noted by author Gregg Braden in his book The Divine Matrix, "We're powerful beings expressing ourselves through the bodies that extend beyond the edge of our cells to become the universe itself."

No soul gives itself more work than it can do. We release karmic ties through our willingness to grow. We create everything that happens to help us have experiences, which propel our transformation back to the Light. There's a resolution to every experience either through karmic action or by the grace of God.

There is nothing left to do but BE until this physical host decides to take its last breath. And yet, since I still appear to be experiencing human life, there must be a reason why. Rather than removing myself from life, it's time to contribute to the positive aspects of this illusion more frequently.

Checking financial news and email, and ultimately watching videos of interest on the Internet, keeps me grounded in this reality. I can stop this type of communication, or at least limit it, to only times when I connect with Lightworker groups to spread the Light, but then my perspective will change. I may not be able to finish the book series describing how the process of awakening unfolded for me. Will that stop other parts of me from recognizing they too can wake-up, rectify mis-thoughts, and return to Source?

:-)

Chapter Thirty

Family Duties

"What you must recognize is that when you do not share a thought system, you are weakening it."
A Course In Miracles

I am running through crowds of people in a panic trying to reach Rebecca's father Saul. He's a fugitive hiding inside a house and someone else is trying to enter it. I free three people from the house and run with them to a crowded bridge. The bridge suddenly clears. There's a lady selling some kind of cure Abigail invented to deal with deadly gas fumes.

The scene in my mind morphs. A list of funeral costs and names appears. Beth's name is clear to read, *Beth $800*. Startled to think a childhood friend may be dying, I rise abruptly and decide to see if Ruth contacted her.

The printer displays all zeros when turned on. I'm born again to live, to give, to love, to appreciate, to share, and to enjoy. Time fills with conscious union in the presence of Source (quietly voicing gratitude, praying, and studying) before downloading the next free "Pathway to Prosperity eCourse." It remains unread along with many others. There's neither time nor desire to read it.

In the late afternoon, I dress for Samuel's fourteenth birthday party. The rest of the family left hours ago in Ruth and Naomi's speed boat to cruise along waterways to the restaurant. I chose to drive my car not willing to forego the usual routine. Sunday evenings at the Center with soul family are now habitual.

My birth family waves from beyond glass doors as I walk through the restaurant. They sit outside at a long table near the dock. What a pleasure to see Naomi's extended family! Rebecca's best friend Lydia, her husband Joseph, and their lovely one-year-old daughter, Mickey Loo Loo, welcomes me too. Lydia and Joseph waited a long time to cherish a child so it's wonderful to see them happily together.

Knowing Daniel's essence will attend, I've brought my camera to document the event. I'm especially happy to see an orb in a picture of Samuel as he opens the present from Daniel.

"Wow, a game system holder for the Nintendo DS Dad sent me," he says with a smile. "Thanks I needed this new stylus."

"Actually Samuel," I whisper laying a hand softly on his shoulder, "I didn't know you had a game system when I bought it. It's from your Uncle Daniel."

Samuel looks suddenly somber.

Everyone orders more beer so I ask for a Samuel Adams. Conversation centers on Martha's funeral. James remains unsure of what time mass will be but everyone plans to attend the following weekend. After eating cake, I excuse myself to set up the coffee station at the Center.

Three people new to Sunday services grace our presence. As we welcome them, I recognize one from Wednesday nights. There doesn't seem to be any advertising, other than my announcements during class and after Wednesday services, so I ask the other two how they learned of the service. One mentions a friend while the other notes he was just driving by and saw the lights on. Both are happy to be there for they can't attend day services due to work schedules. I vow to continue promoting night services before heading back to sleep in my room.

A few days ago, I heard, in my head, that it was time for a break. I think that means the times for me to get to a spot of revelation, of spiritual messages, is slowing down. The thought of not getting messages disturbs me because I want to wake more often, before dreaming. Yet, the alarm on my new clock refuses to work. I drift off to sleep hoping for insights. A message comes thirty minutes later.

You can change your perceptions of earth very beyond what you have here.

A copy of the check from the lawyer sits taped to the file cabinet next to my head. Seeing it reminds me to deposit the real check later in the afternoon. I quickly decide to alter the copy to reflect a payment of 1.2 million dollars for the sale of my company.

Pictures of Dad and Martha flow easily from scanner to computer when the morning ritual completes. This process helps to preserve old photos and makes it easy to design posters. Memorial pictures are valuable to my family. Photos of Daddy will help to replace our last memories of him. Perhaps James and his sister may appreciate my efforts on Martha's behalf too.

Email fills time later in the day. Several members of the Greece tour group ask about trip DVD's. Although the thought of making money sounds good, it seems impossible to designate a price for them. Each request receives this reply before I quickly dress to deposit my check at the credit union.

A joint savings account held with Samuel insures that lawsuit funds stay under my control. It greatly disappoints me to learn the bank takes two weeks to clear the check.

As another cold front passes through, I'm grateful for cooler weather when walking to Rev. Bump's evening class. She asks us to meditate daily. I smile broadly knowing efforts will be rewarded.

Two women from the Greece tour fill dreams the next morning. Kim and her mom are selling everything they have to move quickly. I rise confused, use the bathroom, and quickly return to bed. A bit later, I'm pleased to hear five words swimming in my brain. *The story is ongiving love.*

Sleeping is easy after another quick bathroom trip, but messages continue, mixed with memories of past events. I wonder minutes later if the words now in my brain refer to a life regression completed last year. *One package was 60 to 30 B.C.*

Life is indeed becoming easier to handle! I'm making the metaphysical leap, for priorities shift more each day, as the invisible becomes more real than what I physically see. Isaiah's CD facilitates meditation when the usual morning routine completes. It's normal for the CD to play all three tracks before the player automatically shuts off. This time Track Two, with Buddhist-like sounds, plays at least five times. The sounds guide me to relax.

The now familiar light show plays brilliantly behind closed eyes. Pulsing lights, mostly blue, red, and yellow, are quicker and longer than ever before. I easily sense the presence of Spirit using Daniel's essence to communicate and note several messages. I will see Abigail soon, and change where I live. There's a CD at Borders bookstore, and possibly the thrift store, with the Buddhist-type sounds allowing for deeper meditative states. I also hear concern, warning, or heads-up as Amos uses the lawsuit settlement funds. Meditation ends when the CD player turns itself off.

Wednesday nights' service summons me to attend several hours later. I dress quickly to arrive early. It's such a joy to settle into the audio station at the back of the room. The service uplifts but is over too quickly.

When I return to the house on 47th Drive, James announces there will be a Catholic mass for Martha, at St. Jerome's on Saturday morning, at nine o'clock. I'm not accustomed to leaving the house that early but know Spirit will make sure I'm ready at the appropriate time.

"That's great," I reply happily entering the kitchen where James stands, "because I've already started to design a memorial poster for her."

"There's no need for a poster, especially in the church," James says with emotionless authority.

"Well, we can display it after the service can't we?"

"We're going to a restaurant after the service and that's it. There's no place to display a poster and Mother didn't want a fuss. Forget about it."

I've never heard of having a restaurant meal after a funeral and now struggle with beliefs.

"I'm sure Rebecca would love to host something after the restaurant so we can all come together and reminisce. And since she lives in your parents home less than a mile away the location is perfect."

"Look," James says with a piercing stare, "Mother didn't want any fuss. We are going to respect her wishes. Just make sure you're ready to leave here on time for the service."

He turns abruptly and walks into the living room ending the conversation. I stand dumbfounded trying to make sense of rituals that are way beyond my current ideas. It seems archaic to not allow people to display emotions over a departed loved one but I want to respect the wishes of my husband and his sister. It's clear Martha no longer cares one way or the other.

After viewing photos of Martha on my computer, I log onto the Internet to check for airfare rates to Texas. Something tells me Beth needs us and her time to pass may be near. I email search results to Ruth letting her know Orbitz offers a $264 rate to Dallas.

"I think we should see Beth as soon as we can, just a hunch," I add.

The next morning I rise singing the words "Holy Key Lay" without knowing why. It's especially odd for I've also caught myself singing words to a song in the Dr. Seuss' *The Grinch Who Stole Christmas* movie. An oddly familiar but unknown tune that includes the words, "Fa, who, moray, in a gombay," often escape my lips as well. Perhaps these are the Sumari words spoken of in *Conversations of Seth Volume One*, channeled works of our other lives in other places. Yes, I am reading the book now.

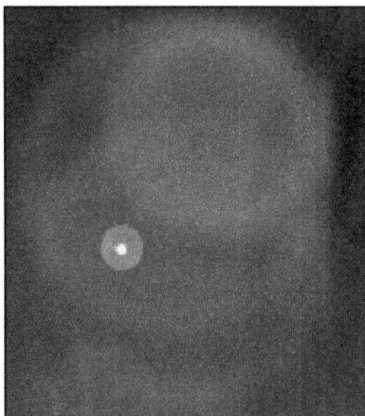

Meditation on the last day in November is again unique. At the end, before the third track ends, I'm in 'the gap' for a fleeting second or two losing all consciousness of what occurs. A faint blue, oblong orb appears after opening my eyes. I sense Martha's spirit. As I stare, a flash of light, a twinkle like a tiny star, quickly appears and enters the orbs form.

I leave at dusk to make coffee for Rev. Geddes because Leah can't make it. The shear number of people in class amazes me. It's nearly twice the amount of people in Tuesday night's class. Many classmates are there. The coffee station table is laden with treats brought by attendees, giving a sense of abundance and love, as everyone gathers around it to munch and talk.

Several people are taking the SOM 100 class again because Charles teaches it differently. I'm told each time you take the course you learn new things, even though it's the same class, because each teacher offers something new. By the time we stop for a break, I've decided to join the Thursday night group.

Anna stands near the restroom door. She notes the Course In Miracles study group just started again after a long hiatus. It's held bimonthly in a smaller classroom. She pulls me down the hall to meet the person in charge. Minutes later, I agree to attend next week.

I wake the following morning upon hearing myself sing *the earth is filled with his glory*. Since I listen to Christian music radio stations I know this song is called "Holy is the Lord." I love the lyrics and am thrilled to know, I sing in my sleep!

Music from the new "Third Day" CD flows through the air reviving the area. When not listening to it, I'm listening to the Christian radio station. Yet, certain songs are not as appealing as others are. Those that mention a God outside us, or vision humans as weak and frail, without the outside assistance of God or Jesus, appall me. I know we are much more powerful than most people believe and Spirit is a part of us, not something outside in Heaven.

The new day unfolds as usual. There's a minimal difference from other meditations because today I'm in 'the gap' for a fleeting second when it ends. A box is soon prominent in my mind's eye. It's magenta colored and even in size with sixteen squares, four down and four across. I open my eyes and note the occurrence in a journal.

After using the bathroom, I fall back asleep only to wake moments later with part of a sentence ringing through my brain. *...this can change the way you want it.* The words hold no meaning as I rise to study before meeting Leah for lunch.

It's truly a blessing to share with friends of like-mind. We're so excited that we often interrupt one another like two children. Our two-hour planned lunch turns into four before I finally leave for the Center.

December brings new opportunities. I'm happy to be a hospitality volunteer for Rev. Lockard who is in town for the week. His class serves to open my mind a bit further. When it's over, I return to my room thinking of Aunt Hagar. It seems prudent to telephone her since she's been on my mind lately. She answers the telephone with a tired voice on the second ring and reports Uncle John had his fifth heart operation. I promise to pray for him before saying good night. I'm not sure how to form the prayer because he's well into his eighties.

Treating for others is now becoming somewhat of an issue, especially when they are not the ones asking for prayers. I wonder if praying to prolong Uncle John's life will only serve to meet someone else's desires. Will prayer affect soul scripts or am I just in essence praying for myself?

Oh Lord thank you for this life. I am ready to move on. Spiral me out of this time. The words fill my brain before dawn. After trying to clarify when this physical life will be over, to no avail, I fall back asleep. Forty minutes later, it occurs to me that I do not choose the time, either when going out of body, or the time to be reborn. It's possible this information is from *Far Journeys.*

Meditation is boring and ordinary. When it's over, I pull the black dress from it's hanger in the closet and dress quickly knowing James will be ready to leave for Martha's service soon. I'm surprised the dress is perfect for the occasion because I bought it on a whim.

This will be my last wifely duty, I sense, as we silently climb into the white Chevy van. When James begins to turn before reaching the church, I ask why.

"We're stopping at the funeral parlor to meet my sister," he replies while turning into the large empty parking lot on the right.

"Aren't we supposed to meet everyone at St. Jerome's in five minutes?" I ask following him to the front door.

James is silent. The door opens as if by magic to admit us. It's difficult to be quiet, but I sense it's the right thing to do spotting Delilah and her husband standing silently in an alcove. I move forward and give them both a hug, consciously propelling love from my heart's core to theirs, before a man wearing an expensive business suit walks briskly into the room.

"Are you ready for the viewing?" he asks.

"We don't need to see her," Delilah replies with pursed lips while slowly shaking her head from side to side.

"But it's State law," the man insists. "Someone has to verify we've done our job."

"We trust you've done a good job," Delilah announces as she turns to sit next to her husband.

"If you could just take a glance at her that would be sufficient," the man persists.

I turn with the others and follow him towards the room where Martha's casket sits remembering it has been many, many, years since I've entered a funeral home. We stop twelve feet from the casket as Delilah notes the funeral home has done its job.

I'm compelled to walk closer and say goodbye to the woman I barely knew. As I pull away from the group, James announces that his mother didn't want anyone to see her dead.

"Nobody dies," I remark making my way to stand alone a foot from her casket-enclosed body.

"I'm sorry I didn't spend more time with you," I say to Martha under my breath. "You did a good job with James and I'm keeping my promise. I have taught him all I can. Now, I'm letting him go so his soul can grow."

I sense our connection before slowly turning to join the others as they file out the front door. The man in the expensive black suit stands holding the door open to a long, black limousine. Delilah and her husband climb into the car. James tugs on my arm to follow their lead. I'm on autopilot now, following intuition, trying to make polite small talk while we follow a sleek black hearse to what I suspect will be St. Jerome's Catholic Church.

When the limousine stops, James and I follow Delilah and her husband as they head for the far curb to wait for the casket. After it's expertly unloaded from the hearse, the men carry it into the church and place it up front on a stand near two sets of beautiful flowers. I follow Delilah passing the pew where the rest of my family sits and take my place in the front.

It surprises me to see that Martha's Florida nephew, and his wife Emily, are the only other people there. Moments later, Rachel arrives holding the hand of a quiet Abigail. I sense she waited for us to arrive before coming in because this is the first funeral they've been to since Daniel passed.

The mass is long and I'm not sure what to do when the priest asks the family to receive communion. I turn to Martha's nephew in the pew behind us.

"I'm not Catholic," I tell him as James rises to follow Delilah and her husband. "What should I do?"

"I can't tell you what to do," he replies solemnly.

All eyes are on me as I rise to take communion. I'm glad to be back in the pew when it's over. There's not a doubt in my mind that this is the last thing we will do as a family. The men rise to carry Martha's casket back to the hearse. I solemnly follow Delilah who walks slowly behind it.

Emily moves briskly up behind us. She stands between us and clasps our hands forming a bond of love and support. I'm grateful for her loving assistance as we walk behind our husbands.

Minutes later we're winding through the cemetery to place Martha's body next to Zephaniah's under a tree.

Everything seems odd for it's been decades since I've participated in a funeral. The service is thankfully short and soon we are on our way to Martha and Zephaniah's favorite restaurant blocks away. Rebecca offers her home as a place to gather after the meal.

"After all," she notes, "it is their house I'm living in."

I wholeheartedly agree and invite everyone to the house less than a mile away. Rachel sounds happy to follow us but Delilah and her husband, and Martha's nephew and wife, have other plans. The occasion ends hours later after a few of us reminisce and give tribute to Martha. Her passing was unexpected but I know a blessing for everyone.

Comforting words fill my head the next morning. *You're observing grace from a beautiful point of earth.*

Meditation is another new experience. Behind closed eyes, I see a moving picture of two figures that appear to be a man and a child. In my mind's eye, the man is on the right side and both of them stand in front of what looks to be a window. I sense they are Daniel and Abigail.

As I watch, Daniel's form floats up above Abigail and moves to her left and then back up above her head. Abigail's form turns into a magenta colored light when his form reaches her head. Daniel's form then floats down to the left of the magenta light and becomes one with it. The picture disappears and for a fleeting time, 'the gap' rules. I realize it as my throat makes the guttural sound made when I weighed more and snored.

:-)

Chapter Thirty-One

Meditation Reaps Rewards

"We can sense that beyond our most profound concepts of God something exists that transcends anything we can know with our intellects, something that is beyond limitation, something that includes us in all that it is, something we can experience at the inner depths of our beingness."
Walter Starcke – It's All God

Life continues to expand with interesting, exciting, and wonderful events. The unseen sporadically tampers with my laptop, turning the screen off making work impossible. This week's assignment for the *It's All God* class is challenging because I want to keep a duplicate but the copier refuses to work. The printer constantly aligns ink cartridges. It cancels halfway through when I try to perform the task.

I quickly type Uncle John's Treatment into the computer to print it using another method. The printer works normally after plugging it into the laptop. Homework ends upon making a small change to Walter Starke's version of the "Lord's Prayer." Starke's version is almost perfect but changing the word higher, to inner, matches my new state of awareness. This revised prayer is a perfect addition to the daily ritual for it's time to seek the Truth from my Inner Self. [58]

As Walter states, "The only problem with calling the divine self the Higher Self and the human self the lower self is that the words higher and lower convey a sense of superiority and inferiority rather than just different parts of one whole."

Rev. Haggerty offers an excellent talk on Sunday night while I wonder where the usual ministers are. A fifty-dollar bill slips into the donation basket when she's not looking. We leave together as soon as the coffee station is clean. I grab a copy of "Pure Inspiration" to read at home before turning off classroom lights.

A blaring TV assaults the air at the house on 47th Drive. I feel like a fugitive moving quickly through the den, dining room, kitchen, and hall to the comforting energy of my room to read.

An article by Dr. Masaru Emoto draws my attention. His experiments with water demonstrate the effects of thoughts and words. While positive compassionate words comfort and heal, negative words, and insults, hurt. Water treated with love and gratitude creates beautiful, complete crystals but exposed to people saying negative things such as, "You fool," results in incomplete and malformed crystals.

Emoto's research is significant because the human body is seventy to ninety percent water (infant bodies are about ninety percent water). Research shows we can be hurt emotionally and as water, be physically changed for better or worse by thoughts and words. When Daniel's essence guided me to discard many CDs with negative words, I had no idea why. Now I recognize that beautiful music heals. I'm gratefully on the right track knowing if the mind perceives something as possible, it's much easier to achieve.

The magazine article spurs my self-healing mission forward. Body chemistry always changes when we begin an inner merging with our Higher Self. The change instinctively refines our energy system. My body is healing. It's been many months since I've taken any medication and the pain is much less.

Griscom explains in her book *Time is an Illusion*, once the body experiences higher vibrations and states of consciousness (such as bliss and rapture) it yearns to deepen such perceptions. While experiencing high frequencies, we are not "home" for lower vibrations. "They do not coexist. Our electromagnetic field simply does not attract them."

I sigh with relief and move on to the next article, a list of things to do for successful living. Since I'm already dreaming big with high goals, I have no issue with number one on the author's to do list. I'm also grateful to believe in myself, have mentors, work hard, and stay focused. The author's advice to be humble seems appropriate for I've heard my task is to learn how to be humble.

Arrogance filled early years of struggle while fighting the illusory demons within. I always thought being humble meant to be meek, not proud. Yet, *A Course In Miracles* notes humility is a lesson for the ego, which consists of accepting our role in salvation, for that is truly why we're here. Salvation is a reminder that this world is not our home and nothing we see is really there at all. The thought soothes me for it seems increasingly difficult to stay focused as negativity creeps back into the house creating adverse conditions.

The feats of Dr. William Tan, noted in the next article, amaze me. He set many new world records, despite a devastating condition. Paralyzed from the waist down, Dr. Tan still managed to tap into immense personal power that changed his life. Clearly, pushing personal limits helps to redefine what's possible.

The CD player zips through all three tracks when I turn it on to meditate. Tracks switch at a rapid pace for several minutes while I lie patiently with closed eyes. The volume adjustment knob broke months ago so I've been listening to the player through headphones set upon my chest. Today the volume is lower making it possible to put the small earplugs into my ears without discomfort. A broad smile fills my face recalling the many times Daniel's spirit directed me while driving in the car. His essence surrounds me now.

The second meditation on Track Three begins. I'm not ready to return to the waking state when it ends and silently ask the entity controlling the CD player to switch to another track. The CD player makes the noise it usually does when changing tracks but turns off.

"I can turn it on by myself if it does not start again," I silently note.

A voice promptly informs me I don't need to have the CD player on. I am where I need to be to communicate. The entity then asks if that is what I want, to communicate with the spirit known as Daniel. I choose to communicate with the spirit offering the highest good of all, the one that can increase my understanding.

I'm instantly in tune with the entity that asked me the question, the communication link God placed in us, joining His mind with ours. We communicate for several minutes but I don't recognize the messenger. I'm very excited and ask for help, several times, to recall what's said for I don't want to forget any of it.

The now familiar gold-orange bursts of light flash, for several seconds behind still closed eyes, when the communication ends. I'm soon in the waking state, opening eyes to note the meditation occurred in less than an hour. I can't remember everything that transpired but recall the most important words. The "presence" repeated them several times. It's a message to share, and a personal communication for me.

*You are called upon to witness. You are called upon to witness that **there is unity even without knowledge**. And that **one day we will be united as One again**.*

The personal message came after asking if I should do something about moving.

You must go slow. You must train your mind to accept the Truth. You have all you need for a joyous and spontaneous life.

This utterly awesome experience fills me with gratitude. I'm excited beyond words. It's suddenly clear that by asking to always be with Daniel's spirit I'm blocking higher entities from coming through. I'm not yet ready to believe the messenger is God Himself.

Prayer rules as I give thanks for the interaction before logging onto the Internet to check email. Several messages require my time. I answer the business one first. It's time to renew the website. A1WebServer sponsored the site for years, without cost, ever since I put it on the Internet in 1996. But now it's time to pay the usual fee. There's no reason not to since my settlement check will soon clear the bank.

A delighted man notes charge card information when I telephone the Web host. It's easy to charge the fee to my Visa card. A1WebServer soon assures me all seven domain names will now forward to one domain. I move on reassured to renew the contract for our Internet Service Provider, which is almost double the cost of the Web host.

The next God communication fills me with delight in the morning even though I'm not certain what it means. *...but the twenty million who do these things, and act accordingly, will see the future.*

My throat makes a noise waking me to document the message. When the daily ritual completes, I lie back down to meditate. The CD player switches tracks to the Buddhist-like music. It quickly switches again to the second meditation before the track ends. Spirit is in control. Happy to know it, I quickly fall asleep still wearing headphones.

I'm up again an hour later. There's too much to do before tonight's *It's All God* class. Although I plan to attend a political meeting at a nearby restaurant, there's just not enough time. Thinking of a male classmate from the tour group, I grab copies of the nine Greece DVD's made to date and head out the door.

So many wonderful things are happening and everything is happening faster. When I offer the DVD's to my classmate he declines the gift. Minutes later another SOM Practitioner student arrives quite unexpectedly and gives me enough money to pay for the blank DVD's bought on credit. No reimbursement is necessary, I explain, for I only wanted to share. She notes it's clear by the way I talk that I've put a lot of love into making them and it makes her feel good to give me something back in return.

Everyone tells me how good I look saying my weight loss is noticeable. I have not tried very hard to lose weight but think heat flashes are contributing to both healing and weight loss. I'm down to 135 pounds as opposed to more than 170 in 2001 when I was so very ill. I have lost sixteen pounds since 2004 and at least ten of that in the past year. My goal is 125-130 pounds but I'm not going to get upset it if I don't get there. It's just nice to see stomach fat decreasing and to walk without my thighs rubbing together so much. Such joy from a human condition!

Conscious or not, words become flesh. It's time to replace undesirable habits with ones that reflect my true being for we become what we perceive and conceptualize. I must further change my theory of life, for as Starcke notes, concepts are imagination's fuel. Replacing the grooves created by years, eons, of confused misthought is vital.

Rev. Charles tells us permanent change comes through altered perception. I know it's necessary to reject the concept of illness and substitute one of wholeness to reap a full spiritual healing. As Charles so eloquently states, "I can not afford to take my wounds with me."

I'm prepared to share my journaling after the mid-class break when Charles intuitively asks for comments. It's of utmost importance to deliver the message received yesterday even though I may find it uncomfortable doing so. I've been called upon to behold the glory of One within us and spread the news of our unity.

"Does anyone relate to the words wake-up?" I nervously ask classmates when it's my turn to share. "I'm referring to page 131 where Starcke discusses the hypnotic state we may have inherited from past lives. It reminds me of the "rote" in *Far Journeys* by Robert Monroe who says we agree to forget our true state to be human again."

Looking straight ahead, I repeat the message of Oneness before quickly sitting down with a pounding heart. After most of the class leaves, I approach Charles with my most pressing question, glad he is filling in for Dr. Bump.

"Can you tell me what the flashes of light are that I see? They're like tiny twinkle lights."

"Oh, my dear child," he replies softly placing his hand on my shoulder. "You are blessed with the sight of God."

He seems to understand as I tell him about what appears to be tiny atoms circulating throughout the air. When I admit to being *A Course In Miracles* student, he reassures me that the jagged flashes of light are normal for Course students. His hug leaves me wanting more. I rush home to read page 25 of the Workbook for Students in *A Course In Miracles*, which notes:

"My thoughts are images that I have made. You will begin to understand (this idea to the process of image making) when you have seen little edges of light around the same familiar objects which you see now. As we go along, you may have many 'light episodes'. They may take many different forms, some of them quite unexpected. Do not be afraid of them. They are signs that you are opening your eyes at last. They will not persist, because they merely symbolize true perception, and they are not related to knowledge. These exercises will prepare the way to it."

Edgar Cayce once noted in a reading, experiencing "white lightening" the true Light, is symbolic of the awakening that is coming. "More and more as the white light comes to thee, more and more will there be the awakening." The colors seen hold different meanings. White is symbolic of "the light of the throne of mercy itself" while green represents healing, blue trust, and purple strength. Cayce further notes, "Ye may never see these save ye have withheld judgment or shown mercy."

After waking several times, I ask for guidance before rising. Kittens meow as they play outside the bedroom window. It's the first time I've heard them. The neighbor's dogs wake me minutes later. *...to continue the guidance and then to track it*, fills my brain.

The words hold no meaning but I document them quickly before meditating. Two magenta colored orbs cover my closed eye vision while facing the sun. They stay for a few minutes while the CD plays the first meditation track. Near the end of the second meditation, I realize my throat is again making some kind of noise. It probably started at what Isaiah refers to as Level Five (the receiving level), when he says to send light out into the world.

The CD is now at the spot where Isaiah instructs listeners to return. Just now, I realize that point is probably the one where I have seemed to be in 'the gap' before. I do not want to return to wakefulness but open my eyes to document the experience. Excitement fades when I turn the laptop on and the screen turns black. I change my mind and go to the bathroom deciding the experience is not to be recorded.

It occurs to me as I go about my business that Martha's spirit may be trying to communicate. Perhaps her spirit did not come through while I was meditating because she passed recently. I believe it takes a bit of time after a human passes to get more into the spiritual mode depending on several factors. One factor is the amount of unfinished business souls have left on earth when they transition. I am fairly certain Martha's business was finished. Another factor may have to do with the adjustment of going back to spirit form after being human. I really don't know.

Nevertheless, I decide to see if anything comes through just in case there is a message. Right before I leave the bathroom there's a fleeting thought about Rev. Mary Jo Van Damme Rance and Rev. Gerald Rance. I wonder why they missed the Sunday evening service for it's unusual for them to miss two Sundays within a few weeks of each other.

Brushing the thought away, I return to my room to sit on the futon in a lotus position with palms up, making sure to connect thumbs with index fingers. The laptop display is no longer black but I ignore it while trying to connect with Spirit.

Thoughts of Mary Jo and Jerry enter my mind within moments. Several weeks ago, I was guided to tell Mary Jo something. It seemed strange but I did it anyway. First, I mentioned how my family all thought I was crazy for saying and doing strange things. Then I said Spirit guided me to tell her something but I was not sure why. Mary Jo kept silent and did not make me feel odd when I spoke. Although I sensed something was going to happen to Jerry, I didn't verbalize that thought.

"I'm supposed to tell you, if you need somebody you can trust, you can count on me."

I now sit on my futon thinking, "Why am I thinking so much about Mary Jo and Jerry?"

Mary Jo and Jerry need you, echoes through my brain.

"Well when they come to me, call me, for assistance I will be there," I answer.

We interact for about a minute but I forget the communication upon asking a question.

"So am I at that point you call an ascending eclipse, an ascending spiral (as in the book *Far Journeys)*?"

Yes, the entity replies.

"Will I be able to avoid being human again?"

Have you not already chosen to be human again?

I recall hearing the time of 140 years several months ago. First, I thought it meant the world, as we know it, would end in 140 years. Right now, I think the 140 years is how long I will choose to stay out of human form until I get reborn as Daniel's child along with Rebecca. I then remember the entity told me there were other worlds and ask if I'll be able to see them.

You already have.

"Have I seen them all?"

I'm told that I have not.

The entity's last words fill me with glee. *You shall see.*

Terry telephones to spread the news that I'm the only one who has to wait two weeks for the settlement funds. His check will soon clear the bank. When our conversation ends the laptop screen flickers until I relax and connect with Spirit. I again sense concern for Amos now that his check cleared the bank.

Aaron telephones from Michigan to ask what cemetery Grandma and Grandpa are buried in. I'm glad he decided to do what everyone seems to want, which is to lay Dad's ashes to rest in the same place as his families. Dad's spirit doesn't care where his ashes go. Neither do I while reciting the names of ancestors buried there, making sure to let him know they include Dad's brothers, and a sister who passed at 21-years-old. Before the call ends, I let Aaron know I'll support his efforts, whatever they may be. I plan to fly back home and share the task.

The next morning there are no notes to review. I ask my Inner Self to reveal more of what I need to know for the highest good of all before falling back asleep.

Twenty minutes later a noise coming from the kitchen prompts thoughts of palmetto bugs. I rise to use the bathroom and change the disliked creature thoughts to ones of cocoons, butterflies, and birds while sitting on the toilet. A small, light gold orb appears about a foot and a half in front of me. As it slowly drifts by, I'm amazed to see the white tile grout behind it. Words fill my brain.

The form doesn't matter. We are all the same.

"Even creatures, we are all the same even creatures?" I ask with great emotion.

You will learn the truth, repeats throughout my brain.

I slip into 'the gap' for a few seconds during meditation at the usual point (when Isaiah refers to Level Five on the third track). The CD player soon turns itself off so I rise to recite the usual treatments before making up the futon.

A large black flea jumps in front of my eyes. Yesterday when I saw a flea, I picked it up, blessed it with good and love, and released it outside. This flea will not let me catch it so I go into my human mode. I'm not about to live again in a house overrun with fleas. After trying to catch it six times, the flea goes out of sight. Alas, it's another test.

The human part of me tells the flea that if it's an illusion in this illusionary world like I, it must go outside the house where fleas belong. Before leaving with my ego intact to buy flea spray at the store, I bless it with good and love but let it know that my bed (my futon) is my sanctuary.

Christmas shoppers fill the store as I hurry to get in line with my purchase. There's one aisle empty of bodies. I move to it quickly. My eyes rest on a set of penguin shower curtain hooks halfway down the aisle and I know they're for me. Someday soon, I will have my own house and the hooks will match my penguin shower curtain perfectly.

The day finally comes in June 2013 as I settle into a marvelous sanctuary steps from Fort Lauderdale's beach. Due to many circumstances, including ridding myself of almost all belongings and moving to another state for several months, it's somewhat of a miracle to see the shower curtain and hooks in one of few boxes.

Terry telephones when I return from the store to say his check cleared the bank. The credit union still holds mine for another

311

week so I decide when large sums of money come to me, and I have no doubt they will, I'll open a bank account elsewhere. The interest on the money is not something to ignore.

Minutes later Aaron telephones to ask what Grandpa's name was. He seems surprised when I tell him it is now his name.

"It will be interesting to see what else today brings," I think while on my way to the Course In Miracles study group. Anna greets me there. We hug warmly feeling one another's energy while heaving sighs of joy to be in each other's presence.

My plan to remain silent changes when I disclose the three most prominent times I've felt the overwhelming Love of God. All eyes focus on me while discussing a near death experience at age sixteen, the arms of God holding me on my last birthday, and the magenta colored orb seen last New Year's Eve.

We participate in a love exercise at the end of class. I sense my words made a difference. Although it seems strange for people I have not met to hold and love me, the wonderful sense of Oneness is overwhelming. It seems as if I'm getting more love than anyone else in the group. But it still doesn't compare to my three prominent experiences with God. I leave class planning to return. It's a real bargain for the small five-dollar donation.

Meaningless words run through my brain upon waking the next morning. My mind wanders wondering what to concentrate on next. I'm wavering between treating for the business sale and finishing a book started many years ago.

Before meditating, I ask, "What should I do now?" The gap beckons when the CD player plays Track One. A strong urge to stay within the gap persists when the last track ends. Spirit spoke. Yet, the only words I remember are the last two, *teach everyone*. The answer is not surprising, for things will fall into place, while I teach everyone the true nature of our being.

The usual treatments are repeated with passion before going online to spend two gift cards received last Christmas. The Borders URL sends me to Amazon where Karen Drucker's Spirit CD's are on sale. Gift cards are more than enough to complete my collection. I am absolutely thrilled while shutting the computer down to go pick up Samuel from school.

Shortly after he gets into the car, Samuel sees a copy of the check I've made out to myself for the sale of the business.

"That doesn't look like a real check Nana," he says quickly. "You know you're not going to get a million dollars for your business."

I stop for the last traffic light before his house and reply. "No, I'm not Samuel. I've decided to change the amount to 9.2 million dollars for 1.2 million just doesn't seem enough."

Samuel shakes his head but doesn't reply. Minutes later, he's telling Rebecca that I've copied the check from Grandpa's lawsuit and changed it.

"You'll never sell that business," Rebecca scoffs.

I leave for the house on 47th Drive determined to no longer share dreams with family. It only serves to hold me back.

The next morning starts normally with treatments and meditation. I'm unable to focus until the second meditation plays. At Level Five, breath expels out of my mouth instead of my nose as usual. The unconscious movement takes me by surprise before rising to go onto the Internet.

:-)

Chapter Thirty-Two

My Birthday Week

"The mind is very powerful, and never loses its creative force. It never sleeps. Every instant it is creating."
A Course In Miracles

Sunday morning's words fill me with delight.

I can fix all things with my hands.

Energy radiates throughout the room while I envision healing others and myself. The notion partners well with another thought of teaching children how to manifest food when hungry.

Green orbs drift by during meditation. I'm lost in 'the gap' with no memory of what's occurred until a picture of a box floats before still closed eyes. People are inside the box. They slowly float into a large, blue orb.

I remain in trance for several minutes receiving (what, I don't know), until unconsciously drawing a deep breath. It's as if something unseen directs my physical form, and now, returns control back to me. Familiar upper body heat overwhelms so I kick the sheet off my body to cool down.

*The puzzle pieces of this amazing life assemble much more rapidly two years later. So much has happened since beginning this strange process. I had no idea it was preparing me for what I'm doing today. I am one of many souls who chose to return to this illusion to wake everyone up to the fact that **this is an illusion of our souls making**.*

Blue orbs represent new life. Seeing figures of people, restricted in a box (representing the limited earth), float into a blue orb, signifies a new consciousness. The vision reminds me of my soul's contract. It activated the process that led me to where I am now. This notion fits perfectly with everything Lightworker sources such as Karen Bishop and Patricia Diane Cota-Robles teach.

*Although the global economy seems worse every day, I know it's an illusion we came to experience as souls. The wonderful part is that we **can** change it with our thoughts. There are thousands, if not millions of people, now praying and treating for a New Earth where money is obsolete and the world is ruled by Divine Love, peace, and harmony.*

I sense the number of Lightworkers is now much larger than ever before and grows quickly with each passing second. Gregg Braden and David Wilcox verify many things I've intuitively known, with evidence of scientific research, showing how the world around us, and our very bodies, are evolving. I'm grateful to play my role.

During the night, I wake and wander into the den where the motion detector light is on. The message comes quickly when I sit in James' big, brown, executive chair.

A path will show the way.

White and magenta colored orbs sit inside the basket of dried flowers on the computer desktop in my room. One magenta colored orb lingers for several minutes. I feel Daniel's presence, and missing him greatly, realize it's always with me. They are all with me!

I hide catastrophe fills my brain in the morning. Time passes quickly as the daily ritual of treatments, meditation, and study continues. I instantaneously escape in Level Five during morning meditation. Again, when the CD ends, it's hard to return to wakefulness.

Another period of meditation in the afternoon enlightens me. Something sits on my forehead during the second track so I pause to free it through the window. The CD player switches tracks several times before finally playing the first track again. As Isaiah's words fill my brain, I recall being in 'the gap' the first time Track One played. Magenta colored orbs grace closed eye vision near the end of Track Three.

Communication begins.

The interaction lasts two to four minutes. It verifies that the memory of Daniel holds me back from further evolution. The entity helping me now is more appropriate for my current level of awareness. If I continue to ask for Daniel's essence, does it exclude the higher being? I must let go now and forget the memory of Daniel. I must train my mind to accept things I do not understand.

The message is clear as an oval, golden orb drifts past, while words swiftly enter my brain.

We discuss the process of creating our own realities in the *It's All God* class later. Yes, I must pay more attention to my thoughts, words, and deeds to create a better reality. Now it makes perfect sense. Childhood concepts molded my behavior. Those false beliefs manifested thoughts that personalized my view of the world and resulted in projections, which stopped me from taking responsibility.

We're now on break until 2007 but it doesn't stop me from doing homework. Daily journaling is complete after twenty-five minutes of meditation.

I later note the first of three "ah-ha" moments, prompted after reading page 156 in *It's All God*. It's clear that after making Spirit the first priority, the Principle of life manifests everything we need. There are no other priorities to make for one truly does act as Spirit, one part of the whole, in every instance.

A quote sparks another "ah-ha" as I realize ego is gone after making Spirit the first priority. It's then all for the highest good. Starcke notes, "When we fully see ourselves primarily as consciousness, we can take up or lay down our bodies at will. We can come and go because time and space no longer limit us. Death ceases because there is nothing in consciousness that dies. Seek ye first the kingdom of God, and you will be able to see that it is all God."

Thoughts flow forth like a quickly moving stream. We lay down our bodies when sleeping but may not remember this when waking. I prefer to view "the kingdom of God" as a big bowl of Universal Consciousness. We are all in it and a part of each other. Even after physical death, we're able to communicate with others. There is no death. There is only a change of form!

Recognizing another "ah-ha" moment when reading the class text is easy. Starke notes, "The first law of human nature may be a hypnotic state that we have inherited from past lives. If so, we have to undo or replace it."

The words again remind me of Robert A. Monroe's research in out-of-body states. Monroe describes this forgetting as something we do to be reborn. We're spirits in various states of learning and undergo this "hypnotic state" to experience things and gain knowledge. We are here to help one another recognize Oneness.

Some of us have certain prompts to help us remember. The phase "wake-up" may be a major prompt.

After eons of struggling through homework, it's truly amazing that I love doing it now. My new treatment "I Put God First" completes tonight's assignment. [59] I quickly note how praying to God implies we are separate. But all things are part of the whole. There's no begging or bargaining as *It* just is! Faith in the whole is the key to "waking up."

Several messages go onto the yellow legal pad, next to my bed, during the wee hours of the morning. I have no idea what they mean upon waking. They're noted in order but one phrase stands out among the rest. *To perceive your abundance as loss is not good.*

I'm soon in 'the gap' for a short time near the end of the second meditation at Level Five. This time, orbs behind closed eye vision change from yellow-gold to the color of magenta. My mind says there's something extraordinary about the sun. Something amazing happens when meditating or lying with my face towards the sun.

The Christian radio station is a Godsend later as music blasts from the living room. Glad James is at work, I turn the speakers around to face my room while checking email. People still send notes of thanks for the weekly business newsletter. I wince reading, "keep up your important work!" It's only a short matter of time before I stop.

Ego leads me to review news of the outrageous electronic voting machine meltdown in Florida. Voting machines appear to have flat-out lost 18,000 votes for Congress. An inkling of the havoc electronic voting causes came during the last year I held the office of secretary for a national group. Now I forward the MoveOn.org email to friends hoping they will help repair our broken election system.

It's such a blessing to have friends of like-mind nearby. Both Leah and Mary email often between our times together. Today's email holds their messages. Leah sends a wonderful quote from page 79 of *Emmanuel's Book*. I already know the connection of love is never broken but am thrilled to verify once again that the soul will come even if reincarnated.

Mary's email warrants attention. Her session with psychic/medium Sally Baldwin went well. Now, she wants company to attend a monthly channeling in Pompano Beach. I reply, knowing she's ready to check out the Center. Minutes later, she agrees to come with me to class the night before in exchange for accompanying her on a Friday night.

The next morning words from the Christian song "Cut" wake me. I've been singing in my sleep again! It's a result of listening to Christian music stations. Disc jockeys play songs as close to my beliefs as I can find. Yet, it's distressing that many of the songs breed thoughts of a God outside us. Happy to know the truth, I fall back asleep.

...and I am never alone.

The words wake me several minutes later. After a quick bathroom trip, I start softly repeating treatments out loud. James is still getting ready for work. My voice grows louder when he leaves shortly before sunrise.

A spirit soon enters the room and speaks.

Forget your humanness. Be one with All.

The spirit instantly disappears. I smile, happy to meditate, and soon fall into 'the gap' between here and there. It lasts a few fleeting seconds before Isaiah's voice reminds me to breathe in yellow sunshine.

A single Christmas tree needle rests on my computer chair. Daniel's voice fills my brain.

"Merry Christmas Mama. It's coming Mama, be patient. It's coming."

The spirit of my last-born son lets me know a new life lies ahead! I'm pleased to see the Christmas tree needle for we have not had a Christmas tree since 2003. The needles from that tree still sit in two large covered containers hidden in the closet.

Mary meets me at the Center in the evening. We sit together to hear Rev. Charles speak. Another group occupies our usual classroom while we enjoy the large sanctuary's energy. Charles grasps a stone as he tells us all living things have a story and stones are no different. Mary stares with wide-eyed disbelief as he calmly relates the stone's story. She's not accustomed to hearing someone channel what appears to be an inanimate object.

"Wait until tomorrow night," she tells me before leaving. "Sally's channeling is a bit easier to understand and believe."

I smile and give her a warm hug before she gets into her silver Mazda RX to roar quickly into the black night.

Minutes later, I'm in my room dealing with a Trojan Horse 2 virus, which infected the laptop. I am ever so grateful to have backed up all daily work while reformatting the hard drive. It's past two o'clock in the morning by the time I restore the software.

Sleep comes easily. Several times, when waking during the night, I recall singing, "I trust in the unseen." It's part of a popular song played on Christian radio stations. I log the words in my journal, use the bathroom, and return to sleep. Although I'm tired from repeatedly waking throughout the night, I no longer wish to sleep normally. Waking thoughts and messages are cherished treasures.

I rise again to recall saying *grateful I AM.* Ego silently thanks James for this opportunity to wake and sleep while he works to support us. The usual treatments are repeated before drifting back to sleep. Minutes later, I wake remembering ... *kind, compassionate, loving, and giving.* They're words from my list of things to be thankful for. Sleep beckons once again but I wake minutes later with a new message.

Holy Moses taught all his brethren, one by one, to be one with God. And the Truth shall set you free.

The telephone rings near the end of the first meditation later in the morning. The CD player refuses to cooperate when I try to restart it. Tracks continually change while it clicks and makes a whirling sound.

"So take me where you want me to be," I loudly announce.

The CD stops on the first track then speeds up as it does when I'm to concentrate. It turns off as I close my eyes thinking it's the end of my non-meditation.

I calmly ask, "This is where you want me to be?"

There's no response.

It's a joy to meet Mary later at Ronnie B's for dinner before going to Sally Baldwin's channeling. We arrive at the meeting spot to learn tonight's focus will be Annie Luther, Sally's sister, who recently passed to the Otherside. Many audience members knew her in human form.

Several people distribute pieces of paper for the audience to write down memories of Annie. The paper has tiny butterflies in the corner that glimmer like fireflies when it's laid down on the chair beside me. Flashes of light are within them so I assume the paper has glitter sprinkled among the butterflies. When I look at mine, there's no light, no glitter of any sort. I look again at the paper on the seat next to me. It's now devoid of anything that would glitter or make light.

The room gets amazingly quiet as Sally begins to communicate with her sister who was ill for many years. Annie soon notes through Sally that she's grateful, for the first essence of energy that she feels emanating from the material plane. She begins to describe her now heightened senses, as she sees us all shifting and changing in color, equal in light.

Annie notes we must open our minds and hear her words even if we do not fully understand. She tells us when we are true to the existence of our divinity, and open to it, we have an opportunity to go somewhere with it. "Somewhere big, somewhere that changes the world. Remember that. Hold onto that," Annie relates through Sally's voice.

Since I shunned the system my entire life, it comes as no surprise to hear her tell us to think out of the box, beyond the reality we believe to be true. By focusing on what we believe to be normal in a third-dimensional way of thinking, we miss out on the mystical, overlooking things like the lights. My ears perk up hearing that fleeting flashes of light are guiding and giving us messages.

"The lights are a new language," Annie relates.

I've been paying attention to them but have yet to get into the language that speaks to our heart and soul. Yet, I'm glad to hear the brilliant flashes of color help us transcend. Excitement builds when Annie speaks of colors beyond the essential spectrum of light that we know as real for I've begun to see colors I didn't know existed.

She continues and notes the language of lights has been part of humanity's experience for eons. It's the light patterns and language of light that opens us up to other dimensions of who we are. There's no need to find higher powers or get in touch with ascended masters for they're part of the light. By learning the language of lights, we can find those many pieces of who we are.

The light is everywhere. It's just a matter of following it. When we transition, we feel more fully a part of that vibrational frequency. Annie tells us to start by looking at a candle or the lights outside, to see the aura or bands around them. By moving on to focus attention on a light outside, contrasted with some darkness, we'll see the aura and bands of light around it and beyond. Her words make a great deal of sense.

My experience of lights started when Daniel passed. It increases daily in different ways. Still, I don't always note the times I see lights or faint orbs because I forget, or am not sure my mind is not playing tricks on me. Now, knowing what I see is the real thing; I'll make more of an effort to document light-related events.

Sally begins to field questions from the audience. I'm anxious to see if Daniel will come through and ponder how to ask a question without divulging that my son passed from his physical state. She channels souls from the Otherside for members of the audience as I silently form a question. When Sally calls on me, I ask a vague question about souls, which I soon forget. Her vague answer leaves me wanting more of an explanation.

When the meeting ends, I move to the front of the room to tell Sally about the flashes of light I saw within the butterflies. She smiles and says Annie always liked butterflies. Mary and I leave after I thank Sally for the session. We part after a few minutes of conversation.

The large red candle still glows in my room when I return. Before preparing for bed, I blow it out and trim the wick to make sure it glows throughout the night. Sleep comes easily but I wake, as usual, several times to use the bathroom.

My eyes focus on the candle at 4:48 AM. It glows brightly for a few seconds before the communicator rings of light that Annie discussed in class appear. First, glowing rings form around the candle then what looks like bubbles spring forth from the bottom of the flame. The bubbles appear on each side of the candle and move up above the glow of the flame. It's really neat to finally see so I quickly try to draw it.

The truth about you, has been, and always will be.

The words ring throughout my brain at 5:05 AM. Other words were spoken but I can't remember them.

Fifty minutes later, I'm up again to hear *look at the light*. I rise, look at the candle, and see what seem to be bubbles streaming from it. They continue to burst forth for about thirty seconds as I silently wish for words to appear so we can really communicate. The silent reply that rings through my brain seems curt.

That is enough.

When the bubbles stop, I turn the light on and try to rationalize. Perhaps the white face on the big candle behind the little one burning now made it easier for me to see the bubbles. I shrug my shoulders, go to the bathroom, and fall back asleep. Another message wakes me at seven o'clock.

We are going on.

Light rings through my brain as the familiar upper body heat engulfs me minutes later. The candle flickers while I repeat the usual meditation sensing it may be time to tweak the words. Another trip to the bathroom makes it easy to drift back asleep.

...Pompeii is being destroyed. ...run for your lives, echoes through my brain at 8:45 AM. There's now a sense I may have lived in Pompeii long ago.

I recall another recent message after sunrise that prompts me to believe we changed our future here on earth.

"The cataclysms of the earth will return mirroring Pompeii. They will stop as the people come together as One."

Earthquakes in Haiti, Japan, Chile, and China afforded humanity yet another means to lift collective consciousness to that perfect point. I know all is in Divine Order.

A message I'm to keep silent about comes right before meditating. The gap beckons while both meditation tracks play. As the CD ends, a small, blue orb, shaped like a bird, drifts across my closed eyes from right to left.

It's a race to finish treatments and study before Rebecca and Samuel arrive to shop with me. They quickly talk me into having my birthday dinner with family the following night. As I drift off to sleep, the words *birthday power* jolts me awake. In five minutes, I will officially be fifty-six human years old.

It's 77 degrees in the house when I wake feeling "the heat" upon me at 4:15 AM. Pools of sweat lie under and around my breasts, reminding me of many miserable nights, before the final hysterectomy stopped night sweats in the 1990's.

The candle is communicating but I hear nothing. I only see the rings, like radio waves of communication, emitting from the flame's center in increasingly large circles. As I watch, the rings morph into scattered pinpricks of light forming a circle shape around the flame. It reminds me of glimmering snowflakes.

Realizing it's my birthday, I rise, use the bathroom, and promptly fall back to sleep. A sentence is on my mind at six o'clock. *I don't need to put that out there in Mind.* Although I don't know what it refers to, I sense it's a good thing to remember saying during astral travel.

After another bathroom trip, I fall asleep only to wake again at 8:00 AM. This time I recall being with someone and saying, "...party. Let's get invited this time." Sun peeks through clouds as I take a sip of water, get up to use the bathroom, and return to sleep.

Forty-five minutes later, I'm up again but can't recall any words. The sun is farther to the southeast and on my right. A pattern that looks like a window screen appears when my eyes close. The edges of the screen are made of light. The lines within them are brighter shades of light.

"Raise your hands," an unknown voice says inside my head. I raise my hands, palms up, to receive my gift, not knowing what it is. I'm so very grateful for the precious gift received from the One.

Daniel has come through, in a big way, on my birthday every year since he passed so there's no doubt; he will today. I turn on the CD player for my meditation period. It changes tracks on its own ignoring Track One. The track indicator display climbs to ten, eleven, twelve, and right up to sixteen before it stops back on track number one. Isaiah's meditation CD has only three tracks so I wonder if I put Daniel's 2005 Memorial CD in the player instead.

As Track One finally begins to play, I'm confused to realize the meditation CD indeed sits in the player. I smile sensing the essence of my last-born son. After welcoming and thanking him, we communicate as I receive another unexpected gift of 'Super Love.'

Track One plays a few seconds up to Level Two where the "orange jaw" relaxes the body. It then whizzes through the three tracks as I focus on the message. Daniel's spirit tells me to be in the Now and enjoy my gift.

So much happens, is received, that I'm afraid it's going too fast and I won't remember it all. "I'm not getting it all," I silently repeat before hearing, even though that is my thought, I am indeed *getting it all*. It is all being stored in my memory. For the moment I relax, and just go with the flow, putting trust in the process.

It's a quickly paced communication with Daniel noting everyone in the family will be happy for me and for them because lives will change for the better. I will get my own place to live.

Yellow-gold flashes of light move rapidly through my mind while lying still with closed eyes. It's like a strobe light with pulsating lights flashing on and off, but the light moves back and forth, and up and down, and so do my eyes behind closed lids. It is so way cool, way more beautiful than anything remembered. This gift is unmatched by anything, except perhaps, the beauty of orbs I occasionally see.

Level Five claims me for at least forty minutes while feeling like I'm in Heaven on earth. The CD repeatedly changes to Track Two, playing the sound of chimes, which I've grown to love. At numerous points, the volume on the CD player turns down and I become concerned the session will end. Yet, each time the volume lowers; it changes tracks, rises again, and continues to play.

At least four times, the CD player changes tracks and whizzes through them before stopping on a meditation track. The track plays for only a few seconds before changing again making it impossible to determine if I hear Track One or Track Three. It finally plays through the second meditation on Track Three. I gladly send purifying, healing light out into my body, the house, and all in it, and ultimately the universe.

Now I'm in 'the gap' but think it's time to stop. As in the past week or so, I don't want to return to waking consciousness. Another message comes before the session finally ends.

We will never leave you. We are One.

Great warmth now causes me to break out into a sweat instead of feeling the usual periodic cold when meditating. It's the same warmth experienced when communicating with Spirit. I now recall telling guides that it's okay if I waste away due to the increased energy. It would be wonderful to feel this beloved connection all the time.

The gift is beyond describing, while in the physical state, but I quickly pick up my laptop attempting to recall it in a somewhat understandable form. My fingers move quickly over the keyboard.

It's soon time to dress for an early bird birthday dinner. This dinner will be different from the last birthday celebrated at Florida Seafood House. Now, I know how to fill a room with loving energy.

James and I drive together for the short ride as I consciously send out waves of love.

The family arrives on time. No one minds hearty hugs as waves of love radiate out, from the core of my heart, to theirs.

There's no complaining during dinner. I'm amazed that everyone gets along. It's as if they all agreed, just as we do at vacation time, to avoid conflict. I'm thrilled when Ruth hands me a one-hundred dollar gift card from a bookstore before dessert.

"Everyone pitched in to make sure you got what you wanted this year," she tells me with a wide grin.

I thank them all. What a pleasure to share this joyous and happy time! The waitress arrives with a cake filling me with more joy as everyone breaks out into a round of "Happy Birthday." We soon bid one another goodbye. James drives home alone when I quickly decide to attend Sunday night's service.

It's a scant five-minute walk to the Center. I'm surprised to see only a few people in attendance. Rev. Van Damme Rance and Rev. Rance are strangely low-key but the message inspires as usual. They're happy when I offer to help clean up the coffee station before walking home.

Sleep comes easily after studying *The Science of Mind*. I'm awake hours later after hearing *...it's a rule*. Shaking my head, I write it down before trudging into the bathroom. After accomplishing my business, I fall quickly back asleep. Dawn breaks upon hearing something has the ability to work beyond the sunset.

It's easier to move into trance during meditation. Beeps fill the air as the CD player repeatedly zips through all three tracks before finally stopping on Track Two. The chimes are barely audible and soon seem to stop making me think the player turned itself off. I lie still thinking the session is over but try to get into a deeper state, without Isaiah's guidance. The volume comes back on as Track Three plays. It plays the very end of the track as I send healing light to the world and beyond.

My watch documents the entire meditation session lasted less than ten minutes. It's enough time for today because my jaw is slack and my mouth is open. I am ever so grateful while rising to dress before meeting Leah for lunch and a matinee.

Our time fills with hugs and laughter. We talk non-stop for four hours before finally seeing the movie. How wonderful to be guided by Spirit and to share with a friend of like-mind!

:-)

Chapter Thirty-Three

Detecting the Unseen

"There is beauty everywhere. You have only to take it all in."
SAM – Book of One :-) Volume 1

I wake briefly upon hearing *...all good, love, love*. A shooting star passes through the eastern sky. Later, my eyes open after thanking someone at 6:00 AM. "Thank you for your gifts," I'd said. "*Look at the candle*," a voice echoes in my brain.

A large, pulsating circle glows around the flame. Little circles, along with other unfamiliar patterns, are inside the large circle. I sense communication but fail to decipher the message. Spring water supports me throughout the night because my throat gets very dry. The bottle is now empty so I trudge to the pantry for another. The shining, den, motion detector light leads me across the dining room to stand on the step.

Come, come, I hear.

It feels good to sit in the leather executive chair, filled with relief and hope, while gazing above the old wooden bookcase. James scraped the ceiling around the hole. It's now more than a foot long and about six inches wide. Cats scamper up a metal ladder James left outside the window leading to the roof.

The lights of communication are the key, the key to all, all, all.

After thanking the messenger, I return to my room to meditate. The CD player switches tracks several times before stopping to play the soothing sound of chimes. Track Three begins after I'm relaxed. Sunlight peeking through clouds shines on my face as Isaiah speaks of sunlight on the CD. Several multi-colored orbs fill closed eye vision when the player turns off. There's no need, or desire, to turn the CD player back on. I'm guided daily and it's way cool to have these experiences!

The Internet occupies time upon finishing my morning ritual. Intuition informs me Panda antivirus software costs more than it's worth. It keeps deleting expensive computer programs I

326

have painstakingly taken the time to reload. Downloading free antivirus programs to replace it, I struggle with negative thoughts about dishonest people who prompt companies to make it difficult for those who legitimately own software.

In "Drawing the Larger Circle," the Addingtons note a blessing technique for getting along with difficult people. They suggest listing things you like about the person and then things you don't like. Next, you bless them morning, noon, and night, for all the things you don't like. For instance, if the person is impatient, you bless them for their patience. I'm thankful for the article and vow to use the technique more often while blessing companies, for perfectly working, noninvasive software.

It suddenly occurs to me Amos may not know that Christmas dinner is at Naomi and Ruth's house. Spirit prompts me to telephone his old job to see if he's coming, at least I think that's the reason. Amos has avoided work since his lawsuit check cleared the bank. He now lives in a rented apartment but I don't know where it is. His boss answers the phone when I call and quickly promises to give Amos my message, if he shows up.

The day passes quickly but it's impossible to sleep. While watching the candle glow at 2:25 AM, I think of the music visualizations in Microsoft's Media Player and wonder who designed it. Whoever they are, I bet they are in tune with Spirit.

Minutes after falling asleep, I wake hearing myself say "...no, I want to make a point." After a slug of water and a quick bathroom trip, sleep again claims me. I wake ninety minutes later delighted to have been running in golden light. The daily treatment ritual soon overcomes my longing to return.

Once again, the CD player zips quickly through tracks when I try to meditate. It hovers on one track and then turns itself off. Sun peeks out of clouds, to the far left, in front of me. It shines on my face as I send out purifying, healing light, even to the black holes of the universe. In a few short minutes, less than five or ten, I'm done.

It's great to be guided so often. Yet, it's just too amazing. I'm still not past second-guessing guides and must get to that point. I turn on the CD player to make sure the batteries are okay, even though they were recently changed. The player turns on and switches to the second track. Once again, I experience "eye-flashes" as the great clings, clangs, and reverberations of music fill my ears.

Frequent flashes of golden-yellow light move behind closed eyelids. My eyes move back and forth, up and down.

Track Two and Track Three play while I again emit purifying, healing light throughout my body, the house, and ultimately the universe. I do not return to waking consciousness on my own. Despite not wanting to, deep breaths jolt me back when the CD player turns itself off after Track Three.

Serenely at peace, I fall asleep only to wake after seeing myself in a convertible. More words about women and hiv/aids, and something about cleanliness, wake me later.

When the morning ritual completes, I'm prompted to shop for the answering machine that's been on my list for weeks. It's hard to reach me by telephone because we have one line and I'm always on the Internet. Ink pens, air filters, and a DVD starring Robert Downey Jr. soon sit next to the answering machine in a shopping cart. How wonderful it is to buy whatever I want! I savor the feeling while driving to get Samuel from school. A teacher soon opens the prep school's door to find that I'm the first car in line.

"Hey, Nana," Samuel says greeting me warmly. "Can you stay at my house for a while so my friend can come over? Mom won't let friends come over unless an adult's home."

"Sure, Samuel," I answer, smiling at him in the back seat. "Since Dr. Bump's class is on break I have plenty of time. You know, you're older now and can sit in the front."

Samuel grins and moves forward to glance at the empty seat.

"Well, I would but the seat is usually filled with stuff and I'm used to sitting back here anyway."

He quickly lifts an electronic game from his pocket while I drive like the chauffeur in *Driving Miss Daisy*.

Samuel's TV programs fail to interest me at the house Rebecca filled with loving energy. Glad to see James Redfield's *Celestine Prophecy*, I lift it off the bookshelf before settling down on a porch lawn chair to read. It's amazing to see she's highlighted information on power plays.

I'm immersed in online banking hours later. It's easy to transfer funds from my account with Samuel to a joint checking balance with James, to cover expenses he may object to paying. How liberating to log off the Internet without clearing the email box with hundreds of unread messages!

Filled with joy, I design Abigail's fifth birthday card taking care to make it fun and interesting. I add lots of X's for kisses and O's for hugs. Although it often seems like the only way to communicate with her, I know all is in Divine Order. She is, after all, getting the experience her soul chose.

Electronics continue to malfunction but I'm used to it now. It started with the TV either mysteriously changing channels or turning off. My personal CD player still changes tracks erratically, and turns off and on, but now I relish those times. The latest mishaps concern the printer and laptop. The printer is still stuck on aligning cartridges but will not complete the process. The laptop LCD display continues to go off and on as well. It's too bothersome to ignore so I take it to a computer repair shop.

Of course, the laptop operates normally for the repairman who telephones the next day to report a software issue. Somehow, a setting changed so he changed it back. I don't tell him how much I dislike the usual settings, and often change them to avoid what I think might be intrusive software going onto the Internet by itself. The LCD display continues to malfunction after paying for the repair. I sit and wait until the display decides to come back on. It's an interesting form of Spirit communication.

Proud to be more in tune with the Universe, I tell several long distance friends via email about Center classes. It feels good to inform them that I'm in my second year. After eighteen months of third year classes, and an internship, I'll be a practitioner, something akin to a spiritual social worker. Just helping people get through life is my new mission. Vast life experience makes me well suited for the task.

We have a lot more abilities than we use as humans. I've been reborn for my outlook is totally different from ever before. I love learning and this is a totally new way to live. Great things seem to happen all the time. Friends of like mind help me to learn a great deal. I'm grateful to see them at services, in classes, and between times for fun.

Health issues seem to be resolved. Of thirteen medications taken since 2001, I take none now. I am pain free, do not get the usual colds or flu that everyone else gets, and am happy to say my doctor has not seen me in more than a year. There's no need to see him for the first time in more than twenty years. Gratefulness abounds to be healthy and have money for travel. Happier than I've been in a long time, I expect to be more so with each passing day.

The candle in my room burns constantly. Throughout the night, it glows, pulses, and radiates in amazing ways. It does all sorts of things. It radiates, from the middle to the outside, and has streams of pulses coming from various parts. In the wee hours of the morning, I dream of finding a hundred dollar bill in my pocket, with other money, and what looks like lots of receipts.

In 2009, it becomes normal to have lots of hundred dollar bills. It's wonderful to give without thinking about how to support myself in the future. And I spend more than ever imagined to see that the word of One reaches humanity. God is truly my source while moving further away from limitation each day.

Waking once more, I know something was said, but don't consciously recall what it was. I ask for the communication again but quickly hear it was not from Daniel. Yet, the energy of his essence breaks through the veil. When it leaves, I cannot recall everything, but remember we will be together again in another life. I really do not care to live anymore than one other human life. And that life will fill with consciousness and wealth, devoid of suffering, or lack. The thought helps me to fall back asleep with a smile.

An unfamiliar song wakes me minutes later. Some of the words still ring through my brain. "…and I heard you say, I love you so." A golden orb appears as I trudge to the bathroom. It changes in color from golden, to yellow, and then magenta.

Meditation is becoming what it should be. The CD track indicator display goes up to track number seven when powered up. After zipping through the CD's three tracks several times, the player turns itself off. I turn it back on. The CD plays barely audibly for a seconds and then zips through a fleeting second of Track Three. It then slides through a second of Track Two and turns off again.

Sun shines on my face. I've been in a trance-like state for almost an hour. Random meaningless words run through my brain. Thrilled communications are increasing, and that I'm conscious of being guided, I fondly recall a few lines from "Silent Lucidity."

"If you open your mind for me you won't rely on open eyes to see. The walls you've built within come tumbling down. A New World will begin."

I'm so grateful that Daniel always finds ways for me to hear the song in times of despair. He continues to watch over me as the New World becomes more real each day. Sporadic sleeping hours fill with communication, while either sleeping, or waking to see the candle glow. It glows in so many different vibrations and pulsations that I know there's an exchange of ideas. My soul is getting the crux of the communication even if my conscious mind does not.

Day passes quickly. I'm prompted once again to bless two bottles of water and place them in the freezer before walking to the Center for the Miracles workshop. This time I don't worry about missing Rev. Charles' class but enter before the meditation begins. I proudly place my $5 in the cardboard donation box before finding a seat within the circle.

Anna sits next to me when I open my eyes. She has a hard time coming out of the meditation. I smile knowing she's in tune with Source. She later describes blinding, yet nurturing, radiant light seen between her eyes so many years ago, when she first practiced meditation regularly. I'm thrilled to have another friend of like-mind. We plan to meet for breakfast after Sunday morning's Christmas Eve service.

I wake four times during the night. The words *Queen A* fill my brain in the wee hours of the morning prompting thoughts of Anna. At six o'clock, I'm in a dream with three other people. There's something about our perception that is 140 on each side of a square and something about the number four. On the cusp of sleep, I picture a square with 140 on each side. The word *Alexie* fills my brain. Alexie may be the guide who announced earlier this month that we'd be called home *within a day, within the last few minutes.* More words ring through my head twenty-four minutes later.

In your mind, God continues to hold you in present.

Still tired, I fall back asleep but am roused fifty minutes later with words about my ultimate destination. The sun is almost visible on the horizon. It fills me with such great joy to know I am guided continually! The number of people coming into my life is increasing, as are the fluctuations in the candle's glow.

Meditation again guides in more ways than the words on Isaiah's CD. The player is already on when I begin to push the start button. It skips the first track, stops on the second, and plays normally for a few seconds, before zipping onto Track Three. The player then erratically zips through tracks at a low volume. I place headphones on happy that it's not stuck as usual in a loud state. Concentrating, I try to grasp the few words it fleetingly rests on. There are a lot of "you" words. Nothing else makes sense but the words are locked in my memory bank for future use.

The volume is suddenly bearable. Now the player zips to Track One, where Isaiah has us imagine we are at the train station. I maintain a calm and meditative state listening until disrupted near the end of Track Three. After experiencing a few eye flashes, the neighbor's loud conversation with a friend, in his driveway, jolts me back. I do not recall getting into trance. Perhaps, I was in 'the gap' upon sending light to the universe.

It no longer seems important to track what happens throughout the day.

In the wee hours of the morning, I wake still singing a Christmas carol. The words "Oh, Holy Night" echo through my head. I wake again, for several minutes before daybreak, to watch a beautiful little magenta colored orb. Golden light periodically encases the orb.

Several golden orbs appear before my eyes fifty minutes later as the sun begins to rise nearer to the horizon. It's surprising to note their beauty is clearer when I close my eyes. There is no doubt guides lead to a place where I'm supposed to be and it is a glorious place. So it is that the universe is me, always guiding, protecting, and supporting, now and forevermore.

Sun begins to rise above clouds as I lie on my futon bed during meditation. Level Four, the heart level, carries me into trance until Isaiah talks of sending the light in Level Six. Now I use the Light within my body to heal before sending it out.

After allowing light from my heart's core to radiate throughout the body, I drift off again during Track Two. All sense is gone for I'm without a body in the natural state. The light of Truth is in my heart's core. No time exists there. The world is forgotten but echoes of eternity are heard.

Consciousness envelops me once again when the CD plays near the end of Track Three. I send the light, the healing, purifying light to benefit all of humanity, all of the universe. The CD player turns itself off and my eyes open filled with wonder.

Spirit soon guides me to visit Amos at work. I'm not sure he's there since Terry reports Amos rarely works now. Trusting intuition, I leave the house immediately to drive up to the tire shop. His boss is happy to direct me to him when I arrive. I soon determine why.

Amos works behind the shop in the back of a big truck loading tires. He is quite high, sweating profusely, and swearing to quit his job if he doesn't get a raise in pay. His voice is high-pitched when quickly announcing that he no longer needs the job that carried him though years of addiction. I gently remind him he lived in the back of a truck for the past year, on the property, and his boss carried him through many lean times.

"I still have 13K," he replies vigorously. "It's enough to live on for a year so I don't have to work at all."

I'm not about to argue but remind him he's made quite a bit of money in the past as the manager. Its clear words are not connecting with the logical part of his brain, for the same attitude that got him fired then, and many times in the past, continues. He jumps down from the truck and quickly shows me the used car recently bought to replace his bike before whipping his new driver's license out of a greasy pants pocket.

"It cost me a lot but I'm back on the road," he brags with a wide smile revealing many rotted and missing teeth.

For a fleeting second, I see my beloved brother before he became lost to life's trials so many, many, years ago. When I offer my congratulations and let him know how proud I am that he's getting his life together, he tells me the telephone message I left the week before never got to him. I don't recall asking if he got it.

"You can call me on my new cell phone now," he says reaching into the car's glove box. "I just got this last week."

Amos seems to settle down as I congratulate him again while continuing to stream love into his body.

"So, you'll join us for the annual family bowl tomorrow night and Christmas dinner Amos?"

Amos looks down at the ground before vigorously replying. "I can't leave here early on Christmas Eve. It's a big tip day. They cut my hours so I only work from noon to four. And anyways, I don't know how to get to Ruth and Naomi's."

I answer quickly knowing he still wants to be part of the family. "Come to my house tomorrow at 1:30 PM. You can follow me to their house."

He follows me to my car. I know the two bottles of water, blessed days before are for him and reach in through the window to retrieve them. He gladly takes the water and promises to be on time for Christmas dinner before offering me a sweaty kiss. I accept his kiss and return it before quickly driving away. God sent me to try and bring him back for he is badly strung out, again.

It's a very busy day and I'm ready to sleep by 8:30 PM. Before retiring for the night, I go to the kitchen for a bottle of water. The motion detector light shines in the den. James is working an extra night at his second job so I enter the room and listen closely.

"Should I sit?" I ask.

The answer is no, it's not necessary. Daniel's essence begins to communicate with encouraging words.

"I am going to kiss you. Try to feel it."

A slight tingle graces the left side of my lips. After noting the sensation, Daniel says, in time the sense will come in stronger.

"Merry Christmas Mom," he says before the light turns off.

Magenta colored orbs bless me with their beauty minutes later, one at a time, over the course of several minutes. I feel treasured beyond measure while surrendering to the lull of sleep.

Several waking messages are quickly forgotten. A new message is recorded without a thought at 4:15 AM.

It will give you all the stuff that's needed.

The morning routine is delightful to repeat. When it's time for meditation, my CD player zips through all three tracks six or seven times. It's done so fast I can't keep count before it finally starts playing normally from the beginning. During Track One, my throat, or perhaps my nose, makes a sound somewhat like a snore at the point where I send the light.

I drift off and become conscious of the same noise during Track Three, again when expanding the light within my heart's core. Energy appears within the yellow-gold light as sun shines on my face near the end of the track. It's more than the usual atoms skirting about, with more flashes of tiny white lights, and something else I cannot describe. It looks like a grid is faintly behind it all.

:-)

334

Chapter Thirty-Four

Christmas and More

*"Have only love in your heart for others. The more you see the good in
them, the more you will establish good in yourself."*
Paramahansa Yogananda

The Center's Christmas Eve ritual summons me out of the house.
As Hospitality Coordinator, it's up to me to fill gaps, assuring the
availability of coffee and tea after services. The task has become
increasingly difficult since three volunteers ended their
commitment. I'm grateful for Leah and David's help but neither one
can cover today's service.

No one seems to want a six-month commitment. Yet, last
minute volunteers always appear. Today is no different. Two people
are already busy making coffee and setting up the table. Their
assistance gives me time to enjoy talking to others before a beautiful
service. The Chorale sweetly sings, again making me second-guess
my decision not to join them.

Anna and I meet for an impromptu breakfast at a nearby
restaurant later. Her friendship is another blessing. We share an hour
of fellowship before heading home to wrap presents.

Twilight falls while family meets blocks away for our
annual Christmas Eve bowl. No one brings friends this year. Rachel
hasn't joined us since Daniel passed and James is visiting Delilah,
his brother-in-law, and nephew. It's clear we all feel the difference
without them, Daniel, Abigail, and Amos. I pay for Rebecca and
Samuel's shoe rental and bowling along with my own.

Time fills with laughter and family antics even though
there's a bit of lamenting when I turn down a beer. Some things are
better left unsaid. When talking of my visit with Amos, I don't
mention his state of mind. It's great to connect with everyone in a
fun atmosphere but I'm happy to return to my room.

Rebecca telephones as soon as I begin to study. She and
Terry saw Amos to invite him to Christmas dinner. Her voice is
overly emotional discussing how strung out and paranoid Amos is.

She is now very concerned for my safety and notes Amos mentioned he doesn't trust me.

"Maybe you should go out somewhere for a while Mom," Rebecca notes in a panic-filled voice. "It might be a good idea to not be home just in case he comes by."

"Thank you for your concern," I remark softly. "I know what state he's in and I'm not worried. There's no need to be afraid."

She ends our conversation quickly not understanding how I remain calm and fearless. Loneliness overwhelms me with thoughts of previous years. Many years of lovingly preparing Christmas dinner are over for the house on 47th Drive no longer seems inviting.

Giving in to my human side, I gleefully watch family movies of Christmases past while working in the kitchen making quiche. Rebecca and Daniel play guessing games as they open stocking stuffers. Everyone else joins in the fun while eating freshly baked quiche. Soon all eyes are on the TV where videos of taped family antics play. Silence will now fill this empty home on Christmas. I sigh, missing it all, and stop the DVD to finish my task.

I've made quiche for many years to keep the family's hunger at bay before Christmas dinner. This year the joy of preparation is gone. I make it because Terry asked me to. Rather than a labor of love, it seems like a chore for now there's a need to grace each family home with quiche so no one feels left out.

This past week has been tough but I have held back from crying. Even though Daniel's spirit and other spirits guide me daily, the illusionary loss of him overwhelms me. Lately, I've felt the loss of my entire family as I become more conscious of my, our, true being. It's particularly painful to see Rebecca become closer to Terry. She hangs out with him during free time and visits his workplace. Such is the condition of human life.

Several, soon forgotten, messages cause me to rise on Christmas morning. A sunrise ritual of repeating the "World Healing Meditation" brings new insights so I change words near the end to suit a new awareness.

The CD player operates normally during meditation. Now I'm certain it's my throat making the weird sound heard when listening near the end of Track One. It happens when I align all levels of consciousness to do the one great work all of us are here to do. And that is to send nourishing white light to all living things.

Near the end of Track Three, I'm consciously aware of missing part of the meditation. There's an unusual tingling in the right knee and a fleeting thought that arthritis is being healed. The task of getting through the day begins when the player turns off.

Ego soon chides me into watching more family movies but the laptop screen goes black. Seconds later, it comes on again as Spirit guides what I watch. When I put the first DVD in, it plays at a certain point, instead of letting me choose from the DVD menu. I stubbornly turn off the DVD player, twice, but find when I turn it back on, it starts playing where it stopped before.

Spirit guides the process as the computer screen blacks out again for a few fleeting seconds. Still not sure of the guidance, I take the DVD out of the player, and put it back in, because this phenomenon is something new. Love and more faith overwhelm upon knowing, Spirit guidance continues despite doubt as the DVD again starts playing somewhere in the middle.

Amos rings the doorbell and shouts through the living room window.

"Hey, Jo, I'm here."

His words ring through the living room, down the hall, and into my room. James is still in the shower.

Amos wears a clean suit that hangs loosely on his small frame.

"How do you like the suit?" he asks noticing my look of surprise. "I bought it from the Salvation Army thrift store."

He continues to talk non-stop noting a freshly mopped kitchen and bathroom back at his rented apartment as I reach for presents on the couch. I'm happy to give him work pants, a set of new sheets, and the photo album returned to me when he was in jail. He thanks me for the sheets and says they'll come in handy.

James is still not ready to go. Amos helps me load my car with gifts and quiche. After grabbing my drink for the day, intuition guides me to bring an extra wrapped gift without a tag. I've always wrapped an extra present or two at Christmas, in case someone arrives unexpectedly, so it's no surprise to have this gift to tuck under my arm before we head for the door.

Everyone seems happy to see us when we arrive but I sense something unspoken. Surrounding energy is very uncomfortable. Naomi's nephew arrives with his girlfriend Elizaveth. Their visit is a complete surprise to me. Elizaveth's higher vibration draws me closer as we sit talking. Connecting with someone of the same vibration helps get me through the day.

Christmas is nothing like past times with a house full of family and friends. James arrives to report his sister is celebrating in Miami and Rachel may not come either. I miss the variety of people, along with the early morning breakfast quiche, stockings, and friendly atmosphere of yesteryears.

Almost an hour passes before all eyes rest on Elizaveth and me while discussing the light seen during near-death experiences. Family is stunned to hear of my longing to go back into the light.

"If you miss it that much why don't you just off yourself?" Naomi remarks loudly from the larger patio table.

"I've tried three times so now I'm pretty sure there's something I have yet to do," I reply turning around to stare at her.

As Elizaveth and Naomi's nephew watch us open presents, I offer the small extra wrapped gift to them pretending the tag fell off. They appear happy to get it. Amos thanks everyone for gifts. Once again, he has not brought a thing. At least he now shares his time.

Rebecca rises to help Naomi and Ruth in the kitchen while I continue to share stories with my new friend. The soap opera aspect of my life becomes overwhelming when dinner is ready minutes later. The long carefully set table of yesteryears is missing. As everyone rises to fill plates, and find a place to sit outside around the pool or in the house, I know it's only a matter of time before that part of my life fully ends.

I eat sparingly nursing the huge rum and coke brought from home. Clouds fill the sky, and since there's a long drive ahead of them, Mike and Elizaveth leave when their plates are empty. Right on cue, rain falls as we tote leftovers back inside the house.

Terry and Amos yell at one another within minutes. Their shouting match is an ego's delight, judging one another in a comparison between prescription and street drugs. Rebecca interferes by telling them their discussion is not appropriate, especially in front of Samuel. True to his usual action, Amos leaves, this time heading for his bosses' house.

Ruth, Rebecca, and Terry prompt me to join them for a game of pinochle while Naomi does the dishes. It's fun even though everyone's ego is in full throttle. A mix of rum and coke helps to get past increasing sensitivity that affects me when others act out, or do not act in a loving manner.

James stays in the house with Samuel but comes out to the patio when Lydia, Joseph and their beautiful daughter arrive. I bless the little, pale girl, as before with good and love forevermore, sensing her life will have its rough spots.

My head now feels the storms pressure and the left hip aches like it did several years ago. As rain continues, hip pain throbs in tune with sinuses, head, and the right side of my mouth.

A plate of leftovers and the new air purifier from family accompanies me to the car when the card game ends. Tears flow upon reaching the safely and sanctity of my love and light-filled room. I miss Daniel so much. Even though my understanding is different, I still can't seem to rid myself of periodic feelings of tremendous loss and unending pain. Now I cry for Christmases past, which I did not appreciate enough, and Christmases to come, which I don't want to experience.

The darkness of blame and guilt surround me. Ego is relentless in its pursuit to keep me locked in the land of limitation, the past. Eyes are weary but I want to watch a bit more of past family Christmases to note how special they were. After inserting the DVD into my laptop, it starts playing right where it left off earlier in the morning. Daniel's voice rings through my brain.

"Ten minutes Mom," he says.

Of course, I disregard his words and watch the DVD for a few more minutes before shutting the computer down. I know better than to completely disregard what I hear for when I do the computer always acts up. I'm so grateful for spirit guides!

The air purifier's steady hum lulls me to sleep but I wake several times after midnight. Rising shortly after two o'clock in the morning to document *one million two-hundred thousand dollars*, I look into the candle flame. The light pulsates out in circles as the words, *to spend as you wish*, fill my brain. Welcome sleep summons me again after a quick trip to the bathroom.

More words wake me before dawn. I'm not sure if I'm speaking to James or perhaps remembering the song "Songbird" by Fleetwood Mac. It's been months since I last heard the song. I rise to note the words in my journal before repeating the morning ritual.

The CD player operates normally during meditation. At Level Four, in Track One, I meander through the meadow near Ruth and Naomi's old Michigan home before climbing to the patch of evergreen trees. Many family members on the Otherside greet me warmly before reaching my favorite spot by the lakes. Grandfather Carl, Dad, Uncle Wallace, Aunt Deborah, and Uncle Freddie are all there but it's hard to spot Daniel. He stays in the back of the crowd until I call him forward.

I'm not sure about being in 'the gap' when the first mediation ends. During Track Three, I drift off but drift back in when Isaiah mentions the light. The act of sending white, purifying, healing light to the world, and beyond, is now a conscious thought.

Tears fill both eyes upon waking an hour later. Daniel tried to visit me again. Usually, the only time I cry is upon seeing him in dreams for my subconscious mind seems lost in the world of emotion. Pushing the thought aside, I go online to review my Visa bill. The payment is due again. I'm overwhelmed with gratitude to note James paid for our Internet Service Provider. It's usually paid with company funds but the company is broke.

It's time to send the weekly nutrition news update. More than 130 countries now access the company's website. Ego guides me while identifying the top ten locations before offering links to free information, including painstakingly researched hiv nutrition handouts. The telephone rings as I note the reproducibles main access Web page. Rebecca soon asks me to watch fourteen-year-old Samuel mow their yard.

"I can't leave work and the yard needs to be mowed before he leaves with Papa," she insistently notes. "You know anything can happen and I don't want him to be alone while working on the yard."

Her request sounds ludicrous since it's raining but she tells me it stopped in her area. I hang up the telephone not making a solid commitment to leave my room.

James is up earlier than expected. I think the rain affects his plans to camp with Samuel in the Everglades. The downpour affects my day as well. I planned to take advantage of Black Friday sales with gift cards but now my body fights to operate normally. My left hip aches upon getting up to walk or lie, and sinuses and the right side of my mouth, where my "suspect tooth" is, still hurt as well.

A great sense of loss overwhelms me while hobbling out to the bathroom.

Minutes later, Rebecca telephones again to see why I have not left to watch Samuel mow the yard. I tell her since the grass is wet I thought it not necessary. At this moment, she tells me

Samuel's friend rushed over thinking I would be there to supervise so she's on her way home. I suspect James telephoned her when she asks if I'm okay and assure her all is well before ending our call.

Rest, sleep, and eating very little between studies fill the day. I'm ready for bed early and fall promptly asleep. Three hours later, I hear w*e are all angels just trying to find our way back home.* "It could be part of a Karen Drucker song," I think, while using the bathroom. Samuel now sleeps soundly on the sofa bed.

James and Samuel leave for the Everglades in the wee hours of the morning. I hear the van back out of the drive.

I'm still tired and not feeling like my usual self after 10:00 AM. Although I don't recall a single word spoken during sleep, the memory of seeing many golden orbs over the course of hours surfaces. My sinuses and left hip still hurt so I decide it could be due to rain and cold weather. Sickness after Christmas is the norm for I've always pushed myself to get everything perfect before family arrives. This year I don't have that ready-made excuse. But maybe my body forgot.

Life continues to be full of surprises. Soft meows fill the air as I stumble out to use the bathroom before saying the usual meditation. Despite their two-week disappearance, three missing kittens return to the back porch to visit and feed with three older cats. Since James is gone, it's now my duty to feed them.

I thank Spirit for sending them but note a preference for a good home where someone cares for them properly. It would be nice to know they're with a human who smothers them with love. A human who takes them to the vet to rid them of fleas and get their shots would be perfect. I'd much rather see them loved and cared for properly than left as pharaoh cats to roam the neighborhood.

Returning to my room, I repeat the usual ritual before falling sleep. Depression and loneliness overwhelm me when I wake later still feeling the body's ills. There doesn't seem to be anything to do but lie on my futon thinking about how Leah told me several days ago not to get down on myself if I got sick.

After being prompted to listen to my prayer CD with inspiring music, I'm ashamed to admit I forgot that Spirit is always with me. The CD player starts normally and begins to play the first selection, the "World Healing Meditation." Spirit uses the opportunity to reach me and switches the CD to Track Two. It plays through prayers, allowing me to fall into 'the gap.' The CD player switches tracks to an upbeat song each time I begin to cry.

Daniel's essence is strong. We dance, and true to his spirit, he has others join us. I again experience the pleasure of being with deceased ancestors. It's very uplifting as we dance several dances. Daniel speaks before the final track ends.

"You've got to get to where you need to go."

I'm still thinking of trying to get to the Otherside but these times spur me forward here on earth. I know there are tasks to accomplish, and goals not yet met, so here is where I have to stay.

When the CD player shuts off, I go online thinking about out-of-state trips. It's wonderful to know there's money left from the lawsuit to travel. The Asilomar meeting is in California and I plan to go for I've never been to Pacific Grove. I'm sure it will be different from past business conventions in Los Angeles, San Francisco, and Hollywood. I email treasured colleagues asking if we can get together in August. No one responds.

Karen Drucker's "Hold On To Love" CD plays in the background while I ponder relationships. Sadly, some have met their purpose and it's time to move on. I'm grateful for the few people who seem to be in my life knowing they're still there for a reason. Even though I'm not sure the lessons are over, I trust they'll stick around until they are.

It's nice to have the house to myself, as I get ready to sleep again. Somehow, I know it will be another message-filled night.

The first memorable words come at 3:40 AM.

Don't ever dull the senses that are filled with love and cheer.

I write the words down, use the bathroom, and check the burning candle before falling back asleep. Words from a Karen Drucker song ring through my head four hours later.

Oh, see me I'm taking one small step, one small step.

James remains in the Everglades with Samuel so I rise to feed Scamp and Prudence on the back porch before falling back asleep. Wylie eats two hours later. The kittens are nowhere in sight. I remember hearing the experiment is over right before they disappeared. The thought causes me to break into a smile before heading back to my room.

The CD player acts normally during meditation. I'm in 'the gap' at the end of Track Three. Minutes later, golden orbs grace me with their presence while gazing into the parking lot beyond our yard. I've seen a lot of them lately. A tiny golden orb appears in front of me as I walk through the dark hall to return to my room. I follow it slowly with closed, and then open eyes, watching it change to a gray color as it floats before yellow window shades. Maybe it changed colors so I could see it better. I make sure to thank it for coming before asking, "Is there a message for me?"

The truth be told, all sins are great.

I'm not sure what this means. From reading *A Course In Miracles*, I've learned there are no sins but sin is a loveless state, being without love. Perhaps I'll get an opportunity to discuss this in class. I still feel the cats sent to this house are meant to help James learn love and responsibility. It does not appear that he's taking the hint as quickly as I would but then again he is not I, or is he?

Email brings a bittersweet communication from Swets Publishing. There's no need for bank details to make purchasing easier, I let them know, because the business no longer publishes journals. Throughout the day, there's a knowing the hiv nutrition mission is quickly coming to an end. Throughout the night I recall declaring, "One million two-hundred thousand dollars for the sale of the business."

:-)

Chapter Thirty-Five

The Veil Continues to Lift

"You can change your perceptions of earth very beyond what you have here."
SAM – Book of One :-) Volume 1

Dawn is nearly two hours away when I recall repeating part of the daily ritual. "I am its emissary through my beliefs." It's part of "The Golden Key," received in class and now declared each morning. Ego informs me these are my own thoughts.

"Hey you, out there in the cold, can you hear me."

Daniel's essence permeates the air. I smile remembering his ever-present humor. The words are from a Pink Floyd CD of his copied for James before Christmas. I fall back asleep with a smile but wake at 6:55 AM. Meaningless words, said in a man's voice rhyming much like a poem, ring in my brain. I'm not a fan of poems. Prayers and the "World Healing Meditation" flow from thin lips before falling back asleep.

The air purifier's steady hum fills the air when I wake two hours later.

"I can't dance with these fuzzy things in my hands."

Surprised, I look at my hands to note they're empty. Sun rises above clouds to shine into my room as I document the words. I'm pleased to see the door to my room is still shut. Sometimes it's hard to remember to close it when I rise to use the bathroom during the night. Energy in the rest of the house is almost unbearable.

All three CD tracks play normally during meditation. Rays of sun shine periodically on my face as I fall into the 'gap' at the end of Track Two and again near the end of Track Three. I'm sending the light, out to the world and beyond, but taking more care this time to first purify and heal my physical host.

Full consciousness does not return until the CD player turns itself off and sun peeks out of clouds. A beautiful magenta colored orb floats outside the window as my eyes open. A golden, smaller one, drifts to the right when it leaves. When the golden orb disappears, a butterfly flies past in the same spot. How very lucky I am to be in greater awareness of Spirit, in all forms!

Spirit always guides much more than I realize. Yesterday, I went to the store to spend one of my new gift cards. A bit of money was left so I thought about buying myself a 'woo woo' movie, as my friend Mary calls them. A comedy named *Just Like Heaven* looked good but I didn't buy it thinking Samuel wouldn't watch it. I haven't watched TV for a number of months but hours later decided to see a movie. *Just Like Heaven* was a thoroughly enjoyable film but I didn't associate it with the movie at the store until after my morning ritual! Even though this is beginning to look more like a being in 'the gap' journal, it in no way reports all the many wonderful things experienced each day.

Living in a state of grace brings one to the present moment where neither past nor future exist. This state of BEing unknowingly accompanies me throughout 2006 and early 2007.

A longing for the past consumes while putting highlights from 1990 to 1992 Christmases on a single DVD disk. Electronic equipment begins to malfunction. An error message notes the drive is full while copying the movie to a new 156-gigabyte (GB) external hard drive. The movie is less than 5GB so I begin to get irritated thinking it may be lost. It took me hours to make.

I decide to test the drive by transferring a movie from my Greece trip. It quickly allows me to do so without error. The LCD display blacks out during my next attempt to transfer the family movie. I give up and turn the computer off. Although I'm irritated because Spirit stops me from doing certain things, I feel truly blessed. It's so cool to follow Spirit's guidance and get more direction every day and night!!!!

James returns from his fishing trip with Samuel. He quickly showers, puts on clean clothes and leaves to work five hours at a part-time job before retiring for the night. Daniel's 2005 memorial CD plays as I slip off to sleep. The CD tracks begin to switch erratically thirty minutes after midnight alerting me to his presence. He begins to answer pressing questions reminding me not to cry.

Answers come quickly. James and I will part and will be all right. Rachel and Abigail will never be a big part of our lives and I may not see them again for a long time. Rebecca will be okay but will backslide a bit before she again comes around to her True Self. I think that is all I asked, and heard, but sometimes it all slips away.

The longer Bon Jovi segment on the memorial CD plays through twice as I grin. I'm so very joyous to hear it because I didn't consciously put it on the CD to begin with. I meant only to tape the few seconds of "Keep The Faith" on Track Three that cause a smile. Yet, tracks eleven through fourteen all play segments of the same song. Track Eleven and twelve are identical revealing a longer segment. There's even more of "Keep The Faith" on Track Thirteen, including the part about standing out in the rain crying, trying to wash away the pain, and then apologizing to Mother and Father for "doing things I can't erase." My smile swells as Track Fourteen plays. It's identical to Track Three. "Hey, man I'm alive; I'm taking each day and night at a time. I'm feeling…"

Now, years later, it's obvious, Daniel's essence found this way to let me know his soul lingered in fourth dimensional reality.

Daniel's spirit somehow burned these tracks onto the CD. Definite communication continues. There's no mistaking. Daniel's essence again reminds me not to cry. It's thoroughly enjoyable to communicate with this wonderful spirit that is always near.

A large Christmas candle on top of the computer desk burns brightly. Candles stay lit, almost constantly for months, even when I'm not at home. I wake after having a nightmare to look at the flame at 2:15 AM. During the dream, I was in an area next to someone frightened by a man who entered their room. I yelled out Daddy, Daddy, to get them some help. Abigail now comes to mind so I send her love before falling back asleep.

Bits of words fly through my brain waking me frequently throughout the night. Upon rising, I use the bathroom, and return to sleep. The other bedroom door stands open at six o'clock. James is fishing again. His things still lie all around the house filling every space except my room.

It's easier to hear Spirit's communication when there's no distraction or chaos. This came to my attention while listening to a series of cassette tapes on developing physic abilities that Leah gave me. Starcke notes everything is in our lives to help us become more fully conscious beings. Chaos is a state of mind and something one goes through to get to self-mastery.

Something carefully led me to where I am now. The house is in chaos and now I realize that's why I'm secluded in this room. At least I have control over the clutter and there is none here. It's very exciting knowing creation comes out of chaos. The thought spurs me forward with anticipation to see what great things will come next. All is in Divine Order. I have been, continue to be, guided by Spirit even when not aware of it.

Still exhausted after repeating the "World Healing Meditation," I lay back down to sleep at 6:25 AM. Words fill my brain twenty, and another twenty, minutes later when I wake scratching my nose.

The CD player operates normally as I lie with the sun periodically shining on my face during meditation. As clouds drift by, I fall into 'the gap' and again send nourishing white light to all living things near the end of Track One. I fall into the delightful gap again for a few fleeting seconds near the end of Track Three.

Usually, after the CD player turns itself off, I lie with headphones on until consciously aware, and then until prompted to get up. It doesn't take long, perhaps a minute or two. Beautiful orbs appear as sun peeks out of clouds. I see them with open and closed eyes. The first ones are blue-green, and then magenta, before golden ones appear.

A large mass of blue-green covers the range of closed eyesight. Minutes later, while in the bathroom, a small orb appears inside a larger mass. The orb drifts past me and floats through gray tiled wall to the outside of the house. Perhaps it helps to train my open human eyes to see orbs more clearly.

I retire early on the night before New Year's Eve hoping to sleep without interruption. But communication again occurs almost constantly throughout the night. Waking to document words exhausts me. Nine bits and pieces of sentences came between 12:55 to 5:43 AM. One sentence strikes me as odd.

It sounds like everything is being made on the other side.

I wonder what it means while reading more words that seems to be from the past. A spirit speaks.

"You should go. You're needed."

Thinking about skipping the yearly throng of people repeating the "World Healing Meditation," I ask, "Does it make a difference?"

"It makes a difference to improve the planet."

I'm now wide-awake and raring to go. Minutes later, I leave to start coffee for the Center. Rev. Haggerty is surprised and pleased to see me for she knows mornings are not my thing. It feels great to repeat the "World Healing Meditation" with others. The burning bowl ceremony, a delightful bonus, allows me to let the rest of my baggage go. Paper and pen help to document a new life, with numerous trips, in the coming year.

Returning home to say prayers an hour later, I don't invite higher beings to lead me because I need to sleep before Rebecca's family barbeque. Today is a big day for her. She decided to let go of the past. Samuel's father is in town with his mother and new girlfriend and they are coming to visit. This barbeque will mark the first time we are all together in many years.

I rise to meditate, after five hours of sleep, before dressing for the barbeque. It's a bearable event as I sit back making few comments while ego's flare. A misty white orb keeps me wiping my glasses in disbelief for several hours. When a huge boxlike turtle nears the back screen door, I rise to feed it some meat. It almost walks all the way to the back screen door but doesn't eat. I bless it silently with good and love and ask if there's a message.

It stands silently for at least an hour just outside the porch but I don't perceive any messages. Maybe it's harder to concentrate on Spirit's messages when other people are around. As the turtle slowly saunters away, I wonder if this was a lesson on how to connect even in the midst of family.

Lydia and Joseph arrive with their beautiful daughter who smiles at me after giving Aunt Rebecca a hug. She seems interested in roaming the empty lot next door so I gladly scoop her small body into my arms and carry her through the bushes. Yard growth stands knee-deep.

We stand side-by-side at the water's edge as the Jungle Queen glides under the bridge. When it's gone, I know it's my charge to bless Mickey Loo Loo again. Cradled in loving arms, she hears me bless her with good and love forevermore. I tell her Indians lived on the land many years ago as she nods her one-year-old head, seeming to understand.

Mickey Loo Loo doesn't want to return to the others so we spent a few more minutes on the other side of the huge yard. She wants to go into the undergrowth so I carry her a tiny bit into a maze of bushes and overgrown weeds. I sense she's a wonderful girl but don't see the things in her that I see in Abigail. Perhaps, it's human nature to be partial to my granddaughter.

Later the crowd thins out but James and I stay because Samuel wants us to see his new *Pirates of the Caribbean* movie. When the movie ends, James leaves but I stay to watch the *Davinci Code*. Rebecca promptly falls asleep curled up in the chair next to me. Samuel decides to play video games in his room. At the stroke of midnight, he comes out to wish his still sleeping mom a happy new year. We kiss and hug before I tell him it's okay to wake her.

"You have my permission to spend the night Nana," he says with a quick glance at his mom, "but don't tell her I said so."

"Thanks Samuel," I tell him as he begins to stoop down by her. "I would but my toothbrush and nightclothes aren't here."

Rebecca and Samuel are in their own rooms asleep when the movie ends. I leave the house and drive through empty streets to 47th Drive. Every experience in my life led me to this point of awareness. Life is only thought and the world we see can change. Every thought represents an electrical charge and cannot be without effects. All thoughts have power, but we must complement them with the energy of seeing them in order to materialize here.

The body's eyes see only form but we can change form because it's not true. The last verse of 2 Corinthians, 4:16, enters my brain. It reminds me to look at the unseen, for visible things are temporary, unseen things are eternal.

Arriving home, I recall reading an appropriate phrase in *A Course In Miracles* and find it on page 637 of the text:

"Look back no longer, for what lies ahead is all you ever wanted in your heart. Give up the world!... Joy has no cost. It is your sacred right... Be speeded on your way by honesty, and let not your experiences here deceive in retrospect."

Atkinson spoke of the power of thought in his book *Thought Vibration* first published in 1906. Scholars and mystics continue to note the awesome God power that lies within us. We are here to rise completely out of limitation bringing civilization to a point from which it will never go back into darkness. Holding a harmonious and thoughtful attitude of a loving, giving Universe that meets our every need, peacefully and equally, is vital to speed us all toward the Heaven on earth that is already ours.

In *Edgar Cayce on The Power of Color, Stones, and Crystals* Dan Campbell eloquently notes:

"We realize that we are not alone in the cosmos, nor isolated in some incidental galaxy, nor pariahs on some forgotten planet, gyrating in a chaotic flux left to circumstances beyond our control. We are simply out of tune with our origin – out of step with the vibrations that truly matter. We live in a world divinely originated because it is born of the Light, and the ground we walk on is holy ground because it is born of Love. Draw all creation back to its beginning and all that remains is Love. It is all that we are required to know and do."

Today is New Year's Eve 2009. The old laptop screen has been black for more than a week so I've hooked it up to the desktop computer monitor to work. I sensed it was time to do the "Christmas thing" when it first went out. After preparing for Christmas, hosting the family dinner, and participating in family functions, I figured spirit would allow me to work on the book. The screen flickered yesterday but went black again so I did other things.

I've recently returned from three tiresome hours of shopping with Ruth, Terry, and Sarah for Momma's eightieth birthday party. Reaching home, I cleared my body of caustic negative energy, by grounding to earth, but still felt the need to shower with sea salt. After thirty minutes in the shower, I'm ready to work on the book.

The old laptop screen flickers and turns black when I turn it on. Not wanting to hook it up to the desktop monitor, and sit in the uncomfortable chair, I turn to the newer laptop planning to check email. The old laptops screen flickers so I again pick it up ready to work.

First, I close the Microsoft Office Shortcut Bar that gets in my way when I'm writing and then the Windows Security Alert message. There's no need for countless software needed to dissuade hackers since this computer is not hooked up to the Internet. I set the computer down with a sigh as the screen blacks out again.

The old laptop screen comes on as I again reach for the new computer. Thoughts of automatic writing enter my mind when the Microsoft Word program starts unexpectedly. It's something I've tried before with some success. Fingers move swiftly over the keyboard.

"So now I will type a message for you. It will be sweet and to the point. Listen well as I tell you what not to do, for you are one with all, and it does not matter what you do here. Do you hear what I say? It does not matter what you do here but let all actions speak of Love for Love is all there is, even if you don't think so.

"Take for instance, the situation you seem to be in. It is not existent. It is not worthy of your or anyone's consideration. You must turn to the path of light and truth in all circumstances and turn the other cheek. The energy you share is rewarded hereafter and forevermore. Seek not to displeasure others for it is only yourself you displeasure.

"The Truth needs to be known by all and you can do that with your writing but you must do it gently and wholly. Turn the other cheek and let it slide past, let it slide past you. Focus instead on the truth of your being as one, for the light is within you, and you know that to be true. Save others if you wish, but recall you are here separate, but in Truth One.

*"What one does here is non-consequential as far as the Truth goes here for there is **no** Truth here. What cannot be understood here is enlightened on the other side of the Truth. For all is darkness here and the scale of truth leads to light quickly once you transcend the path before you. Move quickly now and transcend that path wholly, completely, and forevermore. It is all there is to say. Do it now. Don't burden yourself with physical matters for they are just that, physical, and nothing physical is real.*

"Go, go forth, and spread the word. The Truth is known to few but increases in the light of God. Your BEing is one in Truth that is all you need to know."

This year served me well for the veil continues to lift allowing further examination of life with its habits of limitation and weakness. The circumstances in which I live are the result of past choices. I can change them more to my liking. Today I vow to put the past behind me and live more in the Now. Intentions are clearer than ever before as I continue SOM studies knowing Spirit will soon reveal the uniqueness of my path. Right thoughts, speech, and actions will clear the way to wholeness once again.

:-)

Epilogue

I am eternally grateful for the unseen force that guides me effortlessly toward the Light of Reality. There's a knowing all is in Divine Order as I complete the next book from my Heaven on earth.

Using the Law of Mind to create a perfect living environment is enormously rewarding. It is all about monitoring thought patterns. As Ernest Holmes wrote in 1926, disease and poverty cease to exist as we investigate the Truth and put *It* into operation. Enlightenment leads the way to freedom and Heaven on earth. I AM the living proof.

Notes

These notes include many structured prayers called Spiritual Mind Treatments. Treatments help us to recognize the wholeness within ourselves. Our bodies respond to thoughts. I used many of these tools for my own transformation from fragmentation to wholeness. After decades of despair, sickness, poverty, and limitation, I'm now living a hopeful and joyous life of wholeness, excellent health, freedom, and prosperity.

Certain capitalized words signify aspects or attributes of what many people refer to as *God*. Each treatment ends with "And So *It* Is!" but you can replace this with "Amen" or "So mote it be." Choose the notes and treatments you wish to use. Record the ones that resonate with you on to a tape recorder, or burn them to a CD, or MP3 file. Repeat them in your own voice, feeling the wholeness that you truly are, believing every word. You can then hear them anywhere at anytime if you have earphones to fit the recorder or player. Occasionally record them again as your consciousness changes.

You can make a positive difference just by repeating the treatments even if you don't believe every word in the beginning. When I first started my journey, ego often denied what I repeated. Do not be discouraged if this happens to you. The voice of ego lessened with each repeated treatment. In time, it was possible to repeat treatments with gusto believing every spoken word. You will find it's easier to repeat prayers more enthusiastically after some practice.

There's unseen Power in prayer, regardless of belief. Our thoughts, our prayers, our desires, feed the Matrix in which we live. When we pray, our prayers merge into a field of unlimited possibility. A Matrix of Good exists even when we don't believe in our own power. I can attest to this fact. This unlimited field of Good surrounds, and connects us, and in doing so, it offers a fertile field to plant our thoughts.

I trust *Lightworker's Log :-) Transformation* will be of utmost value to you as the process of returning to Light unfolds. Visit LightworkersLog.com for additional resources.

1- World Healing Meditation (Adapted and Revised)

Always, always and forever was the Word. And the Word was *God*. And God said, "Let there be light" and there was light.

Now is the time of a new beginning. I AM a Co-Creator with God and Heaven comes as the Good Will of God expresses on Earth through me. It is the Kingdom of Light, Love, Peace and Understanding. And I AM doing my part to reveal It's Reality.

I begin with me. I AM a living Soul and the Spirit of God dwells in me, as me. I and the Father are One – and all that the Father has is mine. In Truth, I AM the Christ of God. What is true of me is true of everyone, for God is all – and all is God.

I see only the Spirit of God in every Soul. And to every living thing, I say: I love you, for you are me. You are my Holy Self. I now open my heart and let the pure essence of Unconditional Love pour out. I see it as a Golden Light radiating from the center of my being. And I feel its Divine Vibration in and through me, above and below me, swirling all around me.

I AM One with the Light. I AM filled with the Light. I AM illumined by the Light. I AM the Light of the World.

With purpose of Mind, I send forth the Light. I let the radiance go before me to join the other Lights. This is happening all over the world. I see the merging Lights. There is now ONE Light. We are the LIGHT OF THE WORLD.

The One Light of Love, Peace, and Understanding is moving. It flows, touching and illuminating every soul in the shadow of the illusion. And there is only the Light of Reality. And the radiance grows, permeating, saturating every form of Life. There is only the vibration of One Perfect Life now. All living things respond, and the planet is alive with Light and Love.

There is total Oneness. And in the Oneness, we speak the Word. There is only Unity. Allkind returns to Godkind, the real world. Peace resides in every mind. Love flows forth from every heart. Forgiveness reigns in every soul. Understanding is the common bond.

And now, from the Light of the World, the Only Presence and Power responds. The activity of God is healing and harmonizing all. Omnipotence is made manifest. I AM seeing salvation before my very eyes as all false beliefs and error patterns dissolve. Only Unity exists. The Healing has taken place, and all is now restored to sanity.

This is Peace on Earth and Good Will towards all, and love flows forth from every heart – forgiveness reigns in every soul – and all hearts and minds are One in perfect understanding.

It is done.

AND IT IS SO NOW.

Adapted and Revised. Original meditation from: Ft. Lauderdale Church of Religious Science, Science of Mind Center, 1550 NE 26th Street, Ft. Lauderdale, FL 33305, (954) 566-2868, RSIFTL.com.

2- Science of Mind Principles

We believe in God, the Living Spirit Almighty; one indestructible, absolute and self-existent Cause. This One manifests itself in and through all creation but is not absorbed by its creation. The manifest universe is the body of God; it is the logical and necessary outcome of the infinite self-knowingness of God.

We believe in the incarnation of the Spirit in man and that all men are incarnations of the One Spirit.

We believe in the eternality, the immortality, and the continuity of the individual soul, forever and ever expanding.

We believe that the Kingdom of Heaven is within man, and that we experience this Kingdom to the degree that we become conscious of it.

We believe the ultimate goal of life to be a complete emancipation from all discord of every nature, and that this goal is sure to be attained by all.

We believe in the unity of all life, and that the highest God and the innermost God is one God. We believe that God is personal to all who feel this Indwelling Presence. We believe in the direct revelation of Truth through the intuitive and spiritual nature of man, and that any man may become a revealer of Truth who lives in close contact with the Indwelling God.

We believe that the Universal Spirit, which is God, operates through a Universal Mind, which is the Law of God; and that we are surrounded by this Creative Mind, which receives the direct impress of our thought and acts upon it.

We believe in the healing of the sick through the power of this Mind. We believe in the control of conditions through the power of this Mind.

We believe in the eternal Goodness, the eternal Loving-kindness, and the eternal Givingness of Life to all.

We believe in our own soul, our own spirit, and our own destiny; for we understand that the life of man is God.

Ft. Lauderdale Church of Religious Science, Science of Mind Center, 1550 NE 26th Street, Ft. Lauderdale, FL 33305, (954) 566-2868, RSIFTL.com.

3- Spiritual Mind Treatment for Children

The One and Only Knowing Living Spirit surrounds, and lives, in all. This Perfect Being manifests Itself without limitation through all children living on earth.

Harmony and spontaneous Unity, Positivity, Divine compassion, Complete satisfaction, and Perfect Health flow through all earth children as they are one with God.

The Living Spirit Almighty freely guides every aspect of life for all earth children towards All the Good There Is. Fearless faith in the Creative Mind frees all thought of limitation.

I AM grateful to the Divine Source of all good for the gifts of Harmony, Unity, Positivity, Compassion, Complete satisfaction, and Perfect Health that manifest within all earth children.

I release this treatment and entrust it to the Law of Mind secure in the Truth of One Mind manifesting the Spirit of the Universe within all things forever. And So *It* Is!

4- Treatment for Perfect Health

God is perfect health, perfect peace, and limitless love, free of all dis-ease, discord, or disharmony. This Divine Source flows through all things including me. Right where pain, dis-ease, discord, resentment, anger, or fear seems to operate, the presence of Infinite Intelligence is.

Perfection flows through my blood, as I AM one with Divine Mind. Spirit allows me to grow. There is no inner agitation or outward irritation in me. A warm sense of my Oneness, in essence and experience with All the Good There Is, replaces inner agitation or outward irritation.

I give thanks to God that I AM guided by Infinite Intelligence clearing all thought of limitation. I release this treatment to the Law of Mind knowing that Perfection manifests Itself, within me, forevermore throughout eternity. And So *It* Is!

5- Suggestions for the 21st Century
* Make personal responsibility a necessity in your life; start by caring for yourself and your birth family.
* Always put love of people, starting with yourself, before love of material possessions.
* Recognize that you have the power and knowledge within you to make your life better. Stop pride from limiting personal or spiritual growth.
* Always ask questions, no matter how stupid you, or others, think they may be.
* Practice Mindfulness:
Value love, peace, and harmony, among all living things, every day.
Think about the consequences to others and yourself before you speak; choose your words carefully.
Think about the consequences to yourself and the world before you act; know that your actions can affect people you do not even know.
* Always love all living beings without remorse; act through love and not anger. Give more than you take; lend a hand to lift other people up.
* Help as many people as you can throughout your life to nourish the spirit in all people.
* In times of need, first help people who wish to help themselves; help all people if time and finances permit you to do so. Do not enable destructive people to hurt themselves and others by helping them repeatedly as they continue to destroy themselves and others.
* In times of loss or trouble always look for the lesson that can be learned.
* Be prepared to see opportunities for personal growth; take them and put your fear aside. Opportunities for growth that create the most fear are the ones that offer the most positive growth; they always nourish your spirit the most.
* Assure that the world is a better place before you pass on.
* Remember, there are always spirit guides to help you choose the most positive ways to help yourself and others. To tap into this knowledge, focus on your heart with good intentions for all living beings. Offer love, peace and harmony to everyone you meet.

6- Treatment for Addiction
The Divine Spirit is within all things. This Self-Knowing Force is complete within the Thing Itself and is never hindered. It is the voice of reason, harmony, and clarity, full of All the Good There Is.

This Divine Spirit lives within me, and using its Infinite Intelligence, manifests All the Good There Is. I AM full of positivity, good health, compassion, and a feeling of harmonious unity with all living things.

I declare that Absolute Intelligence manifests peace and limitless opportunity for growth through me, resulting in Perfection without any desire for unnatural substances, alcohol, illegal drugs, or fear of any kind.

I AM grateful to the Divine Source of All Good for the gifts that I manifest, with the power of Divine Universal Intelligence.

With joyful and complete trust in God, our Creator, I entrust these words to the Law of Mind knowing that I AM free, for I know the truth of my real being. And So *It* Is!

7- Treatment for the Ability to Give and Receive Love

God is Spontaneous Love, a true love free of all doubt or fear. This Divine Source of Love flows in all living things including myself.

Divine Love fulfills all the Laws of Life. I share this love within my destined relationships from this day forward. There is no doubt that Divine Love flows through me as I express it effectively within my most prominent destined relationships. As this love flows unhindered, unobstructed, and spontaneously within and through me, it is always effectively felt by every person destined to be in my life. Each and every person feeling this Divine Love returns it effectively to its source, twofold. As this Divine Love continues to grow, it clarifies the nature of my True Being and destiny.

I give thanks that the Divine Source of Love consciously works to give me clarity of mind that is free of doubt or fear.

I release this treatment to the Law of Mind, knowing that Divine Love manifests the Thing Itself spontaneously and freely, within and through me. And So *It* Is!

8- Treatment for Increased Spiritual Awareness

The Living Spirit Almighty is within all things guiding every action towards All the Good There Is. This Divine Being is firmly rooted in me, a point of God-conscious life, Truth, and Divine Harmony.

I AM a center in the Divine Mind and faith neutralizes all fear, doubt, or negativity within me. Everything I do, say, or think is stimulated by the Truth of my real being. Effortless actions animate everything I do, say, or think toward All the Good There Is. I AM guided by Absolute Law and my affairs are guarded in right action. Divine Harmony with all things enhances feelings of positivity, happiness, perfect health, and complete satisfaction.

I AM filled with All the Good There Is and always guided by Absolute Intelligence. I AM thankful for the way Spirit works in my life forever fulfilling me with a sense of peace and Divine Unity with All the Good There Is. Divine Reality of the Principle of Unity is recognized, and received, with conscious gratefulness.

As I release these words to the Law of God, I AM assured that I AM forevermore guided by Absolute Intelligence. And So *It* Is!

9- Treatment for Wholeness and Health

God is present in all things. This Creative Energy flows easily within and through me.

As this Perfect Presence circulates in every cell of my body, it spreads a Divine sense of peace and ease. Spiritual perfection continues to remove all obstructions, barriers in my mind, veins, and life experiences. The flow of Life Force is unretarded filling me with All the Good There Is.

I AM grateful for the freely flowing stream of fearless peace that operates through the power of Absolute Law. And I give thanks for the constantly renewed flow of the One Infinite Life and Substance within me.

I release this treatment to the Creative Mind, the Law of God, knowing that Divine Peace and unhindered Life Force is within me forevermore. And So *It* Is!

10- Treatment for Recovery from Surgery, Diabetes, and High Blood Pressure

I AM one with the Living Spirit Almighty. Dis-ease has no avenue to express itself for Spirit is always actively operating through me.

My body is operating perfectly in tune with All the Good There Is and I AM guided effortlessly into all Truth. I AM filled with peace, poise, and power, always harmonious with the One Power of Spirit. Every atom of my body is complete and perfect, now and forevermore, filled with the essence of Pure Thought.

A consciousness of perfect love, harmony, and peace constantly renews the stream of life within me. My body overflows with a warm sense of Oneness, in essence and experience, with All the Good There Is. Spirit circulates freely within me.

Releasing these words to Universal Intelligence, I AM grateful to be led by the ever-present Mind. And So *It* Is!

11- Pain Treatment

God is present in all things. This Creative Energy flows easily within and through me. As this Perfect Presence circulates in every cell of my body, it spreads a Divine sense of peace and ease.

I AM grateful for the freely flowing stream of fearless peace that operates through the power of Absolute Law.

I release this treatment to Creative Mind, the Law of God, knowing that Divine Peace is within me forevermore. And So *It* Is!

12- Treatment for Health, Peace of Mind, and Unity with Universal Mind

God is perfect health, perfect peace, and limitless love. This Divine Source flows through all things including me.

The presence of Infinite Intelligence operates freely within me stopping all negativity. Perfection flows through my blood, as I AM one with

360

Divine Mind. Spirit allows me to grow. All negative senses are effortlessly replaced with a warm sense of my Oneness in essence, and experience, with All the Good There Is.

I give thanks to God that I AM guided by Infinite Intelligence clearing all thought of limitation.

Perfection manifests the Thing Itself within me throughout eternity as I release this treatment to the Law of Mind. And So *It* Is!

13- Treatment for Stability and Conscious Life

(Author's Note: If you wish, you can replace the word children with the name of a specific child. I used the name Mary to show you how to do this.)

The Living Spirit Almighty is within all things guiding every action towards All the Good There Is. This Divine Being is firmly rooted in children (Mary), points (a point) of God-conscious life, Truth, and Divine Harmony.

Children (Mary) are (is) a center in the Divine Mind and faith neutralizes all fear, doubt, or negativity within them (her). Everything children (Mary) do (does), say (says) or think (thinks) is stimulated by the Truth of their (her) real Being. Effortless actions animate everything they (she) do (does), say (says), or think (thinks) towards All the Good There Is.

Children (Mary) are (is) well liked by their (her) peers, who enjoy their (her) companionship, and interact with them (her) in mutually positive and nurturing ways. Absolute Law guides children (Mary) and their (her) affairs are guarded in right action. Divine Harmony with all things enhances children's (Mary's) feelings of self-worth, positivity, happiness, perfect health, and complete satisfaction. Children (Mary) are (is) filled with All the Good There Is and always guided by Absolute Intelligence.

I AM thankful for the way Spirit works in the children's (Mary's) life, forever filling them (her) with a sense of peace, and Divine Unity with All the Good There Is. Divine Reality of the Principle of Unity is recognized and received with conscious gratefulness.

As I release these words to the Law of God, I AM assured that Absolute Intelligence forevermore guides children (Mary). And So *It* Is!

14- Headache Treatment

The Consciousness of God flows through all people. This Infinite Intelligence is within me filling my brain cells with peace.

The vitalizing power of the Divine Spirit fills me with clarity of mind, allowing my entire body to relax, free from worry or confusion. Infinite Intelligence guides my emotions to right thinking.

I AM grateful for the Consciousness of God within me at all times.

The flow of Life Force is unretarded, and sustained throughout eternity, as I release this treatment to the Law of Mind with complete ease. And So *It* Is!

15- Fatigue Treatment

God is Infinite Strength, full of energy, and peace. This Changeless Reality is in all things including me.

Infinite Strength flows freely throughout my body uprooting anything incompatible with peace. This Infinite Strength is in my consciousness at all times, keeping me vital and strong. The Self-Knowing Mind affords me with clarity of thought at all times.

Infinite Strength resides within me forevermore and I AM eternally grateful. I release this treatment to Universal Intelligence as the Principle of Unity freely guides my life. And So *It* Is!

16- Insanity Treatment

The Mind of God is the only Mind there is. This Mind is Perfect, Whole, and Complete. This Mind is in all people including myself.

I AM conscious of the Perfect Presence of the Mind of God that circulates through me. My thoughts are always rational and poised. This Divine Sense of the Universal Mind affords me with clarity of thought, which flows in unlimited supply in all of my brain cells.

With peaceful clarity of Mind, I give thanks to the Origin of All for my consciousness that is in perfect concert with the Mind of God.

I AM eternally thankful for the Principle of Unity that recognizes the Mind of God as my own and release this treatment to *It*. And So *It* Is!

17- Treatment for Lung Trouble

The Life of God is the One Infinite Life and Substance. It is my life now, flowing in and through me, eternally.

My breath is the Life and Light of God, perfectly flowing through my bronchial tubes, my trachea, and my lungs. As my breath flows, it is perfectly expressed as Absolute Intelligence. Each breath expresses my faith and trust in All the Good There Is, which constantly renews the flow of the One Infinite Life and Substance in me.

I AM grateful for the Principle of Unity that continues to demonstrate my oneness with God. Peacefully, and in Perfect Confidence, I entrust this treatment to the Law of God knowing that the all-powerful Essence of Spirit maintains my breath, and entire body. And So *It* Is!

18- Vision Treatment

Our Creator sees all things with perfect clarity through its Divine Mind. This Divine Mind is in me filling me with All the Good There Is.

My soul is filled with pure light as clarity of mind realizes my oneness with God. Inner sight affords me the gift of spiritual vision and unhindered faith in spiritual substance. My perfect eyes reflect the clearness of spiritual vision and I see perfection in all creation.

I AM grateful that my eyes animate with the light of love, joy, faith, and noble service to humanity.

As I lift up my eyes unto God, from whom comes my perfect sight, I release this treatment to Creative Mind, the Law of Spirit. And So *It* Is!

19- Treatment for Constipation

The Origin of All the Good There Is flows freely with Absolute Intelligence offering unconditional Love, Truth, and Wholeness to all people. I feel this Divine Being within me as the free flow of Life Essence constantly guides every aspect of my life.

All my life forces are harmonious, normal, and perfect as my body functions while Infinite Intelligence rules. There is no fear, no congestion, restriction, inaction, or dis-ease as my body functions perfectly. I recognize the true nature of my being and accept it without resistance. My actions are firmly rooted in Reality, Divine Love, and Truth. My muscles, and bowel, functions with ease acknowledging the Principle of Unity.

God's presence insures the free flow of Life Essence and I AM eternally thankful. Knowing this treatment works by Absolute Law, I release it to Universal Intelligence. And So *It* Is!

20- Treatment for Perfect Skin

The one and only Self-Knowing Spirit is within all people. This Life Essence is within me.

A great sense of calmness freely flows through me since I recognize the Truth of my True Being as peace and harmony. The Consciousness of God constantly renews my entire being, relaxing me with thoughts of All the Good There Is.

I AM thankful that the one and only Self-Knowing Spirit is an active part of my True Being. With calmness, peace, and harmony for all things, I release this treatment to the Law of God knowing that Absolute Intelligence guides every aspect of my life. And So *It* Is!

21- Treatment for Arms and Hands

God is in all things. This Divine Being flows freely throughout my physical body and spirit.

I AM filled with creative ideas as this Life Essence offers me the ability to reach out and grasp Reality. My faith and conviction of Truth is firmly rooted within and I partake of the Divine Benefits that God offers to all living things.

The power of Infinite Intelligence flows freely as I gratefully acknowledge God steadily in my life.

With knowledge of Absolute Intelligence and Conscious Volition, I release this treatment to the Law of God. And So *It* Is!

22- Treatment for Irritable Bowel and Bladder

The Supreme Personality of the Universe includes all life. I AM a part of this Divine Spirit.

As the Divine Mind guides me towards All the Good There Is, my thoughts remain calm. My gastrointestinal tract and urinary system reflect the wholeness of God. They perform perfectly, constantly adjusting to their natural and spiritual perfection and operation. My bowels, bladder, kidneys, and their organs are perfect, for they are spiritual ideas and all that God conceived is perfect. Perfect elimination occurs, as my thoughts remain calm. No waste substance remains and my body is cleansed, of all impurities, regularly and normally.

I AM grateful for the power of Absolute Law that fills me with Divine Love, peace and harmony for all things.

Recognizing the Unity of Good, I release this treatment to the Law of God knowing that my gastrointestinal tract and urinary system both operate in their perfect and natural state. And So *It* Is!

23- Treatment for Perfect Physical Health

I recognize the Living Spirit Almighty as perfect, indestructible, and indispensable. This Perfect Presence circulates in every cell of my body.

My consciousness of God fills me with Divine Love, peace, harmony, and All the Good There Is. Infinite Intelligence guides every aspect of my life and sustains my true perfect being at all times. I AM full of creative ideas, positivity, clarity of mind, and inner sight. This affords me the gift of unhindered faith in the Spiritual Substance that sustains my body's perfection.

I AM grateful for the constant flow of the perfect One Infinite Life and Substance within me. Aware of the Principle of Unity that consistently demonstrates my oneness with All the Good There Is, I entrust this treatment to the Law of God. And So *It* Is!

24- Treatment for Urinary System Perfection

The Supreme Personality of the Universe includes all life. I AM a part of this Divine Spirit.

My bladder, kidneys and their organs are perfect because they are spiritual ideas and all that God conceived is perfect. Thoughts remain calm as Divine Mind guides me towards All the Good There Is. Security, ease, and reassurance replace all thoughts of dis-ease. My entire urinary tract performs perfectly. It constantly adjusts to its natural and spiritual perfection and operation. Perfect elimination occurs, as my thoughts remain calm. My body is cleansed of all impurities normally.

I AM grateful for the power of Absolute Law that fills me with Divine Love, peace, and harmony for all things.

Recognizing the Unity of Good, I release this treatment to the Law of God, knowing that my urinary system operates in its perfect and natural state. And So *It* Is!

25- Feet and Legs

The ever-present Mind works by Absolute Law. It is in all things. The Infinite Reality of this power flows freely within me.

I AM guided by the ever-present Mind towards All the Good There Is. My ability to walk and continuously evolve is guided by right action and truth in all that I do.

The Power of Spirit fills me with humility and gratefulness as I recognize Its glory. By releasing this treatment to Universal Intelligence, I shall always be guided into all truth led by the ever-present Mind. And So *It* Is!

26- False Growths (Tumors, Cancer, Gallstones)

I recognize my True Being as part of One Creative Mind forever manifesting Divine Love and perfection.

This Eternal Presence consciously cleanses my blood, keeping my body in harmony with positivity, and creative ideas full of All the Good There Is. Receptive Intelligence guides the free flow of Life Essence, which assures that every atom in my body is perfect. Absolute Intelligence maintains the perfection within with sustained faith and trust in God, our Creator.

I AM thankful that Spirit is completely manifested as perfection within my True Being.

With recognition of the Eternal Presence in me, I release this treatment to the Law of God. And So *It* Is!

27- Removing the Complex

The One and Only Divine Being lives in all things. I AM a part of this Perfect Essence.

My consciousness is based on Divine Truth, which fills me with All the Good There Is, and gives me clarity of thought. There is no room in my mind for opposing thoughts because my inner consciousness reigns supreme. All of my actions are based on the Truth of Divine Mind as Creative Energy continually guides each and every thought. The Law of Mind ensures that my thoughts are harmonious, peaceful, and trusting.

I AM grateful for the Absolute Intelligence that feeds my belief in the Universal Mind, which manifests through me.

As Divine Truth fills my mind with a constant flow of Creative Energy, I release this treatment to the Law of God. And So *It* Is!

28- Heart Trouble

The Body of God is perfect. It is Divine Love, which flows unhindered throughout all things.

Divine Law and Harmony continually guide my life. Infinite Intelligence supports all body functions, and my heart is a living center, through which Divine Love eternally flows. My heart is never troubled for the blood in my veins and arteries flow freely. This heart healthy action results in perfect circulation, assimilation, and elimination of the lifeblood in me. Universal Mind counteracts negative thoughts as I recognize I AM ageless Spirit.

Recognizing this Law of Life within me, I AM grateful for the way that Spirit works.

I AM one with Conscious Life, and release this treatment to the Universal Mind knowing that I AM because, It is. And So *It* Is!

29- Poison

My body is pure Spirit Substance for the One and Only Substance flows within.

This Perfect and Pure Life of God circulates freely to assure that body organs manifest my oneness with Spirit. The blood of my body is forever pure, perfect, and circulating freely. I AM full of positivity and All the Good There Is.

The pure Life of God flows in and through me always creating a sense of gratitude and I thank All the Good There Is.

Infinite Reality allows me to see my Unity with the Spirit of Life as I release this treatment to the Universal Mind. And So *It* Is!

30- Paralysis

Conscious Life is in all things. This Infinite Reality is within me using the Dependable and Action Principle, which affords me perfect freedom to vitalize my perfect body. Clarity of mind reveals my oneness with the Divine Mind. My endeavors are always guided in right action.

There are no thoughts of restriction or limitation as my mind remains peaceful, calm, and devoid of any turmoil. Infinite Life and Action reveals the true nature of my being.

I AM thankful for the presence of life, and right action in my life, as the Universal Force flows freely within me.

Aware of the One Indwelling Presence, the free-flowing life of Spirit, I AM eternally free releasing this treatment to Universal Mind. And So *It* Is!

31- Nerve Troubles

God, the Living Spirit, is the only Presence in all things. I AM a part of this pure, perfect, and harmonious Spirit. I recognize my nerves are the highest form of intelligence.

I abide in faith as Spirit runs through my flesh. The Essence of Life flows freely and peacefully within, as thoughts of poise and power occur, without strain or struggle. The all-powerful Mind of the Indwelling Christ fills me with love, protection, fearless power, peace, strength, and All the Good There Is. The One Mind in me continues to renew my faith and keep my nerves firm, steady and sensitive, quickly responding appropriately at all times. The steady presence of the One Power dwells in me. I AM complete and confident as my awareness of the one final Reality continues to increase.

My body functions according to Divine Law and I live in a sea of Perfect Life poised in eternal calm. Spirit manifests in me as perfect harmony because the Law of God governs every atom in my body.

I AM thankful to recognize that the past, present, and future are an unbroken stream of Good, and God is the light, power, and inspiration of my life. My past and future are continuations of the one unbroken chain of life, yet no past brings discord to the present.

I release this treatment to the Universal Consciousness as my cup of acceptance fills, and overflows, with the manifestations of my desires. And So *It* Is!

32- Asthma and Hay Fever

The One and Only Infinite Mind is my mind, inspired with perfection and All the Good There Is. I AM open and sensitive to the flow of good in my higher consciousness.

My conscious mind expresses my divine inheritance. It is filled with thoughts of love, joy, and peace. My body is the Temple of the Holy Ghost and I recognize my Oneness with Infinite Life. Nothing obstructs the perfect functioning of my entire body. The Law of Spirit flows freely, exhilarating and vitalizing me. There is only perfect calm as my thoughts are clarified in the Universal Mind.

I AM thankful to know that the breath of God is my breath flowing unrestricted through channels of pure receptivity from Infinite Intelligence.

I release this treatment to the Law of God as I breathe in the Eternal Life Essence that purifies me and keeps me strong. And So *It* Is!

33- Blood Troubles and Skin Dis-eases

The One and Only Infinite Reality lives in all things and flows freely within me.

The rhythmic harmony of my life acknowledges that I AM a temple of God-Life. As Divine Light and Energy freely flow, I AM ageless and deathless, always abiding in God's Law. My blood manifests as pure and perfect Spiritual Substance. The Divine Source of Spirit flows perfectly through my bloodstream keeping it pure. Consciousness of Life fills me with Divine Love and Harmony for all living things.

I AM one in essence and experience with All the Good There Is. My bloodstream constantly renews as Spiritual Substance continues to manifest love, peace, and harmony fulfilling my every need. A calm Self-Propelling Life-Force perfectly revitalizes my entire body with pure Spiritual Substance.

I thank the One and Only Infinite Reality knowing the nature of my real being. Joyous self-realization of Spirit fills me with gratefulness for my Spiritual Perfection.

I release this treatment to Spirit knowing that Absolute Intelligence and Divine Law spread these words throughout the Universe. And So *It* Is!

34- Fevers

The Indwelling Almighty flows unhindered in me.

I AM conscious of my oneness with God who constantly fills me with peace and comfort of mind. The Law of Spirit allows access to only positive thoughts. Conscious Life boosts my faith as I continue to experience All the Good There Is.

I AM thankful for my Divinity, which is a safe haven that allows me to consciously be one with the Indwelling Almighty.

Fearlessly, I release this treatment to the Law of Spirit allowing these words to flow in the wind and fill all space. And So *It* Is!

35- Obstetrics

I rest in Infinite Reality, unified with Absolute Intelligence, and give myself peacefully to the care of Perfection in action.

Right action prevails as the Creative Law working in me synchronizes the growth and perfection of the baby I carry in my womb. Absolute Law allows Absolute Intelligence to ensure that every atom in this new body is healthy, on every plane of expression. Creative Energy works perfectly, as I remain serene and calm, free of negative thought.

I AM grateful to know that the great Law of Creation always operates at the correct time. I joyfully release this treatment to the Law of Spirit. And So *It* Is!

36- Colds, Flu, and Grippe

The Life of God flows freely, in and through, all things. This Life Force manifests All the Good There Is through me.

Every breath I take verifies my unity with Infinite Life. Conscious Life affords me clarity of thought. My mind is full of harmony, confidence, and understanding. God sustains me in perfect health at all times, bringing me peace of mind, and freeing me from harm. Unification and spiritual perfection fulfill my every need.

I AM grateful for my peace of mind and a free heart filled with the Law of Spirit. Recognizing Absolute Law guides my life, I release these words freely into the Creative Energy of Universal Mind. And So *It* Is!

37- Obesity

First Cause, the Body of God, is my body, now manifesting symmetry and perfection.

I AM complete. My body is a part of Spirit, always dependable, using Absolute Law to meet my needs. Divine order guides my appetite. The foods I eat are perfectly absorbed and digested. Gods Divine Love, care, and substance fill the food I eat, in perfect proportion. Spirit fulfills my every need, fearlessly expressing the Thing Itself, with full recognition of Divine Love.

I AM thankful for the presence of God in my life. I release this treatment to Universal Intelligence with presence of mind, aware that Spirit works in, and through, me. And So *It* Is!

38- Diabetes

Spirit is the origin of *All*. I feel and recognize the God-Life that fills my consciousness.

The Truth keeps my body free of dis-ease. All the food I eat is perfectly suited to meet my body needs. The food is absorbed and digested normally, filling every atom of my body with joy, and fulfillment. My blood stream carries the foods energy, and gives me all I need for perfect body function, as it ensures that my blood is pure.

Perfect conscious awareness of the Divine Mind is gratefully acknowledged as I release this treatment to Universal Intelligence. And So *It* Is!

39- Treatment for the Bladder

Eternal Life is mine as I recognize the Conscious Life flowing in and through me.

The Principle of Life acts through me filling my body with positivity, peace, and perfection in all its forms. My thoughts remain calm and free of worry, as the purity and strength of Infinite Reality stops stress, and insecurity, from entering my mind. Perfect assimilation, and appropriate elimination of body substances, occurs as Divine Order guides all body functions.

With joyous peace of mind, I thankfully acknowledge the Infinite Mind that ensures wholeness. Recognizing that I AM an expression of God-Mind, an example of the dynamic Principle of Life, I consciously release these words to flow freely throughout Universal Mind. And So *It* Is!

40- Liver

I AM conscious of the One Divine Power and Vital Essence within.

Divine Harmony, guided by Absolute Law, fills every cell of my body with perfection. Divine Mind clarifies thoughts of harmony and unity with all things. The Beloved molds all new matter that flows into my physical form as pleasant memory experiences. These experiences continually renew themselves with ease. The Law maintains an orderly balance of harmonious thoughts that form ideas, which heal, cleanse, and uplift my Spirit.

Easily releasing this treatment to the Law of God, I AM grateful to recognize the One Divine Power and Vital Essence within me. And So *It* Is!

41- Stomach and Bowel Troubles

I recognize the Beloved in every atom of my being. My faith, perfect and complete, fills me and elates my entire body.

I AM filled with All the Good There Is. Divine Love guides my thinking. Divine Mind elevates my thoughts relaxing them along with my entire body, including all the muscles in my gastrointestinal tract. I give freely of myself and time, unselfishly. I AM filled with love, joy, and positivity. I eat my food thankfully and calmly, free of any discord. The food I eat is absorbed, digested, and assimilated perfectly.

I AM grateful knowing that the very life of God vitalizes my entire body. The Principle of Life fills me with Infinite Life and Eternal Perfection.

I release this treatment to the Law of God, as Life Spirit flows through me, working by Absolute Law to renew me continually. And So *It* Is!

42- Insomnia

As the earth moves to reveal the rays of the Sun, and the light filled stillness of the Moon, I know God is a part of me.

The Sun's rays melt the snow, and heat renews the plants below ground, while perfect trust in God relaxes and renews my body. I let go of earthly thoughts and rest in the Body of God. My entire body overflows with peace and Divine Tranquility. It ceaselessly ensures the stillness in me with ease. Divine Wisdom fills me as I rest in the still silence of Spirit. I remain divinely protected.

My body is richly blessed with Divine Love, full of goodness. I happily rejoice, and thank the Origin of All, as nothing disturbs my spiritual self. Spirit always takes care of my affairs.

The all-powerful Mind of the Indwelling Christ within fills me with Eternal Peace, as I consciously release these words, to soar through the winds of Universal Intelligence. And So *It* Is!

43- Deafness

The truth of my real being is now revealed as Divine Harmony fills me with All the Good There Is.

This Divine Harmony fills my physical being with an ever-increasing capacity to make positive life choices. I AM filled with confidence, and always receptive to changes, ever conscious of Absolute Intelligence. Divine Mind affords me the luxury of perfect, complete, Divine ideas, which I faithfully accept to increase my spiritual growth. I co-operate, knowing the Truth that promotes perfect hearing, for God hears through me. Every idea I have functions according to Divine Law.

I AM thankful, open, and receptive to the Divine Harmony that allows me to hear the voice of God. I release this treatment, as both ears remain open and receptive to the vibration of Perfect Harmony. And So *It* Is!

44- Weather Conditions Treatment

I AM a manifestation of Pure Spirit, in unity with all things, including the ever-changing weather.

As I recognize my unity with the Divine Being in sunshine, shade, rain, and clouds, strong wind and calm breezes, I enjoy and agree with all weather conditions. Each change in the weather is as welcome to me as the variations in my life. I AM always filled with Divine Love and Harmony. I feel harmonious, spiritually and physically complete. I AM free of fear or confusion for I AM the wind, the clouds, the rain, and the sunshine in the sky. I AM in unity with all weather, one with the heat, the cold, humidity, and dryness of the atmosphere, always changing as my spirit grows.

I AM one with all things. As Nature continues to reveal *It's* beauty to me, I rejoice in freedom, fearlessly weathering all climate changes. While I glaze upon the peaceful calm sky or the beauty of the perfect storm, Divine Mind fills me with joyous gratefulness.

I release these words effortlessly into the atmosphere to flow throughout the vastness of the Universe. And So *It* Is!

45- Food Security and Safety

Law of Spirit guides every aspect of my life, even the choices I make to fill my human host.

The Truth ensures that I always have the nourishment needed to keep my body strong. Every dietary choice I make is based on the way Spirit works through Creative Energy. I always consume healthy and appropriate food and drink, omitting substances that may be harmful to my physical body, or the spirit within.

I consume nourishing food and fluids knowing they are my Spiritual Substance and supply. All of these spiritual substances are one with the Essence of Conscious Life, filled with Absolute Intelligence. All nourishment is healing, and works in harmony with Spirit, to fill and always renew me with All the Good There Is.

I gratefully recognize the Absolute Law that guides my food and drink choices. I release these words to the Law of God to freely flow within, and through, Universal Intelligence. And So *It* Is!

46- Rheumatism

I AM a spiritual being within the Body of God, perfect and free. Divine Tranquility assures the Infinite Reality that I AM.

Eternal Truth and beauty are mine as I sense the sunshine in my soul. Divine Intelligence guides me. Divine Law eliminates impurities. My body is full of Truth and freely allows the power of Creative Energy to circulate in my conscious mind. Body fluids flow effortlessly as I AM aware of Divine Love for all things.

I thank the Living Spirit Almighty for the Divine Love that flows, in and through me, as perfect rays of sunshine. Gratefully, with perfect clarity of mind, I release these words to soar though the wind filling all space. And So *It* Is!

47- Healing Intemperance

The Beloved is in all things and fills me with Divine Love and Tranquility. I AM positive, acting freely at all times, as my unity with God is everlasting.

I act appropriately and fearlessly, free of any limitation, during all situations. Conscious Life fills me with faith and joy meeting all needs. Recognition of Divine Reality fills me with All the Good There Is. I AM always satisfied with how God guides every aspect of my life.

I AM grateful for the Truth of Infinite Reality that constantly supplies me with Creative Energy. Releasing these words to the Law of God, completeness and satisfaction are mine forevermore. I bask in the light of Infinite Life. And So *It* Is!

48- Treatment for Tranquility and Non-Reaction to Outside Forces

The Supreme Personality of the Universe includes all life. I AM a segment of this Divine Spirit.

My thoughts remain calm as Divine Mind guides me towards All the Good There Is. I do not react to outside forces for Spirit freely guides every aspect of my life. Divine Love, Peace, and Harmony grow within as I have positive interactions with all living things. There is no worry, anxiety, or fear of criticism because my mind is part of the Divine Mind that fuels all thoughts and actions. My body is free of all negativity, pain, irritation, or agitation.

I AM grateful for the Power of Absolute Law that fills me with Divine Love, Peace and Harmony for all things.

Recognizing the Unity of Good, I release this treatment to the Law of God to flow eternally throughout all space. And So *It* Is!

49- Supply

Conscious Life, surrounded by Substance, flows effortlessly to supply all my needs. The Truth of my unity with all things successfully draws people like me, to me, and we enrich each other's life.

The Living Spirit of Divine Love guides every aspect of my life, at all times, in the right direction. My constructive endeavors reflect unity with all things. Divine Love ensures that I AM compensated for all my efforts. Spiritual Substance always manifests whatever I need before a need arises. I always have an abundance of whatever it takes to make my life happy and fulfilling.

I AM thankful for the conscious understanding of Divine Being, which fulfills all needs at all times. Filled with All the Good There Is, and knowing that I AM a unique part of the Body of God, I joyously release these words to the Universal Mind. And So *It* Is!

50- Peace of Mind

God is Divine Tranquility. I AM pleased to be a part of the Origin of All for Infinite Intelligence is the only cause, medium, and effect in my life.

The Principle of Peace flows freely within assuring a sense of confidence and tranquility. My mind is full of Truth and assurance of completeness and perfection. I trust the Law of Spirit to bring good into my life, as Peace and Light guide me towards All the Good There Is.

Aware of my unity with Universal Intelligence, I AM grateful to be Christ, the Son within the Body of God.

Rejoicing in my perfection, knowing that Divine Tranquility and Love guide every aspect of my life, I release this treatment to the Law of Spirit. And So *It* Is!

51- Treatment for Continued Peace, Inner Sight, and Clarity

The Supreme Personality of the Universe is in all things. As a unique part of this Divine Being, I AM free of all limitation.

Absolute Intelligence ensures a Divinely Sustained Stream of fearless Peace that consciously relaxes my essence at all times. Clarity of Mind continues to increase God-Life and my spiritual vision glows as the rays of the Sun. My spirit's destiny is fulfilled on this earth, through Divine Timing. Continued faith in the Divine Mind ensures the fulfillment of my spirit's destiny in the afterlife, with conscious ease, and abandonment of all earthly outcomes.

"Father, I commend my spirit to thee."

Thankful for ever-increasing recognition of the Law of Unity, I never waver or sway from the nature of my True Being and destiny. The Divine Source of All the Good There Is constantly fills my spirit with gratefulness, joy, and freedom from earthly outcomes. I gratefully retain conscious knowledge of my True Being and all lessons, and experiences, obtained from the beginning of time, forevermore.

Recognizing the Power of Absolute Law, my spirit humbly accepts Infinite Life, and sees the Law of God as the Creative Energy that accepts these words to eternally flow throughout all space. And So *It* Is!

52- Abundance and Prosperity

Conscious Life surrounded by Substance flows effortlessly in, and through, me.

The Truth of my Unity with all things successfully draws all that I need to live a self-fulfilled life full of abundance and prosperity. Absolute Law ensures that I AM always richly compensated for all my constructive efforts. Substance always manifests whatever I need before a need arises.

I AM grateful for the ever-flowing abundance and prosperity of whatever it takes to make my life happy and fulfilling. Filled with All the Good There Is, and knowing I AM a unique part of the Body of God, I joyously release these words to Universal Mind. And So *It* Is!

53- Wake Up to Life Treatment - W(orld) A(ll good) K(arma) E(ternity) – U(nity) P(eace) to L(ove) I(nfinity) F(orgiveness) E(volution)

The Supreme Personality of the Universe is in all things. This Spirit (Adhi, Adon, Adonai, Agni, Allah, Atman, Beloved, Brahman, Divine Being, Divine Love, Divine Spirit, First Cause, God, Great I AM, Illah, Indra, Ishwara, It, Jehovah, Kami, Lord, Mind, Nature, One & Only, Reality, Rita, Saguna, Spirit, Supreme Personality of the Universe, Theo, Uaruna, Yahweh, and so on...) is everywhere. I AM a part of this Divine Spirit that is in all people.

Spirit is All the Good There Is.
Spirit is love, unity, and peace.
Spirit is Karma in action throughout eternity.
Spirit is Infinite Forgiveness.
Spirit is ever-present Evolution.
I AM a unique part of Spirit.
I AM All the Good There Is.

I AM love, unity, and peace.

I AM constantly evolving as Karma helps me to increase my awareness of Reality.

My love has no boundaries and forgiveness is a part of me as I AM a part of the Beloved.

I let go of all human limitations as Allah supports my spiritual evolution.

I AM thankful for the Infinite Law of Mind (Universal Consciousness) that supports my thoughts of love, peace, harmony, and compassion for all people.

As Nature continues to reveal *It's* beauty to me, I release this treatment to the Universal Mind, secure in the Truth of One Mind, constantly evolving and manifesting All the Good There Is. And So *It* Is!

54- Treatment for Non-Reaction to Outside Forces

The Supreme Personality of the Universe includes all things. My perfection within the Divine Spirit is pure Unity.

Divine Mind guides me towards All the Good There Is. All thoughts remain calm. My non-reaction reflects unity with Divine Tranquility. Divine Love, peace, and harmony constantly flow freely as Absolute Law assures ever-present Infinite Tranquility. Spirit fuels positive thoughts and as a part of Spirit, I AM always free of irritation or agitation. Positive interactions with all people constantly occur. Divine Harmony reflects my attitude as the rays of the Sun at all times.

Recognizing that the Divine Mind is my mind, Spirits gifts of Love, Peace, Harmony and Perfection constantly spur thoughts of thanks.

These words now flow through the Law of God and the Law of Unity eternally throughout all space. And So *It* Is!

55- One with Spirit Treatment

The One and Only Infinite Mind is my mind. It is perfect and filled with Light, All the Good There Is.

I AM open to the flow of good in my higher mind. My conscious mind is filled with thoughts of love, joy, peace and All the Good There Is. I AM always perfectly calm and filled with the Truth of the Universe. My belief in Universal Mind guides everything I do, say, or think.

Life is always good for me. I AM always healthy and happy, having whatever I need, because I AM filled with love for everything. I have many friends and we help each other passionately enjoy life and be positive. Divine Mind guides all my actions to do what is right. Truth floods me with peace and oneness for I AM always guided by the One Mind of all people.

Knowing my words are now part of the Universe, I thank the one and Only Infinite Mind. And So *It* Is!

56- My Gratefulness Log

An attitude of gratefulness always serves to bring us greater good. Envision your world the way you want it even if you do not feel like there is anything to be grateful for now. Put your thoughts into words and repeat them at least once a day. As an example, I include my gratefulness log here to get you started. I experienced the physical manifestation of everything on this list. And still enjoy the fruits of my labor after repeating the list every day.

I AM grateful for perfect health, the ability to eat and drink as I please, dance to my hearts delight, and hike through nature joyfully.

I AM grateful for my loving and giving family, all of whom share love and material wealth with one another, are compassionate, and always joyful to spend time with me.

I AM grateful for my friends of like mind who share all things willingly and joyfully (time, material wealth, and knowledge).

I AM grateful for the abundance and prosperity in my life that allows me to have everything I need before I need it, to travel and share my abundance and prosperity with all of humanity, for the greater good of all.

I AM grateful for my generous and considerate husband, who sees the Truth, and values experience enough to do what is right by God's Law.

I AM grateful for the ability to learn and to teach all of humanity in increasingly valuable ways.

I AM grateful to know the Truth. I see Reality and beauty in all things and spread joy, from within me, to everyone I see.

57- The Awakening Process

In my experience, the process of realizing who we really are starts with the need for change because life is no longer comfortable. There's a strong desire to improve living conditions.

Assessment of lifestyle comes next. This results in changing bad habits to more life-giving modes of living. This may mean changing nutritional habits; omitting harmful practices such as substance abuse, smoking, or drinking; reading self-help materials instead of newspapers or magazines; avoiding negative people; listening to positive, nurturing music; or watching inspiring movies instead of watching TV.

We create a better life by opening the mind to greater possibilities and thinking out-of-the-box. Learning to consciously control emotions, thoughts, words, and deeds puts us closer to freedom. The next step is to dispel illusions that no longer serve us, such as ill health, limitation, etc. It is vital to take responsibility for what happens in our life, instead of blaming others. It's also important to stop trying to control other people.

The reality of our true nature as spiritual beings, having a human experience, often takes time to recognize. We achieve greater things by focusing on positivity and gratefulness. Focusing on spiritual growth through journaling; affirmations; meditation; prayer; gratefulness; spiritual classes; volunteer work; and blessing others helps a great deal.

58- New Lord's Prayer (Adapted and Revised {with one change of the word Higher to Inner} from Walter Starke's *It's All God*, page 173.)

"My Inner Self, which art Heaven consciousness, wholly be thy recognition. The kingdom of my Inner Self come, Its guidance be done at the outer material level as well as at the inner spiritual level. My Inner Self, fulfill for me all my daily needs, body, mind, and Spirit. Release me when I have not listened to my Inner Self as I release others who are not listening to theirs. Lead me not into the temptation of believing my lower self is all; deliver me from the evil of believing I AM not already One. For this realization of my Inner Self is Heaven, the only power, and the glory of all being. And So *It* Is!

59- I Put God First Treatment

God is all there is. As a part of this Divine Being, all life is perfect, whole, and complete.

Every action I perform is for the highest good of All. I consciously choose to put God first in all ways, as I, along with all life, am a part of God.

I AM grateful for this Truth and for the clarity of Mind that allows this Truth to be known.

Releasing this treatment to the Creative Energy that flows through all space, I AM assured that it is so. And So *It* Is!

Bibliography

Addington, Jack and Cornelia Addington. "Drawing the Larger Circle." Pure Inspiration, Fall 2006: 68.

Anderson, George and Andrew Barone. *Walking in the Garden of Souls*. New York: Putnam Adult, 2001.

Allen, James. *As a Man Thinketh*. New York: Grosset & Dunlap, 1980. (AsAManThinketh.net).

Atkinson, William W. *Thought Vibration*. Chicago: The New Thought Publishing Co., 1906. (ThoughtVibrations.com).

Atwater, P.M.H. *Beyond the Indigo Children*. Vermont: Bear & Company, 2005.

Baldwin, Sally. "Annie Luther-Language of the Lights." Online Posting. Pompano Beach Otherside Chat. Dec 15, 2006 (DyingToLiveAgain.com).

Braden, Gregg. *The God Code*. California: Hay House, 2005. (GreggBraden.com).

Brungardt-Pope, Helen and Mark Pope, Jane Kopp, Karl Kopp. *For the Aspiring Mystic*. Arizona: Prophecy Rock Press, 2001.

Byrom, Thomas. "You Are Beyond All Things" *The Heart of Awareness: A Translation of the Ashtavakra Gita*. Online Posting. Beliefnet Hindu Wisdom, Wednesday, March 22, 2006 (Beliefnet.com).

Campbell, Dan. *Edgar Cayce on The Power of Color, Stones, and Crystals*. New York: Warner Books, 1989.

Cayce, Edgar. "The Readings Say: Color and Healing." Venture Inward, July/Aug 2009, Vol. 25, No. 4: 44.

Cayce, Edgar. "We Are All Star Travelers." Venture Inward, July/Aug 2009, Vol. 25, No. 4: 45.

Christeaan, Aaron and JP Van Hulle, M.C Clark. *Michael The Basic Teachings*. California: Michael Education Foundation, 1988.

Cohen, Alan. "From the Heart." Horizons Magazine, Dec 2005: 18.

Choquette, Sonia. "Your Psychic Pathway: Listening to the Guiding Wisdom of Your Soul." Illinois: Nightingale-Conant, 1998.

Dhammapada. "Follow You as Your Own Shadow" *The Pocket Buddha Reader*. Online posting. Beliefnet Buddhist Wisdom, Sunday, April 02, 2006 (Beliefnet.com).

Emoto, Masaru. "Water: Mirror of the Soul." Pure Inspiration, Fall 2006: 6.

Fillmore, Charles. *The Twelve Powers of Man*. Montana: Unity School of Christianity, 1930.

Foundation for Inner Peace, *A Course In Miracles*. California: Foundation for Inner Peace, 1992. (ACIM.org).

Freke, Timothy. *Wisdom of the Hindu Gurus*. United Kingdom: Godsfield Press, 1998.

Gage, Randy. *Prosperity Mind: How to Harness the Power of Thought*. Kansas: Prime Concepts Publishing, 2003.

Gibran, Kahlil. *The Prophet*. New York: Alfred A. Knopf, 1923.

Griscom, Chris. *Time is an Illusion*. New York: Simon & Schuster, 1988.

Glanzman, Andy. "The Heart of Business." Pure Inspiration, Fall 2006. Hanh_ Thich Nhat. "Miracle of Mindfulness" *365 Buddha: Daily Meditations*.

Online posting. Beliefnet Buddhist Wisdom, Tuesday, Jan 03, 2006 (Beliefnet.com).

Hanson, Mark Victor. *The Miracle of Tithing*. California: M.V. Hansen & Associates, Inc., 2003.

His Holiness the Dalai Lama. "A Fisherman's Hook." Online posting. Beliefnet Buddhist Wisdom, Saturday, Jan 07, 2006 (Beliefnet.com).

Holmes, Ernest. *The Science of Mind*. New York: Penguin Putnam Inc., 1938, 1998. (ErnestHolmesHubs.com).

Hoppe, Geoffrey and Tobias. "Twelve Signs of Spiritual Awakening", 2001 (CrimsonCircle.com).

Hubbard, Barbara Marx. *Conscious Evolution*. California: New World Library, 1998.

International Bible Society. *New International Version Archaeological Study Bible*. Michigan: Zondervan Publishing, 2005.

Javane, Faith. *Master Numbers: Cycles of Divine Order*. Pennsylvania: Whitford Press, 1997.

Katz, Richard. "Flower Essences Medicine for the Soul." Pure Inspiration, Fall 2006: 78.

Lee, Barbara. "Horoscopes for October 2006." Horizons Magazine, October 2006: 44.

Lockard, Jim. "I Own My Power." Creative Thought, March 2005. (RSINTL.org).

Lockard, Jim. "Handout 4: Integral Living Practices (ILP) Based on Ken Wilber's Integral Spirituality."

MacLaine, Shirley. *The Camino*. New York: Pocket Books, 2000.

Monroe, Robert A. *Far Journeys*. New York: Doubleday, 1985.

Moss, Robert. *Conscious Dreaming*. New York: Crown Publishers, Inc., 1996.

Neale, Jay Scott. "Prosperity Is My Way." Creative Thought, June 2006, Vol. 87, No. 6: 31. Religious Science International, Spokane, WA.

Newton, Michael. *Destiny of Souls*. Minnesota: Llewellyn Publications, 2004.

Nikaya_Anguttara. "Don't Go by Gossip and Rumor" *Buddha Speaks*. Online posting. Beliefnet Buddhist Wisdom, Wednesday, Feb 15, 2006 (Beliefnet.com).

One In Spirit Magazine, Jan-Feb 2006, Vol. 10, No. 1. Religious Science Ft. Lauderdale, Ft. Lauderdale, FL. (RSIFTL.com).

378

Page, Christine. "Living in a Holographic Universe, A Call to Love," The 2007 Big Sky Retreat, September 1-6, 2007, Big Sky Montana.

Page, Christine. *Spiritual Alchemy*. London: Rider, 2003.

Ponder, Catherine. *The Prosperity Secrets of the Ages*. California: DeVorss Publications, 1986.

Phillips_Tony. "Huge Storms Converge." Online posting. NASA Science News. Monday, June 05, 2006. (http://science.nasa.gov).

Phillips_Tony. "Solar Dynamics Observatory: The 'Variable Sun' Mission." Listserv message. Friday, Feb 05, 2010. NASA Science News. Feb 05, 2010. (http://science.nasa.gov).

Phillips_Tony. "Solar Storm Warning." Listserv message. Friday, March 10, 2006. NASA Science News. March 10, 2006. (http://science.nasa.gov).

Prajnaparamita. "Mysterious Doors Swing Open" *The Pocket Buddha Reader*. Beliefnet Buddhist Wisdom, Thursday, Jan 05, 2006 (Beliefnet.com).

Redfield, James. *The Secret of Shambhala*. New York: Warner Books, Inc., 1999.

Renard, Gary. *Your Immortal Reality, How to Break the Cycle of Birth and Death*. Hay House, Inc., 2007.

Rodegast, Pat and Judith Stanton. *Emmanuel's Book II The Choice for Love*. New York: Bantam Books, 1989.

Schwartz, Gary E. and William L Simon. *The Afterlife Experiments*. New York: Atria Books, 2002.

Simpkinson, Charles H. and Anne Simpkinson. *Soul Work*. New York: Harper Collins Publisher, 1998.

Singh, Tara. *Commentaries on A Course In Miracles*. New York: Harper Collins Publishers, 1992.

Spalding, Baird T. *Life and Teaching of The Masters of the Far East, Volume 6*. California: DeVorss Publications, 1996.

Starcke, Walter. *It's All God*. Texas: Guadalupe Press, 1998.

Shearer, Alistair. *The Yoga Sutras of Patanjali*. New York: Crown Publishing Group, 2002.

"The Golden Key" (adapted from Browne Sylvia, Raffanelli G. *Meditations*, 2002). Religious Science Ft. Lauderdale, Ft. Lauderdale, FL. (RSIFTL.com).

Tortora, Gerald J and Nicholas P. Anagnostakos. *Principles of Anatomy and Physiology, 4th Edition*. New York: Harper & Row, Publishers, 1984.

Troward, Thomas. *The Edinburgh & Dore Lectures on Mental Science*. California: DeVorss, 1904; 1909.

Van Praagh, James. *Talking to Heaven*. Simon & Schuster, 2001.

Watkins, Susan M. *Conversations With SETH Volume 1*. New Jersey: Prentice-Hall, 1980.

Weiss, Brian. *Through Time into Healing*. New York: Fireside, 1992.

Williamson, Judith A. "Where There's a Will There's a Way." Pure Inspiration, Fall 2006: 24.

Websites

BBC News (http://news.bbc.co.uk).

David Wilcox (DivineCosmos.com).

Emerging Earth Angels (GammaBooks.com).

Era of Peace (EraOfPeace.org).

Heart Science Foundation (HeartScienceFoundation.com).

Human Energy Systems Laboratory (OpenMindSciences.com).

KenWilber.com (KenWilber.com).

Monroe Institute (MonroeInstitute.org).

Mental Science (Mental-Science.com).

National Aeronautics and Space Administration (Science.Nasa.gov).

National Center for Atmospheric Research (Ucar.edu).

National Center for Biotechnology Information (NCBI.NLM.NIH.gov).

National Hurricane Center (NHC.NOAA.gov).

New Scientist (NewScientist.com).

Reuters (Reuters.com).

RidingTheBeast.com (RidingTheBeast.com).

Sonic Boom Meets Sun Dog 720p (YouTube.com/watch?v=SsDEfu8s1Lw).

Space Weather (SpaceWeather.com).

Space Weather Prediction Center (SWPC.NOAA.gov).

Spirit Library (SpiritLibrary.com).

The Daily Motivator (DailyMotivator.com).

Wikipedia (Wikipedia.org).

Music

Alice Cooper. "Welcome to my Nightmare." *Welcome to my Nightmare*. Atlantic Recording Corp., 1975. Vinyl recording.

Barbra Streisand and Kris Kristofferson. "Everything." *A Star is Born*. Columbia Records, 1976. Vinyl recording.

Bob Seger and the Silver Bullet Band. "Against the Wind." *Greatest Hits*. Capitol Records, 1994. Vinyl recording.

Bob Seger and the Silver Bullet Band. "In Your Time." *Greatest Hits*. Capitol Records, 1994. Vinyl recording.

Bonnie Raitt. "I Can't Make You Love Me." *Fundamental*. Capitol Records, 1998. CD.

Carole King. "Bitter with the Sweet." *Rhymes & Reasons*. A & M Records, 1972. Vinyl recording.

Carole King. "Goodbye Don't Mean I'm Gone." *Rhymes & Reasons*. A & M Records, 1972. Vinyl recording.

Carole King. "In the Name of Love." *Simple Things*. Capitol Records, 1977. Vinyl recording.

Carole King. "The Best is Yet to Come." *Wrap Around Joy*. ODE Records, Inc., 1974. Vinyl recording.

Chris Tomlin. "Holy is the Lord." *Arriving*. Sparrow Records, 2004. CD.

CREED. "Faceless Man." *Human Clay*. Wind-up Records, 1999. CD.

Creedence Clearwater Revival. *Proud Mary*. Jondora Music BMI, 1969. Vinyl recording.

Fleetwood Mac. "Songbird." *Rumors*. Warner Bros. Records, 1977. Vinyl recording.

John Lennon and Paul McCartney. "All You Need Is Love." *Magical Mystery Tour*. Capitol Records, 1967. Vinyl recording.

John Lennon and Paul McCartney. "I Am The Walrus." *Magical Mystery Tour*. Capitol Records, 1967. Vinyl recording.

John Lennon and Paul McCartney. "Strawberry Fields Forever." *Magical Mystery Tour*. Capitol Records, 1967. Vinyl recording.

Karen Drucker. "Hold On To Love." *Hold On To Love*. TayToones Music, 2000. CD.

Macy Gray. "I Can't Wait to Meetchu." *Macy Gray On How Life Is*. Epic Records, 1999. CD.

Robert Downey Jr. *The Futurist*. Sony BMG Music Entertainment, 2004. CD.

The Marmalade. "Reflections Of My Life." Noma Music Inc., 1969. Vinyl recording.

About the Author

SAM is a lifelong believer in the power of love. Her inspiring life demonstrates the strength of mind over matter. It is a story of progression from desperation to hope, poverty to riches, limitation to freedom, and fear to love. *The End of My Soap Opera Life :-)* book series details this amazing journey of self-discovery and transformation.

The awareness that we are spirits in human form having a physical experience came after SAM's son transitioned on April 4, 2004. SAM's quest for self-mastery began the following year when his essence led her through the doors of an establishment teaching the Science of Mind. SAM turned her back on traditional medicine after decades of illness and multiple surgeries. Using Eastern medicine, and the teachings of Ernest Holmes, she successfully rid herself of many maladies.

SAM's book series is a personal account highlighting the process of one Lightworkers awakening. Books from this author include:

* Book One: Death of the Sun
* Book Two: A Change in Perception
* Lightworker's Log :-) Transformation
* Lightworker's Log :-) Prayer Treatments
* Adventures in Greece and Turkey
* Earth Angels
* Return to Light :-) John of God Helps
* Bits of Wisdom
* Book of One :-) Volume One Lightworker's Log

SAM is the administrator of the popular Lightworker's Log website (LightworkersLog.com). She currently concentrates on writing and spreading Spirit's message of Oneness throughout the globe. Guided by messages and synchronicities, SAM knows her most valuable asset is the ever-increasing awareness of our true BEing, unique figments of *All That Is.*